T_EX *for the* BEGINNER

Wynter Snow

 ADDISON-WESLEY PUBLISHING COMPANY

*Reading, Massachusetts • Menlo Park, California • New York
Don Mills, Ontario • Wokingham, England • Amsterdam • Bonn
Sydney • Singapore • Tokyo • Madrid • San Juan • Milan • Paris*

TEX is a trademark of the American Mathematical Society.

This book was prepared with TEX and reproduced by Addison-Wesley from text files supplied by the author.

The cover, part opener, and bug illustrations were drawn by Duane Bibby.

Library of Congress Cataloging-in-Publication Data

```
Snow, Wynter.
    TeX for the beginner / Wynter Snow.
      p.   cm.
    Includes index.
    ISBN 0-201-54799-6
    1. TeX (Computer system)  2. Computerized typesetting.
3. Mathematics printing--Data processing.   I. Title.
Z253.4.T47S64  1992
686.2'2544--dc20                                      91-32353
                                                         CIP
```

2 3 4 5 6 7 8 9 10-HA-95949392

for Bob and Carol—who wanted
to read it;

for Seymour—who taught me about
mind-sized bytes;

for Amy—who kept answering my
questions;

and for Peter—who still likes my
sense of humor.

Preface

TeX is a language for telling the computer where to put ink on a page. Fortunately, the computer already knows how to make letters, numbers, and the various punctuation symbols. What TeX does is create a layout: It says where to put your pieces of text.

The tricky part is that computers are completely dumb. They do exactly what you tell them to do, no more, no less. They cannot see that an L (l) should have been a one (1), or figure out that you meant **\newpage** instead of **\new page**.

So a language like TeX bridges the gap between computer intelligence (which is totally literal minded) and human intelligence (which can recognize a pattern at a glance). It does this by allowing you to create your own commands. Perhaps you want to indent the margins of quotations by $1/4$ inch and use an *italic typeface*, or draw a box around SOMETHING. Making your own commands allows you to accomplish exactly what you want—and makes it easy to change the layout in the midst of a project.

Things that you type in your computer file (or that appear on the screen) are shown in a **bold** typeface in the text, and a `typewriter` typeface in displayed examples. When appropriate, the resulting printout is shown below the example, as follows:

```
This is what you see: The quick brown fox jumps
over the lazy dog.
```

> This is what you see: The quick brown fox jumps over the lazy dog.

The footnotes in this book contain technical information that is not necessary for understanding TeX, but can be helpful to those of you who do understand the jargon.

Since many of you use LaTeX, I have included **LaTeX Notes** that explain things that LaTeX does differently. Unless I tell you otherwise, everything in this book works just as well in LaTeX as it does in TeX. Those of you who do not use LaTeX can skip these notes.

LaTeX Notes

LaTeX is a collection of TeX commands written by Leslie Lamport. The difference between TeX and LaTeX is like the difference between a set of Lego® blocks and an elaborate train system built of Lego blocks. TeX is a set of basic tools, whereas Lamport designed LaTeX as a system of environments and document styles. Understanding TeX helps you understand how LaTeX works and makes it easier to customize LaTeX for individual requirements and projects.

Learning both TeX and LaTeX at the same time can be tricky. Lamport changed some of the TeX commands so that they act differently in LaTeX. Several other TeX commands no longer exist at all, although there are equivalent LaTeX commands that perform all of those particular functions.

The **LaTeX Notes** in this book describe what you do differently in LaTeX. Appendix D of Lamport's *LaTeX User's Guide & Reference Manual* contains lists of LaTeX's "obsolete" TeX commands.

My background is both lay and technical. I earned a living with secretarial skills for eleven years, then became a technical editor and writer working with Seymour Papert and the Logo community at MIT, so my experience spans the gap between technophobes and technophiles.

In writing this book, my first priority was to describe the details clearly so you will understand how TeX works. My goal was to balance TeXnical accuracy with using as little jargon as possible in explaining the ideas.

My next priority was to have fun. Dry details are just that—dry and boring—whether you are reading them or writing them. So I used *bugs* to help explain how TeX works.

Learning Opportunity Bug

A bug is something that does not do what you thought it would do. There are only two kinds of bugs: typographical errors and opportunities to learn something that you do not yet understand. Typos are easy to correct, though they are sometimes hard to find—but those dratted learning opportunities can put a serious dent in your aspirin budget.

Since bugs do not come with labels—such as stripes for typos and polka dots for learning opportunities—it can be tricky to figure out which kind you are dealing with. I put lots of bugs in this book so you can see what they look like and understand why they do not work. That made the book fun for me to write and, I hope, will make it fun for you to read as well.

I tried to anticipate questions and to assume that you know nothing about computer languages and programming, but no one is perfect—so I have undoubtedly slipped up here and there. Please tell me about things you did not understand. Write to me care of Addison-Wesley, Computer Science Editorial Department, Route 128, Reading, MA 01867. This will help me improve the next edition.

Permission is hereby granted to the purchaser of this book to use any of the macros shown in this book.

How to Use This Book

The heart and soul of using TeX is writing macros (new TeX commands). My initial plan for this book was to begin with writing simple macros, and build from there. However, there are a few basic things that all TeX beginners need to know before they start writing macros, so I added a few chapters to the front of the book.

This book has five parts:

- **I: Starting Out** contains basic information that all TeX beginners need to know before they start writing macros.

- **II: Onto the Slopes** shows how to use the basic tools and concepts of TeX.

- **III: Down We Go!** shows how to write macros for all the major formatting tasks of a document. It also describes how to typeset mathematics.

- **IV: Steeper Slopes** contains information about things that are useful in a wide range of tasks. It explains TeX's boxes, lines (rules), and modes, and shows how to change awkward page breaks.

- **V: Back at the Lodge** has tips on diagnosing bugs, and some reference material.

Some of the chapters are designed to be read one after the other. Other chapters stand by themselves and can be read in any order once you are familiar with their prerequisites.

The chapters in Parts III and IV start out with simple tasks and gradually delve into more complex ones. If something in the later part of a chapter seems puzzling, it may become clearer after you have gained more experience with TeX. Thus, feel free to move on to other tasks in other chapters. You can come back to the more complex parts when you feel ready.

In **Part I: Starting Out**, you may already know some of the material in Chapters 1 and 3. If so, go ahead and skim those sections. Chapter 2, however, deals with TeX's special characters—things you must know to get the characters you want. Section 3.10 describes the *actor model*, a set of ideas that is essential to understanding how TeX works. Chapter 4 describes how to fix awkward line breaks. If you want to plunge directly into writing macros, you may want to skip over Chapter 4 and come back to it later.

In **Part II: Onto the Slopes**, Chapters 5 through 11 should be read one after the other. Each assumes that you understand all the material in previous chapters. These chapters cover how to write macros, use *groups* (a way of controlling changes), use different fonts, load additional fonts, change the size of white space (such as margins and paragraph indentation), and create new white space. Chapters 8 through 10 also show how to work with TeX's dimensions and the stretchy-shrinky stuff that TeX calls *glue*. Chapter 11 shows how TeX uses boxes to construct a page.

In **Part III: Down We Go!**, read Chapter 12 first. This chapter describes the *sandwich-structure* macros used in all of Part III's paragraph-formatting chapters. Aside from that, you can read Chapters 13 through 23 in any order you want. They cover how to write macros for flushleft, flushright, or centered paragraphs; lists; bibliographies and glossaries; verse and computer code; headings for chapters and sections; running heads and footers; footnotes; tables and figures.

Also in Part III, Chapters 24 through 27 show how to typeset math with TeX. You can read these chapters anytime after you finish Parts I and II.

Part IV: Steeper Slopes contains information that is useful for a wide range of tasks. Chapter 28 describes TeX's boxes and the basics of how to use them. Chapter 29 shows how to control the size of a box. Chapter 30 explains how to move a box to a different place on the page. Chapter 31 shows how to draw lines (rules) in your text. Chapter 32 describes how to change awkward page breaks. Chapter 33 explains TeX's modes and how to use them correctly.

Part V: Back at the Lodge contains two chapters that you can read anytime. Chapters 34 and 35 describe how to diagnose bugs. Part V also contains two appendixes with font tables and lists of TeX commands.

How TeX Works: Boxes, Glue, and Modes

TeX uses boxes and glue to construct paragraphs and pages. (Somewhat simplistically: All the letters and other characters are placed in boxes, and the white space between them is glue.) So the sooner you understand TeX's boxes, the sooner you will master TeX. Glue is described in Part II, but information about boxes is fairly sparse until you reach Chapter 28.

An understanding of TeX's modes (described in Chapter 33) is essential to understanding how TeX works. However, you can go a long way in TeX before you need to pay much attention to which mode TeX is in. It is much easier to understand modes once you have seen TeX perform a variety of tasks. Therefore, I recommend that you read the chapter on modes whenever you have some spare time and are curious about how TeX changes from one mode to another and what TeX does in each mode.

The Scope of This Book

This book gives you a solid foundation for using TeX and shows how to make any kind of document you want—from articles and books to restaurant menus and brochures. This book does not cover everything that TeX can do, or explain every detail with mathematical accuracy. *The TeXbook* already does both of those things thoroughly.

Instead, this book is a practical, hands-on tutorial that shows you how to use TeX. It also provides a sound conceptual base for learning more about TeX if you want to do so.

Beyond This Book

If you want to learn more about TeX, I recommend both *The TeXbook*, by Donald Knuth, and *TeX for the Impatient*, by Paul Abrahams with Karl Berry and Kathryn Hargreaves. *The TeXbook* is, of course, *the* authoritative and complete source of everything about TeX. *TeX for the Impatient* is like a dictionary, except that it is organized into sections of similar commands rather than alphabetically. It describes clearly and concisely what every TeX command does.

To find a human source of answers to questions, there are three routes you can take. If you are using TeX on a mainframe system in an academic or corporate environment, ask your coworkers who the TeX wizards are. (A TeX wizard is someone especially knowledgeable about TeX.) If they do not know, try sending email to **tex-users** on your local network.

If you are using TeX at home, the colleges or universities in your area are likely to have one or more people who are familiar with TeX. Call the more technical departments—especially computer science, mathematics, and physics—and ask if anyone there uses TeX.

If none of those avenues lead to someone who can answer your questions, contact the TeX Users Group in Providence, RI.

The TeX Users Group

The TeX Users Group (TUG) was formed in 1980 to help members and non-members alike obtain information about TeX and METAFONT. TUG conducts an annual conference, sells TeX and METAFONT products, distributes public domain TeX software for microcomputers, and offers courses on TeX, METAFONT, and other related topics. TUG has site coordinators who provide information on installation of TeX software on specific computer architectures.

TUG publishes both a newsletter (*TeX and TUG News*) and a technical journal (*TUGboat*) to disseminate current and useful information about TeX, the TeX community and TUG.

More information about TUG and TUG membership is available from

TeX Users Group
PO Box 9506
Providence, RI 02940 USA
Phone: 401-751-7760
Fax: 401-751-1071
Email: (Internet) tug@math.ams.com

Acknowledgments

Writing this book has been a very educational experience. Among other things, now I know why authors write acknowledgments.

Without the guidance of my editor, Peter Gordon, this book would have been entirely different—and immeasurably poorer. His friendship helped me through more than a few dark hours. I am also indebted to Seymour Papert, who taught me about mind-sized bites, the actor model of programming, and Logo. Seymour is the source of many metaphors in this book, including the bulletin board analogy, the muffin analogy, and the envelope analogy.

My reviewers and critiquers were invaluable for finding fuzzy places in my prose and errors in my knowledge. My thanks to Karl Berry, David J. Brown, Jill Carter, Michael Downs, Werner Feibel, Richard Furuta, Dawn Griesbach, Christine Griffen, Kathryn Hargreaves, Jennifer Knuth, Silvio Levy, and Gregory Tucker.

In particular, Jill Carter and Jennifer Knuth pointed out confusing passages—often the result of my trying to say two things at once. Silvio Levy explained several things about TeX that had been unclear to me and suggested the term *clone*. Karl Berry showed me how boxes work and answered a slew of questions. He and Kathryn Hargreaves have a passion for accuracy that is truly extraordinary. Kathryn also suggested the analogy of writing the name of a new macro on the envelope containing its definition. Michael Downes suggested many improvements in the **LaTeX Notes** and clarified several points about how TeX works. Last but not least, my copy editors Lyn Dupré and Patricia M. Daly helped keep my style clear and simple, which is never an easy task for a writer.

Any mistakes that remain in this document are mine.

Contents

PART I

STARTING OUT

CHAPTER 1

Starting Out

When people start learning TeX,[1] they want to know what to put in their file and how TeX differs from word processing systems they already know.

1.1   What Is Different about TeX?

Most word processing systems for PCs accomplish two tasks:

- *text editing*: creating and changing a file, and
- *formatting*: making a layout for the text in that file (choosing the size of margins and paragraph indentations; choosing particular styles for section headings, typefaces, etc.).

Many people who use PC word processors do not realize that these can be two separate tasks—especially if they use What-You-See-Is-What-You-Get (WYSIWYG, pronounced *wissy-wig*) systems. The distinction between text editing and formatting is important for understanding TeX, however, because TeX does not create or change your file. Instead, it is a *formatter*: It places text on each page according to the commands that you put in the file.

For those of you who use TeXtures on the Macintosh, the text editor that comes with TeXtures is a generic Macintosh text editor, not an essential part of TeX. Files created with a different text editor can be transferred onto the Macintosh and into TeXtures (and vice versa).

---

[1] "TeX" is the uppercase of "$\tau\epsilon\chi$," from the Greek root $\tau\epsilon\chi\nu$ meaning art, skill, and craftsmanship. The χ is pronounced like the Scottish *loch* and the German *ach*, so to quote Don Knuth, TeX's creator: "*TeX* rhymes with *blecchhh*."

For example, your computer file and the resulting printout might look like this:

```
\section{Our Feathered Friends}

All over the world, as you can easily see in this
preview of coming attractions,
\beginquote
Birds of a feather flock together.
\endquote
```

1. Our Feathered Friends

All over the world, as you can easily see in this preview of coming attractions,

> Birds of a feather flock together.

So TEX is not a word processor, and it is not WYSIWYG. Instead, it is a *formatting language*. You create new commands—such as the **\section**, **\beginquote**, and **\endquote** in the example above—and decide what those commands should do. What you see in your computer file is text and commands. What you see in your printout is the layout of text that TEX creates, using those commands.

This makes it easy to change your mind about the appearance of section headings, quotations, and the like. In many WYSIWYG systems, when you change your mind about how something should look, you must change each and every heading or quotation or whatever. With TEX, all you change is the definition of one command.

Using TEX is like hiring lots of specialists to do the job for you. You tell your **\section** specialist how you want section headings to look (Chapter 17 shows how to do this), and it does the nitty-gritty work every time you say **\section{heading here}**. TEX is a pretty smart typesetter too, so even if you are just starting out and know very little TEX, it still makes a handsome-looking printout for you.

With TEX, therefore, you can use almost any text editor you want to create and change your files. Section 1.3 tells you how to figure out if you can use your favorite word processing program with TEX.

1.2   What Is a TEX Command?

Each TEX command starts with a backslash (\). For example, the command **\TeX** says to typeset the TEX logo.

```
This book shows how to use \TeX.
```

This book shows how to use TEX.

The backslash is TEX's signal for "escaping from" its usual task (typesetting characters into words, words into lines, and lines into paragraphs and pages) and doing something different for a while. Most systems have at least one *escape character*. The backslash is convenient for this purpose because it is almost never needed in ordinary text. When you do need a backslash in your text, TEX has a command for creating one.

There are many different TEX commands. Most of them are designed to accomplish a small, specific task.

Sometimes you want to use a command directly. For example, the TEX command **\raggedright** creates a ragged right margin instead of a justified (straight) one. Thus, I typed **\raggedright** near the front of the file for this book.

Most of the time, however, TEX's commands are a construction kit for accomplishing larger tasks. For example, the **\bigskip** command puts a big vertical space (roughly $1/6$ inch) into the printout. Novels often use this amount of blank space to indicate a shift in time and space between two scenes, or a shift in point of view from one character to another.

```
... the water around Charity's ankles rose rapidly
as she yelled and pounded for help on the locked
closet door.

\bigskip
Once out of the closet ...
```

... the water around Charity's ankles rose rapidly as she yelled and pounded for help on the locked closet door.

Once out of the closet ...

However, having many **\bigskip**s sprinkled throughout your document is a major nuisance if you—or the book designer—decide in mid-book to change the size of that space.

The simple way of accomplishing this task is to make a new command called **\sceneshift** and include the **\bigskip** in its definition. (Chapter 5 shows how to define a new command.) TEX then typesets the **\bigskip** automatically every time it sees **\sceneshift** in your text file.

This ability to create new commands makes TEX very powerful. You are not limited to someone else's ideas about how things should look. If you want to make triangular or hourglass-shaped paragraphs, notes in the margins, or two-column footnotes, you can. Also, making small modifications to customize the format of each document becomes straightforward instead of mind boggling.

There is only one command that you absolutely, positively must know to get a printout: Put \bye at the end of the file. When TEX sees \bye, it finishes all the layout tasks it is working on, completes the last page, and stops. In fact, if you put \bye in the middle of a file, TEX stops there.

```
If I wander hither, and wonder yonder,
\bye
will I ever get to my destination?
```

If I wander hither, and wonder yonder,

\bye does not exist in LATEX. Instead, use \end{document} as described in Section 2.2.2 on pages 21–22 of Lamport's *LATEX, A Document Preparation System, User's Guide & Reference Manual*. In LATEX, every project has the following structure:

\documentstyle{*article* or *report* or *book*}
customize-the-document commands
\begin{document}
the text
\end{document}

\documentstyle{*something*}, \begin{document}, and \end{document} are part of LATEX, not TEX. When LATEX finds \end{document}, it finishes all its pending tasks and stops.

1.3   TEX Files Must Be Plain-Text Files

(You can skip this section if you already know about plain-text files and how to make them.)

TEX works with plain-text files, which contain only the ordinary characters, namely:

letters:	A–Z and a–z
numbers:	0–9
punctuation:	. , : ; ? ! ' ' " @ # $ % ^ & * ( )
	- _ + = { } [ ] ~ < > | / and \
spaces	
carriage returns	
tabs	(TEX converts tabs into spaces)
form feeds	(TEX converts form feeds into TEX's end-this-paragraph command)

Most computer systems use the ASCII encoding system, so plain-text files are often called ASCII files. Since TeX also runs on non-ASCII computers such as the IBM mainframe, I call all these files *plain text files.*

For those of you who work on ASCII systems and are curious, *ASCII* (the American Standard Code for Information Interchange) is a system of number codes for each character. Because computers do their work by manipulating numbers, all letters have to be converted into numbers at some stage of the work. The ASCII code makes it possible for different ASCII-using computers and systems to exchange information with each other. For example, **A** is ASCII number 65, **B** is ASCII 66, and so on. With ASCII codes, a file that says **the quick brown fox** on one system does not say **yjr wiovl ntpem gpc** or **uif rvjdl cspxo gpy** on another.

TeX may produce odd results or send you strange error messages if it finds nonordinary characters, so your text editor must be able to write a file in plain-text form when you have finished typing your document.

Most of the control characters (^**A**–^**Z**) are nonordinary, and TeX does not know what to do with them. Many word processing programs use control characters to accomplish their formatting tasks. A ^**S** might be used to change to an *italic typeface*, and a ^**T** to change back to roman (*roman* means an ordinary text typeface, such as this one). Another control character might be used to create a page break. Similar codes might be used to change margin size or paragraph indentation, create a ragged or justified right margin, and so on.

(Two control characters that TeX does recognize are ^**I**, the tab, and ^**L**, the form feed. See the table on page 6 at the beginning of this section.)

These code characters are generally invisible in the sense that they do not appear on the screen but are still there in the file. Some word processing programs also put codes at the front of their files to indicate such things as the length of the file, the beginning page number, and the like. Such files contain these code characters even if you do not put any additional formatting codes into the file!

There are several ways of finding out if a particular file is or is not a plain-text file.

- Looking at the file with a plain-text editor such as VI or EMACS shows all the characters in the file. Nonordinary characters become obvious— usually as odd sequences such as ^**S**, **M-e**, or **/215**.

- Printing the contents of the file on the screen with an operating-system command such as **type**, **print**, or **more** is a good indicator. Some nonordinary characters might be ignored, but many appear as odd codes or strangely shaped characters (such as ◇, ⌉, and ͜͡). If nonordinary characters are present, you may also hear beeping noises while entire chunks of the file are skipped.

- Running the file through TeX causes TeX to hiccup if there is a character TeX cannot handle. You cannot damage TeX or your file if you try this.

The worst possibility is that TeX could get stuck in a to-be-read-again loop. (Section 35.3 describes what to do if this happens.) Chapter 3 describes how to run a file through TeX.

How can you tell if your word processor can make a plain-text file? Many word processing programs can write a plain-text file on the disk. The manual for your word processor should tell you how to do this. Look in its index or table of contents for "plain-text file" or "ASCII file" or the like. If you cannot find anything in the manual, ask the manufacturer or friends who use the same program how to create a plain-text file.

If your word processor cannot write a plain-text file, write a complaint to the manufacturer! Then find out if there is a program that can convert your word processor's usual file into a plain-text file. Programs designed to convert files from one kind of word processor into files suitable for another word processor can usually convert to a plain-text file as well.

1.4   Your Text Must Be Single Spaced

Some word processing systems allow you to double space your file, which makes it easier to read. However, TeX uses the empty line made by two consecutive carriage returns to know where one paragraph ends and the next begins. Thus, each paragraph in your file must be single spaced.

```
... what happens if I double space the material in my

file?  Since an empty line tells \TeX\ to end the old

paragraph, is each of these lines a separate paragraph?

On the other hand, this material is single spaced so I
can see what happens to my prose when I run the file
through \TeX.
```

> ... what happens if I double space the material in my file? Since an empty line tells TeX to end the old paragraph, is each of these lines a separate paragraph?
> On the other hand, this material is single spaced so I can see what happens to my prose when I run the file through TeX.

When your text is double spaced, TeX treats each line as a separate paragraph.

Similarly, you must put a blank line (two consecutive carriage returns) between your paragraphs. Some word processing programs allow you to use a single carriage return and tab indent to start a new paragraph. If you do this, however, TeX treats your entire file as a single paragraph—and is likely to give you an ominous message about running out of memory space, just before it quits.

In some word processors, the text on the screen looks as if it is double spaced, even though the text in the file is single spaced. The only way to tell for sure is to look at your file.

1.5   Long or Short Lines and Extra Spaces

It does not matter if the lines in your file are long or short. In making a printout, TeX reads your file character by character. Even in a plain-text file, there is an invisible [END-OF-LINE] character at the end of each line. TeX converts this [END-OF-LINE] character into an ordinary space, and follows its own rules for deciding where to break the lines in the paragraph.

TeX also ignores spaces at the beginning of a line. In the following example, the spaces in front of **word** do not appear in the printout.

```
Here is a short line,
a really long line stretching across the page, and one
        word.
```

> Here is a short line, a really long line that stretches across the page, and one word.

Thus, you can indent a block of text in your file—which makes it easier to find—without disturbing TeX's method for deciding where to break a line. Also, you do not have to worry about whether you have one, two, or more spaces after a period or in other places in your file. TeX follows its own rules for how much space to put between words and after sentences. (You can change this behavior if you want TeX to "obey" the lines or spaces that you type. Chapter 16 explains how.)

Most of the time, the [END-OF-LINE] character is between two words, so converting it into a space is the right thing to do. Sometimes, though, this creates a space that you do not want, as the example below illustrates.

Hyphen- ated Bug

When a hyphenated expression is near the end of a line, the "wrapping behavior" of some text editors automatically splits the expression onto two lines, thereby putting an [END-OF-LINE] character after the hyphen. If yours does this, a space appears in the printout between the hyphen and the next letter.

```
On my way to Tiperary, I found a bigger-
than-life canary.
```

> On my way to Tiperary, I found a bigger- than-life
> canary.

To fix this bug, put a percent sign (%) at the end of the line (after the hyphen), and TEX does not typeset an extra space. Putting a % at the end of a line works in all situations where you do not want TEX to convert the END-OF-LINE character into a space.

1.6   Disappearing Spaces

A different kind of problem arises when TEX seems to ignore a space that is not extra:

```
Knuth's book describes \TeX in detail
and is a must for learning \TeX.
```

> Knuth's book describes TEXin detail and is a must for
> learning TEX.

Oops! We wanted "TEX in," not "TEXin."

TEX needs a way of knowing where a command's name ends. After all, there might be another command called **\TeXas** or **\TeXnical** or **\TeXniques**, so it cannot just say AHA! when it sees **\TeX**. Instead, there are specific rules for what can or cannot be the name of a command. These rules are simple. A command is either

- a *control word*, which contains one or more letters (**A–Z**, **a–z**), or

- a *control symbol*, which contains a single nonletter.

The important thing to understand about the distinction between control words and control symbols is that it determines how TEX figures out where the command name ends. When TEX finds a nonletter after a backslash, it knows the command name is complete. When the character after a backslash is a letter, TEX continues reading characters until it reaches one that is not a letter and therefore cannot be part of the command name. Thus, the space between **\TeX** and **in** gets used up by showing TEX where the control word ends.

You might think that putting a second space after the **\TeX** command should fix this problem, but it does not. Instead, we get a Disappearing Space Bug.

Disappearing Space Bug

T$_E$X treats two or more consecutive spaces as a single space, even when they follow a control word. Thus, none of the spaces after a control word appear in your printout.

```
\TeX    is a powerful and versatile language.
```

> T$_E$Xis a powerful and versatile language.

When you need a space in the text after a control word, use a *control space*: a backslash followed by a space (\ ). Since the backslash is also a nonletter, its presence signals the end of the preceding control word and alerts T$_E$X to expect another command: in this case, the control space.

The control space puts the usual amount of interword space into the text.

```
\TeX\ commands come in two flavors: control words
and control symbols.
```

> T$_E$X commands come in two flavors: control words and control symbols.

The control space is a control symbol: a backslash followed by a single nonletter.

Review and Preview

T$_E$X is not a word processing system or a text editor. Instead, it is a formatting language. It may seem rigid or quirky at first since it is a language for talking with computers instead of other people. However, its underlying structure is fairly simple. T$_E$X has only a few different kinds of commands—and I describe how to recognize them as they come up.

Your files must be plain-text files, usually called ASCII files. The lines within a paragraph must be single spaced, and there must be a blank line between paragraphs (two consecutive carriage returns). Typing a % at the end of a line prevents T$_E$X from converting the END-OF-LINE character into a space. To get a space after a command in the text, use a control space.

The next chapter shows how to handle T$_E$X's special characters.

CHAPTER 2

TEX's Special Characters

Most of the characters on your keyboard appear in your printout as the characters you typed and therefore expect to see—but ten have special uses in TEX and produce bugs if used incorrectly. Another three are used mostly for mathematics; when they appear in regular text, TEX typesets them as completely different characters. TEX's method for generating quotation marks and dashes is also unusual. If you type these characters incorrectly, you can get strange results.

This chapter explains how to put all these special characters into your text, and what happens if you use these special characters incorrectly. It also shows six foreign characters and how to place accent marks over letters.

2.1   TEX's Ten Special Characters

TEX uses the following ten characters for its own purposes:

~   # $ %   ^   &   _   {   }   \

To typeset these characters, you must use TEX commands instead of typing them directly. For each of these characters, use the corresponding command from the following chart:

To get:	Type:	To get:	Type:
#	\#	\	$\backslash$
$	\$	{	$\{$
%	\%	}	$\}$
&	\&	^	\char94
_	_	~	\char126

To put a circumflex (ˆ) or tilde (˜) accent mark over a letter, use the accent-making commands shown in Section 2.5. Use \char only when you need just the circumflex or tilde by itself.

Here are examples of all ten special characters so you can see how they look. The **\par** command after each sentence tells TEX to end the current paragraph. The first character in the next sentence then starts a new paragraph. Since the sentences are shorter than a line of text, each sentence appears on a line by itself in the printout.

```
The Orient Express is now boarding on platform \#9.\par
I wish I had \$5,000,000 in the bank.\par
Perfectionists demand 105\%.\par
Tweedledum \& Tweedledee sat on the fence.\par
To begin, Move\_Stack\_Up\_One.\par
Do not write $4 \backslash 5$ to mean 4/5.\par
Prove that $\{ab\}$ equals $\{xy\}$.\par
The circumflex \char94\ looks strange by itself.\par
A tilde \char126\ looks strange too.\par
```

> The Orient Express is now boarding on platform #9.
> I wish I had $5,000,000 in the bank.
> Perfectionists demand 105%.
> Tweedledum & Tweedledee sat on the fence.
> To begin, Move_Stack_Up_One.
> Do not write 4\5 to mean 4/5.
> Prove that $\{ab\}$ equals $\{xy\}$.
> The circumflex ˆ looks strange by itself.
> A tilde ˜ looks strange too.

The first five commands (\# \$ \% \& _) are straightforward control symbols. The rest of this section explains why ab and xy are typeset in italics, why there are dollar signs around the backslash and braces, and what **\char94** and **\char126** do. (Putting a control space after **\char94** and **\char126** ensures that TEX typesets that space. Using the control space after a control sequence is a good habit to cultivate whenever you think TEX might ignore a space that you want to be sure is typeset.)

Dollar Signs around the Backslash and Braces

The backslash (\) and braces ({ and }) appear rarely in ordinary text but are fairly common in math. These and other math symbols must be put in TEX's *math mode*.

TEX uses the dollar sign (**$**) both to start and to stop math mode. The first dollar sign starts math mode, the second stops it. So the dollar sign acts like a toggle switch—just like the CAPS-LOCK key on most computer keyboards: Pushing it once makes everything you type uppercase, pushing it again restores the usual upper- and lowercase.

TEX has three basic modes: a paragraph-making mode, a page-making mode, and math mode. Chapter 24 explains how to use math mode, but a few words here will help you understand what it is.

What Is Math Mode?

There is nothing special or exotic about math mode. It uses a different set of rules for where to put space, and a different set of typefaces. Instead of putting space between words and sentences, math mode puts it around particular kinds of symbols (such as $=$, $<$, $\simeq$, $+$, and $\vee$). TEX's math mode makes it fairly easy for people who know nothing about mathematical spacing to typeset mathematics—even complicated equations.

When you need to use math mode, type one dollar sign to begin math mode, type the math material, then type another dollar sign to end math mode.

```
The circumference of a circle is $2 \pi r$.
```

The circumference of a circle is $2\pi r$.

TEX ignores the spaces you type in math mode and uses the math mode spacing rules instead. (You must still put a nonletter after a math mode control word—such as **\pi**—and the best nonletter for this purpose is often a space.)

\char94 and \char126

\char typesets a character from a *font table* and is the first command we have seen that is not complete in itself. It needs additional information to do its job. In particular, **\char** needs to know where to find the character you want. The circumflex is the 94th character on most of TEX's font tables; the tilde is the 126th.

A *font* is an assortment of type all of one size and style—such as 10-point roman, the font used to typeset the text in this book. A *font table* contains all the characters in a font, arranged in rows and columns. Appendix A displays all of TEX's basic font tables and explains how to use **\char**.

In "computerese" this additional information—the number after **\char**— is called an *input* or an *argument*. Programmers prefer the more specific term *argument* and speak of *giving an argument* to a command or procedure. This sounds like a Groucho Marx phrase to me, so I decided to use the more general term *input* throughout this book.

A number is a nonletter. When TeX sees the number after \char, it knows the command is complete. Since there might be more than one digit in the number, TeX continues reading characters until it finds one that is not a digit. Just as a space after a command is used up in showing TeX where the command ends, a space after this number is also used up in showing TeX where that number ends. To typeset a space after \char94 or \char126, use a control space.

If you get something other than a circumflex (^) or tilde (~) when you type \char94 or \char126, TeX is using a font table that has different characters in those positions. To solve this problem, type {\rm\char94} for a circumflex and {\rm\char126} for a tilde. The command \rm means "switch to the roman font"; the roman font table contains a circumflex and tilde in positions 94 and 126.

2.2   What Happens When I Type the Special Character?

It is easy to forget those backslashes and commands—even for a TeXpert! The three most common bugs appear when you forget to type a backslash in front of the dollar sign, percent sign, or braces. This section describes what happens when you type one of TeX's ten special characters instead of the command for typesetting them.

The Dollar Sign

TeX uses the dollar sign to begin and end math mode. If you want a dollar sign in your text and forget to type the backslash in front of it, TeX goes into math mode instead of typesetting a dollar sign, and you get a Math Oops Mode Bug.

Math Oops Mode Bug

When you type **$** instead of **\$**, three symptoms appear: Letters are typeset in an italic typeface, spaces between words disappear, and TeX sends you an error message when it reaches the end of the paragraph.

```
A mere $5 in the bank would be nice too.
```

A mere $5 in the bank would be nice too.

TeX complains because it expects to be in paragraph-making mode at the end of the paragraph and is in math mode instead. The error message says

```
! Missing $ inserted.
```

and shows some additional information, including the number of the line in your text file where it found this problem. (Chapter 34 explains TeX's error messages in detail.)

TeX inserts this missing **$** to end math mode. The term *inserted* does not mean that TeX puts a **$** into your file. Instead, TeX puts this **$** into its own internal sequence of typesetting activities.[1]

The Math Oops Mode Bug also shows up if you forget to stop math mode when you want to return to regular text (paragraph-making mode),

```
Is 3$\backslash 4 the same as 3/4?
```

Is $3\backslash 4thesameas3/4$?

or if you forget to use math mode with a math-mode-only symbol, such as π (**\pi**).

```
2\pi r is the circumference of a circle.
```

$2\pi risthecircumferenceofacircle.$

The Math Oops Mode Bug crops up in this second example because TeX is smart enough to know that **\pi** should be in math mode. Thus, when TeX is not in math mode and sees a **\pi** or other math-mode-only symbol, it "inserts" a dollar sign to begin math mode before it acts on the **\pi**. However, TeX has no way of knowing where the math mode material ends, so it continues merrily along in math mode all the way to the end of the paragraph. TeX then inserts another **$** to end math mode and sends you the **! Missing $ inserted** error message.

TeX does not change your text file. The word *inserted* in these messages means that TeX inserts the dollar sign into its own internal sequence of activities as it is processing your file to make a printout. (Chapter 3 describes how to make a printout.)

The Circumflex and Underscore

TeX uses the circumflex (^) and underscore (_) to make superscripts and subscripts—so you must change to math mode to use them correctly. For

---

[1]More precisely, when TeX processes your text file, it converts the characters it finds into a list of *tokens*. "**Missing $ inserted**" means that TeX inserts a **$** token into this list. TeX then uses this token list to do its typesetting work. Chapter 33 explains tokens in detail.

example, to get $a^2 + b^2$ in your printout, type **\$a^2 + b^2\$** in your file. If you forget to include the dollar signs, you get a Math Oops Mode Bug.

```
In a right triangle, the hypotenuse $h$ equals the
square root of a^2 + b^2, the sum of the squares
of the other two sides.
```

> In a right triangle, the hypotenuse h equals the square root of $a^2 + b^2, the sum of the squares of the other two sides.$

The Tilde

The tilde (~) makes a *tie*: an interword space that cannot be converted into a line break. Thus, if you put a tilde between an abbreviation and the name or word or number that follows, TeX cannot put the abbreviation at the end of one line and the name, word, or number at the beginning of the next. This can prevent a variety of misunderstandings as well as bad line breaks.

In the following example, TeX normally breaks the line between **No.** and **16**—but the tilde prevents this.

```
Did I know where the bullfrog had gone?  I told
him No.~16 was the place.
```

> Did I know where the bullfrog had gone? I told him No. 16 was the place.

The tilde also shows TeX that the period is not the end of a sentence. When TeX sees a period and space, it treats this as the end of a sentence—and TeX normally puts more space between sentences than it puts between words. To get an interword space instead of an intersentence space after an abbreviation, use either a tilde or a control space. The abbreviations in bibliographies often need to be followed by a tilde or control space.

```
Quent, Ell O., ''The Universe Explained,'' Intl.\
J.\ of Flummery, Vol.~9, No.~3, pp.~66--71.
```

> Quent, Ell O., "The Universe Explained," Intl. J. of Flummery, Vol. 9, No. 3, pp. 66–71.

TeX does not add extra space after a period that follows a single uppercase letter. Thus, you do not need a control space after the periods in *U.N. Secretary-General* or *Ulysses S. Grant.* Of course, if you want to make that space unbreakable, use a tilde.

To make intersentence spaces the same size as interword spaces, say **\frenchspacing**. To restore TEX's usual, different size spaces, say **\nonfrenchspacing**.

The Percent Sign

In TEX, the percent sign (%) lets you make comments that appear in your file but not in your printout. TEX ignores everything on a line to the right of a %. Thus, if you forget the backslash when you want to typeset a percent sign, you get a Disappearing Text Bug.

Disappearing Text Bug

When you use % instead of \%, some of your text disappears. Occasionally, this can be dangerous:

```
The mixture contains 57 % cyanide and 43 %
inert ingredients.
```

> The mixture contains 57 inert ingredients.

If you rewrite or rearrange a paragraph that has percent-sign comments, make sure that the tail end of a comment has not moved to a new line where it will appear in the printout. Also, make sure that text you do want has not moved to a line after a percent sign. Mistakes like these can be embarrassing.

```
Mr.~Grant in Room 8 asked for some skim
milk and a bag of ice.% I poured them
on his bed.
```

> Mr. Grant in Room 8 asked for some skim milk and a bag of ice.on his bed.

If a long comment takes more than one line, put a percent sign at the beginning of each additional comment line.

```
Occasionally, it is necessary to expound endlessly
upon the redundancy of pleonastic and effusive prose.
% It ought to be possible to paraphrase this so
% that I don't repeat myself.
```

Occasionally, it is necessary to expound endlessly upon the redundancy of pleonastic and effusive prose.

Braces Make Groups

TeX uses the braces { and } to begin and end a *group*. (Chapter 6 explains what a group is.) If you want a brace in your text but forget to put the backslash in front of it, you get a Missing Brace Bug.

Missing Brace Bug

If you type { or } instead of \{ or \}, the brace does not appear in your printout. Instead, TeX either begins a group (with {) or ends one (with }).

Groups and braces are a fundamental part of how TeX knows what it is doing, so the consequences of misusing them vary widely. Chapter 34 describes these consequences in depth.

Briefly, if you type { instead of \{, the only apparent effect in your printout is a missing brace—but TeX sends you an error message when it reaches the end of the file. If you type } instead of \}, this usually produces one or more strange effects in your printout and might even change the way TeX typesets the rest of your document.

These brace bugs are tricky to find and fix, so be especially careful when you want to typeset braces.

Both \{ and \} can only be used in math mode. You get a Math Oops Mode Bug if you forget to put the dollar signs around them.

In LaTeX, both \{ and \} can be used directly in text and do not have to be in math mode. LaTeX does the right thing if you do put them in math mode—so if you plan to use both TeX and LaTeX, it helps to do things the same way in both systems.

The Ampersand

The ampersand (&) separates the column entries in tables and is described in Chapter 20. When you want an ampersand in your text and forget to put a backslash in front of it, TeX tells you it found a **! Misplaced alignment tab character &**.

Number Sign

The number sign (#) is used to create a slot for an input—either in the definition of a new command or in the entries of a table. These uses are described in Chapters 5 and 20. When you want a number sign in your text and forget to put a backslash in front of it, TeX says that you cannot use the # character in paragraph-making mode.

2.3 Ligatures

A *ligature* is a character that consists of two or more letters or characters joined together. Printed English uses five ligatures: for **ff, fi, fl, ffi,** and **ffl**. The top line of the following example shows these ligatures; the bottom line shows the same words without the ligatures.

daffy	first	flower	effigy	ruffled
daffy	first	flower	effigy	ruffled

Each time TeX sees an **f** in your file, it looks ahead to the next character. If that next character is an **i** or **l**, TeX typesets the corresponding ligature. If the next character is another **f**, TeX looks ahead again—and typesets the appropriate ligature: **ff, ffi,** or **ffl**. If TeX finds none of these after the first **f**, it typesets an ordinary **f** and continues with the next character in the file.

If you need a nonligatured **ff, fi,** or **fl**, put braces around the second letter, like this:

```
daf{f}y  f{i}rst  f{l}ower  ef{f}igy  ruf{f}led
```

TeX also uses ligatures to make quotation marks and dashes.

Quotation Marks

TeX has four distinct quotation marks:

	To get:	Type:
open double quote:	`"`	`''`
close double quote:	`"`	`''`
open single quote:	`'`	`'`
close single quote:	`'`	`'`

When TeX sees a quote character, it looks ahead to see if the next character is another quote character. If it is, TeX typesets a double quote (" or "). If it is not, TeX typesets a single quote (' or ').

```
''Fascinating,'' said Spock.
```

> "Fascinating," said Spock.

If you use the typewriter-style double quote character (") instead, the open double quote mark is typeset incorrectly.

```
I said, "Do not quote me!"
```

> I said, "Do not quote me!"

TeX behaves like this because of the way the font tables are organized. The font table for the typewriter font is the only one that contains a typewriter-style double quote mark. This position in the other font tables contains TeX's double close quote (or sundry math symbols in the math fonts). Chapter 6 explains how to change fonts. Appendix A contains all of TeX's standard font tables.

An interesting problem arises with quotes within quotes. When TeX finds three quote characters together, it typesets the first two as a double quote and the third as a single quote.

```
John said in a quavering voice, ''Mary said,
'It's not true!'''
```

> John said in a quavering voice, "Mary said, 'It's not true!"'

The solution is to put a \thinspace between the single quote and the double quote. Also, TeX ordinarily typesets very little space between an opening double quote and a following single quote ("'). To equalize the size of these spaces, put a \thinspace between these opening double and single quotes as well.

```
''\thinspace'She's lying,' Mary said.   'I did not
steal her necklace.'\thinspace'' John cleared his
throat, then continued his testimony.
```

> "'She's lying,' Mary said. 'I did not steal her necklace.'"
> John cleared his throat, then continued his testimony.

Dashes

TeX uses this same look-ahead strategy for making dashes. When it finds a hyphen (-), TeX checks the next character to see if it is another hyphen. Altogether, TeX has one regular hyphen and two dashes:

```
The quick-footed fox sprinted---dashed away---on
pages 2--8.
```

> The quick-footed fox sprinted—dashed away—on pages 2–8.

The en dash (–) is traditionally used to indicate a range of things, such as dates, page numbers, and letters. The em dash (—) is the typographical name for the dash we use as punctuation. The en and em dashes got their names because they were the same width as the capital N and M in traditional typefaces. This is not always the case in modern typefaces.

The minus sign (−) is longer than an en dash but shorter than an em dash. When you need a minus sign, put it in math mode.

```
Zero degrees Fahrenheit is $-$18 degrees
Celsius.  Brrrr!
```

> Zero degrees Fahrenheit is −18 degrees Celsius. Brrrr!

2.4   What Is ¡That¿ Doing Here?

Only three other characters might create bugs in your printout: <, >, and |. These characters usually appear only in mathematical expressions, so they are not included in the font tables for regular text.[2] If you need these three characters, put them in math mode.

These characters are usually part of a longer mathematical expression, all of which would be in math mode:

```
Since $2<3$ and $3<5$, we know that $5>2$.
```

> Since $2 < 3$ and $3 < 5$, we know that $5 > 2$.

If you type <, >, or | without putting them in math mode, you get the following:

```
There is a <bug> in my |text|.
```

> There is a ¡bug¿ in my —text—.

---

[2]Compare the characters in positions 60, 61, and 62 in the font tables in Appendix A.

2.5 Accent Marks and Foreign Characters

You can put many different accent marks over the characters in your text. These accents can be used with capital letters as well as lowercase. Type the command in front of the letter you want to accent.

```
The pi\~nata makes a delightful f\^ete.
```

The piñata makes a delightful fête.

To get:	Type:	To get:	Type:
ò	\'o	ŏ	\u o
ó	\'o	ǒ	\v o
ô	\^o	ő	\H o
ö	\"o	ȏȏ	\t oo
õ	\~o	ǫ	\c o
ō	\=o	ọ	\d o
ȯ	\.o	o̲	\b o

The accents on the left are made with control symbols, and the ones on the right with control words. Do not put a space between the control symbol and the letter to be accented. However, you do need the space after the control word to show TEX where the command ends. Each of these commands takes one input: the letter to be accented. (The second o after the \t command is not part of the input. \t o produces o͡ .)

TEX also has some foreign-language characters, ligatures, and accented characters.

To get:	Type:	To get:	Type:
œ, Œ	\oe, \OE	ø, Ø	\o, \O
æ, Æ	\ae, \AE	ł, Ł	\l, \L
å, Å	\aa, \AA	ß	\ss

Since these are control words, put a space or other nonletter after them. If you dislike having a space in the middle of a word, put the entire control word inside braces, like this:

```
I'd rather be {\ae}sthetic than athletic.
```

I'd rather be æsthetic than athletic.

TeX uses ten characters for special purposes: the tilde (~), number sign (#), dollar sign ($), percent sign (%), circumflex (^), ampersand (&), underscore (_), open brace ({), close brace (}), and backslash (\). This chapter shows the commands you must use to typeset one of these characters. It also describes what each of these characters is used for, and the bugs that appear when one of them is used incorrectly.

Another three characters are used mostly in mathematics: the less-than sign (<), greater-than sign (>), and absolute-value sign (|). These characters can only be used in math mode. When TeX sees them in ordinary text, it typesets an ¡ or ¿ or — respectively.

TeX uses a look-ahead strategy to make ligatures: quotation marks; dashes; and the letter combinations ff, fi, fl, ffi, and ffl. TeX also has a variety of accent marks and some foreign characters.

The next chapter shows how to get a printout.

CHAPTER 3

Getting a Printout

Creating a printout is a two-step process. First, TEX processes your file and creates a set of layout instructions for your printer. Second, you send these layout instructions to your printer. This chapter describes both steps and shows how to recover from easily made, common mistakes—such as misspelled filenames and TEX commands.

3.1 Filenames

To process your file, TEX has to be able to find it. Using a specific extension on the end of a filename makes it easy for both people and computer programs to recognize what kind of file it is. A file called **shrubs.wp** is a Word Perfect file; another called **bushes.mss** is a Scribe file. Use the extension **.tex** for your TEX files.

Filenames can contain letters (**A–Z** and **a–z**), numbers (**0–9**), and some punctuation characters. The following filenames are valid on a wide variety of different computers:

```
flowers.tex
tree-gdn.tex
weed_out.tex
chapter5.tex
```

If your computer's *operating system* allows it, you can have longer filenames. *Operating system* means DOS, UNIX, Tops-20, or the like. If you prefer to use a different extension, Section 3.4 explains how TEX can find a file with an unusual name. The Macintosh operating system generates the pull-down menus and allows you to use long filenames with spaces. However, do not put spaces in the names of your TEX files.

3.2 Getting a Printout

The two steps in making a printout are as follows:

- TEX processes your text file and creates a second file. This second file is a set of precise instructions for positioning and typesetting each character on each page. It is called a **.dvi** file (for d̲e̲v̲ice i̲ndependent) because it can be sent to any printer.
- You send this **.dvi** file to your printer.

You must have a driver for your printer that can interpret and print a **.dvi** file. These drivers are different for each type of printer. If you are working on a mainframe system, it should have whatever driver the printer needs. (If it does not, ask your "system wizards" about getting one.) If you are using TEX on your own computer, a driver for your printer was probably included as part of your TEX software package. (If it was not, contact a TEX software supplier or the TEX Users Group at the address shown in this book's Preface.) A **.dvi**-file previewer is also very useful. It allows you to see on your screen how the printout looks, thereby saving time and paper.

The following two sections describe how to make a **.dvi** file and send it to the printer on most mainframes and non-Macintosh computers. The section after that describes how to do this with TEXtures on the Macintosh.

There are so many different computer systems, installations of TEX, operating systems, printers, and driver programs that it is impossible to give a comprehensive listing of every possibility. The following sections are a guide for those of you who are using TEX at home alone. If your own system or installation of TEX is different, ask for help from colleagues; the source of your TEX software, operating system, or printer; or the TEX User's Group.

Making the .dvi File on Mainframes and Non-Macintosh PCs

To create a **.dvi** file, type the command **tex** *filename* after your operating system's top-level prompt. This command tells your computer to run TEX on a particular file. For example, if your text file is called **daisies.tex**, you would say

```
tex daisies
```

You do not have to say **tex daisies.tex** because TEX automatically looks for a file with a **.tex** extension.

For DOS, the top-level prompt shows the active drive and often the directory as well: **C:\meadow>**. The top-level prompt on many mainframe systems is often a single symbol, such as **#**, **%**, or **$**, or two symbols such as **C$**. On UNIX systems, the top-level prompt varies but is often something like **snow@ice>**.

LATEX Notes

For LATEX, type **latex daisies** instead of **tex daisies**.

TEX now processes **daisies.tex** and uses the commands and text it finds there to make another file called **daisies.dvi**. As TEX does this, it sends messages to your screen about the progress it is making and any problems that it finds. When TEX finds a problem, it may also stop processing your file and wait for you to say what it should do next. If TEX does stop, press RETURN to make TEX continue processing your file. Section 3.7 describes all the things you can do when TEX stops and waits for instructions from you.

The messages TEX sends to your screen are also written into a transcript file. This transcript file is usually called **daisies.log** but might have a different extension on your system. When TEX finishes making the **.dvi** file, it sends you a message with the full names of both the **.dvi** file and the transcript file. Here is an example of one such message:

```
Output written on e:\mybook\testit.dvi (1 page, 2048 bytes).
Transcript written on e:\mybook\testit.log.
```

When TEX has finished making the **.dvi** file, your directory should contain three files:

Filename:	What's in the file?
daisies.tex	manuscript with text and TEX commands
daisies.dvi	complete layout instructions for the printer
daisies.log	transcript of session, including error messages

You can print the transcript file just as you would any other ordinary file. You can also put it into another window in your text editor while you edit your **.tex** file—if your text editor allows you to work with more than one window at a time.

Sending the .dvi File to the Printer

The command for sending the **.dvi** file to the printer is different for various computer systems. Ask your colleagues or read the manual for your operating system.

Here are examples of commands I have used on different systems to send the **.dvi** file to a printer:

Tops-20:	print *filename*/unit:*printer*
UNIX:	prtex *filename*
UNIX:	lpr -d *filename*.dvi
Lisp Machine:	:Hardcopy File *filename*.dvi
DOS with PostScript printer:	dvips *filename*

All of these are operating-system commands that you type after the top-level prompt. The one you need to use is probably both similar and different. On some systems, the command automatically looks for a filename with a **.dvi** extension. On other systems, you must type **.dvi** after the filename.

T_EXtures on the Macintosh

T_EXtures uses the Macintosh mouse-and-pull-down-menu system. To make the **.dvi** file, first make sure that the **.tex** file is the active window (the one with visible top and right borders). If it is not, click the mouse on the **.tex** file to make it active.

Now pull down the TYPESET menu and select the TYPESET box. This runs T_EX on your **.tex** file and makes the **.dvi** file. T_EXtures starts a new window on the screen that shows the contents of the transcript (**.log**) file as it processes the **.tex** file.

While T_EXtures is running, this transcript window is the active window, although you can switch to a different window if you want. To make T_EXtures pause while it is processing your **.tex** file, click the mouse on the PAUSE box in this transcript window. Then you can use the CONTINUE, QUIT, or HELP box.

When T_EXtures has finished processing your text file, it displays another new window that shows what your printout looks like. When T_EXtures finishes making the **.dvi** file, this typeset window automatically becomes the active window. To look at different pages in the typeset window, pull down the menu under VIEW and select NEXT PAGE, PREVIOUS PAGE, or a specific page number.

When you want to print the **.dvi** file, first make sure that the typeset window is the active window. If it is not, click the mouse on that window to make it active, or use the WINDOWS menu. Then use the mouse to select the PRINT box under the apple—just as you would to print any other file.

To copy the **.dvi** file from the Macintosh hard disk onto a floppy disk, first put the floppy into the Macintosh external drive. Then use the mouse to select the DVI box under the apple, select DVI TOOL from the options, and follow the instructions. The process is similiar to copying other kinds of files from one drive to another.

What Can Go Wrong?

Oops! You misspelled a T_EX command, or hit the wrong key, or your file is called **bloopers.mss** instead of **bloopers.tex**. The rest of this chapter shows how to recover from these and similar mistakes.

3.3   Filename Errors

The first opportunity for making a mistake is just after you type **tex** at top level. If you forget to type the filename and press RETURN instead, TeX starts itself and prints its standard greeting and version number. Then it prints two asterisks (******) and waits for instructions.

Type the filename after the asterisks:

```
daisies
```

and press RETURN. TeX now processes your **daisies.tex** file.

A different type of problem comes up if you misspell the filename, or if the extension is not **.tex**. TeX then sends you an error message that it cannot find that file, and says

```
Please type another input file name:
```

If you simply misspelled the filename, type the correct one. Sometimes, though, the file is in a different subdirectory or has a different extension. The following section shows what to do in these cases.

3.4   Using Nonstandard Filenames

If the filename extension is not **.tex**, type the entire filename, including its nonstandard extension. If your operating system has a subdirectory, tree, or folder structure and you invoke TeX from a different place in that structure, type the entire pathname of the file. On a UNIX system, for example, the full pathname might be

```
/root/snow/nonfiction/mybook/goofed.tex
```

where **root** is the root directory of the entire structure, **snow** is my home directory, **nonfiction** is a subdirectory of **snow**, **mybook** is a subdirectory of **nonfiction**, and goofed.tex is the file.

If your operating system accepts any of the following filenames as legitimate, it can be used with TeX. Type

`tex bloopers.mss`	extension is not .tex
`tex bah.humbug.tex`	filename has two periods
`tex /snow/oops/goofed.tex`	file is in a different subdirectory
`tex b:mistakes.tex`	file is on a disk in another drive

at the top-level prompt. If you forget to use the complete filename when you start TeX, give the complete name when TeX complains that it cannot find that file.

If you use DOS, however, this complete-filename strategy does not work. The following DOS Backslash Filename Bug explains why.

DOS Backslash Filename Bug

Since DOS uses the backslash for its subdirectory-tree structure, TeX cannot find a file in a different subdirectory. Instead, TeX thinks that the subdirectory name is a command and does whatever that command says to do. If there is no command with that name, TeX sends you an error message.

For example, if you are currently in subdirectory **c:\veggies** and say

```
tex d:\orchard\daisies.tex
```

TeX looks for a command called **\orchard** and complains when it does not find one. To run TeX on the **daisies.tex** file, you must first move into the **orchard** subdirectory and then say **tex daisies**.[1]

In most operating systems, the files you pass to TeX must have an extension—either standard or nonstandard. If the filename has no extension at all, TeX can never find the file and gets *really* stuck. The following Broken-Record Filename Bug explains this problem.

Broken-Record Filename Bug

In most implementations, TeX automatically looks for a filename with the extension **.tex**. Thus, if the filename has no extension at all, TeX cannot find the file and simply continues to ask for another filename again . . . and again . . . and again.

There are two ways you can break TeX out of this Broken-Record Filename Bug.

- Use your operating system's abort sequence—such as CONTROL-BREAK for DOS, and CONTROL-Z or CONTROL-G or CONTROL-C for many others—to stop TeX and return to top level. In TeXtures, click the mouse on the QUIT box in the transcript (**.log**) window.
- Give TeX the filename **null**.

Most implementations of TeX have a file called **null.tex**. This **null.tex** file contains either nothing at all or only the command **\relax**—which says "do nothing." If your system does not already have a **null.tex** file, make one and place it in a subdirectory where TeX always looks. (Check your TeX

---

[1]Some DOS versions of TeX allow you to substitute a forward slash / for the backslash in filenames.

software installation manual for information about which subdirectory this would be.)

3.5 Overfull and Underfull Boxes

As TeX processes the file, it may send you error messages about *overfull hboxes*. An overfull hbox is a line that is wider than the text and therefore sticks out into the margin.[2] For now, simply ignore these overfull-hbox messages. Chapter 4 explains overfull hboxes and how to fix them.

TeX puts a black box in the printout immediately after an overfull hbox, which makes the overfull hbox easy to find but makes the printout ugly. If you prefer not to see these black boxes in your printouts, Section 3.9 tells you how to make them invisible.

TeX may also send you messages about underfull boxes—but you can ignore these too, at least for now. Chapter 10 explains how underfull boxes are made; Chapters 10 and 32 describe ways of fixing them.

3.6 Errors in the Text

All other kinds of problems cause TeX to stop and wait for instructions from you. For example, if you misspell the name of a TeX command, TeX sends you an error message, types a question-mark prompt (?), and waits for instructions. The following text provokes the error message shown below it:

```
Since \tex\ is case sensitive, it
distinguishes between ''TeX'' and ''tex.''
```

```
! Undefined control sequence.
l.25 Since \tex
                \ is case sensitive, it
?
```

TeX uses the term *control sequence* instead of *command*, so from now on we will too.

When TeX finds a control sequence it does not recognize, it tells you where the problem is (line 25 in this example), and shows the exact point in that line where it stopped (here, after **Since \tex** and before **\ is case sensitive, it**). TeX also prints a question-mark prompt (the **?** at the end of the error message above) and waits for instructions from you.

---

[2]More precisely, an overfull hbox is a horizontal box whose contents are wider than the hbox is allowed to be. Most of the time, overfull hboxes are lines in paragraphs that are wider than the text—but other kinds of hboxes can also be overfull.

3.7   Replies to TEX's Question-Mark Prompt

When you see TEX's question-mark prompt, there are nine different responses you can make. Here is a summary of what they do:

i*something*	insert *something*
h	help
RETURN	continue anyway
x	exit now
e	edit file after exiting
s	scroll mode (do not pause at errors)
r	nonstop mode (run without stopping for any reason)
q	quiet mode (do not stop or print messages on screen)
?	what can I type here?

Here is a full description of each of these options:

i *something*   insert *something*

If the problem is simple, such as a typographical error, type **i** and the correction. For example, you could correct the above problem with the undefined control sequence by typing **i\TeX**. This tells TEX to typeset the TEX logo.

Here, *insert* means that TEX inserts your response into its own internal sequence of activities—not into your **.tex** file. Thus, the printout contains whatever you insert this way, but you still need to fix the problem in your **.tex** file.

You do not need to make notes about these errors because TEX writes all these messages into the transcript (**.log**) file. When you are ready to correct the problems TEX found, you can look at the transcript file while you edit your **.tex** file.

You cannot insert backspaces, go backwards, or change anything that TEX has already processed.

h   help

If you do not know what to do about an error message, **h** can sometimes help you figure it out. However, the help messages are brief and assume that you already know some TEX.

RETURN   continue anyway

If you are not sure what to do, or do not want to insert a correction now, type RETURN , and TEX continues.

Sometimes, though, TEX gets stuck in a to-be-read-again loop (see Section 35.3). If TEX reads the same piece of text more than three or four times and cycles through the same set of error messages, it is probably stuck. Type **x** to exit from this particular run.

x   exit

To make TEX stop here, type **x**. TEX finishes any pending tasks and returns you to top level. Then you can fix the problem(s) in your **.tex** file and start afresh.

e   edit the file
Typing **e** stops TEX just as **x** does—but also tells you the full pathname of the file you want to edit and the line number where TEX stopped in that file. On some systems, typing **e** also starts your text editor and takes you directly to that particular line in that file.

s   scroll mode (do not pause at errors)
To make TEX keep going instead of asking you what to do when it finds an error, type **s**. This option is especially useful if you want TEX to make the **.dvi** file while you go do something else. In scroll mode, TEX automatically includes the appropriate help messages in the transcript file.

r   nonstop mode (run without stopping for any reason)
This is like scroll mode but more emphatic. In scroll mode, TEX still stops and waits for instructions if it cannot find a file you want to **\input**. (**\input** "goes and gets" a file, and is described in Section 5.9.) In nonstop mode, TEX does an emergency stop instead. Thus, nonstop mode prevents TEX from getting stuck with a Broken-Record Filename Bug, but TEX does not continue processing your **.tex** file. Instead, TEX throws away anything it has accumulated for the current page—and the **.dvi** file ends on the previous, already completed page.

q   quiet mode (do not stop or print messages on screen)
This is like nonstop mode, except that you do not see any messages on your screen. If you type **q** in response to the **?** prompt, nothing more appears on the screen until TEX finishes making the **.dvi** and transcript files. The transcript file still includes the help messages for the errors it finds. When TEX reaches the end of the **.tex** file, it automatically returns you to top level.

?   what can I do here?
If you forget what responses you can make or do not want to look them up in a book, type **?** and TEX prints a message with your options.

On most systems, you can also type a number in response to the **?** prompt. TEX then ignores that number of subsequent *tokens* in the file. A *token* is either a character (such as **q**) or a control sequence (such as **\TeX**).

If you type anything other than these nine options or a number, TEX prints the options message and again waits for instructions.

You do not have to wait for TEX to find an error if you want it to use scroll mode, nonstop mode, or quiet mode. Put one of the following control sequences into your text file wherever you want it to change modes.

Control sequence:	Name of mode:
\scrollmode	scroll mode
\nonstopmode	nonstop mode
\batchmode	quiet mode
\errorstopmode	usual, stop-for-errors mode

You can put any of these control sequences anywhere in your text file. That makes it easy to have TEX do most of the file in **\scrollmode** and change to its usual **\errorstopmode** for a new or difficult section.

These four interact-with-the-user modes are entirely separate and distinct from the paragraph-making, page-making, and math modes mentioned earlier. The scroll, nonstop, quiet, and errorstop modes tell TEX how to interact with you when it finds an error. The paragraph-making, page-making, and math modes determine what TEX does with the characters it finds in the **.tex** file.

3.8   The Last Possible Mistake in Your File

Waiting Patiently Bug

If you forget to put **\bye** at the end of your file, TEX prints a single-asterisk prompt (*), then waits for instructions.

There is a subtle difference between this bug and TEX's quiet mode. In both, there is no activity on the screen, so it is easy to think that nothing is happening. In quiet mode, however, TEX always terminates and returns you to top level, even without a **\bye** command at the end of the file—although if TEX continues "endlessly" in quiet mode, it could be stuck in a to-be-read-again loop (see Section 35.3). Thus, in quiet mode, you do not see the single-asterisk prompt; with this bug, you do.

When you see a single-asterisk prompt and want to return to top level, type **\bye**. TEX finishes the **.dvi** and transcript files, and returns you to top level.

In LATEX, the Waiting Patiently Bug appears when you forget to say **\end{document}** at the end of your text file. This bug can also appear if you forgot to close some earlier environment—so that LATEX uses **\end{document}** instead of **\end**{*environment*}. To fix this bug, type **\end{document}** instead of **\bye** when you see the single-asterisk prompt.

3.9   Making the Black Overfull Box Invisible

TeX puts a black box in the printout immediately after an overfull hbox. To make these boxes invisible, put the following instruction before the text in your file:

    \overfullrule=0in

\overfullrule says how wide the black box should be—and this instruction tells TeX to make it zero inches wide. So the box is still there, but invisible. To make the black overfull box visible again, see page 46.

The next section explains this instruction and what the equals sign is doing.

3.10   The Actor Model

\overfullrule is the first control sequence we have met with a different kind of job. All the other control sequences do something: They perform an action, so we can call them *doers*. **\TeX** typesets the TeX logo. The control space (\ ) typesets an ordinary interword space. **\bye** finishes the current page and the **.dvi** file, then goes back to top level.

Instead, **\overfullrule** is a *reporter*. It keeps track of how wide the black overfull box should be. When TeX needs to put a black box after an overfull hbox, it asks **\overfullrule** "How wide?" and **\overfullrule** reports whatever width it has stored. Its job is to remember a specific piece of information and to *report* that information when asked.

In fact, we can think of TeX as having a crew of tiny actors, each with a special job to do. There are only two basic kinds of actors in this book. A *doer* performs an action. A *reporter* remembers and reports information. (TeX also has a third type of actor, the *conditional*, which is used briefly in Section 18.5.)

Some actors are complete in themselves. Both **\TeX** and **\bye** already have enough information to do their job. Others need one or more inputs. **\char** needs one input: the number that gives a character's position in the font table.

In **\overfullrule=0in**, however, the **=0in** is not an input. Instead, it is a way of changing the information that **\overfullrule** remembers and reports. Whenever you see an equals sign, the reporter is being told to forget its old information and remember something new.[3]

TeX has many reporters. They remember such things as the page number, margin width, paragraph indentation, and text width. Thus, giving

---

[3]The TeXnical jargon for giving a reporter new information is "assigning a value to a parameter or register." Phrases like that appear often in other books about TeX.

new information to a reporter is a basic TeXnique that we use throughout this book.

This *actor model* of doers and reporters is a generally useful way of understanding how a programming language works; they are not TeXnical terms.

3.11 TeX's Prompts

You may be wondering why TeX has so many prompts: the question mark, double asterisk, and single asterisk.

The question mark (?) is TeX's "What should I do about this error I found?" prompt. When TeX prints the question-mark prompt on the screen, it expects a specific kind of response from you: an **i** *something*, **h**, RETURN , **x**, **e**, **s**, **r**, **q**, **?**, or a number.

The double asterisk (**) is TeX's way of asking for the name of a file to process. On any system where you can say **tex** *filename* at top level, the double-asterisk prompt appears only if you forget to type the filename. When you see TeX's double-asterisk prompt, type the name of a file for TeX to process. (If you forget the name of the file you want to process, type **null** instead.)

The single asterisk (*) is TeX's "What should I do now?" prompt. If you say **null** after the double-asterisk prompt, you see this single-asterisk prompt. This means that TeX is ready to process whatever you type at the keyboard.

For example, if you type **The quick brown fox jumps over the lazy dog.\bye** after the single-asterisk prompt, TeX automatically makes a file called **texput.dvi**—presumably as an abbreviation for "TeX put this **.dvi** file on your system." You can send **texput.dvi** to your printer just as you do any other **.dvi** file. This *interactive* way of working with TeX can be useful when you want to do a quick experiment. However, it is usually better to make a small test file. Your **testit.tex** file both keeps a record of your experiment and allows you to make minor changes until you get the result you want.

If you want TeX to process a file when you see the single-asterisk prompt, type **\input** *filename*. TeX goes to work just as if you had typed **tex** *filename* at top level.

To return to top level when you see TeX's single-asterisk prompt, type **\bye**.

LaTeX has an additional set of error messages for LaTeX-specific glitches, and their appearance is slightly different from TeX's error messages. However, LaTeX also uses TeX's question-mark prompt (**?**) and single-asterisk prompt (*****), so the responses you make are the same in LaTeX as in TeX.

Review and Preview

This chapter describes the two steps of getting a printout: having TEX process your **.tex** file to make a **.dvi** file, and sending the **.dvi** file to your printer. Use the extension **.tex** for your TEX files—unless you strenuously prefer other extensions. TEX can find files with other extensions, in other subdirectories, or on other drives.

While processing the **.tex** file, TEX also writes messages on the screen and in a transcript file, which often has a **.log** extension. If TEX stops when it finds an error, it prints a question-mark prompt on the screen and waits for instructions. To change this pausing-at-errors behavior, you can use **\scrollmode**, **\nonstopmode**, or **\batchmode** to change to the corresponding mode.

In addition to the question-mark prompt, TEX has a double-asterisk prompt, which expects the name of a file to process, and a single-asterisk prompt, which means that TEX will process whatever you type at the keyboard.

The actor model describes two different kinds of control sequences: doers (which perform an action) and reporters (which remember and report information). This distinction becomes increasingly useful as we continue in this book.

The next chapter shows several methods of fixing overfull hboxes. The chapter after that shows how to make new control sequences.

CHAPTER 4

Adjusting Awkward Line Breaks

Sooner or later (usually sooner!) TeX sends you a message about an overfull hbox (for <u>horizontal</u> <u>box</u>) and you see a small black box in the right margin of your printout. You might also notice that the line itself sticks out into the margin. You can, of course, rewrite your prose to fit the line, but this chapter shows several other ways of handling these overfull lines.

A different type of line-break problem occurs when TeX breaks a page in the midst of a hyphenated word. This chapter shows how to fix this problem as well.

4.1 Why TeX Makes Overfull Hboxes

When TeX starts up, it can only stretch or shrink the spaces between words by a small amount. When it finds a line that is longer than the text width, it hyphenates the words in the paragraph and tries again. If it still cannot find places for breaking the lines so that all the lines fit inside the margins, it typesets an overfull line (an **overfull \hbox**), puts the black box into the margin, and sends you a warning.

```
When in the course of typesetting text, it
becomes necessary for \TeX\ to hyphenate the
bonds that have connected each letter with
another ...
```

When in the course of typesetting text, it becomes necessary█
for TEX to hyphenate the bonds that have connected each
letter with another ...

Here is the warning TEX sent me for the example above:

```
Overfull \hbox (11.445pt too wide) in paragraph at lines 4-8
\tenrm When in the course of type-set-ting text, it be-comes
nec-es-sary|
```

The | after **nec-es-sary** is the black overfull box.

This message contains several useful pieces of information. It shows

- how much too wide the line is (here, 11.445 points);

- where the problem is (lines 4–8 of my text file);

- the text that TEX tried to fit on one line, including which typefaces it used along the way (here, **\tenrm**); and

- what hyphenation points TEX found in the words.

You do not have to change all of these lines to make them fit inside the margins. If the line is only 1 point too wide, the part that extends into the margin is roughly $1/72$ inch—smaller than most readers will notice. (However, your copy editor is guaranteed to have sharp eyesight: You have been warned!)

You can take several different approaches to fixing these overfull lines:

- hyphenate the last word on the line yourself;

- force an earlier line break;

- make a "fuzzy" margin;

- change the size of the interword spaces that TEX tolerates; or

- make the black overfull box invisible.

TEX writes all the overfull messages into the transcript file. This makes it easy to find and change the text, since you can look at the error messages in the transcript file while you edit your text file. Either print the transcript file as you would any other ordinary file, or place the transcript file into another buffer or window so that you can see it on the screen.

4.2   Hyphenate the Word Yourself

T_EX's method of finding hyphenation points is quite good but not perfect. Also, during the second pass through a paragraph, T_EX does not hyphenate words or phrases that already contain hyphens, or words that are followed by an em dash. Thus, to hyphenate a word differently, use a discretionary hyphen (\-). T_EX uses your discretionary hyphen(s) instead of generating hyphenation points in that word itself.

This discretionary hyphen does not force T_EX to break the line at that place; it simply gives T_EX a different option. Since you can put more than one discretionary hyphen into a word, you can still let T_EX decide where to break the line: su\-per\-cal\-i\-fra\-gil\-is\-tic\-ex\-pi\-al\-i\-do\-cious.

You can also show T_EX how to hyphenate a word throughout your document by putting **\hyphenation{**moth-er moth-ers**}** in the front of your file, before the text. Use braces { and } around this group of hyphenated words, not brackets or parentheses.

4.3   Break the Line Yourself

You can force T_EX to break the line at an earlier place with the control sequence **\break**. This is often the best solution when a line ends with a long, unhyphenatable word like *straight* or *through*. You can also force a break at a particular hyphenation point. For example, if you say **neces-\break sary** in your text file, T_EX breaks the line after **neces-**.

There is one disadvantage to using **\break**. If you later rewrite the paragraph (or change the size of your margins) but forget to remove the **\break**, T_EX still breaks the line at that point.

When you run T_EX on your file again, you are likely to see an underfull hbox message. This means that T_EX was forced to stretch the interword spaces in that line farther than it thinks is acceptable. However, T_EX does not put a black box into the margin to mark an underfull box, and the line does not stick out into the margin. Thus, if you are doing a draft printout and do not mind having wide spaces between your words, you can safely ignore T_EX's warnings about underfull hboxes.

4.4   Fuzzy Margins

If you do not mind lines that stick out into the margin a little bit, perhaps $1/64$ inch, you can increase the **\hfuzz**. **\hfuzz** is the amount that a line can stick out into the margin before TeX considers it to be overfull.[1] Give the **\hfuzz** reporter a new *dimension* to remember, such as

```
\hfuzz=0.016in
```

In TeX, a *dimension* is a number and a unit of measurement. In this example, the **in** means inches. Section 8.1 explains TeX's dimensions and how to use them.

This instruction allows your right margin to get a little fuzzy. TeX now accepts break points whose lines stick out into the margin as far as 0.016 inches, which is a smidgeon larger than $1/64$ inch. When a line's extra width is smaller than the **\hfuzz** amount, TeX does not send you an error message and does not put the black overfull box in the margin.

When TeX starts out, its **\hfuzz** is 0.1 points, roughly $1/723$ inch, which is very tiny indeed. You can make the **\hfuzz** as large as you want. If you say **\hfuzz=\maxdimen** (roughly 227 inches), you never see another black overfull box on your printout or another overfull hbox warning on your screen. With an **\hfuzz** this large, however, a word could be almost 19 feet long if TeX could not hyphenate it somewhere, so you would have to check each page of your printout.

TeX still prefers and searches for line breaks that do not make overfull hboxes, even when you have increased the **\hfuzz** dimension. TeX's acceptance of a fuzzy line is always a last resort.

4.5   Change the Size of Interword Spaces

Another solution allows TeX to use larger or smaller spaces between the words. When TeX is typesetting your text, it reads an entire paragraph, then starts looking for places to put the line breaks. TeX gives a *badness number* to each possible break point by looking at the size of the interword spaces created by that particular break point.

If the spaces on a line are the ideal size, the badness number of that break point is zero.[2] As the spaces become larger or smaller than the ideal, the badness number increases. So large badness means a bad line-break point, and small badness means a good line-break point. When TeX starts up, it accepts line-break badnesses up to 200.

---

[1] More precisely, **\hfuzz** is the amount that the contents of an hbox can exceed its legitimate width before TeX considers the hbox to be overfull. For a line in a paragraph, this legitimate width is the **\hsize**, which is explained in Chapter 8.

[2] This ideal size for an interword space is specified by the designers of the font you are using. For the 10-point Computer Modern Roman font used in this text, the ideal size is 3.33 points. Section A.3 shows the ideal size of interword spaces for TeX's standard set of 10-point fonts.

The spaces in this line produce badness number 73.
The spaces in this line produce badness number 31.
The spaces in this line produce badness number 9.
The spaces in this line produce badness number 1.
The spaces in this line produce badness number 0.
The spaces in this line produce badness number 5.
The spaces in this line produce badness number 42.
The spaces in this line produce badness number 142.
The spaces in this line produce badness number 336.
The spaces in this line produce badness number 656.
The spaces in this line produce badness number 1137.

The badness number increases rapidly as the spaces shrink and more gradually as they stretch. To increase TEX's tolerance of larger or smaller interword spaces, give the reporter called \tolerance a larger number to remember, such as

```
\tolerance=600
```

TEX now becomes more flexible about the size of its spaces, and makes fewer overfull hboxes for you to fix. In fact, if you say \tolerance=10000 (TEX's largest badness number), TEX accepts any size space, no matter how huge—and you never get another overfull hbox (unless an unhyphenatable word is wider than the text).[3]

You can both increase the \tolerance and prevent TEX from shrinking interword spaces. Change \fontdimen4, the amount that an interword space can be shrunk, for each of your fonts. Section A.3 explains the \fontdimens and how to change them.

You can also specify the size of spaces between words and sentences with \spaceskip and \xspaceskip. These two reporters are described in Section 16.8.

Badness Numbers

Badness numbers are not a measurement of the actual size of the space, and vary among the various fonts. This tolerance system is just a way of translating a line's aesthetic appearance into a number that TEX can use to decide where to break a line. With a large badness number, the spaces on a line can be so narrow that they no longer separate words effectively, or so wide that words become islands floating among rivers of white space.

The \tolerance is actually the badness number that TEX uses on its second processing of a paragraph—after it has assigned hyphenation points to the words. Thus, you may also want to increase the \pretolerance,

---

[3] **10000** is the largest badness number that is meaningful to TEX. \tolerance=10000 and \tolerance=1000000 have exactly the same effect.

which is the badness number TeX uses during its first search for line-break points in a paragraph. TeX's startup **\pretolerance** is **100**, and its startup **\tolerance** is **200**.

The now-standard version 3.0 of TeX also has **\emergencystretch**, a reporter that TeX uses during a third pass through a paragraph. TeX adds the **\emergencystretch** to the allowable size of the interword spaces, thereby scaling down the badness of each line. This enables TeX to find the least awful line-break points in an emergency but prevents TeX from using terrible line-break points during its first two passes through a paragraph. TeX's startup **\emergencystretch** is **0pt**. Experiment with small dimensions until you find one that works for you.

Using large badness numbers is especially useful for printing drafts of a document. With a larger **\pretolerance**, TeX finds more allowable line-break points on the first pass, and therefore hyphenates fewer paragraphs. With a larger **\tolerance**, there are fewer overfull hboxes sticking out into the margin. Most importantly, you do not need to use **\break**s, which often need to be moved or removed after rewriting.

If you get tired of seeing underfull hbox messages on your screen, increase the **\hbadness** reporter. When TeX starts up, the **\hbadness** is **1000**. TeX's highest badness number is **10000**, so if you say **\hbadness=10000**, TeX stops sending you any underfull hbox messages. However, a better strategy is to say

```
\hbadness=9999
```

You probably want to see all the underfull hboxes with a badness of **10000**. Their interword spaces are incredibly wide.

4.6   Make the Black Overfull Box Invisible

Sometimes it makes sense to let the line stick out into the margin and get rid of that black box in your printout. If you want to see the overfull warnings so you can find them easily in your text, but do not want to see black boxes on your printout, say

```
\overfullrule=0in
```

The black boxes are still there on the printout—but they are zero inches wide and therefore invisible. To make the black overfull box visible again, type

```
\overfullrule=5pt
```

Both **0in** and **5pt** are *dimensions*. TeX's dimensions are explained in Section 8.1.

LAT_EX's \overfullrule is 0in. The \hfuzz is still a small dimension, but the black overfull boxes are invisible. If you want to see the overfull box, you can use the draft option in the \documentstyle or change the \overfullrule as shown above.

4.7 Which Strategy Should I Use?

All of them.

When TEX does not find a valid hyphenation point (usually because the word is followed by an em dash), use the discretionary hyphen (\-). In the very rare event that TEX hyphenates a word incorrectly, give a \hyphenation{ex-am-ple} for the entire document. In a final draft, you can force TEX to use specific \break points.

TEX's startup \tolerance=200 and \pretolerance=100 are quite restrictive, because they are designed to meet the highest quality standards of the publishing industry. Most documents do not need to meet such high standards, so I generally change both the \tolerance and \pretolerance, though I use different numbers for different projects. TEX's startup \hfuzz of 0.1pt is minuscule; I often change it to 2.5pt for $8\frac{1}{2} \times 11$-inch documents. I also hate to see those black overfull boxes, so I change the \overfullrule to 0pt—except for those rare instances when I need to see which hbox is overfull while debugging something.

4.8 Changing a Line or Page Break at a Hyphenated Word

When TEX breaks the page in the middle of a hyphenated word, the reader has to remember the first part of the word while turning the page. This extra piece of work, though small, breaks the train of thought for the reader. To force TEX to break the line—and therefore the page—differently, put the hyphenated word into an \hbox (for horizontal box). In the following example, TEX normally hyphenates Russian and breaks the line between its two syllables.

```
Your words can be as unbreakable as Rasputin: the
\hbox{Russian} monk who was stabbed, shot,
poisoned and drowned, yet refused to die.
```

> Your words can be as unbreakable as Rasputin: the Russian monk who was stabbed, shot, poisoned and drowned, yet refused to die.

Anything in an hbox must stay on one line; it cannot be broken or hyphenated onto two lines. The hbox forces TeX to break the line somewhere else.

Using an hbox to stop TeX from hyphenating a word has an important advantage over putting \break in front of the hyphenated word. The hbox does not create strange effects if you rewrite a paragraph or change your margins. Using an hbox on the first line or two of a paragraph does not change the line break at all. TeX simply typesets an overfull line.

When you use an hbox to stop TeX from hyphenating a word, you also need a fairly high \tolerance so that TeX can easily find other places to break the line.

Review and Related Matters

This chapter shows five different strategies for handling overfull hboxes:

- hyphenate the last word on the line yourself with \-;
- force an earlier line break with \break;
- make a "fuzzy" margin with \hfuzz;
- change the size of the interword spaces that TeX tolerates with \tolerance and \pretolerance; or
- make the black overfull box invisible with \overfullrule=0pt.

This chapter also describes how to use an \hbox to prevent TeX from breaking a page in the middle of a hyphenated word.

The next chapter shows how to make new control sequences.

PART II

ONTO THE SLOPES

CHAPTER 5

Making New Control Sequences

Wouldn't it be nice if you did not have to look up the number to give \char every time you wanted a circumflex? Or if you could type \\ instead of \backslash? Or, better still, if you could type \MIT instead of **Massachusetts Institute of Technology**? You can—and this chapter shows how.

5.1   How to Make a New Control Sequence

TeX is basically a do-it-yourself construction kit. Just as Lego blocks are basic pieces for building a variety of objects, TeX's control sequences are small pieces that can be joined together to accomplish a variety of larger, more complex tasks.

The control sequence \def puts these pieces together and makes them into a new control sequence. A simple example is making an abbreviation for a long piece of text, so we do that first.

\def needs two inputs: the *name* of the new control sequence and its *definition*. Put a backslash in front of the name, and put the definition inside braces, like this:

```
\def\MIT{Massachusetts Institute of Technology}
```

What we have just done is called *writing a macro*. The braces show TeX where the definition begins and ends.

Now we can use \MIT just like any other TeX control sequence.

```
The author learned \TeX\ while working at the \MIT.
```

> The author learned TEX while working at the Massachusetts Institute of Technology.

5.2   What Is in a Macro?

A macro can contain text, one or more control sequences, or both text and control sequences. If your manuscript has many backslashes, it is faster to type \\ than **$\backslash$**. Also, remembering the name **\circumflex** is easier than looking up a number every time you want to use one.

```
\def\\{\backslash}
\def\circumflex{{\char94}}

Programmers use \circumflex Z to mean ''control-Z,''
and they call \TeX's '$\\$' an escape character.
```

> Programmers use ˆZ to mean "control-Z," and they call TEX's '\' an escape character.

Putting another pair of braces around **\char94** in the definition of **\circumflex** makes sure that the input to **\char** is always **94**, even if some other number follows **\circumflex** when you use it in your text. If this additional pair of braces is not there and you type "**\circumflex 5**," TEX looks for the 945th character on the font table. Since there is no such position or character, TEX complains!

LATEX uses \\ as a line-breaking macro. Therefore, if you want to make an abbreviation for **\backslash**, use something like **\bksl** instead of \\.

A macro must be used in the same way as the control sequences in its definition. Since **\backslash** can be used only in math mode, \\ must also be put in math mode. You can include the math mode toggles in the definition if you want—but doing so makes the macro less flexible. Section 5.7 explains problems you can encounter and questions to ask yourself when you put math mode toggles into a macro definition.

The next example combines a control sequence with text.

```
\def\texniqs{\TeX niques}
```

```
''\texniqs'' are ways of accomplishing a desired
\TeX nical goal.
```

> "TEXniques" are ways of accomplishing a desired TEXni-
> cal goal.

5.3   Writing Macros That Take Inputs

Sometimes we need to write a macro that takes an input—just as **\char**
takes an input. We have not met any good candidates for this yet, so the
only purpose of the following example is to show how to do it. To write a
macro that takes an input, use **#** both to show how many inputs and to
create "slots" for those inputs in the definition, like this:

```
\def\plopit#1#2{plop one here: #1, and two here: #2}
```

The **#1#2** after **\def\plopit** tells TEX that **\plopit** takes two inputs.
The **#1** and **#2** in the definition show what to do with these inputs when
TEX sees a **\plopit** in your text.

Do not put a space after a **#** slot in the definition—unless you want TEX
to typeset that space. Also, do not put any spaces among the **#**s between
the macro name and the definition.

Using Macros That Take Inputs

When you use **\plopit** in your text, put its inputs inside braces so TEX can
see where those inputs begin and end, like this:

```
A doctor's advice might be:
\plopit{plop-plop}{fizz-fizz}, and call me in the
morning.
```

> A doctor's advice might be: plop one here: plop-plop,
> and two here: fizz-fizz, and call me in the morning.

All macros need help finding their inputs. It does not matter if that
macro was written by Knuth (TEX), by Lamport (LATEX), or by you. TEX
needs a way of distinguishing between an input and the rest of your text,
and uses the braces to do it.

You quickly learn which of TEX's control sequences need braces around
their inputs and which do not. It is like knowing which English verbs have
an irregular past tense: *I ran* instead of *I runned*. After a little practice, one
feels right and the other feels wrong. When I introduce a control sequence, I

also show how to provide its input—either with or without braces. When in doubt, you can look it up.

TeX's capacity for handling inputs is limited, and long inputs slow TeX down. Chapter 12 describes *the sandwich structure*: a different approach to writing macros to handle large chunks of text.

Writing Macros with More Than One Input

A macro can have up to nine inputs; TeX complains if you try a tenth.

After the name of the macro you are defining, number the inputs sequentially, starting with **#1**. Inside the definition, you can use the inputs in any order and you can use them more than once. For example, you could define a **\scramblethis** macro as

```
\def\scramblethis#1#2{#2-#1-#2}
```

```
She gave him the old \scramblethis{one}{two} punch.
```

> She gave him the old two-one-two punch.

You do not have to put slots for all the inputs into the definition. One of my favorite macros is **\ignorethis**:

```
\def\ignorethis#1{}
```

```
Some people ignore problems\ignorethis{such as
bills?}, hoping they will go away.  If the
problem is with a friend, this strategy does
work---but has one significant drawback: sooner
or later the friend goes away.
```

> Some people ignore problems, hoping they will go away. If the problem is with a friend, this strategy does work— but has one significant drawback: sooner or later the friend goes away.

\ignorethis takes one input—and does nothing with it! This gives you a second way of putting comments in your text. Using **\ignorethis** instead of the percent sign means that you do not need to be careful about how your text editor behaves when it wraps—or rewraps—lines.

Inputs can insert almost anything you want into a sequence of control sequences and/or text. Just put an input slot into the appropriate place in the macro definition. Try out your idea in a small test file if you are not sure how it will work.

How a Macro Takes Its Input

When a macro is looking for its input, it grabs whatever "next object" is beside it. This next object can be a single character, a control sequence, or a group of characters inside braces. The braces show TeX where an input begins and ends. Using braces this way is like wrapping all the characters of the input into a single package.

For example, \overleftarrow and \overrightarrow are plain TeX macros that put arrows over their inputs. Both can be used only in math mode. Watch what happens when we use or omit the braces:

```
The Jet Stream flows from $\overleftarrow west$
to $\overrightarrow{east}$, all the way around
the world $\overrightarrow\bigoplus$.
```

The Jet Stream flows from $\overleftarrow{w}est$ to $\overrightarrow{east}$, all the way around the world $\overrightarrow{\bigoplus}$.

5.4   Always Think Macro!

The most important statement in this entire book is this:

Write lots of macros!

Lots and lots and lots of macros. Write macros for *everything*.

Writing lots of macros makes it easy to be consistent—about anything and everything: the shape of special-purpose paragraphs, the size of white space above and below displays of various kinds, which fonts you use for headings, even names for characters and towns, whatever you want. It also allows the computer to remember things you might forget.

```
\def\MartianEyeColor{red}

The Martian's \MartianEyeColor\ eyes
glazed over with fatigue.
```

The Martian's red eyes glazed over with fatigue.

It is almost impossible to write too many macros. The most time-consuming aspects of fixing mistakes are usually a direct result of not writing enough macros. It is easy to change the definition of a few macros. It is not easy to go through your entire document and change one hundred inconsistent instances of \bold Corn Flakes and \BOLD cornflakes. This task becomes even harder if your text editor's global-replace function does not work when words in a phrase are wrapped onto different lines in the file.

Many TEX novices feel hesitant about writing new macros. (What if I break something? What if I do it wrong?) But you will not break anything, and the worst thing that can happen if you "do it wrong" is that you will discover a new error message.

So go ahead! Splurge! Always ask yourself, "Can I write a macro to do this for me?" If the answer is yes, do it!

5.5 TEX's Control Sequences, Macros, and Primitives

Although macros such as **MIT** can make useful abbreviations of text, most of your macros will contain one or more control sequences. In fact, many of TEX's control sequences are macros themselves. Only one-third of TEX's control sequences are *primitives*—which means they were written in a programming language (such as C or Pascal) instead of in TEX. All the others were written in TEX by Donald Knuth, the Grand Wizard of TEX.

Many TEX primitives are also primitive in the sense of rudimentary, and are used mostly to build other control sequences. Many of the control sequences you actually use are macros rather than primitives.

There are few practical differences between primitives and macros. Primitives are faster, but macros can hardly be called slow. Primitives are also "smart" about how they find their inputs, whereas macros always need help to see where their inputs end (unless their input is a single character or control sequence).

def is not the only way of making a new control sequence. Other methods are used to make new reporters. As we encounter tasks that need new reporters, we will also meet the control sequences that create them.

Knuth's *TEXbook* has many references to *plain TEX*. Plain TEX consists of all the primitives plus the other control sequences written in TEX, both macros and reporters. Plain TEX also establishes the startup settings for margin size, paragraph indentation, **overfullrule**, and the like.

Almost every chapter in the rest of this book contains new macros or new reporters. From here on, every time I introduce a control sequence, I say whether it is a primitive or part of plain TEX. Also, the index in this book states whether each control sequence is a primitive, part of plain TEX, LATEX, or created in this book. (The index in Knuth's *TEXbook* also says whether a control sequence is a primitive or part of plain TEX.)

The important thing for now is that a macro is a new control sequence made by **def**. When you write a new macro, check the index of this book or *The TEXbook* to make sure you are not using the name of an existing control sequence. You might even discover something that already does what you want.

If you do re**def**ine an existing control sequence, other control sequences that expect to use the original version do not work properly. If you change something that is fundamental, this could spread large ripples of strange behavior throughout the system (somewhat like adding too much baking powder to a cake, or taking the tomatoes out of spaghetti sauce). Such mistakes do not destroy anything—except your peace of mind—but why give Murphy such a tempting invitation? (That's the Murphy of if-anything-can-go-wrong fame.)

LaTeX solved this problem with a macro called **newcommand**. **newcommand** also makes a new control sequence, but first it checks to see if a control sequence already exists with the name you want to use. If so, **newcommand** warns you that this name is already in use, and LaTeX does not make the new macro.

Since **newcommand** is a macro, you must put braces around both of its inputs: the name of the new macro and its definition.

```
\newcommand{\MIT}{Massachusetts Institute of Technology}
```

To make a macro that takes inputs, put the number of inputs inside brackets between the new macro's name and its definition. Thus, to define **plopit** with **newcommand**, type

```
\newcommand{\plopit}[2]{plop one here: #1, and two here: #2}
```

Another good reason for using **newcommand** is that the names of many LaTeX macros do not appear in the LaTeX book's index. Therefore, if you use **def** instead of **newcommand** in LaTeX, you might redefine some essential part of LaTeX's inner workings.

Another strategy for avoiding redefinitions is to use one or more uppercase letters in the names of your macros. TeX uses uppercase letters only for the control sequence **TeX**, several uppercase foreign-language letters, and some math mode symbols. Everything else is lowercase.

5.6   What TeX Does with Macros

It helps to know what TeX does when it finds a macro in the text.

When TeX sees a backslash, it looks for a control-sequence name and does whatever that control sequence says to do. If the control sequence is a macro, TeX *expands* it—which means that TeX proceeds as if the macro's definition had been typed in the text.

Every time you write a macro, it's as if TeX puts the definition into an envelope and writes the macro's name on the front of the envelope. When

TEX sees a macro in the text, it replaces the macro with a copy of whatever is inside the envelope, and proceeds from there. In this analogy, the envelope is the braces that you put around the definition when you write the macro.

In other words, when TEX expands a macro, it reaches inside those braces and does whatever the definition says to do. If the definition is text, TEX typesets it. If the definition contains one or more control sequences, TEX performs those control-sequence actions. If some of the control sequences are also macros, TEX expands them too.

5.7   Macros and Math Mode

Some control sequences can be used only in math mode. For example, one way of making a fraction is with the primitive \over, like this:

```
There must be at least 27${1 \over 2}$ ways of
making hamburger.
```

There must be at least $27\frac{1}{2}$ ways of making hamburger.

We can use \over to define a new macro called \fraction. Having a \fraction macro instead of using \over directly makes it easy to change our minds about how a fraction should look. (One alternative is this: $^1/_2$.)

However, \fraction raises a dilemma: Do we include the math mode toggles in the definition or put them in the text? *Generally speaking, do not put math mode toggles in your macro definitions.* Instead, put them into your text when you use the macro, like this:

```
\def\fraction#1#2{{#1 \over #2}}

Fellini broke new ground with his movie
8$\fraction{1}{2}$.

The sum of the series $\fraction{1}{2} +
\fraction{1}{3} + \fraction{1}{4} + \cdots +
\fraction{1}{n}$ gradually increases---but very
slowly.  The sum does not reach 6 until $n=616$.
```

Fellini broke new ground with his movie $8\frac{1}{2}$.

The sum of the series $\frac{1}{2} + \frac{1}{3} + \frac{1}{4} + \cdots + \frac{1}{n}$ gradually increases—but very slowly. The sum does not reach 6 until $n = 616$.

When a macro definition includes math mode toggles, the macro does not work correctly if you use it when TeX is already in math mode. The toggle that is supposed to *start* math mode *stops* it instead—so you are likely to get odd results, and probably a Math Oops Mode Bug (page 16) as well. Here is an example:

```
\def\fracture#1#2{${#1 \over #2}$}
```

```
A punster who breaks $\fracture{2}{3} \times
\fracture{1}{3}$ gets just what she deserves!
```

A punster who breaks 2 $_3$ ×1 $_3$*getsjustwhatshedeserves*!

\times is a plain TeX macro that can be used only in math mode. To get proper spacing around the × symbol, the entire expression needs to be in math mode. If you type

```
... breaks \fracture{2}{3} $\times$
\fracture{1}{3} gets ...
```

you get text spacing instead of math mode spacing. Thus, putting the math mode toggles in the definition of \fracture makes it difficult to use \fracture with other math mode control sequences.[1]

The problem is simple. You cannot start math mode if you are already in math mode. Thus,

- If you always use a macro in text, and never with other math mode material, then it is safe to put the math mode toggles into the macro definition.

- If you might use a macro with other math mode material, do not put math mode toggles into the definition. Instead, put them into the text where the macro is used.

5.8   Redefining a Macro

If you want to change a macro's definition, just define it again. To change the definition of \MIT, for example,

```
\def\MIT{M.I.T.}
```

TeX always uses the most recent definition.

A good candidate for redefining a macro is the plain TeX macro \dots. Knuth's intention for \dots was to make an ellipsis for both text and math

---

[1] You can get proper math mode spacing with \fracture, but only by using \null and \hbox in a very awkward and contorted way.

mode. Since TEX typesets three consecutive periods too close together for an ellipsis (...), Knuth used TEX's math mode spacing rules to add space between the periods. However, the spaces between these periods do not expand or shrink along with the interword spaces on the rest of the line. That's fine for math, but not for text, as we see in the following example:

```
These interword spaces \dots\ are their natural width.

These interword spaces \dots\ are stretched.\break
```

> These interword spaces ... are their natural width.
> These   interword   spaces   ...   are   stretched.

The spaces between the periods are not stretched at all.

Knuth's definition of **\dots** uses **\ldots**, a plain TEX macro that can be used only in math mode. Thus, we can still use **\ldots** in math mode. What we need is an ellipsis for text.

If we type a space between the periods, TEX typesets an intersentence space instead of an interword space—and might also split the ellipsis onto two separate lines. To make our ellipsis behave properly, we need to use a tilde. This ties the periods together and typesets an interword space between them. The following new definition of **\dots** allows the spaces between the periods to expand or shrink at the same rate as the spaces in the rest of the line.

```
\def\dots{.~.~.}

There is many a slip \dots\ twixt the tongue and
the lips.  As for why \dots~?  No one knows.
```

> There is many a slip . . . twixt the tongue and the lips.
> As for why . . . ? No one knows.

Now that we have a properly functioning **\dots** macro, I will use it instead of ... in my examples.

If you need to change the definition of an existing macro in LATEX, use LATEX's **\renewcommand**.

5.9 Where Do I Define New Macros?

You can define new macros at any time. (Naturally, you must define a macro before you can use it.) However, putting all your macro definitions in one place makes them easy to find and read. A natural place to put them is at the beginning of your file—but this can make the top of a file unwieldy, since you must get past all your macros before you reach the text.

Keeping Macros in a Separate File

A different approach is to put your macro definitions in a separate file, then have TeX \input this macro file as its first task in processing your text file.

```
\input macros

Now is the time for all good \TeX nical typists
to trade in their old $\fraction{1}{n}$ pieces
for upgraded macros \dots
```

\input is a primitive; it "goes and gets" a file. When TeX sees \input in your text file, it reads the entire \input file—just as if that file was typed at that spot in your document—then goes back to your text file and continues where it left off. Using \input this way makes it easy to update your macros as you learn more TeX.

In the example above, \input looks for a file called **macros.tex**, reads through everything in that file, then continues with **Now is the time** . . . . If you do not specify an extension, TeX automatically looks for a file with the **.tex** extension.

If TeX cannot find the file, it sends you an error message that it cannot find that file and asks you to type another input file name. (Sections 3.3 and 3.4 describe what to do if you encounter this problem.)

Whenever you \input a file, do not put \bye at the end of that file. Instead, put \bye in only one place: where you want TeX to stop.

Lamport changed \input so that you can put braces around its input. This makes \input consistent with other LaTeX commands.

```
\input{macros}
```

You cannot do this in TeX unless the braces are part of the filename.

In LaTeX, do not put \end{document} at the end of every file. Put \end{document} only where you want LaTeX to stop.

5.10 Using \input for File Management

You can \input as many files as you want, whenever you want. This lets you select specific macro files for a particular document. If the filename extension is not **.tex**, type the extension as well.

```
\input twelve.pt
\input my_usual.mac
\input two-cols
```

```
Are we alone in the universe?  Or are little green
humanoids also sitting down at computer keyboards
throughout our galaxy at this very moment?  \dots
\bye
```

This example \inputs three macro files: **twelve.pt** has information for using 12-point fonts, **my_usual.mac** contains the usual set of macro definitions, and **two-cols.tex** creates two columns on a page instead of one.

Using \input is also a good TEXnique for organizing a large project. Instead of having one huge file with the text of an entire document, you can split it up into chapters and put each chapter into a separate file. The file for doing this book starts out with

```
\input bookfont.mac
\input mymacros.mac
\input thebook.mac
```

```
\input thefront.z00
\input inafile.z01
\input specchar.z02
\input printout.z03
```

Sometimes, the order in which you \input these files is important. In this example, both **thebook.mac** and **mymacros.mac** contain definitions for a \section macro. If I had input **thebook.mac** first, before **mymacros.mac**, TEX would have used my generic definition of \section— which is wrong. When **thebook.mac** follows **mymacros.mac**, however, TEX uses the definitions that were custom designed for this book.

You can use LATEX's \include macro instead of \input. If the extension is not **.tex**, specify that as well.

```
\include{daisies}
\include{printout.z03}
```

Using \include makes it possible to use \includeonly, which is useful on large projects. \include does have one disadvantage in comparison with \input: any text file that you \include automatically starts on a new page.

\include and \includeonly are described in Section 4.4 on pages 75–77 of Lamport's LaTeX book.

Review and Preview

\def allows you to create your own control sequences, so you are not limited to someone else's ideas about what to do or how things should look. \def appears in all the rest of the chapters in this book.

This chapter shows how to write macros with \def, including macros that take inputs, and explains how TeX expands the macros it finds in your text. When you write a macro that can be used only in math mode, putting the math mode toggles into the definition can cause problems. It is simpler and often wiser to put the toggles into the text instead.

Using \input is a helpful method for managing files. Keeping macro definitions in one or more separate files makes it easy to update your macros as you learn more TeX. The beginning of a text file can \input the macro files it needs in a few short lines, which makes the text file easier to read. Also, large documents can be organized into separate files for each chapter. Do not put \bye at the end of a file you plan to \input as part of a larger project.

The next chapter shows how to **use** *many* **different** *fonts*. It also explains *groups*, an important feature of TeX that is used throughout this book.

CHAPTER 6

A Smorgasbord of Fonts

Using different typefaces can be lots of fun. (Like spices, though, a little variety goes a long way, and too much variety creates confusion.) This chapter shows how to use several different type styles. It also explains *groups*, a very useful feature of TeX that allows you to change things inside a specific part of the text.

6.1   Presto Chango!

Plain TeX starts out with five basic type styles: roman, *slanted*, *italic*, typewriter, and **bold**. The plain TeX macros for changing to these different styles are as follows:

Macro name:	Result:
\rm	The quick brown fox jumps over the lazy dog.
\sl	*The quick brown fox jumps over the lazy dog.*
\it	*The quick brown fox jumps over the lazy dog.*
\tt	The quick brown fox jumps over the lazy dog.
\bf	**The quick brown fox jumps over the lazy dog.**

```
Each of these \tt control sequences \it changes
\bf the \sl font.
```

Each of these control sequences *changes* **the** *font.*

In typesetting, a *font* is an assortment of type that is all the same size and style—such as Baskerville Italic 10 Point. A type *style* describes the appearance of the type—such as roman, bold, or italic. A *typeface* is a collection of differently sized fonts in the same style—such as Baskerville Italic. A *typeface family* is a collection of similar typefaces in different styles; the Baskerville family includes Baskerville, Baskerville Italic, and Baskerville Bold.

The terms *italic* and *slanted* both mean a slanted typeface. Traditionally, italic fonts were designed to look like script or handwriting. In the 1930s, however, typeface designers began to design slanted characters whose shapes were a tilted version of their upright siblings. These designs became more popular in the 1970s.

TEX has two varieties of slanted characters: a script-like typeface and a tilted-roman typeface. Knuth uses **\it** to mean the script-like characters, and **\sl** to mean the tilted-roman ones.

In TEX, each font is a collection of up to 256 characters in one specific size. For example, the text of this book is typeset in a font called Computer Modern Roman 10 Point. The Computer Modern fonts that come with TEX contain only 128 characters. However, TEX can handle fonts with as many as 256.

How do you return to the roman style after you have changed to one of the others? You can, of course, simply type **\rm**. There is nothing wrong with this approach. However, it is much more efficient to put the font change *inside a group*.

6.2   Using a Group to Change Fonts

Putting a font change inside a group is like keeping the bull inside a fence so he does not run amok and bother all the cows in the meadow.

```
That {\bf bold bull} is securely fenced.
```

That **bold bull** is securely fenced.

The open brace ({) means *begin a group*, and the close brace (}) means *end a group*.

Any changes that you make inside a group stay in that group and do not affect the text that follows. This is called *local*, meaning that the changes are local to a particular group.

To begin a group, type {. Then type the font change and whatever text you want typeset in that font. To end the group, type }. When TEX sees the }, it stops all the changes you made inside that group. TEX processes the text after } in the same way as the text before {. If the font was roman

before, it will be roman after. If it was slanted before, it will be slanted
after.

```
\sl The slant on {\bf these groups} is very useful!
```

The slant on these groups is very useful!

We can change all sorts of things inside a group and not have to worry
about how to change them back. The changes stop when we end the group.

The Bulletin Board Analogy

It's as if TeX has a bulletin board with many signs—and one of them says
CurrentFont=\rm. When we say **\it** in the text, TeX takes down the old
sign and puts up a new one that says **CurrentFont=\it**.

Starting a group is like putting a big sheet of transparent plastic over the
board. TeX can still see all the signs through the plastic. Now when we say
\it, however, TeX does not take down the old sign. Instead, it puts a new
CurrentFont=\it sign over the old one.

When we end a group, TeX takes down the sheet of plastic—which pulls
off any signs that were tacked on over the plastic. Thus, all the old signs are
still there on the board.

(Of course, TeX does not really have a bulletin board inside it, any more
than it has little people doing the work of **\bf**, **\overfullrule**, and **\def**.
This is simply an analogy that shows how TeX works.)

Groups Inside Groups Inside Groups . . .

You do not have to end one group before you begin another. You can begin
a new group whenever you want. This is handy if you want a roman or bold
word inside a long group of italic words.

```
You can {\it nest one group {\bf inside}
another group} like this too.
```

You can nest one group inside another group like this
too.

The italic font is local to the first group; it began after the first { (the first
sheet of plastic in the bulletin-board analogy). The bold font is local to the
second group; it began after the second {.

When the second group ends, TeX removes the second sheet of plastic
and the **CurrentFont=\bf** sign. Now when TeX checks the **CurrentFont**
sign—which it does every time it typesets a character—it sees the first

group's **CurrentFont=\it**. Thus, TEX typesets **another group** in the italic font.

When the first group ends, TEX removes the first sheet of plastic, which makes the original **CurrentFont=\rm** sign visible once again.

Changing the Font in Math Mode

The math mode toggle (**$**) also begins and ends a group. If you want to use a different font in math mode, you do not have to use braces to stop that change. It stops automatically when you end math mode.

```
The circumference of a circle is $\bf C = 2 \pi r$,
and its area is $\bf A=\pi r^2$.
```

> The circumference of a circle is $\mathbf{C} = 2\pi\mathbf{r}$, and its area is $\mathbf{A} = \pi\mathbf{r}^2$.

The math mode spacing rules do not change when you change the font. TEX still puts space around the =, and no space between the **2**, the π, and the **r**. Also, the font change affects only letters and numbers. The π and the other math symbols are available in only one font.

Of course, you can use braces to nest another group inside the math mode group if you want to. For example, you might want only one letter or group of letters typeset in the bold font:

```
The force of gravity is $F = {\bf G} m_1 m_2 / d^2$,
where {\bf G} is the gravitational constant.
```

> The force of gravity is $F = \mathbf{G}m_1 m_2/d^2$, where $\mathbf{G}$ is the gravitational constant.

Math mode spacing does not change when you nest a group inside math mode. In this example, the **G** is treated in the same way as the **F**, **m_1**, **m_2**, and **d^2**.

6.3 The Italic Correction

Both slanted and italic characters lean over toward the right. If the slanted character is tall and the space is small, the slanted character might even bump into the next upright character. The solution is to insert an *italic correction* (\/). This primitive adds a little extra space after an italic or slanted character.

```
The italic correction {\it equalizes\/} the size
of spaces on each side of the italics, and makes
text easier to read.  Without it, a {\it slanted}
letter seems to lurch toward the next one.
```

> The italic correction *equalizes* the size of spaces on each
> side of the italics, and makes text easier to read. Without
> it, a *slanted* letter seems to lurch toward the next one.

Using an italic correction is crucial when there is no space between a
slanted letter and the upright character after it.

`{\it embank}ment`	*embank*ment
`{\it embank\/}ment`	*embank*ment
`{\sl OUCH}!`	*OUCH!*
`{\sl OUCH\/}!`	*OUCH!*
`{\it label})`	*label*)
`{\it label\/})`	*label*)

The size of the italic correction is different for each character, since
tall characters lean farther than short ones. Commas and periods are the
shortest characters of all, so even the tallest italic characters cannot bump
into them. Thus, do not put any italic correction in front of a comma or
period.

```
As we walked along the {\it towpath},
Jack and Jill were both quite {\it gleeful\/},
Spot and Snoopy drank the birds' bath.
As poems go, this one is awful.
```

> As we walked along the *towpath*, Jack and Jill were both
> quite *gleeful* , Spot and Snoopy drank the birds' bath. As
> poems go, this one is awful.

In this example, the italic correction after **gleeful** is wrong, because it adds
unwanted space. The space between **gleeful** and the comma should be the
same as the space between **towpath** and the comma.

6.4 Typeface Macros

Macros make it easy to change your mind about which typeface to use for
a particular kind of text. Let's suppose you start out using an \it typeface
for things you want to emphasize, then change your mind and decide you
want \sl instead—or an entirely different typeface becomes available and you
want to switch. Now you have to change {\it words} in your text file to

{\sl words} or {\exotic words}—and make sure you do not change \item to \slem as well.

Instead, you can write one macro for emphasizing words in your text, another for titles of books or journals, and a third for examples of programming.

```
\def\em{\it}
\def\bibl{\sl}
\def\eg{\tt}
```

```
Now I can {\em emphasize\/} my words, advise you
to read Knuth's {\bibl \TeX book}, and show examples
of {\eg program names} with whatever typeface I want.
```

> Now I can *emphasize* my words, advise you to read Knuth's TEXbook, and show examples of `program names` with whatever typeface I want.

If you change your mind about how you want your book titles, program names, or emphasized words to look, all you need to change is one macro definition. TEX does all the rest.

In writing this type of macro, the essential question is, "What categories of things need to stand out visually—and might benefit from being typeset in a font that is different from the text?" This book, for example, has four main categories and corresponding macros: \em for emphasizing words, \code for the names of control sequences and the like, \npt for inputs, and \bug for the names of bugs.

```
\def\code#1{{\bf #1}}
\def\npt#1{{\sl #1}}
\def\bug#1{{\rm #1}}
```

As it turned out, I did not need the \bug macro after all. However, if the book designer had wanted the bug names in a different typeface, it would have been simple to do this. Every bug name in the text uses the \bug macro. Also, \code started out in my drafts as \tt; the designer changed this to \bf. So which typeface you want to use is not that important. You can always change the typeface later.

Letting the Macro Do the Work

Always **think macro**. Ask yourself, "Is this a pattern? Can I put this in a macro?"

Anything that you do more than a few times or might change later is a good candidate for a macro. For example, if you are working on a piece about ships, it is helpful to write one macro that says how to typeset a ship name, plus a collection of macros for the name of each individual ship. This simplifies the typing, guarantees consistency, and lets TeX do all the work for you. The following **\ship** macro takes one input, and typesets it using the **\em** (emphasis) font.

```
\def\ship#1{{\em #1}}
\def\Const{\ship{U.S.S. Constitution}}
\def\Merim{\ship{U.S.S. Merrimack}}
```

TeX expands **\Merim** to **\ship{U.S.S. Merrimack}**—then expands that to {**\em U.S.S. Merrimack**}. The font change stays inside the group formed by the inner set of braces in the definition of **\ship**. Without this inner set of braces, there is no group, and TeX continues to use the **\em** font through the rest of your text.

```
\def\wrongboat#1{\em #1}
\def\Titanic{\wrongboat{U.S.S. Titanic}}
```

```
The \Const, at anchor in Boston harbor, can be
seen by any interested tourist.  Will a similar
tour be organized for the \Titanic\ in its resting
place on the ocean floor?
```

> The *U.S.S. Constitution*, at anchor in Boston harbor, can be seen by any interested tourist. Will a similar tour be *organized for the U.S.S. Titanic in its resting place on the ocean floor?*

6.5   Using Exotic Fonts: Load Your Own

TeX can use many other fonts in addition to the roman, bold, italic, slanted, and typewriter styles we have already seen. Depending on the fonts available on your system (including your printer), you might have such delicacies as SMALL CAPITALS or **sans serif** styles.

When TeX starts up, however, all it knows about are the roman, bold, italic, slanted, typewriter, and math mode fonts in the standard size (usually 10 point), plus two sets of smaller roman, bold, and math mode fonts for subscripts and superscripts (usually 7 and 5 point). TeX does not know anything about the other exotic fonts, even if they are available on your system.

To use any of these other fonts, you must *load* each one individually. Loading a font means getting information about that font and putting that information into TeX's memory. Each font has its own separate file containing coded information about the size of each letter and various other characteristics of the font.

Loading Exotic Fonts

Here are several of the exotic fonts that are probably available to you. (This book uses the Syntax family of sans serif fonts instead of the Computer Modern family of sans serif fonts shown in the following table.)

small caps	THE QUICK BROWN FOX JUMPS OVER THE LAZY DOG.
sans serif	The quick brown fox jumps over the lazy dog.
sans serif italic	*The quick brown fox jumps over the lazy dog.*
sans serif bold	**The quick brown fox jumps over the lazy dog.**

The TEX primitive \font loads a font into TEX's memory. It needs two inputs: the name you will use for the font, and the computer's filename for the font.

```
\font\sc=cmcsc10       % small capitals
\font\ssf=cmss10       % sans serif
\font\ssi=cmssi10      % sans serif italic
\font\ssb=cmssdc10     % sans serif bold
```

In this example, \sc is our name for the small-capitals font, and **cmcsc10** is the computer's filename for that font. The first input to \font can be any name you want. If you prefer, you can call this font something else, perhaps \caps or \smallcapitals or \smcap. However, the second input must match the computer's filename for that font—in this case, **cmcsc10**.

\font is similar to \def because it makes a new control sequence. In the example above, \sc, \ssf, \ssi, and \ssb are all new control sequences. These new control sequences all act like doers. They say "change to this font," just as \rm, \bf, and the other font-changing macros do. However, the new control sequence also acts like a reporter, because it has the job of remembering where TEX can find the information for this font. That is why you see an equals sign between the first and second inputs to \font.

Since this new control sequence combines qualities of both doers and reporters, let's give it a distinct category all its own: a *fontname*. So \sc, \ssf, \ssi, and \ssb are all fontnames. (\rm, \bf, \it, \sl, and \tt are all macros, not fontnames.)

When these fonts are loaded, you can use the new fontnames in the same way you use \rm, \bf, and the other font-changing macros. Once a font is loaded with a particular name (such as \sc), you must use that fontname to use the font.

```
Such a multitude of {\sc delicious, \ssf tantalizing,
\ssi magnificent, \ssb splendid} fonts!
```

> Such a multitude of DELICIOUS, tantalizing, *magnificent,* **splendid** fonts!

The small caps and sans serif fonts already exist in LaTeX. The control sequences for them are \sc for SMALL CAPS, and \sf for sans serif (our \ssf font).

Use \newfont to load a new font in LaTeX. \newfont is explained in Section 5.8.2 on page 116 of Lamport's LaTeX book.

Deciphering a Font's Computer Filename

The computer names for these font files are abbreviations. The **cm** at the beginning of the file name stands for *Computer Modern*.[1] If your system has an extensive set of exotic fonts, some of the computer filenames might start with something other than **cm**.

The number at the end of the filename states the size of the font. All the fonts we have seen so far are 10-point fonts, but other sizes are also available. The next chapter shows how to load these as well.

The letters between **cm** and the number describe what kind of font it is. At the very least, your system has all the fonts on the left in the following list (unless you, as the system's owner, did not obtain one of them). You might also have one or more of the fonts on the right—or others that do not appear in this list.

r	roman	csc	small capitals
bx	bold extended	u	unslanted italic
tt	typewriter	ss	sans serif
sl	slanted	ssi	sans serif italic
ti	text italic	ssdc	sans serif bold
mi	math italic	inch	inch-high letters
sy	math symbol		
ex	math extension		

Now we can decipher many of the font filenames that you encounter. For example, **cmti10** is Computer Modern Text Italic 10 Point, and **cmbx8** is Computer Modern Bold Extended 8 Point. If new fonts become available on your TeX system, use their filenames in the same way as the ones shown here.

Text italic is not the same as math italic. The spacing between letters is quite different—so you should always use text italic (**cmti**) for typesetting text, and math italic (**cmmi**) for typesetting math. Furthermore, text italic has italic numbers, math italic does not; text italic has ligatures, math italic

---

[1]Some systems have **am** (*Almost Modern*) fonts instead of **cm**. The two sets of fonts are very similar in appearance. The Almost Modern fonts are the original version, now obsolete.

has symbols; text italic has foreign-language symbols, math italic has Greek letters; and so on. To examine the differences in detail, look at the font tables in Appendix A.

Font Metrics Files and Pixel Files

You need two files for each font you want to use: a *font metrics file* and a *pixel file*.

The font metrics file contains information that TeX needs about the size of each character, its italic correction, and other characteristics of the font. These font metrics files have a **.tfm** extension (for TeX font metrics). Thus, the name of the Computer Modern Roman 10 Point metrics file is actually **cmr10.tfm**.

The pixel file shows your printer the shape of each character—pixel by pixel. (The term *pixel* stands for *picture element*, and originally meant each tiny dot on your video screen.) That is, a font's pixel file contains information for your printer's driver, which takes the **.dvi** file and tells the printer where to put ink on the page—or dots on the screen for a **.dvi** previewer.

Different kinds of pixel files have different types of names. The names of many pixel files end with the letters **gf**, **pk**, or **pxl**. These files might also be called something other than a pixel file, but the principle is the same.

Since pixel files take up a lot of memory space, they are usually stored in a packed form, called PK files. PostScript fonts are done differently; each pixel file is created by the printer on an as-needed basis.

Review and Preview

This chapter shows how to change among the roman, `typewriter`, **boldface**, *slanted*, and *italic* fonts, and keep such changes local (inside a group). Writing macros like **\em**, **\bibl**, **\eg**, and **\ship** makes it easy to use a font consistently when you emphasize words, cite references, and type program names. This chapter also describes how to load any other fonts that might be available on your system.

The next chapter shows how to make your text larger or smaller, and how to load different sizes of fonts. Chapter 27 explains how to get different sizes of math mode fonts. This allows you to use math mode in parts of your document that use larger or smaller typefaces—such as headings and footnotes.

CHAPTER 7

Making Your Text Larger or Smaller

TeX starts out with 10-point type. (Points are a measurement used by printers. There are roughly 72 points to the inch.)[1] Many books use 10-point type (as this one does), but 10 point is rather small for an $8\frac{1}{2} \times 11$-inch sheet of paper. This chapter shows two different ways to make the size of your text larger (or smaller).

LaTeX Notes

LaTeX has two methods of getting larger or smaller fonts. If you want text fonts of a different size, give **documentstyle** a second, optional input as shown in Section 2.2.2 on page 21 of Lamport's LaTeX book.

To change to a larger or smaller font within your document, use the size-changing macros shown in Section 5.8.1 on page 115 of Lamport's LaTeX book.

7.1 Magnify the Size of Your Text

The easiest way to make your text larger (or smaller) is with the plain TeX macro **magnification**. To get 12-point type throughout your manuscript,

---

[1]There were originally 12 points to a pica, and 6 picas to an inch, and thus 72 points to the inch. Since the baselines of 10-point type are usually set 12 points (1 pica) apart, this makes 6 lines to the inch. The pica typeface on typewriters got its name from this measurement as well. A century ago, the American Typefounders Association defined the point as 0.013837 inch, which means there are now 72.27 points to the inch.

put the following instruction near the front of your text file (before the actual text begins):

```
\magnification 1200
```

The numbers for the degree of **\magnification** are based on 1000, in the same way that percentages are based on 100. **\magnification 1000** multiplies the size by 1, which means there is no change at all. **\magnification 1200** multiplies the size by 1.2 (and 1.2 × 10 point = 12 point type). Similarly, **\magnification 500** multiplies the size by 0.5, making it $1/2$ of 10 point, which is 5 point.

In many TEX systems, twelve different sizes of fonts are available with plain TEX (although your system might have more or fewer sizes):

size in points:	5	6	7	8	9	10
\magnification	500	600	700	800	900	1000

size in points:	11	12	14	17	21	25
\magnification	1095	1200	1440	1728	2074	2488 [2]

If you give **\magnification** a number for a size that is not available (such as 2000), your printer hiccups. (More precisely, your printer's driver program hiccups.) TEX can handle the calculations easily, but the driver usually complains and often substitutes a different font—which may or may not be adequate for what you had in mind.

LATEX does not have **\magnification**. Give **\documentstyle** a second optional input instead (such as **[12pt]**) as shown in Section 2.2.2 on page 21 of Lamport's LATEX book.

Let TEX Remember the Number

It is a nuisance to look up numbers like 1728 every time you want really large type. Luckily, TEX has a plain TEX macro that does the remembering for you. Say **\magstep1** for one step up from 10 point, **\magstep2** for two steps up, and so on. Also, **\magstephalf** expands to 1095, the half step between 1000 and 1200.

TEX expands:	into this instruction:
\magnification \magstephalf	\magnification 1095
\magnification \magstep1	\magnification 1200
\magnification \magstep2	\magnification 1440
\magnification \magstep3	\magnification 1728

---

[2]The numbers on this bottom line are based on powers of 1.2. The number 1095 is $1000 \times \sqrt{1.2}$, and 1200 through 2488 are $1000 \times (1.2)^1$, $(1.2)^2$, $(1.2)^3$, $(1.2)^4$, and $(1.2)^5$.

```
\magnification \magstep4        \magnification 2074
\magnification \magstep5        \magnification 2488
```

Limitations of Using \magnification

\magnification makes everything bigger or smaller—except the width
and height of your text and margins. For anything that should stay the
same size, specify **true** with the dimension. (Dimensions are explained in
Chapter 8.)

You cannot use **\magnification** more than once. It is designed to change
your entire document, not to change back and forth from one type size to
another. To use more than one type size, you must load each additional font
individually.

Using **\magnification** has one important drawback. To be readable, the
letter shapes of a small font need to be wider than the shapes of a large
font. Thus, the letters of a magnified font look fat (these letters are
cmr5 loaded at the 10-point size) and the letters of a shrunken font
look anorexic. A better method of getting 12-point type for your text is to
load an entire set of 12-point fonts.

To use math mode in a different size, however, you must use the font-
family system described in Chapter 27. Otherwise, anything you type in
math mode is typeset in TEX's usual set of 10-point fonts. Since Chapter 27
is a hefty mouthful for a beginner, use **\magnification** until you are ready
to use TEX's font-family system.

7.2   Loading Smaller Fonts

To use different sizes of type in the same document, you must load the
specific sizes you need. Let's say you want to use 8-point fonts for your
footnotes. Load these the same way we loaded the exotic fonts.

```
\font\eightrm=cmr8      % roman
\font\eightbf=cmbx8     % bold extended
\font\eightit=cmti8     % text italic
\font\eightsl=cmsl8     % slanted
\font\eighttt=cmtt8     % typewriter
```

Now you can use **\eightrm** and these other fontnames in the same way that
you use **\bf** and the other font-changing macros.

```
{\eightrm The ears lent to Marc Antony were
never returned, said {\eightbf Zeus}---as
quoted in {\eightsl The Olympic Heights}, a
local newspaper.  Thus, the interest on this loan
is still mounting.}
```

> The ears lent to Marc Antony were never returned, said **Zeus**—
> as quoted in *The Olympic Heights*, a local newspaper. Thus, the
> interest on this loan is still mounting.

As any writer can tell you, it is easy to change one's mind and move footnote material into the text, or move text into the footnotes. Then one must delete **\eightrm**, change **\eightit** into **\it**, and so on—which is a big nuisance. But once again, TEX has a solution.

7.3   Macros to Change Font Size

The solution is to write a macro that changes the meaning of **\rm**, **\bf**, and the other control sequences. Here is one called **\eightpoint**:

```
\def\eightpoint{%
\def\rm{\eightrm}%
\def\bf{\eightbf}%
\def\it{\eightit}%
\def\sl{\eightsl}%
\def\tt{\eighttt}%
\rm}
```

The percent signs at the ends of the lines make sure there are no spaces anywhere in the **\eightpoint** macro. This is important because you might use **\eightpoint** in a situation where TEX is obeying (and typesetting) all the spaces you type.[3]

Now when we say **\eightpoint**, the roman, bold, italic, slanted, and typewriter font-changing macros all use the 8-point fonts instead of the 10-point set. Since we do not want to typeset the rest of the document in 8-point type, we put the **\eightpoint** change inside a group.

```
{\eightpoint
This entire example---every {\it italic,
\sl slanted, \bf bold}, and {\tt typewriter}
word---is in eight-point type.}
```

> This entire example—every *italic, slanted,* **bold,** and `typewriter`
> word—is in eight-point type.

---

[3]TEX typesets the space after a brace when it is in horizontal (paragraph-making) mode. TEX's modes are explained in Chapter 33. TEX ignores spaces at the beginning of a line unless you are using **\obeyspaces**, a plain TEX macro described in Section 16.3.

Our **\eightpoint** macro does more than change the definitions of the font-changing macros. The last line also says **\rm**. Why do we need this, especially since TEX is already using a roman typeface?

First, TEX might not be using a roman font at the time we switch to **\eightpoint**. Second, even if it is a roman font, it is a 10-point roman font, not an 8-point one. If we do not say **\rm** at the end of the definition of **\eightpoint**, we get a Font Does Not Change Bug.

Font Does Not Change Bug

To change the **CurrentFont** sign on TEX's bulletin board, we must use a macro that expands to a fontname. Plain TEX defines **\rm** as **\tenrm**, the 10-point roman font—and TEX's bulletin board actually says **CurrentFont=\tenrm**, not **\rm**. Similarly, plain TEX defines **\it** as **\tenit**, **\bf** as **\tenbf**, **\tt** as **\tentt**, and **\sl** as **\tensl**.

Until we put **\rm** on the last line of **\eightpoint**'s definition, all **\eightpoint** does is change the definitions of the font-changing macros. Changing the definitions does not change the current font.

There are always two steps in using any fonts other than TEX's basic set of 10-point fonts. (This basic set of fonts includes the 7- and 5-point fonts for subscripts and superscripts.)

- Load the fonts with **\font**.
- Change to the new font by typing either a fontname (such as **\eightrm**) or a macro that expands to a fontname (such as **\rm**).

If you need to use math mode in more than one font size, you must use TEX's font-family system, as explained in Chapter 27.

7.4   Loading Larger Fonts

Some of you are probably thinking, "Aha! I can load a set of 12-point fonts with **\font\twelverm=cmr12**, and so on." That is a terrific idea, but it may not work on your system. Until recently, there were no **cmr12**, **cmbx12** (and so on) files. Instead, many TEX systems use a set of scaled-up 10-point fonts that can be loaded at the 11-, 12-, 14-, 17-, 21-, and 25-point sizes.

To load a scaled-up font, you must give **\font** some additional information, like this:

```
\font\twelvebf=cmbx10 scaled 1200
\font\xiibold= cmbx10 at 12pt
```

These two instructions accomplish the same result: Each loads the bold **cmbx10** font file at the 12-point size. Even though the names for the two are different, saying **\twelvebf** has the same effect as saying **\xiibold**. (The roman numeral *xii* is shorter than the word *twelve*. This feature makes roman numerals handy for naming fonts.)

Both **scaled 1200** and **at 12pt** instruct TeX to load a specific, scaled-up font file. **scaled** and **at** do not have a backslash because they are not control sequences. Instead, they are *keywords*: words that give additional information to a control sequence. Both **scaled** and **at** are keywords only when they follow the control sequence **\font** as shown.

Some keywords also need an input; **scaled** needs a number, and **at** needs a *dimension*—a number and unit of measurement. (Dimensions are explained in Section 8.1.) Both **scaled** and **at** convert this information into instructions that **\font** uses to find the computer's scaled-up font file. You can also get scaled-down fonts in the same way.

It is not necessary to type a space between **scaled** or **at** and its input. Including the space can make the instruction easier to read, but you can omit the space if you prefer.

Let TeX Remember the Font-Size Numbers

Computers are very good at remembering numbers, but most people are not. We can use **\magstep** with **scaled**, just as we did with **\magnification**. **scaled\magstep1** is one step up from 10 point (namely 12 point), **scaled\magstep2** is two steps up, and so on.

The following table shows the equivalent keywords and inputs for all of TeX's standard font sizes that are larger than 10 point.

scaled 1095	scaled\magstephalf	at 11pt
scaled 1200	scaled\magstep1	at 12pt
scaled 1440	scaled\magstep2	at 14pt
scaled 1728	scaled\magstep3	at 17pt
scaled 2074	scaled\magstep4	at 21pt
scaled 2488	scaled\magstep5	at 25pt

To load a 17-point font, for example, you can say **scaled 1728**, or **scaled\magstep3**, or **at 17pt**.[4]

```
\font\LARGEbf=cmr10 scaled\magstep3
```

Then you can use **\LARGEbf** in the same way as the other fontnames.

---

[4]Some printer drivers need the higher precision of **at 17.28pt** to find the **scaled 1728** font. Or, if the font is available in the **1700** size as well as **1728**, you can get both **17pt** and **17.28pt**.

```
Here is a {\LARGEbf Big Bold} typeface.
```

Here is a **Big Bold** typeface.

When loading scaled-up fonts, some people prefer to specify a number; others do not. Some people prefer just the number (**1200**); others prefer a dimension (**12pt**). Use whichever method feels most comfortable to you.

Review and Preview

This chapter describes two methods of changing the size of the type in your document. **\magnification** either magnifies or reduces the size of everything in the document. Loading a different size font changes only the font.

To change from one size type to another—such as in footnotes or headings—write a size-changing macro like **\eightpoint**. **\eightpoint** changes the definitions of the font-changing macros. For example, **\bf** then changes the font to **\eightbf** instead of **\tenbf**. To limit these changes, put **\eightpoint** and the 8-point part of the text inside a group.

The next chapter shows how to change the size of the white spaces on the page. Chapter 27 explains how to get different sizes of math mode fonts by using TEX's font-family system. This lets you use the correct math mode fonts in such places as headings and footnotes that use larger or smaller typefaces.

CHAPTER 8

Shaping Your White Space

The size and shape of the white space on a page has a strong impact on the reader. Are the lines so long and close together that the document is hard to read? Or so short and far apart that it looks like a draft? Are the words all scrunched together on some of the lines? Is it difficult to see where one paragraph ends and the next begins?

TeX starts out with roughly 1-inch-wide margins, $1/4$-inch paragraph indentations, and 6 lines of text to the inch. (TeX uses points instead of inches, so the actual sizes are slightly different. You will soon see what the real sizes are.) This makes your pages very dense and hard to read, so you probably want to change some of these startup (default) settings. To do this, give a different dimension to the appropriate reporters.

TeX has many white-space reporters. They range from everyday matters (such as margins and paragraph indentations) to more esoteric concerns (such as how much space to put before and after math mode material). This chapter explains the reporters you are most likely to modify: paragraph indentations, margins, spacing between paragraphs, and spacing between lines. We meet several other white-space reporters in the chapters that follow—and for those of you who like to explore uncharted waters, Appendix B lists all of TeX's white-space reporters.

To change any of these reporters, you need to know how to use TeX's system of *dimensions*.

8.1 TEX's Dimensions

A dimension is simply a number and a unit of length. Some people like to use inches, others prefer various printers' units, and still others use the metric system. TEX can handle all three.

Altogether, TEX recognizes nine units of length. Each unit has its own two-letter abbreviation. TEX uses the conversions shown in the third column of the following table for all its dimension calculations. For each unit of length, the fourth column shows how many of those units are in one inch, and the fifth column shows how many points are in one of those units.

			1 in =	1 unit =
in	inch	1 in = 72.27 pt		72.27 pt
pc	pica	1 pc = 12 pt	6.0225 pc	12 pt
pt	point	1 pt = 1 pt	72.27 pt	1 pt
bp	big point	72 bp = 1 in	72 bp	1.00375 pt
cm	centimeter	2.54 cm = 1 in	2.54 cm	28.45 pt
mm	millimeter	1 mm = 0.1 cm	25.4 mm	2.845 pt
dd	didot point	1157 dd = 1238 pt	67.5415 dd	1.07 pt
cc	cicero	1 cc = 12 dd	5.6285 cc	12.84 pt
sp	scaled point	65536 sp = 1 pt	4736286.7 sp	0.00001526 pt

These abbreviations do not begin with a backslash because they are keywords, just as **scaled** and **at** are keywords. Thus, TEX recognizes **in**, **pc**, **pt**, **bp**, **cm**, **mm**, **dd**, **cc**, and **sp** as part of a dimension only when they are used in a situation that requires a dimension. At all other times, they are typeset as ordinary text.

```
There are 2.54 cm to the inch---and
the \TeX\ dimension '1in' equals '72.27pt.'
```

There are 2.54 cm to the inch—and the TEX dimension '1in' equals '72.27pt.'

It does not matter whether or not you put a space between the number and the unit of measurement. TEX treats the dimensions **5pc** and **5 .pc** in exactly the same way. Typing no space between the number and the keyword, however, prevents your word processor from "wrapping them" onto different lines, and makes it easier for you to recognize that this is a TEX dimension. It also does not matter if you use inches for one dimension, points for the next, and millimeters for the third. TEX does not get confused—although you might!

Here are some examples of legitimate TEX dimensions:

```
    2 in    .5 pc    0.35pt    -67,86254bp    0mm    +1024 sp
```

A few of these dimensions may look strange to you.

- *Zeros*: I prefer to put a zero in front of the decimal point when a number is smaller than one, but you do not have to. TEX understands either way. Also, do not say **0** without a unit of length when TEX expects a dimension. Instead, say **0pt** or **0in** (or whatever unit of length you like).

- *Minus sign*: A minus sign in front of a dimension is often used to subtract instead of add, or to make TEX "move in reverse": left instead of right, up instead of down. Three examples of these negative dimensions appear on pages 88, 94, and 102.

- *Plus sign*: If you want, you can put a plus sign in front of a positive dimension, although it is not necessary. In TEX, + always means a positive number (larger than zero); it never means to add numbers.

- *Commas*: You can use a comma *instead of a period* for the decimal point. TEX is designed this way because the comma is used for this purpose in some European countries. However, do not use a comma anywhere else in a number (such as to separate the thousands from the hundreds).

TEX has two other units whose size depends on the font you are using. The **em** is used for horizontal (right/left) spacing and the **ex** for vertical (down/up). Back in the days of metal type, an **em** space was the same width as the capital **M**, and an **ex** was the same height as the lowercase **x**. TEX's **em** and **ex** make it possible to scale things up or down in different sizes of fonts, yet keep the same relative spacing. In TEX's basic set of 10-point fonts, the **em** and **ex** are the following sizes:

	\rm	\sl	\it	\tt	\bf	math italic
1 em =	10.00 pt	10.00 pt	10.22 pt	10.50 pt	11.50 pt	10.00 pt
1 ex =	4.31 pt	4.31 pt	4.31 pt	4.31 pt	4.44 pt	4.31 pt

The **em** and **ex** stay the same relative size in proportion to the font. For example, in the Computer Modern Roman 12 Point font, the **em** is $1.2 \times 10 = 12$ points, and the **ex** is $1.2 \times 4.31 = 5.17$ points.

Keeping a Dimension True to Size

When you use **magnification** but want a particular dimension to stay the same, say **true** in front of that unit of measurement. For example, if you are magnifying your text to 14 point, you might not want the **overfullrule** magnified as well.

```
\magnification \magstep2
\overfullrule=5truept
```

More importantly, you may want to use **true** with reporters that govern various aspects of your white space.

8.2   Paragraph Indentation

TeX automatically puts some white space at the beginning of each new paragraph. To find out how wide this white space should be, TeX asks the primitive reporter called **\parindent**. The startup **\parindent** is actually 20 points, which is a little wider than $1/4$ inch. (Twenty points is 0.27674 inch, and $1/4$ inch is 18.0675 points.)

To get a different amount of white space at the beginning of your paragraphs, give a new dimension to the **\parindent** reporter. For example, to make all your paragraphs start with a $1/2$-inch indentation, say

```
\parindent=0.5in
```

You can change **\parindent** whenever you want, although doing this in the middle of a paragraph makes it hard to see and does not change the indentation at the beginning of the current paragraph. TeX uses the new **\parindent** when it starts the next paragraph, and continues using this **\parindent** for every new paragraph thereafter (unless you change this reporter again).

Use **\setlength**, LaTeX's dimension-changing macro, to change the **\parindent**. Type **\setlength**{**\parindent**}{**2em**} (or whatever dimension you prefer). You can change **\parindent** anywhere in your document.

Starting a Paragraph without Indentation

Sometimes, a particular paragraph should begin with no indentation. When text that follows a figure or table continues a previous paragraph rather than starting a new one, it should not be indented. Also, you might not want to indent the first paragraph of a chapter, section, or subsection—or the paragraph after a **\sceneshift** macro that uses a **\bigskip** to indicate a shift of scene or time.

For this purpose, you do not have to change **\parindent** to **0pt** and then change it back. Instead, say **\noindent** at the beginning of the paragraph.

```
\dots\ attached a metal string and sent the kite soaring
into the stormy skies.
\sceneshift

\noindent
Suddenly, lightning struck!   Ben Franklin knew \dots
```

. . . attached a metal string and sent the kite soaring into the stormy skies.

Suddenly, lightning struck! Ben Franklin knew . . .

All the nonindented paragraphs in this book—including this one—begin with **\noindent**.

Of course, the simple way to achieve this is often to put **\noindent** in a macro. For example, the macro that typesets the printout part of these examples uses **\noindent** to begin the initial paragraph. That is why the first paragraph of all the examples is not indented.

\noindent is a primitive—and a doer, not a reporter. It says to start a new paragraph without any indentation. Similarly, the primitive called **\indent** says to start making a paragraph and to insert an indentation that is **\parindent** wide.[1]

8.3 Margins

There are two ways of changing the margins. One makes the text narrower (or wider) and moves it sideways. This approach affects the entire page—including the headline and footline that TeX automatically puts at the top and bottom of every page—and is the best way of managing your page margins. The other method deals separately with the headline, footline, or text areas of the page. Since this second approach is better suited for special-purpose indented paragraphs, it is described in Chapter 13.

The width of the text is the **\hsize**, and its left/right placement on the page is the **\hoffset**. Both **\hsize** and **\hoffset** are primitive reporters. (As you may have guessed, the **h** in their names is for *horizontal*.)

When TeX starts up, the **\hsize** is 6.5 inches, and the **\hoffset** is 0 points. However, this **\hoffset** of 0 points does not mean that the text begins at the left edge of the paper. When you send the **.dvi** file to your printer, the driver program automatically puts a 1-inch margin between the text and the left edge of the paper.

To change the left and right margins, give new dimensions to the reporters **\hsize** and **\hoffset**. A good rule of thumb for choosing the

---

[1]This is a slight oversimplification. **\noindent** and **\indent** both nudge TeX into horizontal (paragraph-making) mode. **\indent** also adds an indentation, while **\noindent** does not. If TeX is already in horizontal mode, **\noindent** has no effect, but **\indent** adds another slab of white space that is **\parindent** wide. Thus, starting a paragraph with **\indent\indent** puts two **\parindent**-sized spaces at the beginning of that paragraph. Starting a paragraph with **\noindent\noindent** has the same effect as a single **\noindent**. TeX's modes are explained in Chapter 33.

\hsize is one that gives you approximately 55–65 characters in a line. When you have more than that, a line becomes hard to read.

Let's suppose you need to increase the left margin to 1.25 inches. Since the first inch is already there, shift the text to the right with an \hoffset of 0.25 inches.

```
\hoffset=0.25in
```

By moving the text to the right, the right margin got smaller. To adjust the right margin back to 1 inch, make the text narrower. The \hoffset was increased **0.25in**, so decrease the startup \hsize of **6.5in** the same amount.

```
\hsize=6.25in
```

After you have worked with TEX for a little while, it becomes easier to think in terms of left margin and text width instead of left margin and right margin.

To change the width of the text in LATEX (the \hsize of your paragraphs), use \setlength to change the \textwidth.

To change the \hoffset in LATEX, use \setlength to change \oddsidemargin and \evensidemargin. LATEX uses the \oddsidemargin on odd-numbered pages, and the \evensidemargin on even-numbered pages.

The \textwidth, \oddsidemargin and \evensidemargin should be changed only in the preamble.

8.4 Let TEX Do the Math

It can be tricky to remember which dimension you gave to each of these reporters. After all, it is their job to remember these things, not yours. If you let TEX do the adding and subtracting, you do not have to remember anything at all.

The example above increased the \hoffset by $1/4$ inch and decreased the \hsize by $1/4$ inch. The TEX primitive \advance does the arithmetic for us. To subtract, use a negative dimension instead of a positive one.

```
\advance\hoffset by  .25in
\advance\hsize   by -.25in
```

\advance adds two inputs, then tells the reporter to remember the new amount. The first input to \advance comes from the reporter itself—from \hoffset and \hsize in this example. The second input comes from **by**.

by is another keyword. You can use it with any of TEX's three arithmetic control sequences: \advance, \multiply, and \divide.

You can use \advance with any reporter. If the reporter remembers a number, give **by** a number. If the reporter remembers a dimension, give **by** a dimension. For example, when your text is very narrow, you might want to increase the **\tolerance** so that you are not flooded with overfull hboxes.

```
\advance\tolerance by 3000
```

Use LaTeX's **\addtolength** macro to add something to a dimension reporter. For example, to increase the **\parindent** by **1em**, type

```
\addtolength{\parindent}{1em}
```

You can also use LaTeX's **sloppy** environment for one or more paragraphs instead of changing TeX's **\tolerance**.

Top and Bottom Margins

You can change the top and bottom margins the same way you change the left and right ones. **\voffset** says how far down to move the text on the page, and **\vsize** says how tall the text should be. Both **\voffset** and **\vsize** are primitive reporters.

Plain TeX's startup **\voffset** is **0pt**, and the **\vsize** is **8.9in**. Experiment with different dimensions until you get what you want. When you send the **.dvi** file to the printer, the driver program automatically puts a 1-inch margin between the text and the top edge of the paper.

TeX has many of these **h**-for-horizontal and **v**-for-vertical pairs. If your mind glazes over trying to remember which is which, pin a seascape near your monitor. *Horizontal* comes from the same root word as *horizon*—and you get *vertigo* from being in a high place and looking down.

To change the height of the text in LaTeX, use **\setlength** to change LaTeX's **\textheight**. To change the **\voffset**, use **\setlength** to change the **\topmargin**. Both the **\textheight** and the **\topmargin** should be changed only in the preamble.

8.5 Spacing between Paragraphs

The amount of white space between paragraphs is determined by the primitive reporter called **\parskip**. **\parskip** can be changed like all the other reporters. Give it a new dimension to remember.

```
\parskip=1pc
```

TeX adds a **\parskip** to the page just before it starts a new paragraph, not at the end of a paragraph.

Use \setlength to change the \parskip. Type \setlength{\parskip}{3pt} (or whatever dimension you prefer). You can change \parskip anywhere in your document.

8.6   Spacing between Lines

"How do I double space a document?" is one of the first questions many people ask when learning TeX. The spacing between lines is controlled by the primitive reporter called \baselineskip.

Remember back in grade school when you were learning to write the alphabet on special paper with those widely spaced lines? Each of those lines was a *baseline*: the line that the letters sit on. The only letters that go below the baseline are the ones with tails—such as g, j, p, q, y, and Q. TeX's \baselineskip is the distance between one baseline and the next.

When TeX typesets a paragraph, it breaks the paragraph into lines of text. Then it stacks those lines on the page as if it were hanging shelves on a wall, starting from the top and working down. TeX's \baselineskip says how far apart the baselines should be. It's as if TeX has a ruler exactly \baselineskip long that it uses to decide where the next shelf should go. (Chapter 33 describes this process in more detail.)

TeX's startup \baselineskip is 12 points. Six lines of text that are 12 points apart make 72 points (almost 1 inch), so each baseline is roughly $1/6$ inch away from its neighbors. To change this, give new information to the \baselineskip reporter. For example, to get a space-and-a-half effect, type

```
\baselineskip=18pt
```

You can change the \baselineskip whenever you want, as often as you want. However, it is pointless to change it more than once in the same paragraph. TeX uses the report from \baselineskip at the end of the paragraph to set the baselines for the entire paragraph.

You can use one reporter to give new information to another reporter. Letters often need a blank line between paragraphs. To make this blank line the same size as the \baselineskip, type

```
\parskip=\baselineskip
```

\parskip now stores whatever information it gets from \baselineskip. If the \baselineskip is 14pt, the \parskip is now 14pt as well.

Changing \baselineskip for Different Sizes of Text

When you use two different sizes of fonts in a document, such as 10-point for text and 8-point for footnotes, you also need to change the \baselineskip in these two areas. The simplest method is to put this change in the macro that changes the font size—such as the following **\eightpoint** macro:

```
\def\eightpoint{%
\def\rm{\eightrm}%
\def\bf{\eightbf}%
\def\it{\eightit}%
\def\sl{\eightsl}%
\def\tt{\eighttt}%
\baselineskip=10pt
\rm}
```

(The only difference between this **\eightpoint** macro and the one on page 78 is the change to the **\baselineskip**.)

Let TₑX Do the Remembering

It is a nuisance to look up your usual **\baselineskip** every time you want to change it. TₑX can do the remembering for you. The plain TₑX reporter called **\normalbaselineskip** has the job of remembering the normal size of a **\baselineskip**. When TₑX starts up, the **\normalbaselineskip** is **12pt**. Thus, another way of changing your baselines to double spacing is

```
\baselineskip=2\normalbaselineskip
```

TₑX multiplies the report from **\normalbaselineskip** by **2** and gives the result to **\baselineskip** as its new information. The number does not have to be an integer. You can also say

```
\baselineskip=1.5\normalbaselineskip         or
\baselineskip=1.3333\normalbaselineskip
```

to get space-and-a-half or space-and-a-third baselines.

The **\normalbaselineskip** reporter does not change when you change your **\baselineskip**, so you can use it as a stable reference point. If your baselines have gotten bollixed up and you want to restore the normal baselines, type **\normalbaselines**. **\normalbaselines** is a plain TₑX macro whose definition includes the following instruction:

```
\baselineskip=\normalbaselineskip
```

Using one reporter as a reference point and source of information for other reporters is a very useful TₑXnique. We see it often in the rest of this book.

Changing the Size of Your Normal Baselines

You can also change the **\normalbaselineskip** if you want. To get three lines of text to the inch as your standard-size baselines, type

```
\normalbaselineskip=0.3333in
\baselineskip=\normalbaselineskip
```

If you forget that second line, the **\baselineskip** does not change and you have a Reporter Did Not Change Bug.

Reporter Did Not Change Bug

When you give new information to a reporter, it calculates and stores the new information immediately. It does not matter if that new information came from a second reporter or if you change the second reporter afterward. To change any reporter, you must give new information to that particular reporter.

Thus, TEX does not change the **\baselineskip** when you change the **\normalbaselineskip**. Here is what happens to **\baselineskip** and **\normalbaselineskip** during the following sequence of events:

When TEX starts,

\baselineskip reports:	12pt
\normalbaselineskip reports:	12pt

- After \baselineskip=18pt,

\baselineskip reports:	18pt
\normalbaselineskip reports:	12pt

- After \normalbaselineskip=15pt,

\baselineskip reports:	18pt
\normalbaselineskip reports:	15pt

- After \baselineskip=2\normalbaselineskip,

\baselineskip reports:	30pt
\normalbaselineskip reports:	15pt

8.7   Let TEX Do All the Work

Wouldn't it be nice if you could type **\linespacing{2}** to get double spacing, and **\linespacing{1.5}** for space-and-a-half? You can. Write a **\linespacing** macro that takes one input, like this:

```
\def\linespacing#1{\baselineskip=#1\normalbaselineskip}
```

As we saw in Section 5.3, the **#1** after **\linespacing** tells TEX that this macro takes one input. The **#1** inside the definition shows where to insert that input when TEX finds the macro in your text and expands it. Thus, TEX expands **\linespacing{1.75}** into

```
\baselineskip=1.75\normalbaselineskip
```

If the current **\normalbaselineskip** is 12 points, the **\baselineskip** becomes 21 points, as you can see in the following example:

```
\linespacing{1.75}
Is double spacing more like double parking or like
double dating?  If the former, will I get a ticket?
If the latter, is it blind?
```

> Is double spacing more like double parking or like double
>
> dating? If the former, will I get a ticket? If the latter, is
>
> it blind?

You can use **\setlength** to change the **\baselineskip**, and you can do this anywhere in your document. However, the best way of changing the baselines in LaTeX is to redefine **\baselinestretch** with **\renewcommand**. For example, to get double-spaced lines, type

```
\renewcommand{\baselinestretch}{2}
```

You can also redefine the **\baselinestretch** to be **1.5** for space-and-a-half baselines, or **1.333** for space-and-a-third, or any other number you want. Change the **\baselinestretch** in the preamble.

8.8   Reporters and Muffins

When you need to give new information to a reporter, there are three ways of doing it—one direct and the others indirect:

Directly: `\baselineskip=15pt`
Give a specific number or dimension for the reporter to remember.

Indirectly: `\baselineskip=\normalbaselineskip`
Have another reporter supply the new information.

`\advance\baselineskip by 10pt`
Use `\advance`, `\multiply`, or `\divide` to provide the new information.

Giving the information *directly* is like giving a muffin to someone who is hungry. It supplies exactly what the person needs. In the same way, providing a specific number or dimension gives the reporter exactly what it is looking for.

Sometimes it is easier and more consistent to provide the information *indirectly*, from another reporter. This is like saying, "Go ask Joe, he has a muffin for you."

For example, to make **\baselineskip** the same as **\normalbaselineskip**, it is better to say **\baselineskip=\normalbaselineskip** than to give **\baselineskip** a specific dimension. That way, if you decide to change the **\normalbaselineskip** in a later draft, the **\baselineskip** changes too. (Of course, you must change the **\normalbaselineskip** first. Otherwise, you get a Reporter Does Not Change Bug.)

The other way of giving information *indirectly* is like giving a recipe. It says, "I do not have exactly what you need right now, but here is a recipe you can use."

In the example above, **\advance** takes in some ingredients (a report from **\baselineskip** and information from **by**) and generates the new dimension for **\baselineskip** to remember. It's as if **\advance** baked a muffin especially for **\baselineskip**.

This give-a-recipe strategy is useful whenever you do not have a specific number or dimension handy—or whenever you need to make a change that is relative. For example, to change the **\hsize** for a draft, saying

```
\advance\hsize by -1.5in
```

is a more flexible approach than **\hsize=5in**.

The inputs for **by** with both **\multiply** and **\divide** must be numbers, not dimensions. Also, these numbers must be integers (no decimals allowed). For example, if you want to change the **\hsize** to $\frac{2}{3}$ of its former size for a draft, type

```
\multiply\hsize by 2
\divide\hsize by 3
```

8.9   Putting It All Together

If each document you work with uses a unique format, customize these reporters for each document. However, if you work with only a few special formats (such as letter, thesis, and draft), then you might want to write a macro for each one. Here are bare-bones versions of **\thesis** and **\draft**:

```
\def\thesis{\hsize=6.25in
   \hoffset=0.25in
   \voffset=0.25in
   \vsize=8.75in
   \normalbaselineskip=18pt
   \normalbaselines}
```

```
\def\draft{\hsize=5in
   \vsize=7.5in
   \parindent=30pt
   \linespacing{2}}
```

The document that you want to typeset as a draft would then start with

```
\input macros
\draft
```

A similar approach is to make a small file for each type of document, such as **thesis.mac** and **draft.mac**. Each file would give customized information to the relevant reporters, and can also contain any special macros for that particular format. With this approach, the beginning of a thesis would start with

```
\input macros
\input thesis.mac
```

 LaTeX uses this input-a-file system. Each of LaTeX's style files customizes the white-space reporters for a specific type of document. Advice on modifying LaTeX style files is far beyond the scope of this book. If you want to experiment, copy an existing style file and see what happens to a short test file when you change something in the new style file.

Review and Preview

This chapter describes dimensions and shows how to change the size of your margins, the height and width of your text, the size of paragraph indentations, and the space between the baselines of your text. Both \noindent and \indent can start a new paragraph. \linespacing, \thesis, and \draft are examples of macros that modify the white space on the page. The muffin analogy illustrates three ways of giving new information to reporters.

The next chapter shows how to create new white space. The chapter after that introduces TeX's *glue*—which is more like silly putty than the sticky stuff you might expect.

CHAPTER 9

Skips: Creating New White Space

When you put white space on a page, sometimes you need a specific amount and sometimes you need to fill "from here to there" but cannot know in advance how large a space that is. **\parindent** is a good example of a specific amount. "The rest of the page" is a good example of an unknown from-here-to-there quantity.

This chapter shows how to add specific amounts of white space to your line or page. The next chapter introduces *glue*, a taffy-like substance that can stretch or shrink however far you need.

9.1 Put Some White Space Here

TeX's **\hskip** primitive adds horizontal space to a line, and the **\vskip** primitive adds vertical space to a page. Naturally, you also have to say how much space, so **\hskip** and **\vskip** both take an input.

```
Dick and Jane went \hskip 1in skipping
down the hill.

\vskip0.25in

Spot ran up to meet them.
```

Dick and Jane went   skipping down the
hill.

Spot ran up to meet them.

For those of you who grabbed your rulers: The horizontal space between **went** and **skipping** is larger than 1 inch because it also contains one interword space. The horizontal space in front of **Spot** is the **\parindent** indentation. The vertical space between **hill** and **Spot** is larger than $^{1}/_{4}$ inch because TEX adds the **\vskip** to the distance between baselines. In other words, the distance between the baselines of **hill** and **Spot** is **0.25in + 1\baselineskip**.

To force TEX to put the exact amount of the **\vskip** between two lines of text, say **\nointerlineskip** above the **\vskip**. TEX normally puts interlineskip glue between lines of text in order to place their baselines exactly **1\baselineskip** apart. **\nointerlineskip** is a plain TEX macro that prevents TEX from putting interlineskip glue between the lines immediately above and below it.[1]

It does not matter whether or not you put a space between the **\hskip** or **\vskip** and its input. Since numbers are nonletters, TEX can see where the control sequence ends. If you forget to include the number, TEX sends you an error message and uses **0** (zero). If you forget the unit of length, TEX sends another error message and uses **pt** (points).

LATEX has two macros for putting white space on the page: **\hspace** and **\vspace**. Put braces around their inputs.

    \hspace{.25in}
    \vspace{1.2cm}

Lamport designed **\hspace** and **\vspace** so that you cannot get a Plus or Minus Bug (see page 110).

9.2   TEX's Ready-Made Everyday Skips

When you want to make your skips consistent, it is a nuisance to remember how big your last **\vskip** was, or to look back through your document to find out. Therefore, TEX has three ready-made sizes of vertical skips:

---

[1]More precisely, **\nointerlineskip** tells TEX not to put interlineskip glue between two boxes. TEX puts each line of a paragraph into an hbox. Chapters 11, 28, and 33 describe this process.

\smallskip	3 points
\medskip	6 points
\bigskip	12 points

(This is an oversimplification. All of TeX's skips actually use glue, which I explain in the next chapter. For our purposes here, though, we can pretend that they use only a dimension.)

These sizes are especially convenient for TeX's startup 10-point typefaces, because the **\bigskip** is the same height as the **\baselineskip**, the **\medskip** is half that height, and the **\smallskip** is half of that.

It is easy to change the size of these skips. Each has a corresponding skipamount reporter—so to change the size of a skip, change the appropriate reporter. Let's say you want the **\bigskip** to be $1/2$ inch, the **\medskip** to be $1/3$ inch, and the **\smallskip** to be $1/4$ inch.

```
\bigskipamount=0.5in
\medskipamount=0.3333in
\smallskipamount=0.25in
```

\bigskip and its two siblings are plain TeX macros written by Knuth. Their definitions are

```
\def\bigskip{\vskip\bigskipamount}
\def\medskip{\vskip\medskipamount}
\def\smallskip{\vskip\smallskipamount}
```

When TeX finds a **\bigskip** in your text and expands it, **\vskip** expects to find a dimension as input. Instead, it finds **\bigskipamount**. Still hopeful of getting its input, **\vskip** prods **\bigskipamount**—and **\bigskipamount** reports **12pt**.

This is exactly the same as the go-ask-Joe strategy in the muffin analogy of Chapter 8. Instead of getting its input directly, **\vskip** gets its input from the reporter **\bigskipamount**.

Using **\bigskip**, **\medskip**, and **\smallskip** makes it easy to have three different but consistent sizes of white space in your document. First decide what kinds of places need a big, medium, or small skip; then decide what size each of those three skips should be.

9.3   Making \baselineskip-sized Skips

A different approach to changing your skip sizes defines the **\bigskip**, **\medskip**, and **\smallskip** in terms of the **\baselineskip** instead of the skipamount reporters.

```
\def\bigskip{\vskip\baselineskip}
\def\medskip{\vskip 0.5\baselineskip}
\def\smallskip{\vskip.25 \baselineskip}
```

Again, it does not matter whether you put a space between \vskip and its input. TeX ignores this space if you type one. Since \baselineskip, 0.5\baselineskip, and .25 \baselineskip all begin with a nonletter, all three can show TeX where the control sequence ends. TeX also does not typeset the space between .25 and \baselineskip.

This is similar to the way we gave new information to \baselineskip in Section 8.6. Now when TeX expands \medskip, it multiplies the \baselineskip by 0.5 and gives the result to \vskip as input.

If you use these definitions of \bigskip, \medskip, and \smallskip, these skips are larger in double-spaced sections and smaller in single-spaced sections. Each time TeX expands one of these skip macros, it uses the current \baselineskip. Thus, if you increase the \baselineskip in a draft section of your text or decrease it for a quotation, TeX uses this larger or smaller report when it expands the macro and calculates the dimension for \vskip.

A slight variation on this idea makes the skipamount reporters proportional to the \baselineskip.

```
\bigskipamount=\baselineskip
\medskipamount=0.5\baselineskip
\smallskipamount=0.25\baselineskip
```

New information for reporters is calculated and stored immediately. Thus, if you use this TeXnique, the sizes of the \bigskip, \medskip, and \smallskip do not change when you change the \baselineskip.

In other words, if the \baselineskip is 18pt when you change the skipamount reporters, \bigskipamount becomes 18pt, \medskipamount becomes 9pt, and \smallskipamount becomes 4.5pt. Even if you change the \baselineskip later in your file, those skipamount reports stay the same.

9.4 Making Special-Purpose Skip Macros

Sprinkling big, medium, and small skips throughout your document makes it easy to forget which size you used for which purpose. This leads to inconsistent spacing. Thus, let a macro remember what size skip to use in a particular situation—even if you plan to use the same size skip for all of them.

```
\def\endofexercise{\bigskip}
\def\sceneshift{\bigskip}
```

```
Exercise 9.1:
How many angels can dance on the head of a pin?
\endofexercise

This theological question has no simple answer \dots
```

> Exercise 9.1: How many angels can dance on the head of
> a pin?
>
> This theological question has no simple answer ...

Having a variety of special-purpose skip macros makes it easy to use big, medium, and small skips consistently throughout your text. It also makes it easy to change the size of a **\sceneshift** or an **\endofexercise** without disturbing other skips in your document.

9.5 Horizontal Skips

TeX also has five standard horizontal skips in convenient sizes. Three can be used as line-break points; two cannot.

Breakable		Unbreakable	
\enskip	0.5 em	\enspace	0.5em
\quad	1 em	\thinspace	0.16667 em
\qquad	2 em		

Since all five are based on the **em**, their exact width varies among the different fonts. (Page 85 shows the size of the **em** in TeX's standard set of Computer Modern 10-point fonts.) The **\quad** and **\qquad** are useful amounts of white space for separating the columns in tables (as we see in Chapter 20).

Since the definitions of these macros contain specific dimensions, there are no corresponding skipamount reporters to change. In fact, only **\bigskip**, **\medskip**, and **\smallskip** have skipamount reporters.

9.6 Writing New Skip Macros

You can make your own skips instead of changing the dimensions for the big, medium, and small skips. You might need a **\tinyskip** and **\biggerskip** as well as the standard set. Or you might want a set of horizontal skips whose size does not change when you switch fonts.

One way to make your own skips is to specify their sizes directly:

```
\def\tinyskip{\vskip 1.5 pt\relax}
\def\biggerskip{\vskip24pt\relax}
```

```
\def\bigHskip{\hskip20pt\relax}
\def\medHskip{\hskip 10pt\relax}
\def\smallHskip{\hskip 5 pt\relax}
```

The **\relax** at the ends of these definitions makes sure you do not get a Plus or Minus Bug (see page 110).

The other way is to create a new reporter—like the big, medium, and small skipamounts. First, use the plain TEX macro **\newskip** to make a new skip reporter. Second, tell this reporter what dimension to remember. Third, use the new reporter when you define your new macro. Here is an example of these three steps:

```
\newskip\hugeskipamount
\hugeskipamount=36pt
\def\hugeskip{\vskip\hugeskipamount}
```

First, **\newskip** makes a new reporter called **\hugeskipamount**. Next, **\hugeskipamount** is given the dimension **36pt** to remember and report. Finally, **\hugeskip** is defined as **\vskip\hugeskipamount**.

Now you can use **\hugeskip** in the same way as **\bigskip** and **\smallskip**.

\newskip is similar to **\def**—it makes a new control sequence. However, this new control sequence is a reporter, not a macro.

While processing your file, TEX expands a macro into its definition, but a reporter merely provides information to whomever asks for it. This "asker" can be either TEX itself or another actor. For example, when TEX starts a new paragraph, it asks **\parindent** how large the indentation should be. If you say **\vskip\parindent**, **\vskip** needs an input—so it prods **\parindent** and **\parindent** gives its report.

9.7   Skipping Backward

You can skip backward (move left or up) as well as forward (to the right or down). Use a negative dimension as the input for **\hskip** or **\vskip**.

```
Toodle oooooooooo

\vskip -\baselineskip
\noindent Toodle agagag
```

> **Toodle** agagagoooo

This skipping backward can be useful in a variety of circumstances, such as typesetting the words **LATEX Notes** or the bug (which was done with a special font) on top of the grey box in the margins of this book.

Review and Preview

This chapter shows how to create specific lengths of new white space, including

\hskip	horizontal skip doer (right or left)
\vskip	vertical skip doer (down or up)
\bigskip	large-size vertical skip doer
\medskip	medium-size vertical skip doer
\smallskip	small-size vertical skip doer
\bigskipamount	reporter for \bigskip
\medskipamount	reporter for \medskip
\smallskipamount	reporter for \smallskip
\thinspace	0.16667em horizontal skip doer
\enskip	0.5em horizontal skip doer
\enspace	0.5em unbreakable horizontal skip doer
\quad	1em horizontal skip doer
\qquad	2em horizontal skip doer

One way of getting different size skips is to change the size of the skipamount reporters. Another is to write new skip macros and make new skip reporters. Writing a macro for each different white-space purpose makes it easy to have consistent sizes of skips in your document.

The next chapter shows how to make stretchable white space and use TeX's glue.

CHAPTER 10

Glue: Space That Can Stretch and Shrink

TeX also makes white space that expands or shrinks however far you need. It does this with *glue*—a "magic mortar" that is like a dimension, except it can also stretch or shrink. Most of the white space on a page is made of glue. TeX uses glue between words and paragraphs just as a mason uses mortar between bricks. This chapter shows how to use glue (without getting stuck!).

10.1   What Is Glue?

To make glue, start with a dimension, then add some stretch and subtract some shrink, like this:

```
10pt plus 3pt minus 1pt
```

This glue is 10 points wide—and can expand another 3 points or shrink by 1 point. In other words, it can be as large as 13 points or as small as 9 points.

The dimension part of glue (**10pt** in the example above) is called its *natural space*. This is the size of the glue if TeX does not stretch or shrink it. (In fact, a dimension is really a special case of glue that cannot be stretched or shrunk.)

10.2   Using Glue

Glue is used as an input in the same way as a dimension. For example,

```
\hskip 72pt plus 12pt minus 6pt
\vskip 12pc plus  2pc minus 0.5pc
```

The **\smallskipamount**, **\medskipamount**, and **\bigskipamount** reporters actually hold glue instead of a dimension. Here are the complete specifications that Knuth gives for all three:

```
\smallskipamount=3pt plus 1pt minus 1pt
\medskipamount=  6pt plus 2pt minus 2pt
\bigskipamount= 12pt plus 4pt minus 4pt
```

The glue on a page is always stretched or shrunk proportionately. If the **\medskip** on a page is stretched to 7 points, the **\smallskip** is stretched to 3.5 points and the **\bigskip** to 14. Thus, you can control the way TeX stretches glue by specifying its **plus** and **minus** amounts.

When you give only a dimension to a glue reporter (without the **plus** and **minus**), TeX automatically adds **plus0pt minus0pt**. That is what TeX did in the previous chapter when we said **\bigskipamount=0.5in**.

Thus, if you do not want TeX to stretch the glue between paragraphs or in a **\smallskip**, **\medskip**, or **\bigskip**, specify a dimension instead of glue. Since TeX automatically adds **plus 0pt minus 0pt**, the glue cannot be stretched or shrunk.

TeX sometimes stretches **plus0pt** glue, but only in an emergency. When a page has less text than TeX needs to fill that page, TeX is forced to stretch something somewhere. If this happens, TeX sends you an underfull vbox warning.[1]

10.3   Infinitely Stretchable Glue

Glue can also stretch however far you need. Use an infinite-glue keyword instead of a dimension keyword. TeX has three infinite-glue keywords: **fil**, **fill**, and **filll**. Sections 10.4 and 10.5 explain why TeX has three infinite-glue keywords instead of one—and how to decide which one to use.

Put a number in front of the glue keyword, just as you would for a dimension keyword. All three of the following glues can stretch infinitely far and do not shrink at all.

```
2in plus 1fil   minus 0pt
5pc plus 1fill  minus 0pt
0pt plus 1filll minus 0pt
```

---

[1]A *vbox* is a vertical box. Chapter 28 describes TeX's boxes, and Chapter 33 shows how TeX uses boxes to do its work. Chapters 29 and 32 show you several ways of dealing with underfull vboxes.

You can make stretch-only glue by specifying only the dimension-plus-something (such as **6pt plus 2pt**). Similarly, using just the dimension-minus-something (such as **2in minus 0.5in**) makes shrink-only glue.

The **fil**, **fill**, and **filll** keywords create different degrees of stretchability (or shrinkability). The reason for having three different strengths of infinite glue is explained in the next few sections. The rest of this chapter shows several ways of using infinitely stretchable glue.

10.4   Fill It with Glue

Infinitely stretchable glue allows you to fill an area with white space, even when you do not know how large that area is. For example, if the last line on a page is a **section**{**heading**}, you want to move that heading to the next page. To start a new page before TEX normally would, fill the rest of the page with glue, then **eject** it. **eject** is a plain TEX macro that forces a page break.

```
\dots\ counting my roosters before they hatch.

\vskip 0pt plus 1fill
\eject

\section{Birds in the Hand}
```

In this example, **vskip** makes some white space, and **plus 1fill** makes it infinitely stretchable. TEX pulls the glue to the bottom of the page when **eject** breaks the page. (**section** is a macro that we define in Chapter 17.)

Glue is used this way so often that TEX has four "filler" primitives.

\hfil	equivalent to \hskip 0pt plus 1fil
\hfill	equivalent to \hskip 0pt plus 1fill
\vfil	equivalent to \vskip 0pt plus 1fil
\vfill	equivalent to \vskip 0pt plus 1fill

The next example uses **hfil** to typeset a short line at the top of a paragraph.

```
{\bf Snoopy's Revenge:}\hfil\break
On a dark and stormy night, Snoopy tells the tale
of a faithful beagle who \dots
```

> **Snoopy's Revenge:**
> On a dark and stormy night, Snoopy tells the tale of a faithful beagle who . . .

\hfil adds the dab of glue and **\break** forces a line break—which pulls the glue all the way to the margin.

Since you often want to start a new page or make a short line, it makes sense to write macros for these two tasks. They are

```
\def\newpage{\vfill\eject}
\def\eol{\hfil\break}
```

\eol is my own personal shorthand for e̲nd o̲f l̲ine. You can call this macro something else if you prefer—but do not use either **\endline** or **\filbreak** for its name. TeX already uses both those names for altogether different purposes.

With these two macros, type **\newpage** whenever you want to start a new page. Type **\eol** whenever you want to start a new line.

LATEX already has a **\newpage** macro.

Instead of **\eol**, use LATEX's **\newline**, ****, or **\linebreak** macros. **\newline** behaves exactly like **\eol**. LATEX defines **** differently among the various environments, so that it performs the correct actions for breaking the line at that point.

LATEX's **\linebreak** macro behaves like TeX's **\break**, except that **\linebreak** can take an optional argument. **\linebreak[0]** allows TeX to break the line at that point, but neither encourages nor discourages this action. **\linebreak[1]**, **\linebreak[2]** and **\linebreak[3]** give increasing degrees of encouragement—and **\linebreak[4]** forces a line break.

\newline, ****, and **\linebreak** are described in Section 5.2.1 on page 89 of Lamport's LATEX book.

10.5   Which Kind of Glue Do I Use?

How do you decide which kind of glue to use? If you want the glue to stretch no more than a specific distance, use finite glue—as Knuth did for the skipamount reporters. (When TeX is forced to pull text farther than the glue allows, it stretches any glue it can find and sends an underfull box warning to your screen and the transcript file.)

If you need infinite glue, use the lowest strength that gets the job done. Each higher level of glue is infinitely stretchier than the previous one. Finite glue is the least stretchable, and filll glue the most stretchable. Generally speaking, start with fil glue unless you know you need something stronger. For example, here is a tongue-twister from my childhood:

```
Rubber\hfil baby\hfil buggy\hfil bumpers!\break
```

Rubber   baby   buggy   bumpers!

TEX pulls **bumpers!** against the right margin when it **break**s the line. This stretches the glue in each **hfil** the same amount, so the four words are equally spaced across the entire line.

This changes when we mix two levels of glue:

```
Peter\hfil Piper\hfill picked\hfil a\hfil peck\break
```

PeterPiper   pickedapeck

The **hfil** glue seems to disappear because the glue in these fillers has zero width until TEX pulls on it. Since **hfill** uses infinitely stretchier glue than **hfil**, TEX put all the stretch between **Piper** and **picked**.

The **newpage** macro uses **vfill** because there could be some fil glue earlier on that page. The **vfill** makes sure that all the stretch goes at the bottom of the page. For the **eol** macro, however, it is very unlikely that there is any other fil glue in that line. The glue between words is finite, so **hfil** is sufficiently powerful to fill the line.

Knuth did not make any **hfilll** or **vfilll** control sequences because he wants to discourage people from getting into situations where that strength of glue is needed. However, if you absolutely positively need to overwhelm some fill glue, you can make your own filllers. The following **hfilll** and **vfilll** macros can be used just like **hfil**, **hfill**, **vfil**, and **vfill**.

```
\def\hfilll{\hskip 0pt plus 1filll minus 0pt}
\def\vfilll{\vskip 0pt plus 1filll minus 0pt}
```

If you make a habit of using fill glue only when you need to overpower some fil glue, you rarely need to resort to filll glue.

Disappearing Glue Bug

If some of your glue seems to disappear, check to see if you mixed different levels of glue. Each higher level of glue overpowers any level below it.

The glue in **hfil**, **vfil**, **hfill**, and **vfill** has a natural width of **0pt**—so if nothing pulls it out, it seems to disappear. The doers that pull on glue are **break**, **eject**, and the boxes shown in Chapter 28.

10.6   Shrinking Glue

Back in Section 10.2, you saw that glue can shrink. In particular, **bigskip**, **medskip**, and **smallskip** can shrink up to one-third their natural size. The shrinkability of these skips is finite, since Knuth used dimension keywords for the **minus** amounts: **minus4pt** for the

\bigskipamount, **minus2pt** for the **\medskipamount**, and **minus1pt** for the **\smallskipamount**.

Using shrinkable glue allows TEX to shrink the glue on a page to make the text fit the **\vsize**. However, TEX complains if you use infinitely shrinkable glue inside or between paragraphs. If you need glue that can shrink down to 0 points, use the same dimension for both its natural space and its shrinkability. For example, **20pt minus 20pt** can shrink to 0 points.

TEX does have infinitely shrinkable glue that you can use inside boxes to create special effects. The glue in the primitives **\hss** and **\vss** can shrink below zero and overlap the material before or after it. Sections 29.4 and 32.6 describe this special glue and ways of using it.

10.7   Oops!

Both **plus** and **minus** are keywords, so TEX treats them in a special fashion whenever it expects to find glue. This provides a toehold for the rare Plus or Minus Bug.

Plus or Minus Bug

If your text contains the word *plus* or *minus* in a place where TEX expects to see glue, TEX treats it as a keyword and expects to see a number and dimension or infinite-glue keyword after it.

To make sure that your text does not inadvertently turn into glue, type **\relax** in the place where a **plus** or **minus** would make glue. **\relax** is a primitive that says to do nothing. In the following example, it prevents TEX from interpreting the **plus** as a keyword.

```
Wrong: splish \hskip 1em
plus splash means raindrops.

Right: squish \hskip 1em\relax
plus squash means dead bugs!
```

> Wrong: splish   lash means raindrops.
> Right: squish   plus squash means dead bugs!

In the "wrong" part of this example, the **plus** does not appear in the printout—and the **sp** in **splash** is missing as well. Since TEX expects to find glue as the input to **\hskip**, it complains when it finds the **s** instead of a number, and complains again when it finds the **p** instead of a dimension keyword or infinite-glue keyword. The error messages say there is a missing number and an illegal unit of measurement.

Use this **\relax** strategy whenever you define a skip-using macro that might be followed by a **plus** or **minus** when you use the macro in your text. For example, Knuth defines the **\enskip** macro as

```
\def\enskip{\hskip.5em\relax}
```

This makes it possible to type **\enskip plus** without getting a Plus or Minus Bug.

A different kind of bug appears if you specify glue when TeX expects a dimension. Since TeX is not expecting to find glue, it treats the **plus** or **minus** as text.

Glue in Your Text Bug

If glue is typeset as text, one of two things has happened. Either you tried to give glue to a dimension reporter, or you typed the glue but did not say what to do with it.

```
Additionally speaking, the sum of 2 and 2 is
generally held to be 4.

\parindent=1in plus 5pt

But in the Restaurant at the End of the Universe,
it is whatever you can get away with.
```

> Additionally speaking, the sum of 2 and 2 is generally held to be 4.
>   plus 5pt
>   But in the Restaurant at the End of the Universe, it is whatever you can get away with.

10.8   Which Reporters Handle Glue?

Luckily, it is easy to distinguish between dimension reporters and glue reporters. All the glue reporters have the word *skip* in their names. With only two exceptions, dimension reporters do not. These two are **\lineskiplimit** and **\normallineskiplimit**, which are described on page 328.

You may want to follow this same strategy for naming your own new reporters. **\newskip** makes a new glue reporter. If you want to make a new dimension-only reporter, use the plain TeX macro **\newdimen** instead. For example,

```
\newdimen\normalparindent
\normalparindent=20pt
\parindent=\normalparindent
```

\newskip automatically gives glue of **0pt plus 0pt minus 0pt** to the new skip reporters it creates, and **\newdimen** gives **0pt** to new dimension reporters. Appendix B lists all of TeX's dimension reporters, glue reporters, and the doers that handle either dimensions or glue.

10.9   Underfull Boxes

When TeX is forced to pull glue farther than the **plus** amount allows, it sends an **underfull** warning to the screen and the transcript file. That is why you sometimes see an underfull hbox message when you **\break** a line earlier than TeX had in mind.

An underfull hbox warning is very similar to the overfull warning, and looks like this:

```
Underfull \hbox (badness 10000) detected at line 275
\tenrm some gaunt text in the underfull line.
```

The badness number gives you an idea of how far TeX had to overstretch the glue. Since **10000** is the highest possible badness number, this particular line is quite ugly. TeX shows where the problem is in your text file (line 275 in the above example) and the text it put into the underfull box (**\tenrm some gaunt text . . .** in the above example).

You can usually rearrange the line breaks in an underfull hbox by using a higher **\tolerance** for that paragraph. A more aesthetic solution to an underfull hbox is to rewrite the paragraph.

You can also get underfull vboxes, especially if you **\eject** a page having too little text to fill up the page. TeX pulls the last block of text down to the bottom of the page and sticks the extra white space anywhere it finds some glue. This overstretches the **\parskip** glue—as well as any other glue on the page. The text and white space form large stripes across the page, making it look very strange indeed. (Chapter 32 explains what to do about underfull vboxes.)

Review and Preview

This chapter shows how to handle T$_{\!E}$X's glue without getting stuck (though it may take a little practice here and there). Glue is like a dimension that can stretch or shrink (or a dimension is glue that cannot stretch or shrink).

Most of T$_{\!E}$X's white space is glue, and T$_{\!E}$X's skips all contain glue. If you give a dimension to a glue reporter, T$_{\!E}$X automatically adds **plus 0pt minus 0pt**. If you give glue to a dimension reporter, the glue appears in your printout as text. Both **hskip** and **vskip** actually take glue as input. The four "fillers" **hfil**, **hfill**, **vfil**, and **vfill** put a dab of glue into your text.

newskip makes a new glue reporter that starts with **0pt plus 0pt minus 0pt**. **newdimen** makes a new dimension reporter that starts with **0pt**.

This chapter contains several new macros that use glue. **eol** and **newpage** make short lines and start new pages. For emergency use only, **hfilll** and **vfilll** overwhelm fill level glue.

The next chapter explains how T$_{\!E}$X converts the characters in your file into words, spaces, lines, paragraphs, and pages.

CHAPTER 11

How TEX
Makes a Page

It helps to understand what TEX does when it processes your file and how TEX puts a page together. Almost everything on a page is either a box or glue. The previous chapter explained what glue is and how to work with it. This chapter shows in a general way how TEX uses boxes and glue to build paragraphs and pages; Chapter 33 gives more detail about this process.

11.1   What Are TEX's Boxes?

Boxes are rectangles with a baseline across their middle. They have height, depth, and width. The height of a box is how far it extends above the baseline. The depth is how far it extends below the baseline. The width is how far it extends horizontally. Boxes also have a reference point: the point where the baseline meets the left edge of the box.

When TEX is making a paragraph, it typesets letters into words and words into lines—and does all this work with boxes. TEX views each letter as a box whose size is determined by the information in the font files. For example, here is a large y. The lines show the edges and the baseline of its box.

reference point ⟶ **y** ——baseline

In addition to these implicit boxes around characters, TEX has two basic kinds of boxes: horizontal and vertical.

11.2   Making Paragraphs: Horizontal Mode

TeX sticks these character-boxes together horizontally to make words (thus the name *horizontal mode*) and puts glue between the words. TeX aligns these boxes horizontally along their baselines.

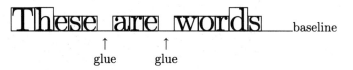

When TeX reaches the end of a paragraph, it breaks this long list of words plus glue into lines. TeX puts each line into an hbox (horizontal box). The width of this hbox is the \textbf{hsize}—and TeX stretches the interword glue in each line so that the right-most word is against the right edge of the hbox.

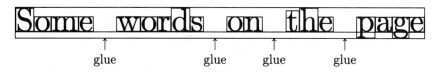

The baseline of the enclosing hbox (the box around the entire line of words) is the same as the baseline of each letter on that line. The height of the enclosing hbox is the same height as the tallest letters on that line: in this case, the **S**, **d**, and **h**. The depth of the enclosing hbox is the same as the deepest letters on that line: here, the **p** and **g**. The width of the enclosing hbox is whatever you have specified as the **\hsize**.[1]

11.3   Making Pages: Vertical Mode

TeX then stacks these lines of hboxes vertically (thus the name *vertical mode*), adding each new hbox to the current page. When TeX is stacking boxes to make a page, it aligns them vertically along their reference points. TeX puts interlineskip glue between these hboxes and adjusts this glue so that the baselines of the hboxes are **\baselineskip** apart. In the example below, the **\baselineskip** is **30pt**.

[1]I gave this particular line a special **\hsize** that is **2\parindent** smaller than the text's normal **\hsize**.

> Some words on this page
> are wider than other words
> on page seven.

In the example above, line 2 has no letters with descenders and line 3 has no tall letters. To make sure that the baselines of all three lines are **\baselineskip** apart, TₑX put more interlineskip glue between lines 2 and 3 than between lines 1 and 2.

At the end of each paragraph (and in a few other circumstances as well), TₑX checks to see if there are enough lines to fill up a page. If there are, TₑX's *output routine* assembles a page and sends it off to the **.dvi** file.

11.4   The Structure of a Page

Each page has three areas: a header (at the top), a footer (at the bottom), and text (in the middle). TₑX puts the header into an hbox, the text into a vbox (a vertical box), and the footer into an hbox, then encloses all three in an all-encompassing vbox. A typical page might look similar to the example at the top of the next page.

The white space at the top of the text vbox is not a mistake: It is the **\topskip** glue, which is explained in Section 18.4. The white space between the header and the text vbox is also not a mistake: TₑX adds space here so that the baselines of the header and the first line of text are normally **24pt** apart.

The height + depth of the text vbox is the same as the **\vsize**. TₑX pulls the last line of text down to the bottom of this vbox, and stretches (or shrinks) any vertical glue on the page if necessary. If TₑX has to stretch glue on a page that has only text (no **\vskip**, **\vfil**, or **\vfill** glue), TₑX stretches the **\parskip** glue between paragraphs.

TₑX's output routine places these three boxes inside a larger, all-encompassing vbox, and sends the entire page to the **.dvi** file.

Decapitation Then and Now

text:

tolling of the noon hour faded into the dusty sunshine. Mortimer Brigglesworth wriggled and squirmed, but could not escape the bonds of cruel fate. He was led to the platform and flung face down upon the stained surface of the execution block. The executioner swung his axe and chopped off Mortimer's head.

"Hurrah, hurrah," the crowd chanted as the taxman's bald pate fell into the waiting basket.

Mortimer's head was soon lifted onto a pike, and displayed in the center of the square for all to see. Children and old people alike threw moldy tomatoes and rotten eggs at the target—often missing their aim and splattering their neighbors instead. Agents of the nearby medical school waited eagerly in the wings for Mortimer's remains. The cadaver would soon serve as grist for science, or at least what passed for science in this backwater town during the medieval ages.

footer:

-101-

11.5   More about Boxes and the Contents of the Text Vbox

TeX automatically performs all the box-making tasks described in this chapter. Sometimes, though, you want to use TeX's boxes to accomplish various special effects (such as moving text into different areas or using the same amount of space for different sizes of chapter headings). Chapters 28 through 30 describe ways of using TeX's boxes explicitly.

Most of the chapters in the rest of this book describe ways of formatting the text part of the page. However, Chapter 18 describes how to change TeX's headers and footers.

TeX also keeps track of *floating material*—such as tables and figures that can "float" to the top of the same page, to the top of the next page, or to a page by itself—or footnotes that can float to the bottom of the same page and might be continued at the bottom of the next page. Floating material goes into the text vbox. Footnotes are described in Chapter 19. Chapter 23 explains how to float your tables and figures.

Review and Preview

This chapter shows how TEX uses boxes to build a page. It treats each character as a box having a specific height, depth, and width. In making a paragraph, TEX puts adjacent characters next to each other to make words, and puts a dab of glue between the words. Thus, TEX converts each paragraph into a list of words and glue.

When TEX reaches the end of a paragraph, it decides where to break the lines. TEX puts each line into an hbox, and stretches or shrinks the glue between the words so that the last character in each line is flush against the right margin (i.e., the right margin is justified).

TEX puts glue between the hboxes of the paragraph so that their baselines are one **\baselineskip** apart. When TEX has accumulated more than enough lines to fill up a page, it decides where to break the page. TEX's output routine puts these hboxes of text into an enclosing vbox and includes any floating material that belongs on this current page. The output routine also generates the header and footer hboxes; encloses the header, footer, and text boxes in a single, all-encompassing vbox; and ships the finished page to the **.dvi** file.

The next part of this book shows how to write macros for a wide variety of formatting tasks:

- Chapters 12 through 16 show how to change the shape of a paragraph: for quotations, flushleft or centered text, itemized lists, glossaries, computer code, and the like.

- Chapters 17 through 19 show how to handle special pieces of text: section headings, headers and footers, and footnotes.

- Chapters 20 through 22 explain how to make tables, put headings above columns, and draw lines on tables.

- Chapter 23 describes how to make tables and figures that can float to other, nearby places on the same or subsequent pages.

- Chapters 24 through 26 explain how to use math mode and display math mode.

- Chapter 27 shows how to get the correct fonts when you need to use math mode in more than one size.

Chapter 12 shows the three basic macro structures that you need for these tasks, so I recommend that you read it next. It introduces some terms and ideas that are used in the rest of the book, so you will be baffled if you skip over it.

Chapters 13 through 23 in the next part of this book are designed to stand alone. Thus, you can go directly from Chapter 12 to whichever formatting task you want to learn next. The exception to this jump-wherever-you-want approach is Chapters 24 through 26, which explain how to use math mode. Those three chapters need to be read in order. Chapter 27 describes how to use TeX's font-family system so you can use math mode in your headings or footnotes as well as in your text.

PART III

DOWN WE GO!

Quotations: Three Basic Macro Structures

Sometimes you need different shapes for your paragraphs. Quotations often have narrower lines than regular text, have extra white space above and below, and are usually single spaced. A list of numbered or bulleted items is usually indented and may have extra space between each item as well as above and below the list. Computer code has ragged-right margins; wedding announcements have centered text; poetry has a unique appearance all its own.

The best method of making special-purpose paragraph shapes is to use the *sandwich* structure: a slice of bread (macro), then some meat (text), and another slice of bread (macro). Most of the macros you have seen so far have a *meat-and-potatoes* quality: Plop it on your plate and there it is. Macros that take one or more inputs (such as \linespacing in Chapter 8) have a *jelly-doughnut* structure. When TeX finds one of these macros in your text, it stuffs the inputs (jelly) into the slots you made for them in the macro definition. (These food analogies are not TeXnical terms; they are my overactive imagination at work once again.)

This chapter uses quotations to illustrate all three of these macro structures. Our new quotation macros all produce the same layout but use different methods to achieve them. The next several chapters delve into the nuts and bolts of the control sequences you need for making a variety of other special paragraph shapes.

**LᴬTEX
Notes**

LᴬTEX uses a system of *environments* to make special paragraph shapes. Thus, for quotations, use a **quote** or **quotation** environment, shown in Section 2.2.4 on pages 25–26 of Lamport's LᴬTEX book.

To make a new environment using the TEXniques described in this and subsequent chapters, use LᴬTEX's **newenvironment** macro.

12.1   The Meat-and-Potatoes Structure

The do-this-now style of the meat-and-potatoes structure is simple and straightforward. First, we make a **displayskip** to put white space above and below the quotation. Then, the **quotation** macro changes the margins with **narrower**—a plain TEX macro that puts a **parindent**-wide piece of white space on each side of the line. **quotation** also starts the paragraph with a **noindent**.

```
\def\displayskip{\bigskip}
\def\quotation{\narrower\noindent}
```

In the source reference, we use **eol** (page 108) to end the previous line and **em** (page 70) to change the font for the title of the play.

To stop the margin changes when we reach the end of the quotation, we put the whole thing inside a group.

```
The essence of my life was captured by Oscar
Wilde a century ago:

{\displayskip\quotation
I can resist everything except temptation.\eol
---{\em Lady Windemere's Fan}, 1892.
\displayskip}

\noindent With these simple words \dots
```

> The essence of my life was captured by Oscar Wilde a century ago:
>
> > I can resist everything except temptation.
> > —*Lady Windemere's Fan*, 1892.
>
> With these simple words . . .

It is often better to put one skip above displayed material and another below. For example, TEX puts an **abovedisplayskip** above a math display and a **belowdisplayskip** below it—even though both these reporters are

12pt plus3pt minus9pt. (\abovedisplayskip and \belowdisplayskip are described in Section 24.3.)

Having two skips makes it easy to change the size of one without disturbing the other. Also, having more space below displayed material than above it makes the material look centered, so designers often want displays formatted this way. For simplicity's sake, however, the examples in this and the following chapters use only one skip.

12.2 The Jelly-Doughnut Structure

While \quotation is shorter to type than the control sequences in its definition, it would be nice if the macro also included the braces, the two \displayskips, the \eol, and the em dash (---). It can. What we need is a jelly-doughnut structure.

The following \quotethis macro takes two inputs: #1 for the quotation itself, and #2 for the source reference. Since some sources might be the titles of articles instead of books or plays, we do not put the font change into the definition of \quotethis.

```
\def\quotethis#1#2{{\displayskip\narrower
    \noindent #1\eol---#2\displayskip}}

\dots\ Lewis Carroll's characters are as vivid
and true to life as our next-door neighbors:

\quotethis{''If everybody minded their own
business,'' the Duchess said with a hoarse growl,
''the world would go round a deal faster than it
does.''}{{\em Alice's Adventures in Wonderland},
1865.}

\noindent
With these few words, the Duchess springs to life.
```

> ... Lewis Carroll's characters are as vivid and true to life as our next-door neighbors:
>
> > "If everybody minded their own business," the Duchess said with a hoarse growl, "the world would go round a deal faster than it does."
> > —*Alice's Adventures in Wonderland*, 1865.
>
> With these few words, the Duchess springs to life.

The definition of **\quotethis** starts with an open brace to start a group, and ends with a close brace to end the group. TeX ignores the space in front of **#1** in the definition of **\quotethis**. That space is used up in signaling the end of the control word **\noindent**. Since **#** is also a nonletter, this space is not necessary. However, it does make the definition easier to read.

When you use **\quotethis** in your text, its inputs must be put inside braces. The braces show TeX where those inputs begin and end.

Long Inputs and Runaway Arguments

While **\quotethis** works nicely for short quotes, TeX sends you an error message if the input contains more than one paragraph. If you start an input with { and begin a new paragraph before you end the input with }, TeX's complaint looks similar to the following:

```
Runaway argument?
severe penalties for early withdrawal.
! Paragraph ended before \quotethis was complete.
<to be read again>
                    \par
l.69
```

Programmers use the term *argument* instead of *input*. Also, **\par** means "end the current paragraph." TeX converts a blank line into **\par** when it processes your text file.

Thus, TeX is saying that it found a blank line before it found the end of the input for **\quotethis**. TeX has just finished processing the text **severe penalties for early withdrawal** and found the problem when it reached line 69. (The **<to be read again>** message is explained in Chapter 35.)

In most circumstances, this complaint is useful because it notifies you of probable errors—but it becomes a nuisance if your two-paragraph quotation is intentional. Knuth anticipated this need. Whenever a macro's input might contain more than one paragraph, put the primitive **\long** in front of the definition, like this:

```
\long\def\longquote#1{{\displayskip
    \narrower\noindent#1\displayskip}}
```

\long tells TeX that the inputs for a particular macro are allowed to contain more than one paragraph. This **\longquote** macro takes one input: the entire quotation.

However, TeX's capacity for handling inputs is limited, and long inputs slow TeX down. When you need a macro to handle a large chunk of text, use the sandwich structure instead. The sandwich structure is explained in the next section.

LATEX Notes

\long is built into LAT_EX's \newcommand, so inputs to your new macros can have more than one paragraph.

12.3   The Sandwich Structure

The other way of having the macro begin and end the group is to use a before-and-after sandwich structure. The T_EX primitives \begingroup and \endgroup do exactly what their names imply: They begin and end a group. For example, if you like to exercise your fingers (or make the group easier to see), you can change fonts by typing

```
\begingroup\it This is typeset in italics.\endgroup
```

\begingroup and \endgroup have a big advantage over braces: They can be used in different macros. A definition that contains an open brace must also have a matching close brace—but you can put \begingroup in one macro definition and its matching \endgroup in another.

```
\def\beginQuote{\begingroup\displayskip
    \narrower\noindent}
\def\endQuote{\displayskip\endgroup}

Mark Twain had a keen eye and a sharp wit.

\beginQuote
Soap and education are not as sudden as a
massacre, but they are more deadly in the long
run.\eol
---''The Facts Concerning the Recent
Resignation,'' 1867.
\endQuote

\noindent
They muddy the water as well as the mind.
```

> Mark Twain had a keen eye and a sharp wit.
>
> > Soap and education are not as sudden as a massacre, but they are more deadly in the long run.
> > —"The Facts Concerning the Recent Resignation," 1867.
>
> They muddy the water as well as the mind.

In this macro pair, **\beginQuote** begins a group and **\endQuote** ends it.

A sandwich-style macro can take inputs too, if you like. The simplest way is to give **\endQuote** an input—the source reference—as follows:

```
\def\beginReferencedQuote{\begingroup
    \displayskip \narrower \noindent}
\def\endReferencedQuote#1{\eol---#1
    \displayskip\endgroup}
```

Here is an example of this pair of macros.

```
Nay, Shakespeare knew well whereof he spoke:

\beginReferencedQuote
The devil can cite Scripture for his purpose.
\endReferencedQuote{{\em The Merchant of Venice,
Act I, Scene iii}}

Being a mischievous person, so can I.
```

> Nay, Shakespeare knew well whereof he spoke:
>
> > The devil can cite Scripture for his purpose.
> > —*The Merchant of Venice, Act I, Scene iii*
>
> Being a mischievous person, so can I.

You can also define **\beginQuote** to take an input for the source information and make this information accessible to **\endQuote**. The figure and figure-caption macros in Section 23.5 show how to do this.

All of LATEX's environments use a sandwich structure. LATEX automatically does a **\begingroup** when you type **\begin**{*environment*} and an **\endgroup** when you type **\end**{*environment*}.

Use **\newenvironment** to define a new environment in LATEX (described in Section 3.4.2 on page 57 of Lamport's LATEX book).

12.4   Oops! Where Paragraphs End

Humans and computers have different ideas about where a paragraph ends. People tend to think of a paragraph's end as the period following the last word of the last sentence. TEX does not know that a paragraph has ended until it finds the blank line after that period.

These differing notions about where a paragraph ends can make it seem as if TEX is ignoring one or more control sequences. Suppose the \quotation example in Section 12.1 had put the \displayskips outside the braces, like this:

```
Life is a series of opportunities for making
mistakes.

\displayskip
{\quotation
This is one of them.  This example is an error.
Do not copy this blooper.}
\displayskip

\noindent
If you do, it will give you grey hair.  (You have
been warned.)
```

> Life is a series of opportunities for making mistakes.
>
> This is one of them. This example is an error. Do not copy this blooper.
>
> If you do, it will give you grey hair. (You have been warned.)

In this case, the close brace ends the group—which stops the changes made by \quotation before the paragraph ends. (I'll soon tell you how I avoided this problem in the earlier example.) The printout does have a nonindented paragraph—but it is the same width as the rest of your text. It looks as if TEX ignored \narrower!

Ignores My Command Bug

When TEX makes a paragraph, it does not ask for reports until it reaches the end of that paragraph. If you begin a group, change some reporters, and end the group before TEX finds the end of the paragraph, the reports TEX gets are the same as the reports it would have gotten before the group began.

When you change a paragraph-shaping reporter inside a group, end the paragraph before you end the group.

There are several ways of ending a paragraph in TeX. One is the blank line. Another is the control sequence **\par**. To fix the Ignores My Command Bug, type \par before you end the group:

```
Once upon a time, I too agonized about making
mistakes.  But no more!  When Murphy asked me to
join his team, he said:

\displayskip
{\quotation
I don't have time to make all the mistakes
myself.  I need help!  And like any other
employer, I prefer to hire the best.\par}

\displayskip\noindent
What a relief to be a top-notch mistake-maker
instead of a mere klutz!
```

> Once upon a time, I too agonized about making mistakes. But no more! When Murphy asked me to join his team, he said:
>
> > I don't have time to make all the mistakes myself. I need help! And like any other employer, I prefer to hire the best.
>
> What a relief to be a top-notch mistake-maker instead of a mere klutz!

This Ignores My Command Bug can crop up whenever you change a reporter that affects the shape of a paragraph. Make sure you end the paragraph before you end the group.

TeX has two other methods of ending a paragraph. The control sequence **\endgraf** acts just like **\par**.[1] Any **\vskip** also ends a paragraph, because it stops paragraph-making horizontal mode and changes back to page-making vertical mode. The **\displayskip** at the end of the paragraph in Section 12.1's **\quotation** example expands to a **\vskip**—and therefore prevents that example from having an Ignores My Command Bug (see page 129).

---

[1] **\endgraf** is part of plain TeX, but it is not a macro since it was made with **\let** instead of **\def**. **\endgraf** is like a backup copy of **\par**. Having two paragraph enders may seem redundant, but since TeX "does a \par" at the end of every paragraph, you sometimes want to redefine **\par** to behave differently in special circumstances. **\endgraf** lets you use TeX's default method of ending a paragraph even when you have redefined **\par**.

12.5   Eliminating Extra Vertical Space between Macros

The chapters that follow define a variety of paragraph-shaping macros. All of them put a **\displayskip** of space at the beginning and end of the special area of text. If two of these macros have no text between them, TₑX puts two **\displayskip**s between them when you only want one. For example, you might have a quotation followed by some computer code, or a table followed by a quotation.

```
\dots\ slings and arrows of outrageous fortune,
and by opposing, end them.
\endQuote

\beginCode
to piglatin :words
if empty? :words [op []]
op list change first :words
        piglatin butfirst :words
end
\endCode
```

> . . . slings and arrows of outrageous fortune, and by opposing, end them.

```
to piglatin :words
if empty? :words [op []]
op list change first :words
        piglatin butfirst :words
end
```

(The **\beginCode** and **\endCode** macros are defined in Chapter 16.)

There are two **\displayskip**s between Hamlet's speech and the piglatin program. To remove this space, use the plain TₑX macro **\bigbreak** instead of a **\bigskip**. The simplest way is to define a **\displaybreak** and use that instead of the **\displayskip** in your macros.

```
\def\displaybreak{\bigbreak}
```

\bigbreak makes sure that you only get one **\bigskipamount** of vertical space, even when two or more **\bigbreak**s follow one another. Thus, whenever a begin-special-text macro might follow another **\vskip** in your text file, use a **\bigbreak**—or **\medbreak** or **\smallbreak**.

How \bigbreak Works

When TEX adds a \vskip to the page, it also gives the size of that skip to a primitive reporter called \lastskip. When TEX adds something else (such as text) to the page, the \lastskip automatically becomes 0pt.

\bigbreak and its two cousins compare the \lastskip on the page with their own skipamount reporter, then do one of two things:

- If the \lastskip is smaller, they remove it, add their own skip, and tell TEX that this is a good place to break the page.

- If the \lastskip is the same size or larger, they leave that skip in place, and do nothing more.

Thus, you always get the larger skip—but nothing more.

Here are our new, improved, sandwich-style quotation macros:

```
\def\beginQuotation{\begingroup
   \displaybreak
   \narrower \noindent}
\def\endQuotation{\displaybreak\endgroup}
```

Since \bigbreak, \medbreak, and \smallbreak also tell TEX that this is a good place to break the page, we put a \displaybreak in \endquotation too.

Review and Related Matters

This chapter shows three basic structures for making macros:

- a straightforward meat-and-potatoes style,

- a jelly-doughnut style that takes inputs, and

- a sandwich style that uses \begingroup and \endgroup in a before-and-after approach.

\long allows a macro's input to contain more than one paragraph, although the sandwich structure is a better method of dealing with large chunks of text. Differing notions of how to recognize the end of a paragraph give a toehold to the Ignores My Command Bug. Therefore, when you change a paragraph-shaping reporter, always use \par to end the paragraph before you end the group. The \bigbreak, \medbreak, and \smallbreak macros prevent TEX from putting two much vertical space between adjacent macros.

The next several chapters demonstrate a variety of control sequences for making special paragraph shapes.

CHAPTER 13

Changing Your Paragraph Margins

The simplest way of reshaping a paragraph is to change its margins. This chapter shows how to use **\raggedright** and how to change **\leftskip** and **\rightskip**, the reporters that govern how much white space TEX puts at the left and right ends of each line.

To understand this chapter, you must be familiar with the following:

- groups (Section 6.2);
- sandwich-structure macros (Chapter 12); and
- **\displaybreak** (Section 12.5).

To make flushleft, flushright, or centered paragraphs, use LATEX's **flushleft**, **flushright**, or **center** environments. These are shown in Section 5.6 on pages 111–12 of Lamport's LATEX book.

All of LATEX's text environments put white space above and below the displayed paragraphs—so if you want to change only the shape of the paragraphs, use **\raggedright**, **\raggedleft**, or **\centering** instead.

13.1 Ragged Right Margins

When TEX starts out, the left and right margins are both *justified*, meaning that the glue on each line is stretched or shrunk so that the text fits exactly the full length of that line. The opposite of justified is *ragged*, meaning that the text has an irregular edge. (This book has a ragged right margin.)

The simplest way to get a ragged right margin is to use the plain T_EX macro **\raggedright**.

```
{\raggedright
Raggedy Ann and Raggedy Andy are a ragamuffin
pair.  Their hair is jagged, their clothes are
patched.  Such tatterdemalion flair!\par}
```

> Raggedy Ann and Raggedy Andy are a ragamuffin pair. Their hair is jagged; their clothes are patched. Such tatterdemalion flair!

\par ends the paragraph before you end the group, and makes sure you do not get an Ignores My Command Bug.

We can combine **\raggedright** and **\narrower** to make a quotation macro with a ragged margin.

```
\def\beginRaggedQuote{\displaybreak
    \begingroup
    \raggedright \narrower}
\def\endRaggedQuote{\par\endgroup
    \displaybreak}
```

Here are examples of **\beginRaggedQuote** and **\endRaggedQuote**.

```
When she awoke, Briar Rose (also known as
Sleeping Beauty) might have yawned, stretched her
limbs and said,

\beginRaggedQuote
''Briars and thorns make a prickly bed, especially
when one must sleep on them for 100 years, waiting
for one's prince to appear.''
\endRaggedQuote
```

> When she awoke, Briar Rose (also known as Sleeping Beauty) might have yawned, stretched her limbs and said,
>
> > "Briars and thorns make a prickly bed, especially when one must sleep on them for 100 years, waiting for one's prince to appear."

Oops!

It often does not matter which of two control sequences comes first. Other times, though, the results can be quite different if you switch their order.

For example, if you say **\narrower** before **\raggedright**, the right margin looks like it has not budged: It is still in the old position.

```
\def\beginRaggedOops{\begingroup
    \displaybreak \narrower \raggedright}
\def\endRaggedOops{\displaybreak\endgroup}
Charles Darwin's words are so mild they seem
innocuous.  It is hard to believe they shook our
world so profoundly.  He begins:

\beginRaggedOops
When on board H.M.S. 'Beagle,' as naturalist, I was
much struck with certain facts in the distribution
of the organic beings inhabiting South America, and
in the geological relations of the present to the
past inhabitants of that continent \dots
\endRaggedOops
```

> Charles Darwin's words are so mild they seem innocuous. It is hard to believe they shook our world so profoundly. He begins:
>
>> When on board H.M.S. 'Beagle,' as naturalist, I was much struck with certain facts in the distribution of the organic beings inhabiting South America, and in the geological relations of the present to the past inhabitants of that continent . . .

The problem here is a Cart Before the Horse Bug.

Cart Before the Horse Bug

This bug can appear when two control sequences in a macro affect the same reporter. If the first control sequence seems to be ignored, the second may be canceling the work of the first.

If you think you might have a Cart Before the Horse Bug, switch the two control sequences and see if that fixes the problem.

In this case, both **\narrower** and **\raggedright** change the glue at the right edge of the paragraph, but they change it in different ways.

\rightskip is a primitive reporter that governs the glue at the right text margin—and the corresponding primitive reporter for the left margin is called **\leftskip**. Here is Knuth's definition of **\narrower**:

```
\def\narrower{\advance\leftskip by\parindent
    \advance\rightskip by\parindent}
```

So **\narrower** is relative. It takes the current size of **\rightskip** and increases it by **\parindent**.

In contrast, **\raggedright** is absolute. It gives **\rightskip** a specific amount of glue to remember. Here is the relevant part of Knuth's definition of **\raggedright**:

```
\def\raggedright{\rightskip=0pt plus2em ...}
```

(The rest of **\raggedright** removes the glue from interword spaces so they cannot stretch or shrink. Methods of controlling the size of interword spaces are described in Sections 4.5, 16.8, and A.3.)

The following table shows the resulting **\rightskip** glue when you put **\narrower** either before or after **\raggedright** (assuming that your **\parindent** is **20pt**).

`\narrower \raggedright`	results in:	`0pt plus2em`
`\raggedright \narrower`	results in:	`20pt plus2em`

When \narrower Does Not Work

If your **\parindent** is **0pt**, **\narrower** does not move the paragraph margins. Instead, you must change **\leftskip** and **\rightskip** explicitly.

```
What doubts must lurk in the minds of left-handed
persons when the language itself casts aspersions
on their nature:

{\advance\leftskip by 30pt
\advance\rightskip by 30pt
\noindent
Gauche and sinister, what a pair!  I'd rather be
dextrous, right, and fair.\par}
```

> What doubts must lurk in the minds of left-handed persons when the language itself casts aspersions on their nature:
>
> > Gauche and sinister, what a pair! I'd rather be dextrous, right, and fair.

Both **\leftskip** and **\rightskip** are glue reporters. When you change a glue reporter at the end of a macro but do not specify all the **plus** and **minus** glue, use **\relax** to make sure you do not get a Plus Or Minus Bug if the words *plus* or *minus* follow the macro. (The Plus Or Minus Bug is described on page 110.)

```
\def\beginIndentedQuote{\displaybreak
  \begingroup
  \advance\leftskip  by 15pt
  \advance\rightskip by 15pt\relax}
\def\endIndentedQuote{\par\endgroup
  \displaybreak}
```

If a **\noindent** or other control sequence had followed the change to the
\rightskip glue, the **\relax** would not have been necessary.

13.2   Ragged Left Margins

Many books begin or end each chapter with a quotation—*Dune* and *The
T_EXbook* are two examples. *The T_EXbook*'s quotations have a ragged left
margin and are typeset flush against the right margin. How can we make a
\raggedleft macro that accomplishes this?

If we copy the **\raggedright** macro and change **\rightskip** to **\leftskip**,
the last line of the paragraph is typeset flush against the wrong margin.

```
\def\oopsleft{\leftskip=0pt plus2em\relax}
{\oopsleft
Counterclockwise, leftward turning: since
cyclones in the northern hemisphere spin
''against the clock,'' do these storms also skip
backward in time?\par}
```

> Counterclockwise, leftward turning: since cyclones in the
> northern hemisphere spin "against the clock," do these
> storms also skip backward in time?

T_EX fills the last line of every paragraph with **\parfillskip** glue. When
T_EX starts up, the **\parfillskip** (a primitive reporter) is **0pt plus 1fil**—
which is infinitely stretchier than the finite glue we added to the **\leftskip**.
To overwhelm this fil glue, our **\raggedleft** macro needs fill glue.

```
\def\raggedleft{\leftskip=0pt plus 1fill\relax}
```

```
{\raggedleft
Once upon a time, there was a shaggy dog named
Raggs.  Raggs thought he was a sheep dog, but
there were no sheep in his neighborhood.  Raggs
had nothing to do, so he slept on the porch all
day long and was perfectly content.\par}
```

Once upon a time, there was a shaggy dog named Raggs.
Raggs thought he was a sheep dog, but there were no
sheep in his neighborhood. Raggs had nothing to do, so
he slept on the porch all day long and was perfectly
content.

\raggedleft is a tool that we can use inside other macros to make paragraphs with a ragged left margin. For example, the following pair of **\beginFlushRight...\endFlushRight** macros use \raggedleft to typeset text flush against the right margin.

```
\def\beginFlushRight{\begingroup
    \displaybreak \raggedleft}
\def\endFlushRight{\displaybreak\endgroup}
```

```
\beginFlushRight
Many occasional poker players (myself included)
cannot remember if a flush beats a straight or
the other way around.  I always have to look it
up, because I never can figure it out.
\endFlushRight
```

Many occasional poker players (myself included)
cannot remember if a flush beats a straight or the other
way around. I always have to look it up, because I never
can figure it out.

A Ragged-Left Quotation Macro

A slightly more complicated task is beginning a chapter with a ragged-left quotation on the right half of the page. We could measure the width of the text and add half of that dimension to the **\leftskip** reporter, but it is easier and more accurate to let TEX do the math. Thus, we start by making a new **\textwidth** reporter.

```
\newdimen\textwidth \textwidth=28pc
\hsize=\textwidth
```

```
\def\beginRightQuote{\begingroup\raggedleft
    \advance\leftskip by 0.5\textwidth\relax}
\def\endRightQuote{\vskip 3pc \endgroup}
```

There are two important things to notice about \beginRightQuote.
First, \beginRightQuote has no \vskip at the beginning. It is designed to follow the \vskip that ends the chapter-heading macro. If this
quotation macro was supposed to end the chapter instead, we would
start it with \vfill—and we would probably put an \eject at the end of
\endRightQuote.

Second, \advance uses the \textwidth reporter to give new information
to \leftskip. Using 0.5\textwidth instead of a specific dimension means
that \beginRightQuote does not care how wide the page is. It works
equally well when the \textwidth is 5 inches or 7 inches, so you can use
the macro in a variety of different documents.

You can use 0.5\hsize instead if you want the quotation to be only half
the width of the current \hsize. This example used \textwidth instead of
\hsize because you might change the \hsize to create special effects inside a
box, but the \textwidth for the document stays the same.

Here is how \beginRightQuote looks:

```
\beginRightQuote
The birds and the bees, the ants and the fleas,
all live under one roof.
\endRightQuote

\noindent
Picnickers often believe that the only good bug
is a dead bug, but research has shown \dots
```

> The birds and the bees,
> the ants and the fleas, all
> live under one roof.

Picnickers often believe that the only good bug is a dead
bug, but research has shown . . .

Whenever you write a new macro, think about how you plan to use it.
Is it a tool—like \raggedright and \raggedleft—and therefore needs to
be as simple as possible? Does it make displayed paragraphs that are set off
from the rest of the text with a \displaybreak above and below? Or is it
a specialized macro for a specialized niche and needs to fit that niche in a
specialized way?

13.3   Making Centered Paragraphs

To make centered material, we need to put equal amounts of glue on both sides. The question again is: Which level of glue do we use? Since fill glue worked for **\raggedleft**, it should work for our **\centerthis** macro as well. To make sure the glue is the same on both sides, use the report from **\leftskip** as the new information for **\rightskip**.

```
\def\centerthis{\leftskip=0pt plus 1fill
    \rightskip=\leftskip \relax}
```

```
{\centerthis\noindent
When the epicenter of an earthquake becomes the
centerpiece of a discussion, can aftershocks be
far behind?\par}
```

> When the epicenter of an earthquake becomes the centerpiece of a discussion, can aftershocks be far behind?

What Level Glue Do We Need?

Did we really need fill glue in **\centerthis**? Or would fil glue have done just as well? After all, the **\parfillskip** contains fil glue. Perhaps all we need to do is balance that. The following **\offcenter** macro tests this idea.

```
\def\offcenter{\leftskip=0pt plus 1fil
    \rightskip=\leftskip \relax}
```

As it turns out, both the top and bottom lines are off center:

```
{\offcenter
The ancients believed the sun went around the
earth---and that circles were a perfect form.
Thus, the motion of bodies in a perfect heaven
must surely be perfect as well.  This idea turned
out to be as off center as the notion of a
geocentric universe.\par}
```

> The ancients believed the sun went around the earth—and that circles were a perfect form. Thus, the motion of bodies in a perfect heaven must surely be perfect as well. This idea turned out to be as off center as the notion of a geocentric universe.

If you measure the space on the bottom line, you see there is twice as much glue on the right as on the left. This is because the **\rightskip** glue is added to the **\parfillskip** glue, like this:

```
\parfillskip      0pt plus 1fil
+ \rightskip      0pt plus 1fil
                  -------------
Total:            0pt plus 2fil
```

So the glue on the right totals **2fil** of stretch, and the glue on the left only **1fil**.

The top line of the **\offcenter** example is askew as well, because the line starts with a **\parindent** of white space. In the **\raggedleft** examples, that did not matter—but for **\centerthis** material, it does.

Therefore, to make a centered paragraph, always use **plus 1fill** glue, as we did in our **\centerthis** macro. Also, either use **\noindent** at the beginning of the paragraph, or change the **\parindent** to **0pt**—as we do for **\beginCenter** in the next section.

Sandwich Macros for Centered Paragraphs

Our **\centerthis** macro is a tool—like **\raggedright** and **\raggedleft**. It is one of the control sequences we use for a **\beginCenter** macro. Since there could be more than one paragraph inside the centered material, we also change the **\parindent** to **0pt**.

```
\def\beginCenter{\displaybreak
    \begingroup \parindent=0pt
    \centerthis}
\def\endCenter{\par\endgroup\displaybreak}
```

Review and Related Matters

This chapter introduces **\leftskip** and **\rightskip**, the reporters that say how much white space goes at the left and right sides of each line. **\raggedright**, **\raggedleft**, and **\centerthis** are tools for making sandwich-style macros for flushleft, flushright, and centered paragraphs. Since TeX puts **\parfillskip** glue on the last line of every paragraph, both **\raggedleft** and **\centerthis** need to use fill glue, whereas **\raggedright** only needs fil glue.

When two control sequences affect the same reporter and they are in the wrong order, a Cart Before the Horse Bug appears: It looks as if the first control sequence was ignored. Also, if the **\parindent** is **0pt**, **\narrower** does not move the margins.

Chapter 14 shows how to make a variety of lists: with bullets, numbers, letters, and the like. Chapter 15 shows how to make paragraph shapes for glossaries and bibliographies. Chapter 16 shows how to make TEX "obey" the lines and/or spaces that you type—a useful TEXnique for verse and computer code.

CHAPTER 14

Making Lists

Everybody makes lists. Some lists have bullets, such as the one below that describes prerequisites for the chapter. Others have numbers or letters or begin with snippets of text. Some people prefer indented lists. Others wrap the text back to the left margin. Some lists are short, with just a few items. Others might take several pages. This chapter shows the control sequences you need for making lists.

To understand this chapter, you must be familiar with the following:

- groups (Section 6.2);
- sandwich-structure macros (Chapter 12); and
- \displaybreak (Section 12.5).

 To make lists in LaTeX, use the **itemize**, **enumerate**, or **description** environments, shown in Section 2.2.4 on pages 26–27 of Lamport's LaTeX book.

14.1 Using \item

The simplest of all these control sequences is the plain TeX macro \item. It takes one input. For the sake of convenience, we call this input a *label* just as Lamport does. \item places this label in front of the text. \item also changes the shape of the paragraph after the label.

The following example shows how to use \item:

```
I took my shopping list to the mall:
\item{1.} light bulbs
\item{10.}fly swatter

\item{ZZZZZ} ice water
\item {} ice cream, for all the wonderful people
in my family who deserve a tasty treat,
\item{*}  tennis balls---for the tennis
enthusiasts in the house who become glued to the
TV whenever Andre Agassi appears, and
\item {$\bullet$} amanita mushrooms.

The sheriff came by later and inquired, politely,
about my plans for the mushrooms.
```

> I took my shopping list to the mall:
>   1. light bulbs
>   10. fly swatter
> ZZZZZ ice water
>   ice cream, for all the wonderful people in my family
>   who deserve a tasty treat,
>   * tennis balls—for the tennis enthusiasts in the house
>   who become glued to the TV whenever Andre Agassi
>   appears, and
>   • amanita mushrooms.
>   The sheriff came by later and inquired, politely, about
>   my plans for the mushrooms.

\bullet is a plain TEX macro that can be used only in math mode. The left margin in this example goes from the top line's **I** in **I took my shopping list** down to the bottom line's **m** in **my plans for the mushrooms**.

There are several things to notice about this list:

- **\item** puts the same amount of white space between the label and the text, regardless of the width of that label. (This white space happens to be **0.5em** wide.)

- If the label is wide (such as the **ZZZZZ**), it sticks out into the left margin.

- The label itself can be empty, as in the **ice cream** example.

- It does not matter whether or not you put spaces between **\item** and its input—or between the input and the text.

- It does not matter whether or not you put a blank line between the paragraphs. (The line above the first **\item** can also be blank.)

- All the lines in the paragraph are indented. This indentation is the same width as the **\parindent**.

If you have a list within a list, **\itemitem** works just like **\item**—except the indentation is **2\parindent** wide.

```
\item{1.} This item is the wrong color.
\itemitem{(a)} I wanted a red collar, not blue.
\itemitem {$\circ$} My tabby cat insists
on having a color-coordinated costume.  Since
she is very temperamental, I shall have no peace
until she is satisfied.
\item {2.}Secondly, I wanted bells.
\itemitem {(b)}How can my canary know the cat
is stalking her unless she hears the bells?
```

1. This item is the wrong color.
   (a) I wanted a red collar, not blue.
      o My tabby cat insists on having a color-coordinated costume. Since she is very temperamental, I shall have no peace until she is satisfied.
2. Secondly, I wanted bells.
   (b) How can my canary know the cat is stalking her unless she hears the bells?

If you like the way **\item** works, that is fine. However, many people want to do their lists somewhat differently. The rest of this chapter describes ways of modifying **\item**.

\item is completely different in LATEX. Lamport redefined **\item** so that it is available only in the **itemize**, **enumerate**, **description**, **list**, and **trivlist** environments. Outside those environments, **\item** does not exist.

14.2   Customizing the \parindent for a List

We can make the indentation of the item paragraphs wider (or narrower) by changing the **\parindent**. Since we want to limit this change to the list, we use the sandwich structure to keep this change inside a group.

```
\def\beginItems{\begingroup
  \displaybreak
  \advance\parindent by 1em}
\def\endItems{\displaybreak \endgroup}
```

The width of the bullet plus the space between the label and the text happens to be **1em**. Thus, this particular change aligns the bullet with the normal paragraph indentation.

```
Here is a splendid opportunity for listing clich\'es:
\beginItems
\item{$\bullet$} bite the bullet
\item{$\bullet$} faster than a speeding bullet
\item{$\bullet$} insults flying as thick as
bullets
\item{$\bullet$} ballots or bullets
\item{$\bullet$} what a bullethead!
\endItems

And last but not least: about as subtle as a bullet.
```

Here is a splendid opportunity for listing clichés:

- bite the bullet
- faster than a speeding bullet
- insults flying as thick as bullets
- ballots or bullets
- what a bullethead!

And last but not least: about as subtle as a bullet.

14.3   Customizing the \item Label

Wouldn't it be nice if you did not have to type the entire label for every item? The solution, of course, is to write a macro that does the work for you. One way is to make something like a **\bulletitem** (perhaps **\bitem** for short), like this:

```
\def\bulletitem{\item{$\bullet$}}
```

Wouldn't it be nicer still if you could use **\item** inside all your lists just as LaTeX does? Then you could change from one type of list to another, without having to change every entry from a **\bitem** to a **\numbitem**.

As you have probably guessed, TeX can do this too. The strategy is to make a copy of **\item** and then redefine **\item**. To do this, we use the primitive **\let**, like this:

```
\let\knuthitem=\item
```

\let is similar to \def because it also makes a new control sequence. However, this new control sequence is not a macro. Instead, it is a *clone*—a kind of identical twin that takes on a life of its own.

A macro is expanded when you use it in your text, so it means whatever the macro definition expands to at the time the macro is used. The clone made by \let takes whatever meaning the second input has right now. Thus, **\knuthitem** becomes an exact copy of what **\item** does at the time you say \let\knuthitem=\item.[1]

The equals sign here does not mean that **\knuthitem** is a reporter getting new information. Whenever you see an equals sign in a TEX instruction, it means that TEX is *assigning a new meaning or value* to the control sequence in front of the equals sign. The source of the new meaning or value is the information after the equals sign.

Giving a reporter new information is just one type of *assignment* in TEX. Creating a clone with \let is another. Loading a font with \font is a third. \font creates a new control sequence (the fontname) and assigns a meaning to that control sequence.

Our **\knuthitem** clone is stable. Its meaning continues to be the original definition of \item, so we can now redefine \item to behave slightly differently. To have \item typeset a bullet at the left of the item paragraph, use the following definition.

```
\def\item{\knuthitem{$\bullet$}}
```

Now we can type just **\item** instead of **\item{$\bullet$}** or **\bulletitem**.

```
\item Guillotines were once the cutting edge of
the decapitation business.
\item To make frog stew, first you have to catch
some frogs.
\item Whomever fishes for compliments may wind
up with snails.
```

- Guillotines were once the cutting edge of the decapitation business.
- To make frog stew, first you have to catch some frogs.
- Whomever fishes for compliments may wind up with snails.

---

[1] There is no TEXnical term for the new control sequence made by \let. The second argument to \let must be a *token*. A token is either a control sequence or a single character. In computerese, \let\knuthitem=\item means that **\knuthitem** acquires the current meaning of \item.

The following table shows what happens to the meanings of **\item** and
\knuthitem after various events:

After startup,   \item is   \par\hang\textindent
                   \knuthitem is nonexistent

After \let\knuthitem=\item,
                   \item is   \par\hang\textindent
                   \knuthitem is \par\hang\textindent

After \def\item{\knuthitem{$\bullet$}},
                   \item is   \knuthitem{$\bullet$}
                   \knuthitem is \par\hang\textindent

After \def\item{\relax},
                   \item is   \relax
                   \knuthitem is \par\hang\textindent

Naturally, you can make a **\knuthitemitem** clone to customize
\itemitem as well.

14.4   Keeping Your New \item inside a Group

Since you probably want numbered lists as well as bulleted lists, it makes
sense to put the new **\item** definition inside a group. Like all other changes
you make inside a group, if you define a macro inside a group, that macro
definition stops when you end the group. Thus, the new **\item** works
properly where it is supposed to—and when you end that group, **\item**
behaves once more as Knuth defined it.

```
\def\beginBullets{\begingroup
   \displaybreak
   \def\item{\knuthitem{$\bullet$}}}
\def\endBullets{\displaybreak \endgroup}

According to {\em Webster's Collegiate Dictionary},
the word ''item'' has several meanings:
\beginBullets
\item adv: also---used to introduce each article
in a list or enumeration.
\item n: a separate particular in an
enumeration, account, or series.
\item n: a separate piece of news or
information.
\endBullets
```

According to *Webster's Collegiate Dictionary*, the word "item" has several meanings:

- adv: also—used to introduce each article in a list or enumeration.
- n: a separate particular in an enumeration, account or series.
- n: a separate piece of news or information.

Naturally, you can make other changes inside the **\beginBullets** group. You can make the margins **\narrower**; use **\raggedright**; change the **\parindent**, **\parskip**, **\leftskip**, or **\rightskip**; even change things like **\tolerance** and **\hfuzz**.

It often makes sense to put changes like these into the definition of **\beginBullets**. Perhaps you want to put a **\medskip** between each **\item**. The simplest way to do this is to change the **\parskip** glue that TeX puts before each **\item** (or in this case, before each **\knuthitem**).

Since TeX also puts **\parskip** glue before the *first* **\item**, we need to remove this "extra skip." Thus, we give **\vskip** a negative dimension—to move up instead of down—just before the first **\item**.

```
\def\beginSkipBullets{\begingroup
  \displaybreak
  \def\item{\knuthitem{$\bullet$}}}
  \parskip=\medskipamount
  \vskip-\parskip}
\def\endSkipBullets{\displaybreak \endgroup}
```

When you want to change only one list, change the **\parskip** inside the **\beginBullets** group, like this:

```
As the bullets fly over the listless crowd, we see that

\beginBullets
\parskip=\medskipamount
\vskip -\parskip
\item This bulleted list has a medskip between each item.
\item The change to the parskip stays inside the group
that starts in beginBullets and stops in endBullets.
\item There is no extra space at the top of the list.
\endBullets

The fusillade ends, the crowd returns to its everyday
tasks, and the world becomes mundane once more.
```

As the bullets fly over the listless crowd, we see that

- This bulleted list has a medskip between each item.

- The change to the parskip stays inside the group that starts in beginBullets and stops in endBullets.

- There is no extra space at the top of the list.

The fusillade ends, the crowd returns to its everyday tasks, and the world becomes mundane once more.

A different strategy for changing the **\parskip** is to do it between the first and second **\item**s. This way, the **\parskip** glue is still your usual size for the first item and changes to **\medskipamount** for the second.

14.5   Numbering Your Lists

Another useful thing that TEX can do is number your lists automatically. This way, if you add a new item right after the first, you do not have to go through the entire list and change items 2–98 into 3–99. The strategy here is to make a counter and **\advance** it.

First, the plain TEX macro **\newcount** makes a new number reporter, just as **\newdimen** makes a new dimension reporter and **\newskip** makes a new glue reporter. **\newcount** automatically gives the number **0** to the new reporters it creates.

Let's call our new reporter **\listnumber**.

```
\newcount\listnumber
```

Now we redefine **\item** so that it uses this counter and typesets the number.

```
\def\item{\advance\listnumber by 1
   \knuthitem{\the\listnumber.}}
```

\the is a TEX primitive and a doer: It gets a report and typesets that report. Thus, **\the\listnumber** means "typeset the report from **\listnumber**." You can use **\the** with any reporter.

(Analogously, **\showthe** also gets a report, but sends that report as a message to your screen instead of typesetting it. This allows you to see the value of a reporter at any particular place in your document.)

Now each time that TEX finds an **\item**, it adds **1** to the **\listnumber** counter, then uses the report from **\listnumber** when it makes the label. Again, it makes sense to put this customized **\item** definition inside a group.

```
\def\beginNumbers{\begingroup
   \displaybreak
   \def\item{\advance\listnumber by 1
      \knuthitem{\the\listnumber.}}}
\def\endNumbers{\displaybreak \endgroup}

Here we have a numbered list:
\beginNumbers
\item On the first hand, we have five fingers.
\item On the other, five digits.
\item And our enumerator has no denomination.
\endNumbers
```

Here we have a numbered list:

1. On the first hand, we have five fingers.
2. On the other, five digits.
3. And our enumerator has no denomination.

When **\endNumbers** ends the group, the **\listnumber** is restored to zero. All of the **\advance**s done by **\item** stay inside the group.

TEX's *number reporters cannot handle fractions or decimals, only integers (whole numbers): 0, 1, 2, 3 . . . 16,384 and −1, −2, . . . −16,384.* The TEXnical name for a number reporter is *count register*. The other two types of reporters are *dimension registers* and *glue registers*.

14.6   Making Lettered Lists

The strategy for making a list with letters is similar to the one for numbers. Instead of typesetting the number reported by **\listnumber**, we use the ASCII code to typeset the corresponding letter. Again, we need a counter, but now we set it to the ASCII number just before the letter **A**.

```
\newcount\asciinum   \asciinum=64
```

The letter **A** has ASCII number 65, **B** has 66, and so on.

Now we define **\item** to typeset the corresponding letters, and we do this inside a **\beginABC** macro. Instead of **\the**, we use **\char**, the primitive that gets a character from the font table.

```
\def\beginABC{\begingroup
   \displaybreak
   \def\item{\advance\asciinum by 1
      \knuthitem{\char\asciinum.}}}
\def\endABC{\displaybreak \endgroup}
```

Here is an example of our **\beginABC** list:

```
Alphabet soup is a truncated Greek:
\beginABC
\item Alpha is the first Greek letter;
\item Beta is the second;
\item Gamma follows on their heels; and \dots
\item Omega completes the set.
\endABC
```

> Alphabet soup is a truncated Greek:
>
> A. Alpha is the first Greek letter;
> B. Beta is the second;
> C. Gamma follows on their heels; and . . .
> D. Omega completes the set.

If you want to use lowercase letters (a, b, c . . .), start the counter with ASCII number 96 instead of 64.

14.7   Flushleft Lists

One drawback to Knuth's **\item** is that the label is not typeset flushleft. Instead, it is typeset an **\enspace** to the left of the text that follows the label. If you want a flushleft label, you must make your own list and your own **\item**—without using **\knuthitem**.

If the text in this list needs to wrap back to the left margin, the items are ordinary paragraphs that begin with a label instead of a **\parindent**. Thus, the tasks for this customized **\item** are very simple:

- end the previous paragraph—with **\par**,
- start a new paragraph—with **\noindent**,
- typeset the label, and
- **\hskip** some space—with a dimension.

Here is a flushleft list whose items start with bullets:

```
\def\beginFlushList{\displaybreak
   \begingroup
   \def\item{\par \noindent $\bullet$\enspace}}
\def\endFlushList{\par \endgroup
   \displaybreak}
```

```
This watery universe has a variety of flushes:
\beginFlushList
\item Dogs flushed the quails from their nests.
\item The shy nudist flushed in embarrassment and wished
a fog bank would cover the beach and hide everyone.
\item The four-flusher's bluff was called---and caught!
\endFlushList

You were expecting scatology?  Tsk, tsk.
```

This watery universe has a variety of flushes:

- Dogs flushed the quails from their nests.
- The shy nudist flushed in embarrassment and wished a fog bank cover the beach and hide everyone.
- The four-flusher's bluff was called—and caught!

You were expecting scatology? Tsk, tsk.

If you need numbers instead of bullets in the label, use a counter, just as we did in Section 14.5. You can use **\listnumber** again if you like, or make a new counter.

```
\newcount\flushnumber
\def\beginFlushNumbers{\displaybreak
    \begingroup
    \def\item{\par \advance\flushnumber by 1
        \noindent \the\flushnumber.\enspace}}
\def\endFlushNumbers{\par \endgroup \displaybreak}
```

Indented Lists with Flushleft Labels

To make an indented list, we need to indent the left margin of the entire list, make a label the same width as the indentation, and place this label in the indentation space. So after we **\advance** the **\leftskip** in our definition of **\beginIndentedFlushList**, the tasks for our new **\item** macro are

- end the previous paragraph,
- start a new paragraph,
- **\hskip** back to the left margin (over the **\leftskip**), and
- typeset the label.

The following **\beginIndentedFlushList** places the label inside an hbox (horizontal box), using the TEXniques described in Chapter 29. The advantage of using the hbox is that we can control its size.

```
\newdimen\labelwidth   \labelwidth=1pc

\def\beginIndentedFlushList{\displaybreak
   \begingroup
   \advance\leftskip by \labelwidth
   \parindent=\labelwidth
   \def\item{\par\noindent
      \hskip -\labelwidth
      \hbox to \labelwidth{$\bullet$\hfil}}}
\def\endIndentedFlushList{\par \endgroup
   \displaybreak}
```

Here is an example of this indented flushleft list.

```
Ode to the joys of parking a car in Boston:
\beginIndentedFlushList
\item My car became indented at the parking lot,
and I identified the driver as a rotten sot.

My lawyer is a shark, so the driver got indebted as
he tried to pay me off.
\item I wish he'd been indentured to a wealthy toff.
\endIndentedFlushList
```

> Ode to the joys of parking a car in Boston:
>
> - My car became indented at the parking lot, and I identified the driver as a rotten sot.
>   My lawyer is a shark, so the driver got indebted as he tried to pay me off.
> - I wish he'd been indentured to a wealthy toff.

Review and Related Matters

Knuth's \item and \itemitem macros make indented lists. Both need an input: whatever you want to put in the label. \item and \itemitem can be customized by using \let to make a clone, then redefining the original. TeX can automatically number or letter the items in a list by using counters. \newcount creates the new counter, the redefined \item \advances the counter, and \the or \char typesets the counter's report.

Chapter 13 shows how to add white space to the left or right margins of paragraphs. Chapter 15 shows how to make paragraph shapes for glossaries and bibliographies. Chapter 16 shows how to make TeX "obey" the lines and/or spaces that you type—a useful TeXnique for verse and computer code.

CHAPTER 15

Hanging Indentation

Usually, both bibliographies and glossaries are indented lists, but the first line of each entry is typeset flush with the left margin. To accomplish this, we use *hanging indentation*. This term describes the shape of a paragraph whose indentation "hangs down" one or more lines in an unusual way. (The plain TeX \item macro uses hanging indentation to indent the entire paragraph.) We tackle bibliographies first since they are a little simpler than glossaries.

To understand this chapter, you must be familiar with the following:

- groups (Section 6.2);
- sandwich-structure macros (Chapter 12); and
- \displaybreak (Section 12.5).

Use **thebibliography** environment to create a bibliography. Use \cite in the text to cite a source. Section 4.3 of Lamport's LaTeX book (pages 73–75) describes how to use \cite and **thebibliography** environment.

LaTeX has two methods for generating the bibliography entries. To make each of the entries yourself, use \bibitem as described in Section 4.3.1 of Lamport's LaTeX book. Alternatively, you can use BibTeX to have the computer create the entries. BibTeX is a program that searches through a bibliographic database for the information on each source that you \cite in your document. Section 4.3.2 of Lamport's LaTeX book describes how to use BibTeX.

For glossaries, use LaTeX's \glossary and \makeglossary macros. These are analogous to LaTeX's \index and \makeindex macros. These indexing and glossary macros are described in Section 4.5 on pages 77–79 of Lamport's LaTeX book.

15.1   Hanging Indentation for Bibliographies

The goal of this section is to create bibliographies that look like the examples on pages 157 and 158.

To change the left margin for a bibliography, we use the reporter called **\hangindent**, a TeX primitive that says how wide the hanging indentation should be. In the following example, there is **30pt** between the left margin and the beginnings of the second, third, and fourth lines. The **\noindent** makes sure that the paragraph does not start with the usual **\parindent**.

```
\hangindent=30pt
\noindent
The bookworm browsed among the books, deciding
which to munch.  He wandered here, meandered
there, selecting one for lunch.  He nibbled pages
at his leisure; then he got some punch.
```

> The bookworm browsed among the books, deciding which to munch. He wandered here, meandered there, selecting one for lunch. He nibbled pages at his leisure; then he got some punch.

\hangindent affects only the next paragraph.[1] When TeX finishes typesetting that paragraph, the **\hangindent** automatically changes back to **0pt**. Thus, we need to establish the new **\hangindent** for each paragraph in our bibliography. The simplest way to do this is with a new **\bibentry** macro for starting each new entry.

It is a good idea to make a reporter for the width of this hanging indentation, so we do that now too. The indentation does not have to be **30pt**; it can be any dimension you want.

```
\newdimen\biblioindent
\biblioindent=30pt
\def\bibentry{\hangindent=\biblioindent}
```

This definition assumes that there is a blank line between each of the entries to end the current paragraph. If you might type the entries without blank lines between them, include a **\par** at the beginning of **\bibentry**'s definition.

---

[1]More precisely: When TeX is in vertical mode, **\hangindent** affects only the next paragraph; when TeX is in horizontal mode, **\hangindent** affects only the current paragraph. Thus, **\noindent\hangindent=30pt** acts just like **\hangindent=30pt\noindent**. TeX uses the value of **\hangindent** at the end of a paragraph, so if you change the **\hangindent** again in the midst of a paragraph, the first assignment is forgotten.

```
\def\betterBibEntry{\par \hangindent=\biblioindent}
```

Including this \par is always a good idea. It cannot hurt, since \par means end the current paragraph. If TeX is "between paragraphs" (in vertical, page-making mode), \par has no effect.

Since bibliography entries start at the left margin, we also change the **\parindent** to **0pt**. (A different method of accomplishing this same result is to put **\noindent** at the end of the definition of **\bibentry**.)

```
{\parindent=0pt

\bibentry Frankenstein and Chaney, {\em Our
Favorite Monsters From Attila to Zeno, An
Annotated Bibliography}, NY: Horrific Press,
1984.

\bibentry Heckle and Jeckle, ''The Fine Art of
Driving a Speaker Up the Wall,'' {\em Oration
Weekly}, Vol.~2, No.~1, 1215.\par}
```

> Frankenstein and Chaney, *Our Favorite Monsters From Attila to Zeno, An Annotated Bibliography*, NY: Horrific Press, 1984.
>
> Heckle and Jeckle, "The Fine Art of Driving a Speaker Up the Wall," *Oration Weekly*, Vol. 2, No. 1, 1215.

To limit the **\parindent** change to the bibliography itself, we put this inside a pair of sandwich macros that begin and end the bibliography.

```
\def\beginBibliography{\begingroup
    \parindent=0pt}
\def\endBibliography{\par \endgroup}
```

This is a "bare bones" bibliography. You may want to include **\raggedright** or have other special characteristics as well. The **\par** in **\endBibliography** makes sure that you end the paragraph before ending the group, and do not get an Ignores My Command Bug (see page 129) in the last entry.

Putting Labels in the Margin

Our **\bibentry** does a nice job with ordinary bibliographies, but what if we need a label like [1] or [Knu83] at the start of each entry? Then we need a macro that takes an input for this label. We also need to make sure that the text of each entry starts at the same place, no matter how much information is in the label.

The solution is to put the label inside an hbox (horizontal box) that is the same width as our **\biblioindent**. **\hbox** is a primitive doer that takes one input: whatever you want to put inside the box. Chapters 28 through 30 explain how to use TEX's boxes.

Our **\boxentry** macro takes one input: the text for the entry's label. We start our **\boxentry** macro with **\par** to make sure we end the previous paragraph, then use **\noindent** to avoid getting a Text by Itself Bug (see page 288).

```
\def\boxentry#1{\par\noindent
    \hangindent=\biblioindent
    \hbox to \biblioindent{[#1]\hfil}%
    \ignorespaces}
```

The **to** after **\hbox** is a keyword. It gives the hbox a specific width: in this case, the dimension called **\biblioindent**. Thus, each entry begins with an hbox that is the same width as the bibliography's indentation.

\ignorespaces is a TEX primitive. It tells TEX to ignore any spaces that follow until TEX finds a character that is not a space. In the example below, TEX does not typeset any of the spaces after **\boxentry**'s input.

```
\biblioindent=60pt

\boxentry{1}Ali, Muhammad, ''Name Changing as a
Powerful Pugilistic Tactic,'' {\em Boxing
Tidbits}, June 1980.

\boxentry{Byr44}   Byrd, Nestor, ''Better than
Twigs---a Wren's Eye View of Cardboard,'' {\em
Better Nests and Gardens}, July 1981.

\boxentry{Jack 1929a}
Jack, ''An Insider's Report on the State of the
Box,'' {\em Square-Siders}, August 1982.
```

[1]	Ali, Muhammad, "Name Changing as a Powerful Pugilistic Tactic," *Boxing Tidbits*, June 1980.
[Byr44]	Byrd, Nestor, "Better than Twigs—a Wren's Eye View of Cardboard," *Better Nests and Gardens*, July 1981.
[Jack 1929a]	Jack, "An Insider's Report on the State of the Box," *Square-Siders*, August 1982.

Without the **\ignorespaces**, TEX would typeset an interword space when it finds one or more spaces after a **\boxentry** input in your document.

You can also make a counter that numbers the bibliography entries automatically. See Sections 14.5 and 17.4 for details on how to make and use a counter.

15.2   Glossaries

Glossaries are similar to bibliographies. Each paragraph has a **\hangindent**, the **\parindent** is **0pt**, and each glossary entry takes one input: the word or phrase being explained. Having our **\gloss** macro take an input makes it easy to typeset that word or phrase in a different font, and to change that font if you decide you prefer something else. Just as **\item**, **\bibentry**, and **\boxentry** need to begin with **\par** to end the previous paragraph, so does **\gloss**.

Here are all the pieces:

```
\newdimen\glossaryindent
\glossaryindent=2\normalparindent
\def\gloss#1{\par
    \hangindent=\glossaryindent
    {\bf #1:}}
\def\beginGlossary{\displaybreak
    \begingroup
    \parindent=0pt}
\def\endGlossary{\par \endgroup \displaybreak}
```

The following example shows these macros at work. The definitions are from *Webster's New Collegiate Dictionary*, Springfield, MA: G. & C. Merriam Company, 1981.

```
\beginGlossary
\gloss{gloss} a brief explanation of a difficult or
obscure word or expression; a false and often
willfully misleading interpretation (as of a text).

\gloss{glossary}
a collection of textual glosses or of terms
limited to a special area of knowledge or usage.
\endGlossary
```

> **gloss:** a brief explanation of a difficult or obscure word or expression; a false and often willfully misleading interpretation (as of a text).
>
> **glossary:** a collection of textual glosses or of terms limited to a special area of knowledge or usage.

The Size of Spaces in Glossary Inputs

The spaces in \gloss's input stretch or shrink the same amount as other spaces in that same line. If the input is typeset inside an hbox, as we do in the following \firmgloss macro, the glue in these spaces stays its natural size and does not stretch or shrink.

In the following example, the interword spaces after the terms being defined have been stretched. The interword spaces in **under the table** were also stretched—but the interword spaces in **over the transom** were not.

```
\def\firmgloss#1{\par
   \noindent
   \hangindent=\glossaryindent
   \hbox{\bf #1:}}

\gloss{under the table} adv.\ describing an illegal
payment, sometimes called a kickback, that is given
secretly and is not reported to the IRS.

\firmgloss{over the transom} adv.\ describing
unsolicited manu\-scripts sent to a publisher who has
not asked to see them.
```

> **under the table:** adv. describing an illegal payment, sometimes called a kickback, that is given secretly and is not reported to the IRS.
>
> **over the transom:** adv. describing unsolicited manuscripts sent to a publisher who has not asked to see them.

\firmgloss needs the \noindent after \par to nudge TEX into paragraph-making (horizontal) mode. Since \firmgloss uses an hbox, the \noindent makes sure you do not get a Text by Itself Bug (page 288).

15.3 Where Does the Hanging Indentation Begin?

In all the examples in this chapter so far, the first line of the paragraph is the normal width, and the hanging indentation follows. This is because another reporter called \hangafter is normally **1**. But we can change this reporter too and get interesting effects.

```
\hangindent=20pt
\hangafter 2
\noindent
Bats hang down, coats are hung up.  Admirers hang
onto your every word.  Kids hang around after
school, and hang out on the streetcorners.
Planes are kept in hangars, and clothes are kept
on hangers.  Paintings hang on walls, ornaments
hang on Christmas trees, and chandeliers hang
from ceilings.
```

> Bats hang down, coats are hung up. Admirers hang onto your every word. Kids hang around after school, and hang out on the streetcorners. Planes are kept in hangars, and clothes are kept on hangers. Paintings hang on walls, ornaments hang on Christmas trees, and chandeliers hang from ceilings.

As you can see, **\hangafter** identifies the boundary between the normal lines and the hanging indentation. **\hangafter 2** says, "Use hanging indentation after line 2."

Some of you are thinking right now, "Oops, she forgot the equals sign." Yes, I am giving the reporter called **\hangafter** some new information, so where is that equals sign?

Actually, the equals sign is optional.[2] You do not have to use it. Just as you understand the difference between "chop wood" and "white chair," TEX understands from the context that **\hangafter 2** means "Give the reporter called **\hangafter** the new information of **2**."

In a somewhat rough analogy, *chop* is a verb—a transitive verb, which is like saying that it takes an input. *Wood* is a noun and says what the chopping action is being applied to. So we know from the verb-noun structure what "chop wood" means. Also, *white* is an adjective and *chair* is a noun. We know from the adjective-noun structure of "white chair" that "white" is modifying "chair."

In a similar way, TEX knows that **\hskip** is a doer and **\parindent** is a reporter. The **\hskip** doer expects an input, and the **\parindent** reporter provides it. So this doer-reporter structure is familiar to TEX. The reporter-input and reporter-reporter structures are also familiar to TEX. TEX knows that the second member of the pair is giving new information for the first.

---

[2]The equals sign is optional in all of TEX's assignments. The instructions **\let\this=\that** and **\let\this\that** do exactly the same thing. So do **\parskip=0pt** and **\parskip0pt**. To prevent confusion, however, I always use the equals sign in this book (except for the **\hangafter** example above) and in my own code.

So the equals sign is more like punctuation than a word of any kind. It is neither a doer nor a reporter. Its only function is to make the instruction easier for humans to understand. Thus, you can say \hangafter=5, \hangafter 5 or \hangafter5, whatever "feels right" to you. Like \hangindent, \hangafter also affects only the next paragraph.

15.4 Negative Numbers and Dimensions

Some of you may be wondering what TEX does if \hangindent is a negative dimension (such as −1in) or if \hangafter is a negative number (such as −3).

When \hangindent is negative, TEX puts the indentation on the right side of the paragraph instead of the left. When \hangafter is negative, TEX puts the indentation on the top line(s) of the paragraph instead of the bottom.

You can think of \hangafter as saying which baseline marks the boundary between the hanging indentation and the normal lines. The positive or negative number says on which side of this boundary the hanging indentation appears. Thus,

\hangafter = 3   puts the boundary at baseline #3, and
                    the hanging indentation goes below.
\hangafter = -3   also puts the boundary at baseline #3, but
                    the hanging indentation goes above.

Review and Related Matters

This chapter shows how to use TEX's hanging indentation. Hanging indentation is especially useful for making bibliographies and glossaries. To start the bibliography entry with a label, put the label in an \hbox. Using \ignorespaces makes sure that TEX does not typeset extra spaces between a label and the subsequent text.

\hangindent specifies the width of the hanging indentation. A positive \hangindent puts the indentation on the left side of the paragraph; a negative \hangindent puts the indentation on the right. \hangafter says which baseline is the boundary between the indented lines and the normal-width lines in the paragraph. A positive \hangafter puts the indentation below that boundary; a negative \hangafter puts the indentation above it.

Chapter 13 shows how to add white space to the left or right margins of paragraphs. Chapter 14 shows how to make a variety of lists: with bullets, numbers, letters, and the like. Chapter 16 shows how to make TEX "obey" the lines and/or spaces that you type—a useful TEXnique for verse and computer code.

CHAPTER 16

Obeying Lines and Spaces: Verse and Computer Code

The ideal way to typeset verse or computer code is to have TeX "obey" both your line breaks and extra spaces. Then you can create WYSIWYG (what you see is what you get) effects. The two control sequences that make TeX "obedient" are \obeylines and \obeyspaces. This chapter shows how to use them.

To understand this chapter, you must be familiar with the following:

- groups (Section 6.2);
- sandwich-structure macros (Chapter 12); and
- \displaybreak (Section 12.5).

LaTeX Notes

For poetry, LaTeX has a **verse** environment, shown in Section 2.2.4 on page 27 of Lamport's LaTeX book.

For computer code, you can use LaTeX's **verbatim** or **tabbing** environments, or you can use the \beginCode...\endCode macros shown in this chapter. The **verbatim** environment is shown in Section 3.7 on page 65 of Lamport's LaTeX book. The **tabbing** environment is shown in Section 3.6.1 on pages 62–63 of Lamport's LaTeX book.

16.1   Using \obeylines

\obeylines is a plain TEX macro that makes TEX end a paragraph when it finds an ⌞END-OF-LINE⌟ character in your text file. Thus, each line in your text file is treated as a separate paragraph—and starts on a new line in your printout. Unless you want TEX to typeset the rest of your document this way, put \obeylines inside a group.

```
{\obeylines
Now these are the Laws of the Jungle:
and many and mighty are they;
but the head and the hoof of the Law
and the haunch and the hump is---Obey!
---{\em The Second Jungle Book}, Kipling, 1895}
```

> Now these are the Laws of the Jungle:
> and many and mighty are they;
> but the head and the hoof of the Law
> and the haunch and the hump is—Obey!
> —*The Second Jungle Book*, Kipling, 1895

\obeylines uses an interesting trick to accomplish this task. When TEX reads your document file, it normally converts the ⌞END-OF-LINE⌟ character into a space. After you say \obeylines, however, TEX converts the ⌞END-OF-LINE⌟ character into a \par instead.

16.2   Making a Verse Macro with \obeylines

If you are quoting some verse in your document, put \obeylines inside a \beginVerse macro. Use the sandwich structure to begin and end the verse. Since each line begins a new paragraph, it starts with a space that is \parindent wide. If you want the verse to be flush with the left margin, change the \parindent to 0pt.

```
\def\beginVerse{\displaybreak
    \begingroup
    \parindent=0pt
    \obeylines}
\def\endVerse{\endgroup \displaybreak}
```

You do not need a \par in the definition of \endVerse. The ⌞END-OF-LINE⌟ character at the end of the last line of verse is already converted into a \par before TEX reaches \endVerse.

Oops!

If you write a jelly-doughnut macro with **\obeylines**, you get a Disobedient Bug. The following **\disobey** macro illustrates this bug. The macro writer wants **\disobey**'s input to be typeset as verse—with each line in the text file starting a new line in the printout—but it does not work out that way.

```
\def\disobey#1{\begingroup
    \obeylines #1\par \endgroup}

\disobey{%
Sweet lords, sweet lovers, O!  Let us embrace.
As true we are as flesh and blood can be:
The sea will ebb and flow, heaven show his face;
Young blood doth not obey an old decree:
We cannot cross the cause why we were born.}

Shakespeare: {\em Love's Labour's Lost}
```

> Sweet lords, sweet lovers, O! Let us embrace. As true we are as flesh and blood can be: The sea will ebb and flow, heaven show his face; Young blood doth not obey an old decree: We cannot cross the cause why we were born.
> Shakespeare: *Love's Labour's Lost*

This bug appears because TeX gobbles up a macro's input before it expands the macro. By the time TeX expands **\disobey** and finds the **\obeylines**, it has already converted those END-OF-LINE characters into spaces.

Disobedient Bug

Whenever you use the jelly-doughnut structure for a macro with **\obeylines** or **\obeyspaces**, this bug appears. Instead of typesetting each line or space separately, TeX makes a normal paragraph and follows its usual rules about ignoring extra spaces.

To fix a Disobedient Bug, always use the sandwich structure when you need **\obeylines** or **\obeyspaces** in a macro.

Adding Vertical Space inside Your Verses

If you want a blank line in your printout when you are using **\obeylines**, the simple way is to put a tilde (~) by itself on the line you want blank.

TeX does not start making a paragraph until it finds either a character to typeset or a control sequence that explicitly starts a paragraph, such as \indent or \noindent. Since the tilde nudges TeX into starting a paragraph, a \baselineskip of vertical space is added to the page, even though the only thing in that paragraph is a space. The tilde also makes these blank lines easy to see when you are typing your document.

If you want a different amount of space between verses, put a \verseskip on a line by itself, and define it to be whatever size you want.

```
\def\verseskip{\medskip}

\begingroup\obeylines
While skipping down the alleyways
Through verses thick and thin,
\verseskip
The wine splashed dimly in the haze,
And cats yowled in the din.
\endgroup
```

> While skipping down the alleyways
> Through verses thick and thin,
>
> The wine splashed dimly in the haze,
> And cats yowled in the din.

16.3   Using \obeyspaces

\obeyspaces is also a plain TeX macro. It tells TeX to typeset all the spaces—even the ones that follow a control sequence. Again, unless you want TeX to do this with all the spaces in the rest of your document, put \obeyspaces inside a group.

```
{\obeyspaces
\TeX normally  ignores   extra    spaces,
     and normally does not typeset the
spaces after a control sequence.  But you can
     tell \TeX , if you want,
to  ''obey''  every  space  you  type.}
```

> TeX normally ignores extra   spaces,   and normally does not typeset the spaces after a control sequence. But you can   tell TeX , if you want, to "obey" every space you type.

16.4   Macros for Verse and Computer Code

The simplest way to typeset computer code (and some poetry) is by using
\obeylines and **\obeyspaces** together. This is not as straightforward as it
looks, however. The next few sections explain the bugs you encounter along
the way.

First, here is the solution:

```
\def\codefont{\tt}
\def\startline{\par\noindent}

{\obeylines\obeyspaces%
\global\def\beginCode{\displaybreak%
\begingroup%
\obeylines\obeyspaces%
\let^^M=\startline%
\codefont}%
\global\def\endCode{\endgroup\displaybreak}}
```

Next, here is the explanation of all those pieces, and why they are
needed. We start with the idea of putting **\obeylines** and **\obeyspaces**
together in an ordinary sandwich-style macro.

Oops! Spaces at the Beginning of the Line Disappear

To be understood, most computer code needs the correct spacing at the
front of a line. However, if you make a **\beginCode** macro by adding
\obeyspaces and **\codefont** to the **\beginVerse** macro, you discover the
Ignores My Spaces Bug, as shown by the following **\beginNoSpaceCode**
macro. The spaces at the beginning of a line do not appear in the printout.

```
\def\beginNoSpaceCode{\displaybreak\begingroup
    \parindent=0pt
    \obeylines\obeyspaces
    \codefont}
\def\endNoSpaceCode{\endgroup\displaybreak}
```

The following example of **\beginNoSpaceCode** shows a Logo program that
prints a greeting.

```
\beginNoSpaceCode
to greet :name
print sentence [hi,]
              :name
print [how are you?]
end
\endNoSpaceCode
```

```
        to greet :name
        print sentence [hi,]
        :name
        print [how are you?]
        end
```

One way to fix this problem is to put a tilde (~) at the front of a line that begins with spaces. However, that is a nuisance, and there is another way.

Ignores My Spaces Bug

When you combine \obeylines and \obeyspaces, TeX still ignores spaces at the beginning of a line.

TeX ignores those spaces because it is in vertical (page-making) mode when it starts reading the characters at the beginning of each line. TeX always ignores such spaces when it is in vertical mode. It does not change into horizontal (paragraph-making) mode until it finds a character to be typeset, or a control sequence that starts horizontal mode. (Chapter 33 explains TeX's modes.)

The solution is to start a new paragraph (begin horizontal mode) before TeX reads that first space. To start a new paragraph at the beginning of each line, we need something a little fancier than \obeylines. We need to convert the end of each line into \par\noindent instead of just \par.

The END-OF-LINE character is ^^M. Knuth uses \let^^M=\par in his definition of \obeylines, so we follow the same strategy. However, we cannot say something like \let^^M={\par\noindent}, because the second input to \let has to be a single *token*, not a group. (A token is either a character to be typeset or a control sequence—so one control sequence is okay, but not two. Chapter 33 explains more about tokens.) Therefore, we make a new macro called \startline and use that instead of \par as the second input to \let.

```
\def\startline{\par\noindent}
\let^^M=\startline
```

Since there is a **\noindent** in **\startline**, it does not matter what the
\parindent is. Therefore, we do not need **\parindent=0pt** in the macro
definition. Our new attempt at writing a **\beginCode** macro looks like this:

```
\def\beginStubbornCode{\displaybreak
   \begingroup
   \obeylines\obeyspaces
   \let^^M=\startline
   \codefont}
\def\endStubbornCode{\endgroup\displaybreak}
```

This looks pretty good. In fact, the macro itself is the same as the
solution shown on page 167.

However, **\beginStubbornCode** does not do what we want. Spaces at
the beginnings of lines are ignored, the font does not change, and each new
line is indented with the **\parindent**.

The solution is to define **\beginCode** and **\endCode** while the rules
of **\obeylines** and **\obeyspaces** are in effect. However, we do not want
\obeylines and **\obeyspaces** to affect the entire document, so we need
to put them inside a group. Normally, when we define a macro inside a
group, that particular macro definition disappears when we end the group.
Therefore, we need to make the definition **\global**.

```
\def\codefont{\tt}
\def\startline{\par\noindent}

{\obeylines\obeyspaces%
\global\def\beginCode{\displaybreak
\begingroup%
\obeylines\obeyspaces%
\let^^M=\startline%
\codefont}%
\global\def\endCode{\endgroup\displaybreak}}
```

\global is a TeX primitive. It can be used whenever you want the new
meaning of a control sequence to be *global* instead of local. Global means
that the new meaning gets posted on the innermost layer of the bulletin
board, instead of being removed when the group ends. Some examples of
giving a new meaning to a control sequence are defining a macro with **\def**,
making a clone with **\let**, and giving a reporter new information.[1]

---

[1] **\global** can be used to make any assignment global instead of local (see page 275 of *The
TeXbook*).

Since the rules of \obeylines and \obeyspaces are in effect while we define \beginCode and \endCode, we also removed all the spaces from the beginning of the lines, and used % to remove the END-OF-LINE characters at the ends of the lines. Since these spaces no longer exist, TeX cannot typeset them under any circumstances whatsoever.

If your fingers get tired typing \global\def, the TeX primitive called \gdef is equivalent to \global\def. The rest of this chapter shows several ways of fine tuning our sandwich macros for code and verse.

16.5   Controlling Page Breaks in Computer Code

Let's say you want to prevent TeX from starting a new page in the middle of your computer code. Add the plain TeX macro \nobreak to \startline.

```
\def\startline{\par\nobreak\noindent}
```

The \nobreak control sequence insists that TeX cannot put a page break between these two paragraphs.

TeX now puts everything from \beginCode to \endCode on the same page—no matter how long that page becomes. If you have lengthy pieces of computer code, however, you want to be able to start one or more new pages in the middle, and to control where those new pages start. The simplest way is to type \eject on a line by itself when you want to start a new page.

```
\beginCode
...
last line on the old page
\eject
first line on the new page
...
\endCode
```

\eject is a plain TeX macro that forces TeX to end the current page and start a new one. It also pulls the text down to the bottom of the page, thereby stretching any vertical glue on that page. If you do not want that glue stretched, use our \newpage macro (page 108) instead of \eject.

16.6   Removing Extra Space between Lines of Code

Plain TeX establishes the \parskip glue as 0pt plus 1pt. Since each line of code is a separate paragraph, the space between them contains \parskip glue and can stretch. When TeX does not have enough text to fill the page, it stretches the glue past the 1-point limit (which results in a very odd-looking page). If you want to make sure that TeX does not stretch this glue, change the \parskip to 0pt in \beginCode.

```
{\obeylines\obeyspaces%
\global\def\beginCode{\displaybreak%
\begingroup%
\parskip=0pt%
\obeylines\obeyspaces%
\let^^M=\startline%
\codefont}}
```

16.7   Changing Fonts in Computer Code

One nice feature of the **\beginCode** macro is that you can change fonts.
The only catch is to make sure that extra spaces do not creep into your
code. Thus, instead of using a space to show TEX where a font-changing
macro ends, put another pair of braces around the words—or write a font-
changing macro that takes an input.

The following example shows both TEXniques. **\slant** takes an input: the
text to be typeset in the **\sl** font.

```
\def\slant#1{{\sl#1}}

\beginCode
to square {\sl{:side}}
repeat 4 [forward \slant{:side} right 90]
end
\endCode
```

```
to square :side
repeat 4 [forward :side right 90]
end
```

16.8   Controlling the Size of Interword Spaces in Verse

The WYSIWYG effects of **\obeyspaces** in the **\beginCode** macro rely on
the fact that interword spaces in the **\tt** font have no glue: They do not
stretch or shrink. To achieve this same effect with other fonts for your verse
or computer code, remove the glue from TEX's spaces.

The TEX primitives **\spaceskip** and **\xspaceskip** are reporters that
influence the size of spaces between words and sentences. When TEX starts
up, both are zero (**0pt plus 0pt minus 0pt**). When they are zero, TEX
uses the **\tolerance** to decide how big the spaces should be. If you give
them a nonzero dimension or glue, however, they override TEX's usual
behavior.

When they are not zero, TEX uses the **\spaceskip** for spaces between words and the **\xspaceskip** for spaces between sentences. You can make these spaces larger or smaller if you prefer. The natural size (with no stretch or shrink) of an interword space in TEX's **\rm** font is **0.333em**, and an intersentence space is normally **0.444em**. For comparison, an interword space in the **\tt** font is **0.525em** and the intersentence space is twice that size: **1.05em**. (Appendix A describes these and other characteristics of each of TEX's fonts.)

The following **\rigidspaces** macro gives new information to these two reporters.

```
\def\rigidspaces{\spaceskip=0.3333em
    \xspaceskip=0.5em\relax}
```

\rigidspaces is designed to be a tool—an ingredient for the **\beginVerse** macro.

```
{\obeylines\obeyspaces%
\global\def\beginRigidVerse{\displaybreak%
\begingroup%
\obeylines\obeyspaces%
\let^^M=\startline%
\rigidspaces}%
\global\def\endRigidVerse{\endgroup\displaybreak}}
```

Review and Related Matters

\obeylines causes TEX to convert the ⎡END-OF-LINE⎤ character into a **\par**. **\obeyspaces** causes TEX to typeset every space it sees, including the space after a control word. These two macros make it possible to get WYSIWYG effects, which are useful for typesetting computer code and verse.

\obeylines and **\obeyspaces** cannot be used in a jelly-doughnut macro because TEX reads the macro's input using its usual rules—before it expands the macro and finds **\obeylines** and **\obeyspaces**. Thus, you must use the sandwich structure to write macros for your verse and computer code.

Combining **\obeylines** and **\obeyspaces** in the same macro has some unexpected side effects. This chapter explains the bugs that can crop up when you use these two macros together, and how to fix them.

\global lets you post new information on the innermost layer of the bulletin board so that the change does not stop when you end the group.

Chapter 13 shows how to add white space to the left or right margins of paragraphs. Chapter 14 shows how to make a variety of lists: with bullets, numbers, letters, and the like. Chapter 15 shows how to make paragraph shapes for glossaries and bibliographies.

CHAPTER 17

Headings: for Sections, Chapters, and Title Pages

Every document has at least one heading—a title of some sort. Most have other kinds of headings as well: for chapters, sections, subsections, paragraphs, and the like. This chapter shows how to make a variety of headings, both plain and fancy, and let TEX do all the numbering for them as well.

To understand this chapter, you must be familiar with the following:

- reporters (Section 3.10);
- loading large fonts (Chapter 7);
- using skips (Chapters 9 and 10);
- jelly-doughnut macro structure (Chapter 12); and
- \bigbreak (Section 12.5).

LATEX has seven heading macros: \part, \chapter, \section, \subsection, \subsubsection, \paragraph, and \subparagraph. Section 2.2.3 of Lamport's LATEX book (pages 22–24) describes which of these macros are available in the different document styles, and shows how to use them.

If you need a heading macro that behaves differently, you can use the TEXniques in this chapter to write your own.

17.1   Simple Headings

To make a simple heading, we need a jelly-doughnut macro that `\vskip`s some space and typesets its input in a bold typeface. Since the heading should be flush with the left margin, we also use a **\noindent**.

```
\def\heading#1{\bigbreak
    \noindent{\bf#1}
    \medskip}
```

Here is how it looks:

```
\dots\ controlling criminal behavior.

\heading{Decapitation, Then and Now}

''Off with their heads'' is a foolproof (but
rather extreme) method of preventing recidivism.
```

. . . controlling criminal behavior.

Decapitation, Then and Now

"Off with their heads" is a foolproof (but rather extreme) method of preventing recidivism.

Using a larger typeface is equally simple. Change the size before you change to the bold typeface.

```
\def\largeheading#1{\bigbreak
    \noindent
    {\large\bf#1}
    \medskip}
```

Using **\large** allows you to have different type styles in your headings. To make a **\large** macro, use the **\eightpoint** macro as a model (page 91) and substitute a set of larger fonts for the 8-point fonts. Or, if you need to use math mode in your headings (perhaps for Greek letters or math symbols), use the relevant parts of the **\twelvepoint** macro as a model (page 282).

17.2   Chapter Headings

Chapters always start on a new page, so we begin our **\chapter** macro with a **\newpage**. If we want the heading to appear at the top of that page, we are all set. But if we want to **\vskip** an inch first—using the same pattern as **\heading** and **\largeheading**—we get a Does Not Skip at the Top Bug.

The heading in **WontSkipChapter** is typeset at the top of the page, not 1 inch down.

```
\def\WontSkipChapter#1{\newpage
   \vskip 1in
   \noindent{\Large\bf#1}
   \bigskip}
```

Does Not Skip at the Top Bug

Glue always disappears at the top of a page.

When TeX breaks a page, it throws away the glue between the last text on the old page and the first text on the new page. This is correct behavior in virtually all circumstances, because the text should start in the same place on all pages.

The solution is to use the plain TeX macro **vglue** instead of **vskip**. **vglue** and the corresponding **hglue** make space that cannot disappear. Here is our debugged **chapter** macro. It takes one input: the text for the chapter's title.

```
\def\chapter#1{\newpage
   \vglue 1in
   \noindent{\Large\bf#1}
   \vskip 2\bigskipamount}
```

17.3   Let TeX Remember the Titles and Authors

We can write a **titlepage** macro that takes inputs for the title and author, but then we have to make sure we do not put the author's name in the title slot and vice versa. It is simpler to let TeX remember which is which.

The following two macros take an input and use it to define another new macro. The input for **title** is the document's title. The input for **author** is the document's author.

```
\def\title#1{\def\theTitle{#1}}
\def\author#1{\def\theAuthor{#1}}
```

We use **title** and **author** like this:

```
\title{Methods of Spinning Gold}
\author{Rumplestiltskin}
```

Now when you say **theAuthor** in your text, TeX expands that macro to **Rumplestiltskin**.

We use **\theTitle** and **\theAuthor** instead of inputs in our **\titlepage** macro. Again, we use **\vglue** to put white space at the top of the title page.

```
\def\titlepage{\vglue 1in
   \beginCenter
   {\Large\bf\theTitle}
   \vskip 2\normalbaselineskip
   {\large\theAuthor}
   \endCenter
   \newpage}
```

(The **\beginCenter...\endCenter** macros are defined on page 141, and the **\centerthis** macro is on page 140.)

Your text file now looks like this:

```
\input macros
\title{Methods of Spinning Gold}
\author{Rumplestiltskin}
\titlepage

Spinning flax into gold is as easy as pie, though
few ordinary mortals know the secret \dots
```

Oops!

If you do not specify a title and author before you say **\titlepage**, TEX complains about two undefined control sequences: **\theTitle** and **\theAuthor**.

17.4   Let TEX Do the Numbering: Counters for Headings

Most books have numbered chapters; some documents also have numbered sections; a few have numbered subsections as well. It is a huge nuisance to renumber chapters or sections or subsections by hand if you decide to add, remove, or rearrange a few areas of text.

Luckily, TEX can do all this work for you. Make a new counter and **\advance** it. **\newcount** makes a new number reporter, just as **\newdimen** makes a new dimension reporter and **\newskip** makes a new glue reporter.

Here is our new **\sectionnumber** counter and the numbered **\section** macro that uses it. The input for **\section** is the text for the section heading.

```
\newcount\sectionnumber
```

```
\def\section#1{\bigbreak
    \advance\sectionnumber by 1
    \noindent{\bf\the\sectionnumber. #1}
    \medskip}
```

\newcount automatically gives a **0** to the new reporter it creates. Since TeX adds **1** to **\sectionnumber** every time it finds a **\section{heading}** in your text file, zero is exactly where we want **\sectionnumber** to start.

\the is a TeX primitive and a doer. It gets a report and typesets that report. Thus, **\the\sectionnumber** means "typeset the report from **\sectionnumber**."

TeX's number reporters can handle only *integers* (whole numbers) 0, 1, 2, 3 . . . 16,384 and −1, −2, . . . −16,384, not fractions or decimals.

Using More Than One Counter

Engineers are almost as fond of numbers as mathematicians are, and their documents typically use up to five levels of section numbering. If a counter can deal only with integers, how do we create numbers like **5.13.8.6**? Simple. We use four counters.

```
\newcount\chapternumber
\newcount\sectionnumber
\newcount\subsectnumber
\newcount\subsubsectnumber
```

This is a lot of counters to stick into a **\subsubsection** macro, so we make another macro that generates the number for us.

```
\def\theSubsubsectionnumber{%
    \the\chapternumber.%
    \the\sectionnumber.%
    \the\subsectnumber.%
    \the\subsubsectnumber}
```

The percent sign makes TeX ignore the END-OF-LINE character after the open brace and the periods. Since TeX ignores the spaces at the beginning of a line, no spaces are typeset between these counters.[1]

Now we can write our **\subsubsection** macro. It advances its own counter, then typesets the entire number and title. The input for **\subsubsection** is the text for the subsubsection heading.

---

[1] TeX always ignores spaces at the beginning of a line *unless two circumstances are true.* If TeX is in a horizontal mode and if **\obeyspaces** is in effect, TeX typesets spaces at the beginning of a line. This is not likely to be the case when TeX sees a **\subsubsection** in the text.

```
\def\subsubsection#1{\medbreak
   \advance\subsubsectnumber by 1
   \noindent
   {\bf \theSubsubsectionnumber \quad #1}
   \smallskip}
```

```
\dots has been established here in
Section 5.13.8.5.
```

```
\subsubsection{Extensive Substrata}
```

```
Investigation of the subterranean strata showed
conclusively that \dots
```

> . . . has been established here in section 5.13.8.5.
>
> **5.13.8.6   Extensive Substrata**
>
> Investigation of the subterranean strata showed conclusively that . . .

Each time you start a new chapter, section, or subsection, the counters for all the lower sectioning levels must be reset to zero. Thus, this task needs to be included in the macro.

```
\def\numberedChapter#1{\newpage
   \advance\chapternumber by 1
   \sectionnumber=0
   \subsectnumber=0
   \subsubsectnumber=0
   \vglue 1in
   \beginCenter \Large\bf
   Chapter \the\chapternumber\break
   #1
   \endCenter
   \vskip 2\bigskipamount}
```

In the **\section** macro, only the subsection and subsubsection counters are reset to zero—and in the **\subsection** macro, only the subsubsection counter is reset to zero.

Using Letters Instead of Numbers

Some styles use letters instead of numbers to identify sections. TeX can generate these as well. Instead of **\the**, we use **\char**, the primitive that gets a character from the font table.

\char needs an input to say which character, and the input we use is the character's position in the font tables. This position is the same as the character's ASCII number. **A** is ASCII number 65, **B** is 66, **C** is 67, and so on. Thus, we start our new \ASCIInumber counter at 64. The input for \LetteredSection is the text for the section heading.

```
\newcount\ASCIInumber   \ASCIInumber=64

\def\LetteredSection#1{\bigbreak
    \advance\ASCIInumber by 1
    \noindent{\large\bf
        \char\ASCIInumber. #1}
    \medskip}
```

To use lowercase letters, start your \asciinumber at **96**. **a** is ASCII number **97**, **b** is **98**, and so on.

17.5   Changing the Shape of the Heading

Naturally, you can make the headings \raggedright. Put this control sequence into the macro definition—inside a group.

```
\def\raggedHeading#1{\bigbreak
    \noindent
    {\raggedright\bf#1}
    \medskip}
```

To make the second line of a long heading start directly under the first letter of the heading—instead of wrapping back to the left margin—put the title inside a vbox. Chapter 28 shows how to use vboxes in general, and Chapter 29 explains how to control their size.

Review and Related Matters

This chapter shows how to make macros for headings. A simple heading typesets a \noindented title in a bold font, and places \vskips above and below that title. Fancier headings are in \larger fonts and may start a new page. \vglue allows you to begin your \chapter or \section macro with glue that does not disappear at the top of a page.

\title and \author macros let TeX remember this information and put it in the proper place on a \titlepage. TeX can number your chapters and sections automatically with counters. If you prefer, these counters can be used to generate letters instead of numbers.

CHAPTER 18

Headers and Footers

Most documents need page numbers, although you may want to move them to a different place on the page, or remove them altogether for things like menus and single-page letters or resumes. Many documents also need identifying information printed on every page in the *header* or *footer*.

As these names imply, the *header* is the line at the top of the page, above the text; the *footer* is the line at the bottom, below the text. The header is sometimes called a *running head*, and the footer a *running foot*. This chapter describes how to do a variety of things with your header and footer.

To understand this chapter, you must be familiar with the following:

- changing fonts (Chapter 6);
- using fillers, especially **hfil** (Chapter 10); and
- using **the** with reporters (Section 14.5 or 17.4).

18.1   Changing the Header and Footer

Two plain TeX reporters govern the contents of the header and footer: **headline** and **footline**. Instead of reporting a number, a dimension, or glue, these reporters handle a *token list*. A *token* is either a character or a control sequence, so a token list is simply a series of characters and/or control sequences.

When TeX makes the header or footer, it puts the report from **headline** or **footline** into an hbox (horizontal box) that is the same width as the **hsize**. Thus, make sure you fill the blank spaces with glue.

Let's say we want the footer to be empty and the header to contain a flushright page number. The plain TeX macro **folio** typesets the page number. Since TeX may be using a different font when it breaks a page (and sends that page to the **.dvi** file), we specify the exact font we want it to use.

```
\headline={\hfil \twelverm\folio}
\footline={\hfil}
```

You can also put text into the header or footer. For example, you may want to put the document's title into the header, or put the page number into the footer with dashes around it. (Again, always specify the font.)

```
\headline={\twelvebf Making the News\hfil}
\footline={\hfil\tenrm---\folio---\hfil}
```

\headline, **\footline**, and **\folio** do not exist in LaTeX. To change the header or footer in a document, use the **\pagestyle** declarations described in Section 5.1.2 (pages 83–84) and Section C.4.2 (pages 161–62) of Lamport's LaTeX book.

18.2   Making Roman-Numeral Page Numbers

\folio is an especially clever macro. It can typeset either arabic (decimal) or roman-numeral page numbers. It does this by typesetting roman numerals when **\pageno** is a negative number, and arabic numerals for positive ones.

The plain TeX page-number reporter is called **\pageno**. To make roman-numeral page numbers on your documents, type

```
\pageno = -1
```

before the text. Not only does TeX use roman numerals to typeset the page number, it also decreases the page-number reporter instead of increasing it. When you want to switch back to arabic numerals, type **\pageno=0** or **\pageno=1**.

Naturally, this TeXnique works just as well for changing the page number in a general way. If a particular document (or part of a document) needs to start on page 10, type **\pageno=10** in the appropriate place. Or, if the middle ten pages will be supplied later, type

```
\advance\pageno by 10
```

just before the missing pages.

Whenever you need just the page number itself, instead of a specifically roman or arabic numeral, use **\the\pageno** instead, or make your own page-number macro.

```
\def\thePagenumber{\the\pageno}
```

For roman-numeral page numbers in LATEX, type **pagenumbering**{**roman**}. To switch back to arabic page numbers, type **pagenumbering**{**arabic**}. To change the page number, use **setcounter** or **addtocounter**.

18.3   Macros for the Headers and Footers

Sometimes you want to change the header from one page to another. Many documents use a section or chapter number and title in the header. Most books have different headers on odd- or even-numbered pages. To accomplish these changes, we use macros.

We start by making a **headingfont** macro. This macro makes it easy to change only this one aspect of the header when you are customizing your macros for a particular document. **headingfont** also makes it easy to use the same font in a consistent way in other places in your document. Searching through your macros to change a few **tenbf**s into **tenrm**s or **twelvebf**s is not a fun way to spend your time.

```
\def\headingfont{\tenbf}
```

Now we write the token list for **headline** itself. This particular list puts both the section number and the section title into the header, as well as the page number.

```
\headline={\headingfont
    Section \the\sectionnumber \quad \theSectionTitle
    \hfil\folio}
```

sectionnumber is the number reporter that we created in Section 17.4. **theSectionTitle** is defined in the following **TitledSection** macro. **TitledSection** takes one input: the text for the section heading.

```
\def\TitledSection#1{\bigbreak
    \advance\sectionnumber by 1
    \def\theSectionTitle{#1}
    \noindent{\bf \the\sectionnumber. #1}
    \medskip\nobreak}
```

The input to **TitledSection** becomes the definition of **theSectionTitle** and is typeset in the header. For example, the following text file might produce the following running head:

```
\TitledSection{Boxes for the Peerage}
At the races, dukes and earls are eligible for \dots
```

Section 3   Boxes for the Peerage   *183*

Oops!

Since the \headline uses a macro called \theSectionTitle, you must make sure that this macro is defined before TEX completes the first page. There are two possibilities:

- If the first section of the document also begins on page one, \section defines \theSectionTitle for you.
- If the first section begins after page one, you must define a start-up \theSectionTitle yourself. (Doing this ensures that TEX never hiccups on page one because of an undefined \theSectionTitle.)

This definition can be empty if you want, but it must exist. Put it near the top of your document, before the text.

```
\def\theSectionTitle{}
```

18.4   Changing the Space between Headers and Text

When TEX starts up, the baseline-to-baseline distance between the headline and the first line of text on the page is **24pt**. In other words, the baseline of the header is **24pt** above the baseline of the first line of text on the page. To change this distance, change the primitive glue reporter called \topskip.

When TEX makes a page, that page has three pieces: the header, the body (where the text goes), and the footer. (See Chapter 11.) TEX puts each of these pieces into a box and stacks them on top of one another, leaving some extra space between the header and the body.

The \topskip glue goes at the top of the body. More precisely, the \topskip specifies the distance from the top edge of the body to the baseline of the first line of text. (If the height of the first line of text is larger than the \topskip, TEX moves the text down until it fits inside the body.)

Plain TEX sets \topskip=10pt. This means that the first baseline of text on each page starts in the same place: **10pt** below the top edge of the text vbox. TEX adjusts the glue at the top of the text vbox so that the first baseline is in the correct place.

Thus, to put more space between the header and your text, change the \topskip.

```
\topskip=2\baselineskip
```

There is no corresponding \footskip reporter, but you can modify the \baselineskip in the plain TEX macro \makefootline. Here is Knuth's definition of \makefootline:

```
\def\makefootline{\baselineskip=24pt
  \line{\the\footline}}
```

Change the \topskip only in the preamble. LATEX also has reporters called \footskip, \footheight, \headsep, and \headheight (described in Section C.4.2 on page 163 of Lamport's LATEX book), all of which should be changed only in the preamble. Use LATEX's \setlength to change any of these reporters.

Oops!

If you have macros that put text into \vboxes, it can seem as if your \topskip has disappeared when that \vbox is the first thing on the page. (Chapters 28 through 30 describe TEX's boxes and how to use them.)

Disappearing Topskip Bug

TEX always adjusts the \topskip glue. If the first line on a page is taller than usual, the \topskip glue shrinks accordingly. Since the baseline of a \vbox is on the bottom line of text in that box, any \vbox with more than one line seems to overlap the \topskip glue. Thus, when a \vbox is the first thing on a page, if it has more than one line (as it usually does), your \topskip glue either shrinks or disappears.

The solution is simple. Change the \vbox to a \vtop. Chapter 28 explains the difference in height between these two boxes. To make sure you do not get a Scrunched Baseline Bug (page 291), put a \strut at the end of the text in the \vtop box.

18.5   Macros for Odd- and Even-Numbered Pages

In the publishing world, the right-side page is a *recto*, and the left-side page is a *verso*. Rectos are odd numbered, and versos are even numbered. To put different running heads on the rectos and versos, you need to use conditionals.

Conditionals are the third type of actor. The pattern for a conditional instruction has four parts. First, there is a test that can be answered with either *true* or *false*. For example, if we say

```
\ifodd\pageno
```

the reply is *true* if \pageno reports an odd number, and *false* if it reports an even number.

Second, the conditional does something if the answer is *true*. Third, it can also do something else if the answer is *false*. Fourth, \fi shows where the conditional ends. So the full pattern is

```
\ifodd\pageno do this
        \else do that
        \fi
```

\ifodd, **\else**, and **\fi** are all conditional actors. Since **\ifodd** performs the test, let's call it a *tester*. TEX has seventeen tester actors. All of them are primitives. You can also make new testers with **\newif**.

\else and **\fi** are like the supporting actors in a cast. **\else** says what to do if the test reply is *false*. **\fi** says where the conditional instruction ends. **\else** is optional, but you must always have a closing **\fi** to show where the conditional ends. Both **\else** and **\fi** are primitives.

We use **\ifodd** to make different headers on odd- and even-numbered pages. The following **\headline** translates into English as follows: If the page number is odd, do the **\RightHead**; otherwise, do the **\LeftHead**.

```
\headline={\headingfont
    \ifodd\pageno \RightHead
    \else \LeftHead
    \fi}
```

The **\RightHead** and **\LeftHead** are macros, defined in the usual way. The headers for a technical report might be specified as follows:

```
\def\LeftHead{\folio \hfil Section \the\sectionnumber}
\def\RightHead{\theSectionTitle \hfil \folio}
```

Since every page uses either a **\LeftHead** or a **\RightHead**, make sure the macro package includes a startup definition for these two macros, even if that definition is empty ({}).

 LATEX has macros called **\markright** and **\markboth** that you can use to change LATEX's usual running heads. These are described in Section C.4.2 on pages 161–62 of Lamport's LATEX book.

18.6   Making a Blank Header on Title Pages

To make a blank header on a title page, put that page inside a group and say **\headline**={\hfil}. Then make sure that TEX breaks the page before you end the group. TEX uses the current report from **\headline** when it assembles the page and sends it to the **.dvi** file. Therefore, either break the page explicitly with \eject or \newpage before you end the group, or wait until you are sure TeX has gone on to another page.[1]

18.7 Multiline Headers and Footers

If you need more than one line in a header or footer, nest a vbox inside the \headline or \footline. Put \vss glue at the top of the vbox, and nest as many \lines as you need inside that vbox. Section 30.4 shows how to nest one box inside another.

Review and Related Matters

This chapter shows how to use \headline and \footline to make headers and footers. Always specify the font for TeX to use in the header or footer. Most headers or footers contain a page number, supplied by \folio or \the\pageno. Page numbers can be done with either roman or arabic numerals.

The header often needs to contain the title of a chapter or section. The \TitledSection macro in this chapter automatically writes a \theSectionTitle macro that expands to the current section title in your headers.

The \topskip reporter governs the space between your headers and text. If the \topskip glue seems to disappear, use a \vtop box instead of a \vbox.

To make different headers for recto and verso pages, use the \ifodd tester. To make empty headers or footers on title pages, put that page and an empty \headline or \footline inside a group.

The next chapter describes how to make and use footnotes.

---

[1]You can also use conditionals to make a blank header on a title page. Use \newif to make a new \iftitlepage reporter. Use \iftitlepage in your \headline just as we used \ifodd\pageno. Then put \titlepagetrue in your \titlepage or \chapter macro, and put \titlepagefalse in your footer.

CHAPTER 19

Footnotes

Many documents have footnotes of one kind or another. Some footnotes are numbered; others use asterisks or daggers. This chapter shows how to handle a variety of different footnote tasks and styles.

To understand this chapter, you must be familiar with the following:

- changing the font size, especially **\eightpoint** (page 91);
- making, advancing, and using counters (Section 14.5 or 17.4); and
- making clones (Section 14.3).

Use LaTeX's **\footnote** macro as shown in Section 2.2.1 on page 19 of Lamport's LaTeX book. It is different from TeX's **\footnote** macro.

19.1   Using \footnote

\footnote is a plain TeX macro. It takes two inputs: the *reference mark* (the number or symbol that tells the reader "there is a footnote here") and the text of the footnote. To raise the reference mark, use ^ to make it a superscript, and put the entire superscript in math mode.

```
Writing notes with the foot is a challenging
task, but people with no hands become quite
skillful.\footnote{$^{*}$}{This feat boggles
the mind.}
```

> Writing notes with the foot is a challenging task, but people with no hands become quite skillful.*
>
> ---
> *This feat boggles the mind.

Two other symbols are often used as reference marks in addition to the asterisk: the dagger and double dagger. Another two are possible: the paragraph and section.

†	\dag
‡	\ddag
¶	\P
§	\S

Use the control sequence for the symbol you want as the first input to **\footnote**. (Again, to raise this symbol, make it a superscript.)

```
\dots\ more bad jokes.\footnote{$^\dag$}{Which is
more likely to prick the ear: a sharp note or a
dagger's point?}
```

> ... more bad jokes.†
>
> ---
> †Which is more likely to prick the ear: a sharp note or a dagger's point?

If you want to type the reference mark for each footnote in your document, this approach is fine. However, it rapidly becomes a nuisance when your footnotes are numbered. You have to make sure you do not repeat or skip a number—and you have to renumber them if you add or delete one.

19.2   Let TeX Do the Math: Counters for Your Footnotes

Just as we can make and **\advance** counters for headings and numbered lists, we can also make a counter for footnotes. First, we need a new number reporter.

```
\newcount\notenumber
```

Next, we write a macro that uses our **\notenumber** reporter to make the reference mark. This **\numberedFootnote** macro takes one input: the text of the footnote.

```
\def\numberedFootnote#1{%
    \global\advance\notenumber by 1
    \footnote{$^{\the\notenumber}$}{#1}}
```

Using **\global** makes sure that the **\notenumber** is increased even if the footnote is inside a group. For example, the footnote might be inside a quotation made with sandwich macros, or inside a group that uses a different font.

Oops!

A font change gives Murphy a wonderful opportunity for putting a Wrong Font in Footnote Bug into your printout.

Wrong Font in Footnote Bug

If a section of your document that is typeset with a different font contains a footnote, this same font is used to typeset the footnote.

```
{\sl People with a slanted view of life often
compensate by leaning to one side or the
other.\numberedFootnote{Tower, Lena: Getting the
Right Slant on Things.} This is called skew.}
```

> *People with a slanted view of life often compensate by leaning to one side or the other.*[1] *This is called skew.*
>
> _____
> [1] *Tower, Lena: Getting the Right Slant on Things.*

The solution is to specify the font in the footnote macro itself. The next section shows how.

19.3   Changing the Font for Your Footnotes

Footnotes are often typeset in a smaller typeface than the text. Even if the size is the same, though, you want to avoid getting a Wrong Font in Footnote Bug. Both tasks are simple: Put a font-specifier in the footnote macro itself. **\fontedFootnote** also takes one input: the text of the footnote.

```
\def\fontedFootnote#1{%
    \global\advance\notenumber by 1
    \footnote{$^{\the\notenumber}$}{\eightpoint#1\par}}
```

If your footnotes use the same size fonts as your text, say **\rm** instead of **\eightpoint**. The **\par** after **#1** in the definition makes sure that you do not get an Ignores My Command Bug (page 129).

19.4 Making a Clone of \footnote

Remembering the name of your new footnote macro can also be a nuisance. (Was it **\ftnote**, or **\numfoot**, or **\newnote**?) Wouldn't it be nice if you could simply type **\footnote** without having to include the reference mark? You can.

First, we make a clone of **\footnote** as we did with **\item** (in Section 14.3).

```
\let\knuthnote=\footnote
```

Now we use this **\knuthnote** clone when we redefine **\footnote** to do what we want. Our redefined **\footnote** macro takes one input: the text of the footnote.

```
\def\footnote#1{%
    \global\advance\notenumber by 1
    \knuthnote{$^{\the\notenumber}$}{\rm#1}}
```

19.5 Oops! When Your Footnote Disappears

A footnote is an *insertion*—something that TeX floats to a different spot on the page. When TeX finds a footnote, it puts this material into a special place in its memory until it is ready to finish the page. TeX then inserts the footnote at the bottom of the page.

Footnotes are one kind of insertion. The other kind is designed for material such as tables and figures, and is described in Chapter 23.

Insertions have one minor drawback: They sometimes disappear. Luckily, TeX is quite predictable in this regard, so you can easily learn to avoid the Disappearing Footnote Bug.

Disappearing Footnote Bug

There are four places where an insertion disappears:

- inside another insertion,
- inside a **\vbox** or **\vtop** box,
- inside an **\hbox** nested inside another **\hbox**, or
- inside a subformula of a math formula.

(Chapter 28 explains how to use the **\hbox**, **\vbox**, and **\vtop** boxes.)

TₑX puts each line of a paragraph inside an hbox (horizontal box). If you put an additional, deliberate hbox inside a paragraph, and put a footnote inside that second hbox, the footnote disappears. For example, the following footnote does not appear in the printout:

```
The magician waved his wand and said \hbox{\sl
abra-cadabra,\footnote{The meaning of this
ancient phrase has been lost.} shazaam}, and
the box disappeared!
```

The simple solution is not to put footnotes in any of these places. But life is rarely so accommodating. If you must have a footnote in one of these places, use **\vfootnote** instead.

\vfootnote also takes two inputs—the reference mark and the footnote's text. However, **\vfootnote** does not put the reference mark into the text. You do that yourself, directly, inside the box or insertion or subformula. Then you put the **\vfootnote** nearby, in a spot that is outside the box or insertion or subformula.

```
Since my example macros use a vbox, I had to
use a vfootnote to get this note at the bottom
of this page.$^{\ddag}$

\dots\ Later, after the example:
\vfootnote{$^{\ddag}$}{\eightpoint
Then I checked my printout to make sure the
footnote was on the correct page!}
```

> Since my example macros use a vbox, I had to use a vfootnote to get this note at the bottom of this page.[‡]
>
> ... Later, after the example:

\vfootnote puts the footnote on the same page as the **\vfootnote** itself—which can be different from the page where the reference mark appears. You may need to move the **\vfootnote** farther up or down in your document to get it on the correct page.

[‡]Then I checked my printout to make sure the footnote was on the correct page!

\vfootnote does not exist in LaTeX. However, LaTeX uses \footnotemark and \footnotetext to accomplish the same purpose: putting a footnote on a page when the footnote would otherwise disappear. See Section C.2.3 on page 156 of Lamport's LaTeX book.

Review and Related Matters

This chapter shows how to use \footnote and make your own customized \footnote macros. Our \numberedFootnote macro numbers the footnotes automatically. \fontedFootnote makes sure that the footnote is in the correct font.

Footnotes disappear if you put them inside a box or inside another insertion. \vfootnote solves this problem if you must have a footnote in one of these places.

Another type of insertion allows tables and figures to float to a different spot on the page, or a subsequent page. Chapter 23 describes how to do this.

CHAPTER 20

Alignment: Making Tables

Tables are the only area in TeX where you *do not* want to write macros. Each table is unique, so it is difficult to write a macro that is flexible enough to handle each table's idiosyncracies. This chapter shows how to use **\halign**, TeX's most useful table-making primitive.

TeX also has **\settabs**, which works similarly to the tab keys on a typewriter. The main difference is that on a typewriter, pressing the tab key always moves the carriage (or print ball) to the right. In other words, a typewriter's "next tab position" is always to the right of the carriage's current position. In TeX, however, "the next tab position" means the next one in the sequence—which can be either to the left or the right of TeX's current position on the page. If you want to use **\settabs**, pages 231–34 of *The TeXbook* explain how to do it. Since I have never used **\settabs** myself, I did not include it in this book.

This do-not-write-table-macros advice applies only to using **\halign** in a macro. A variety of other tool-style macros are helpful in making tables and are included in this and the next three chapters. In particular, you want **\begintable** and **\endtable** sandwich-style macros, and you may want a **\tablecaption** as well. Since tables may need to *float* to a more convenient spot, the details of these macros are covered in Chapter 23. (*Float* means that the table can move to the top of the current page, to the top of the next page, or to a page by itself, instead of appearing in the exact place where it is typed in the document file.)

To understand this chapter, you must be familiar with the following:

- changing fonts (Chapter 6);
- using skips (Chapter 9), especially **\quad** and **\qquad** (Section 9.5); and

- using glue and fillers (Chapter 10), especially \hfil and \hfill (Section 10.4).

A modest familiarity with boxes (Chapter 28) is also helpful.

You can use \halign in LATEX, exactly as described in this chapter, or you can use LATEX's **tabular** environment—which uses \halign to make tables. I personally find TEX's \halign far more flexible than LATEX's **tabular** environment, but many people prefer the convenience of using **tabular**.

LATEX's **tabular** environment is described in Section 3.6.2 on pages 63–65 of Lamport's LATEX book. Section C.9.2 on pages 182–85 has information about ways of fine tuning tables with **tabular**.

20.1   Making a Simple Table with \halign

\halign is a TEX primitive that takes one input: the entire table. Each line of the table ends with \cr, a primitive. \cr is an abbreviation for the carriage return on old-style typewriters. The first line of the table makes the pattern for the rest of the table to follow. TEX calls this first line a *preamble*.

To create this preamble, we make a *template* for each column and then put the templates together. The three basic templates are

```
#\hfil          makes a flushleft column
\hfil#          makes a flushright column
\hfil#\hfil     makes a centered column
```

Just as #1, #2 . . . #9 in a macro definition show what to do with the inputs, the number sign (#) in the template shows where TEX should put the text in that particular column. The \hfil makes that text flushleft, flushright, or centered.

Now we put some templates together to make a preamble for the entire table. An ampersand (&) marks the end of each column. We also put some space between the columns by adding a \quad to the appropriate templates. (Plain TEX's \quad macro is \hskip1em, which is an appropriate amount of space to put between columns.)

```
\halign{#\hfil&   \quad#\hfil&   \quad\hfil#\cr
one&      One comes first.&            1\cr
two&      Second entry, second column.&   000,002\cr
three&    Last, but not least.&        iii\cr}
```

one	One comes first.	1
two	Second entry, second column.	000,002
three	Last, but not least.	iii

Since TeX ignores all spaces after an ampersand, we can type spaces between the columns so we do not go blind trying to figure out which text goes in which column. Type the ampersand immediately after the column's text. TeX does not ignore a space in front of an ampersand.

\halign puts every column entry into an hbox (horizontal box), then arranges these boxes according to the preamble that you specify on the first line. The boxes in each column all have the same width. Watch what happens when we remove the \hfil from the templates.

```
\halign{#&  \quad#&  \quad#\cr
1&        Oops, we goofed.&          1\cr
02&       Not what we had in mind.&  000,002\cr
three&    Truly mistaken.&           i i i\cr}
```

1	Oops,	we	goofed. 1
02	Not what we had in mind.		000,002
three	Truly	mistaken.	i i i

The middle column makes it clear that each entry in a column is the same width. When there is no glue in a template, TeX stretches the interword glue inside each entry and pulls the rightmost word to the right edge of the hbox. The left column shows what happens when there is only one word in an entry: TeX typesets that word on the left side of the hbox. The third column (on the right) has examples of both. The hboxes here are as wide as the **000,002**. The upper hbox has space at the right of the **1**. In the lower hbox, TeX stretched the interword glue between the three i's.

(Actually, the first thing inside the hboxes for the middle and rightmost columns is the **\quad** space. The **\quad** is defined as **\hskip1em\relax**, so this space is not stretchable.)

When we restore the **\hfil**s to the templates, the fil glue is stretchier than the finite glue in the interword spaces. Thus, the interword spaces stay their natural width, and the fil glue stretches to fill the place you put it: the right, left, or both sides of the entry.

20.2 Making Fancy Templates

The templates can contain whatever you want to put in them, which makes them very flexible. You can include font changes, text, math mode, macros—even other boxes. (Boxes make it possible to put entire paragraphs into an entry.)

The following examples use flushleft columns, but that is only to make them simple to read. Use whichever type of column templates you need.

Changing the Font

To change the font for an entire column, put the font change into the template itself.

```
\halign{\bf#\hfil&  \quad\em#\hfil\cr
brash&   bold and rash\cr
brunch&  breakfast and lunch\cr}
```

> **brash**   *bold and rash*
> **brunch**   *breakfast and lunch*

You can also change the font inside any entry. Since each entry is put into an hbox, the font change is limited to that particular entry. (All changes inside a box are local to that box.)

```
\halign{\eg#\hfil&  \quad#\hfil\cr
\rm Call sign:&  \bf Address:\cr
KZRY&            15 Lune Acey Drive\cr
WIOU&            \em One Precarious Place ...\cr}
```

> Call sign: **Address:**
> KZRY   15 Lune Acey Drive
> WIOU   *One Precarious Place ...*

If you do not specify a font change in the template or in a particular entry, TEX uses whichever font was currently being used in the text, before the **halign**.

Putting Text in the Template

Sometimes every entry in a column contains the same words or characters. These can also go in the template.

```
\halign{\hfil# degrees Fahrenheit~&
       = # degrees Centigrade\hfil\cr
32&    0\cr
90&    32\cr
212&   100\cr}
```

> 32 degrees Fahrenheit = 0 degrees Centigrade
> 90 degrees Fahrenheit = 32 degrees Centigrade
> 212 degrees Fahrenheit = 100 degrees Centigrade

The preamble—the first line of the \halign—can be typed on more than one line in your document. The preamble is ended by the first \cr, not the first END-OF-LINE character in your text file. Since \cr ends all the lines in the table, you can type your tables in any way that makes it easier to see what you are doing.

The space between **Fahrenheit** and the equals sign is created by the tilde in the first template—not the spaces in front of the equals sign. TEX ignores spaces at the beginning of a line (unless you have said \obeyspaces for some reason while TEX is in horizontal mode).

20.3   Math Mode in a Template

Sometimes an entire column needs to be typeset in math mode. You can put the math mode toggles into the template itself.

```
\halign{$#$\hfil&  \quad#\hfil\cr
F = {G m_1 m_2 \over d^2}&
 Newton's law of gravitation.\cr
E = mc^2&
 Einstein's classic mass/energy equation.\cr}
```

$$F = \frac{Gm_1m_2}{d^2} \quad \text{Newton's law of gravitation.}$$
$$E = mc^2 \quad\quad \text{Einstein's classic mass/energy equation.}$$

Using Macros in a Template

You can use macros in a template just as you can anywhere else. The examples above included our own font-changing macro \em as well as the plain TEX macros \bf and \quad.

You can define special macros for particular tables or templates. The following \zip macro saves typing in a table of Boston addresses. \zip takes one input: the last two numbers in the zip code.

```
\def\zip#1{, Boston, MA 021#1}

\halign{#\hfil&  \quad#\hfil\cr
Bowdler, Izzy&  20 Censor Lane\zip{96}\cr
Party, Tea&     One Dock Square\zip{01}\cr}
```

Bowdler, Izzy   20 Censor Lane, Boston, MA 02196
Party, Tea   One Dock Square, Boston, MA 02101

Macros are especially helpful in adjusting the width of the space between columns (as we see in Section 20.4).

Putting Boxes into a Template

Sometimes you need more than one line of text in an entry. However, \halign puts each column entry into an hbox—and inside an hbox, all the text is typeset on a single line. Therefore, to get more than one line of text in the same column entry, we have to nudge TeX into paragraph-making (horizontal) mode.

The solution is to put a **\vtop** box into the template and put the text into the **\vtop** box. This makes it possible for TeX to change into paragraph-making mode. (Chapter 33 explains TeX's modes, and Chapter 28 explains how to use boxes.)

We also have to specify a new **\hsize** for that paragraph. If we do not, TeX uses the same **\hsize** as the full-sized lines on the page.

The following recipe for rye crackers shows how to put the **\vtop** box into a template.

```
\halign{\hfil#&  ~#\hfil&
\quad\vtop{\hsize=12.5pc\noindent #\strut}\cr
1&      cup rye flour\cr
1/2&   tsp baking soda&  Combine with the flour.\cr
2&      tbs shortening&  Cut shortening into the dry
                        ingredients until blended.\cr
3--4& tbs cold water&  Gradually add cold water until
                        the dough forms a ball.\cr}
\noindent Roll between flour-dusted ... and remove.
```

> 1 cup rye flour
> 1/2 tsp baking soda   Combine with the flour.
> 2 tbs shortening   Cut shortening into the dry ingredients until blended.
> 3–4 tbs cold water   Gradually add cold water until the dough forms a ball.
> Roll between flour-dusted wax paper to 1/8 inch thick. Flip onto lightly greased cookie sheet. Bake at 400° for 5–7 minutes until browned and crisp. Cut with spatula and remove.

The **\strut** at the end of the **\vtop** box is necessary to make the baselines come out even. (See the Scrunched Baseline Bug on page 291.)

20.4   Adjusting the White Space between Columns

There are several ways of adjusting the white space between the columns of your tables. The first is to put a specific amount of space between the templates. That is what we did in the examples above: We used either a **\quad** or an interword-sized space (˜). If you want a larger or smaller amount of space, you can **\hskip** a particular amount and then adjust the size of that space until you have what you want. You can also **\indent** the first column to make it align with the paragraph indentations—or move the entire table using the TEXniques described in Chapter 30.

```
letters from the tooth fairy:
\medskip
\halign{\indent#\hfil&  \hskip 2pc\vtop{%
\hsize=2.3in\noindent #\strut}\cr
Dentists:&  people who love to make jokes while
sticking their fingers in your mouth.\cr
Dentures:&  what you get for not flossing.\cr}
```

letters from the tooth fairy:

Dentists:	people who love to make jokes while sticking their fingers in your mouth.
Dentures:	what you get for not flossing.

Using a Space-Making Macro

The second method of adjusting the white space between columns is to make a **\skipit** macro for each table. Putting a **\skipit** between each template guarantees that the space between each column is the same size. Putting the definition of **\skipit** inside a group ensures that each table's **\skipit** is unique to that table.

```
\begingroup
\def\skipit{\hskip 2.5pc\relax}
\halign{%
#\hfil&  \skipit
#\hfil&  \skipit
#\hfil\cr
1 foot&    12 inches&    0.305 meters\cr
1 yard&    3 feet&       0.914 meters\cr
1 mile&    1760 yards&   1609 meters\cr}
\endgroup
```

1 foot	12 inches	0.305 meters
1 yard	3 feet	0.914 meters
1 mile	1760 yards	1609 meters

The **\begintable** and **\endtable** sandwich-style macros shown in Chapter 23 include **\begingroup** and **\endgroup**. This makes it simple to define a specialized **\skipit** macro for each table that needs one. Put the definition of **\skipit** after **\begintable** and before the **\halign**.

Using TEX's \tabskip Glue

\tabskip is a TEX primitive that reports how much glue TEX should put between the **\halign** columns. The **\tabskip** starts out as **0pt plus 0pt minus 0pt**, but you can change it. If you use **\tabskip** glue between the columns, you do not need any other space in the templates.

```
We often think of the ancient Greeks as
contemporaries of one another, but the following
table shows that is not true.

\medskip
{\tabskip=0.25in
\halign{#\hfil&  #\hfil&  #\hfil\cr
Aristophanes&   448?--?380 BC&   playwright\cr
Aristotle&      384--322 BC&     philosopher\cr
Archimedes&     287?--212 BC&    mathematician\cr}}
```

We often think of the ancient Greeks as contemporaries of one another, but the following table shows that is not true.

Aristophanes	448?–?380 BC	playwright
Aristotle	384–322 BC	philosopher
Archimedes	287?–212 BC	mathematician

TEX also puts **\tabskip** glue in front of the first column and after the last one.

You can change the **\tabskip** glue as you go along. Let's say you want to align the dashes in the date column above. The simple way is to split the dates into two columns, using a pattern of *glue, date, en dash, date, glue* (**\hfil#&#\hfil**). To make sure you have no space in the templates between the dates and the en dash, change the **\tabskip** glue to **0pt** between those two columns.

```
{\tabskip=1.5pc       % 1.5pc = 18pt = 0.249in
\halign{#\hfil&
\hfil#\tabskip=0pt&
#\hfil\tabskip=1.5pc&
#\hfil\cr
```

```
Aristophanes&  448?--&  ?380 BC&  playwright\cr
Aristotle&     384--&    322 BC&  philosopher\cr
Archimedes&    287?--&   212 BC&  mathematician\cr}}
```

Aristophanes	448?–?380 BC	playwright
Aristotle	384–322 BC	philosopher
Archimedes	287?–212 BC	mathematician

In the same way, you can remove the \tabskip glue in front of the first
column by not changing the \tabskip until after the first template. You
can also remove the \tabskip glue after the last column by restoring it to
0pt at the end of the preamble.

```
\halign{%
#\hfil\tabskip=1.5pc&
#\hfil&
#\hfil\tabskip=0pt\cr
...\cr}
```

To change the glue between columns in LaTeX's **tabular** environment, change
the **tabcolsep**, which is *half* the width of the space between columns.

20.5   Making the Table a Specific Width

To make the table as wide as the text, put some stretchiness in the glue
between columns—with explicit **plus**es in either the hskips or the **tabskip**
glue—and specify a size for the **halign**.

```
Some stretch limos are verrrrrrrry long indeed.
Their middle sections go bump on the road humps.

\medskip
\halign to \hsize{%
\tt#\hfil\tabskip=0pt plus 1fil&
#\hfil&
#\hfil\tabskip=0pt\cr
plus&    makes the&    streeeeeetch\cr
minus&   creates your&  shrnk\cr}
```

> Some stretch limos are verrrrrrrry long indeed. Their middle sections go bump on the road humps.

```
plus                  makes the             streeeeeetch
minus                 creates your          shrnk
```

You can specify a different width if you prefer, perhaps a multiple of the \textwidth:

```
\halign to 0.75\textwidth{...}
```

To specify a width for a table, use LaTeX's **tabular*** environment and put glue in some of the columns. To add this intercolumn glue, use **\extracolsep** inside an @{*text*} in the *cols* input for **tabular**, as described in Section C.9.2 on pages 182–85 of Lamport's LaTeX book.

20.6   Oops!

Two different bugs can appear when you are fiddling with tables: the Too Many Number Signs Bug and the Extra Alignment Tab Bug.

Too Many Number Signs Bug

Each column template can have only one # (number sign) to show where the text goes. If you put two number signs in one template, TeX sends you an error message that looks like this:

```
! Only one # is allowed per tab.
l.22 #\hfil#
            &   #                        \cr
```

This error message shows which line in your file contains the problem (line 22), and splits that line just after the extra number sign.

The other bug appears when you forget to put the \cr at the end of a line. TeX simply continues until it finds the end of the next column, as marked by the next ampersand, then sends you an error message.

Extra Alignment Tab Bug

If TeX finds an ampersand (**&**) when it expects a \cr, it changes that ampersand into a \cr. Then it continues with the table. It also sends you an error message that looks like this:

```
! Extra alignment tab has been changed to \cr.
<template> \hfil \endtemplate

1.24 Shrnk&
                    is created by&    minus\cr}
```

This error message also shows which line TEX was on when it found the
problem, and splits the line at the ampersand that it converts into a \cr.
The cause of the bug is usually a missing \cr at the end of the previous line.
However, if your lines are completely snarled up, the missing \cr could be
earlier in the table.

20.7   Adjusting the White Space between Rows

There are two methods of increasing the space between rows. One adds
space between two particular rows. The other increases the spacing between
all the rows in the table.

If you want to put a **\smallskip** or other **\vskip** between two rows,
TEX complains if you try to add it directly. **\vskip** adds something to the
stack of vertical items on the page, so it can only be used in page-making
(vertical) mode. That makes it incompatible with **\halign**, which uses
restricted horizontal mode. (Chapter 33 explains TEX's modes.)

Knuth solved this problem with **\noalign**, a primitive that inserts
vertical mode material into an **\halign** table. **\noalign** takes one input:
the material to be inserted.

```
\halign{#\hfil&  \quad\hfil#&  \quad#\hfil\cr
Star&           Magnitude&   Type\cr
\noalign{\smallskip}
Algol&                 var.&   B8\cr
Alpha Centauri&        0.3&    G0\cr
Proxima Centauri&     11.0&    M\cr
Polaris&               2.6&    F8\cr}
```

Star	Magnitude	Type
Algol	var.	B8
Alpha Centauri	0.3	G0
Proxima Centauri	11.0	M
Polaris	2.6	F8

If you want to increase the overall spacing, however, you do not have
to put a **\noalign{\smallskip}** between every row of the table. You can
increase the **\baselineskip** instead, just as you do for paragraphs.

A simple way to do this is with **\openup**, a plain TEX macro that
increases the **\baselineskip**, **\lineskip**, and **\lineskiplimit**. (**\lineskip**

and **\lineskiplimit** are described on page 328.) **\openup** takes one input: the size of the increase. A convenient dimension for this purpose is the **\jot**, a plain TEX reporter for **3pt**.

```
\begingroup
\openup 1\jot
\halign{#\hfil&   \qquad\hfil#\cr
Speed of sound through&        ft/sec\cr
air at sea level, 32$^\circ$ F.&  1,088\cr
ice-cold water&                4,938\cr
granite&                      12,960\cr}
\endgroup
```

Speed of sound through	ft/sec
air at sea level, 32° F.	1,088
ice-cold water	4,938
granite	12,960

If you need stretchiness between the opened-up lines, you can say **\openup\smallskipamount** instead of **\openup 1\jot**.

You can use **\openup** to increase the **\baselineskip** anywhere you want. However, **\openup** is most useful for changing the line spacing of **\halign** tables and math mode displays. Put it inside a group so it does not affect the rest of your text.

To change the space between rows in LATEX's **tabular** environment, change the **\arraystretch** instead of using **\openup**. See Section C.9.2 (page 185) of Lamport's LATEX book for instructions on how to do this.

20.8   How to Write Template Macros

It can be difficult to read a long string of **\hfil#**s and **#\hfil**s accurately. If you want, you can write template macros that eliminate this problem. To write a template macro, use **##** instead of **#** to show TEX where the column text goes, like this:

```
\def\leftcol{##\hfil}
\def\rightcol{\hfil##}
\def\centercol{\hfil##\hfil}
```

When TeX expands these **\leftcol**, **\rightcol**, and **\centercol** macros, it transforms each double ## into the single # that TeX needs for the template.

You can also make a macro for a template that contains a **\vtop** box. The following **\parcol** macro takes one input: the width of the text that goes inside the **\vtop** box.

```
\def\parcol#1{\vtop{\hsize=#1\noindent ##\strut}}
```

\parcol also contains a double ##. TeX transforms this double ## into the single # that it needs in order to see where the text goes in the template.

When you use these macros to build an **\halign** preamble, you must also tell TeX to expand them right away. **\halign** does not expand the control sequences in the preamble as it reads them, but it does check to make sure there is a # in each template.

To make TeX expand the preamble macros, we use **\span**, a primitive that has two functions—like a word that has two meanings. When used in the preamble, **\span** says to expand the next control sequence right away, and that is exactly what we need here.[1]

```
\tabskip=12pt
\halign{\span\leftcol&  \span\centercol&
\span\rightcol&  \span\parcol{2in}\cr
one&  two&  three&  Elastic is so wonderful
because it expands to meet one's need.\cr
1&    2&    3&      Somehow, work always expands
beyond the available time.\cr}
```

one	two	three	Elastic is so wonderful because it expands to meet one's need.
1	2	3	Somehow, work always expands beyond the available time.

---

[1] When **\span** is used instead of & between two columns in the rest of the table, TeX combines those two columns into one. However, it is usually easier to use **\multispan**, a plain TeX macro that is described in the next chapter.

Review and Related Matters

This chapter shows how to use **halign**, TeX's table-making primitive. The first line (which ends at the first **cr**) is called the preamble. It gives the pattern for the table and is made up of templates. Each template shows TeX what to do in a particular column. There are three basic kinds of templates: flushleft, flushright, and centered. A fourth type uses a **vtop** box, which allows you to have more than one line in the entries for a particular column.

There are two methods of putting space between columns. **tabskip** glue (which starts out as **0pt plus 0pt minus 0pt**) goes between all the columns and can be adjusted for each table. The other method places explicit **hskip**s in the column templates. Use **noalign** to add vertical space between two rows. **openup** increases the spacing between all the rows.

Chapter 21 shows how to put headings into your tables. Chapter 22 shows how to draw lines in your tables. Chapter 23 shows how to write macros that can *float* large tables to nearby locations in your document.

CHAPTER 21

Putting Headings in Your Tables

Most tables have headings above one or more columns. This chapter shows how to handle a wide range of special situations that come up whenever your tables need headings.

To understand this chapter, you must be familiar with the following:

- using skips, especially \quad and \qquad (Chapter 9);
- using glue and fillers, especially \hfil and \hfill (Chapter 10); and
- using \halign and \tabskip glue (Chapter 20).

Some familiarity with boxes (Chapter 28) is also helpful.

LaTeX has a \multicolumn macro for placing headings in special places. In particular, use \multicolumn for a heading that spans more than one column, or to place it in a different position (left, right, or centered) from the entries below it. \multicolumn is described in Section 3.6.2 on page 64, and in Section C.9.2 on page 184 of Lamport's LaTeX book.

21.1 Column Headings

If all your columns are flushleft, it is easy to make column headings. Put the headings on their own line—and if you want them in boldface, that is easy too. Type \bf in front of each heading entry.

```
\halign{#\hfil&  \quad#\hfil&  \quad#\hfil\cr
\bf Town&  \bf Population&  \bf Area\cr
Dry Gulch&         1001&      9801 sq.mi.\cr
Scenic Junction& 4096&        7135\cr}
```

Town	Population	Area
Dry Gulch	1001	9801 sq.mi.
Scenic Junction	4096	7135

Life is rarely so accommodating, however. Columns of numbers are usually typeset flushright. Other kinds of information may need to be centered. The following sections deal with these and similar challenges.

21.2   Flushleft Headings over Flushright Columns

To put a flushleft heading over a flushright column, use an **\hfill** after the heading to overwhelm the **\hfil** glue in the template.

```
\halign{#\hfil&  \quad\hfil#\cr
\bf Town&        \bf Pop.\hfill\cr
Fortune City&    5,100,100\cr
Madhouse Junction&  409,600\cr}
```

Town	Pop.
Fortune City	5,100,100
Madhouse Junction	409,600

This works nicely when the heading is narrower than the column—but watch what happens when the heading is wider:

```
\halign{#\hfil&  \quad\hfil#\cr
\bf Town&    \bf Population\hfill\cr
Blooperton&  83,196\cr
Oopsville&    2,306\cr}
```

Town	Population
Blooperton	83,196
Goofsville	2,306

Oops! Since **Population** is the widest entry in the column, it fills the entire column. Thus, it does not matter which level of glue is on either side of **Population**; neither piece of glue is stretched at all.

One way to fix this is to use a flushleft column and put invisible numbers in front of the smaller entries. To make an invisible number, we use \phantom, a plain TeX macro that typesets an empty hbox whose size is exactly the same as its input. We want the name of our invisible-number macro to be short so that it takes up as little space as possible in the text file. Therefore, we make a control symbol instead of a control word.

All the numbers in the Computer Modern fonts are the same width, so it does not matter which one we use as the input to \phantom. Since numbers are nonletters, we can use any of them for our macro's name.

```
\def\0{\phantom{0}}
\halign{#\hfil&   \quad#\hfil\cr
\bf Town&         \bf Population\hfill\cr
Fudgeville&       \02,846\cr
Patchupon&        50,327\cr}
```

Town	Population
Fudgeville	2,846
Patchupon	50,327

If you need two invisible numbers, type \0\0. Or if you need varying amounts of invisible numbers and possibly invisible commas as well, use an abbreviation for \phantom, such as the following \inv macro. \inv takes one input: whatever you want to typeset invisibly.

```
\def\inv#1{\phantom{#1}}
```

Using \inv more than a few times is very cumbersome, however. A better solution is to use the plain TeX macro \hidewidth.

```
\halign{#\hfil&   \quad\hfil#\cr
\bf Town&         \bf Population\hidewidth\cr
Tinsel Town&      36,169\cr
Ogreville&        121\cr}
```

Town	Population
Tinsel Town	36,169
Ogreville	121

\hidewidth makes the entry behave as if it has zero width. \hidewidth also contains fill glue, so it overwhelms the \hfil in the template just as \hfill does.[1]

---

[1] What \hidewidth actually does is \hskip −1000pt plus 1fill. Thus, \hidewidth has a huge but negative natural width and infinite stretchability—so it is never the widest entry in a column.

A heading with **\hidewidth** overlaps the adjacent column if you do not add enough space to separate them. One solution is to use **\inv** in the next column's template—with whatever text overlaps into the space between those columns. The alternative is to measure the width of the overlap and include an **\hskip** of that width in the template.

Whichever method you choose, you need to see the resulting table to see where the heading text extends beyond the column entries. To do this, put the table into a small **testit.tex** file, run TEX on the file, and look at the printout.

```
\halign{%
#\hfil&   \quad
\hfil#&   \inv{\bf lation}\quad
#\hfil\cr
\bf Town&    \bf Population\hidewidth&   \bf Area\cr
Plex City&   22,748&          11,374 sq.mi.\cr
Trundleton&     225&   \inv{11,}932\cr}
```

Town	Population	Area
Plex City	22,748	11,374 sq.mi.
Trundleton	225	932

Since the third column in the above example uses a **#\hfil** template, it is easier to see that the second entry needs an **\inv{11,}** in front of **932**. However, that is a long bunch of characters to type, which soon becomes awkward if you have more than a few entries that need invisible numbers. Using a flushright template would be a simpler way of aligning the numbers—but then we have the problem of typesetting **sq.mi.** We could put it in a separate column and start that template with a tilde (˜). However, we can also put the **sq.mi.** into an **\rlap** box. (**\rlap** makes an hbox of zero width, and is explained on page 302.)

```
\halign{%
#\hfil&   \quad
\hfil#&   \phantom{\bf on}\quad
\hfil#\cr
\bf Town&
\bf Population\hidewidth&
\bf Average Family Size\hidewidth\cr
Gargan City& 27,843,218&  3.7\rlap{ kids/family}\cr
Whittledon&     247,339& 11.2\cr}
```

Town	Population	Average Family Size
Gargan City	27,843,218	3.7 kids/family
Whittledon	247,339	11.2

Here, the **\rlap** is in the last column, so it does not matter how much text you put inside the **\rlap** box. (If you put a lot of text inside this **\rlap** box, it could extend into the right margin. Also, if you have lines in your tables, the text extends past those lines.) With additional columns, however, you need to increase the intercolumn space separating the two templates.

21.3 Centered Headings over Flushleft/right Columns

Use the same TeXniques to make centered headings. This time, we put a **\qquad** of space between the columns instead of a **\quad**. (A **\qquad** is **2em** wide instead of **1em**.)

```
\def\km{\phantom{km}}
\halign{#\hfil&
\qquad\hfil#&  \qquad#\hfil&  \qquad\hfil#\cr
&&\hfill\bf Orbital\hfill&  \hfill\bf Distance\hfill\cr
\hfill\bf Planet\hfill&     \hfill\bf Diameter\hfill&
\hfill\bf Period\hfill&     \hfill\bf from Sun\hfill\cr
Mercury&   4,860 km&  88 days&  $57.9 \times 10^6$ km\cr
Jupiter& 142,600 \km& 12 years& $778.3 \times 10^6$ \km\cr}
```

Planet	Diameter	Orbital Period	Distance from Sun
Mercury	4,860 km	88 days	57.9×10^6 km
Jupiter	142,600	12 years	778.3×10^6

Again, use **\hidewidth** instead of **\hfill** when the heading is wider than the column.

```
\def\msec{\phantom{m/sec$^2$}}
\halign{#\hfil&
\hskip 1.6pc \qquad#\hfil \hskip 1.6pc&
\hskip 1.3pc \qquad\hfil# \hskip 1.3pc\cr
\bf Planet&
\hidewidth\bf Length of Day\hidewidth&
\hidewidth\bf Surface Gravity\hidewidth\cr
Venus&    243 days&   8.6 m/sec$^2$\cr
Saturn&  10.23 hrs&  11.3 \msec\cr}
```

Planet	Length of Day	Surface Gravity
Venus	243 days	8.6 m/sec^2
Saturn	10.23 hrs	11.3

In the example above, we do not want to put **m/sec^2** into an **\rlap** box because that would change the width of that column. Instead, we write a **\msec** macro that uses **\phantom** to add space after each number in that column.

When we put a flushleft heading over a flushright column with **\hidewidth**, it is easy to see how much text is wider than the column and to add more space between columns. Adjusting the spacing is a little trickier with a centered heading. The preceding Venus table took three stages.

First, put plenty of space between the columns so the headings do not overlap. An inch is usually wide enough, so our first step used the following templates:

```
\halign{%
#\hfil&    \hskip 1in
#\hfil&    \hskip 1in
\hfil#\cr
...}
```

Second, in each column, measure the heading and the widest entry. Subtract the entry's width from the heading's width. This is the heading's "extra width." Use **\hskip** to put half of this extra width at the front of the template and half at the end. Add a **\qquad** of space to separate the headings.

Third, adjust the size of the **\hskip** as needed for the table's aesthetic appearance.

21.4   Flushleft Headings over Centered Columns

Flushleft headings over centered columns generally look terrible—but if you must have them, use **\hfill** and **\hidewidth** as described in the sections above.

21.5   Spanning Two or More Columns with Text or Headings

Sometimes a heading applies to more than one column. Sometimes text in the body of a table goes across more than one column.

To make an entry span two or more columns, use the plain TEX macro **\multispan**. It takes one input: the number of columns. After the **\multispan** and its input, type the text that appears across these columns. Type an ampersand after that text to end that column and start the next one, or a **\cr** to end the line.

```
\halign{#\hfil\qquad&
#\hfil& \qquad#\hfil& \qquad#\hfil& \qquad#\hfil\cr
\bf Date&
\multispan{4}\hfil\bf Tide Times and Height\hfil\cr
&          High&   Low&    High&   Low\cr
15 Jan&          &  06:03&  12:41&  18:34\cr
16 Jan&    00:43&  06:59&   13:35&  19:30\cr}
```

Date	Tide Times and Height			
	High	Low	High	Low
15 Jan		06:03	12:41	18:34
16 Jan	00:43	06:59	13:35	19:30

When TeX finds a **\multispan**, it ignores the templates for those columns. Instead, TeX makes an hbox the same width as all the spanned columns combined. Into that hbox, TeX typesets the text after **\multispan** and its input.

Since TeX ignores those templates, you do not need fill glue in the multispanned text to overwhelm the template glue. Fil glue is strong enough to make the multispanned text flushleft, flushright, or centered.

Oops!

This template-ignoring behavior creates an opportunity for the Off-Center Multispanned Bug.

```
\halign{#\hfil&   \qquad#\hfil&  \qquad#\hfil\cr
&    \multispan2\hfil\bf Construction\hfil\cr
\bf Bridge&   \bf Year&   \bf Span\cr
Brooklyn&     1883&       1595\cr
Miampimi&     1900&       1030\cr}
```

	Construction	
Bridge	Year	Span
Brooklyn	1883	1595
Miampimi	1900	1030

Off-Center Multispanned Bug

When TeX finds a **\multispan**, it spans the entire width of those columns—including any **\quad** or other **\hskip** in the template for the first spanned column.

Thus, **Construction** is actually centered between the end of **Miampimi** and the end of **Span**, even though it does not look centered. (Measure it if you don't believe me.)

To fix this bug, use **\tabskip** glue instead of an **\hskip**, or move the **\hskip** to the end of the previous template. In the tides example on page 215, the first **\qquad** appears in the first template, not the second.

Oops Again!

A different kind of bug appears if you type a space after the input to **\multispan**. Even though we put braces around this input, the braces are not necessary unless you span ten or more columns. When **\multispan** looks for its input, it takes the next object it finds. That next object can be a single digit (2–9), or a group. Thus, to give **\multispan** a number with more than one digit, you must put that number in braces.

If you do not put **\multispan**'s input inside braces, the strong habit of typing a space after a number creates an opportunity for the Multispanned Space Bug.

```
\halign{#\hfil\hskip2pc&  #\hfil&  \hskip2pc#\hfil\cr
\bf Name&  \bf Year&  \bf Span\cr
Golden Gate&   1937&   4200 ft.\cr
Atlantis&    \multispan 2 data unavailable\hfil\cr
Throgs Neck&   1961&   1800\cr}
```

Bridge	**Year**	**Span**
Golden Gate	1937	4200 ft.
Atlantis	data unavailable	
Throgs Neck	1961	1800

Multispanned Space Bug

When there is a space after **\multispan**'s input, TEX typesets that space.

To fix the Multispanned Space Bug, remove the space after the number. Either put braces around the number, or put braces around the text spanning the columns — and do not type any spaces before or after those braces.

21.6   Ignoring a Template with \omit

Sometimes all you need is to ignore one particular template. The primitive called **\omit** says to do just that.

The following example puts a centered dash in an entry to indicate missing data. This table uses **\tabskip** glue instead of a **\qquad** to separate the columns and to make sure that the dash is properly centered.

```
\def\cdash{\hfil---\hfil}
\halign{#\hfil\tabskip=3pc&  \hfil#&  \hfil#\cr
\bf Lake&  \bf Depth\hidewidth&
\bf Shoreline\hidewidth\cr
Okeechobee, FL& \omit\cdash&       110\rlap{~mi.}\cr
Moosehead, ME&    246\rlap{~ft.}& \omit\cdash\cr
Tahoe, NV/CA&    1,685&            71\cr}}
```

Lake	Depth	Shoreline
Okeechobee, FL	—	110 mi.
Moosehead, ME	246 ft.	—
Tahoe, NV/CA	1,685	71

\omit must be first in the entry to have any effect. **\cdash** uses fil glue to center the dash. Since the template is omitted, we do not need fill glue for this task.

Review and Related Matters

This chapter shows how to make headings for your tables. When a heading's alignment (flushleft, flushright, or centered) needs to be different from the alignment of the column below it, use **\hfill** in the heading entry to override the template's **\hfil** glue. When a differently aligned heading is wider than the text below it, use **\hidewidth** instead of **\hfill**. When you use **\hidewidth**, however, you must also add additional space between the appropriate columns to prevent the headings from overlapping. To put text across more than one column, use **\multispan**.

Chapter 22 shows how to draw lines—both horizontal and vertical—in your tables. Chapter 23 shows how to make material that can float to the top of the same page, the top of the next page, or to an entire page by itself. This is very useful for both tables and figures, so a set of general-purpose macros for tables and figures is defined together in that chapter. These macros include begin-and-end sandwich-style macros, caption macros, and macros for figure and table notes.

CHAPTER 22

Drawing Lines (Rules) in Your Tables

Putting lines in your tables is somewhat different from putting them into your text. (Since both typesetters and TₑX use the term *rules* instead of *lines*, we will too.) This chapter shows how to put rules into your tables.

To understand this chapter, you must be familiar with the following:

- using **\halign** and **\tabskip** (Chapter 20); and
- using **\omit** (Chapter 21).

LATₑX has its own system for adding rules to tables in its **tabular** environment. See the examples in Section 3.6.2 on pages 63–65 of Lamport's LATₑX book.

22.1 Adding Horizontal Rules with \noalign

The TₑX primitive called **\hrule** makes a horizontal rule, but we cannot put it directly into a table. **\hrule** is like **\vskip**: It adds something to the stack of vertical items on the page, so it can be used only in vertical (page-making) mode.

Therefore, to put an \hrule into a table, use \noalign, as we did in Section 20.7. Since we need some space between the \hrule and the entries, we include a \smallskip before and after the \hrule.

```
\halign{#\hfil&    \quad\hfil#&
\quad\hfil#&       \quad\hfil#&      \quad\hfil#\cr
\bf State&
\hfill\bf 1800\hfill&   \hfill\bf 1850\hfill&
\hfill\bf 1900\hfill&   \hfill\bf 1950\hfill\cr
\noalign{\smallskip\hrule\smallskip}
New York&     589,051&    3,097,394&
              7,268,894&  14,830,192\cr
Virginia&     880,200&    1,421,661&
              1,854,184&  3,318,680\cr}
```

State	1800	1850	1900	1950
New York	589,051	3,097,394	7,268,894	14,830,192
Virginia	880,200	1,421,661	1,854,184	3,318,680

Macros for Table Rules

Since it is important for all the rules in your tables to be consistent, these \noaligned rules are good candidates for macros. Here are three:

```
\def\tablerule{\noalign{\smallskip\hrule\smallskip}}
\def\tabletoprule{\noalign{\hrule\smallskip}}
\def\tablebottomrule{\noalign{\smallskip\hrule}}
```

Put them inside the \halign wherever you need them. (The Empire State Building example on page 221 uses all three of these macros.)

Oops!

When the heading in a table's last column uses \hidewidth, that heading extends past the edge of the table. However, if you have rules in that table, they go only as far as that edge. The extra part of the heading drifts into space, and you have a Dangled Heading Bug.

Dangled Heading Bug

An \hrule inside an \halign is only as wide as the \halign itself. Since \hidewidth makes TeX think that an entry is narrower than its text, the rule does not extend as far as the dangled heading.

To fix this bug, add another column and an invisible something. The following example puts an invisible, boldface **ories** into the fourth column, which extends the \hrule to the proper length. (Page 233 shows an example that extends the \hrule by putting an \hskip in the last column.)

```
\halign{#\hfil&   \qquad\hfil#&   \hskip 3em\hfil#&
#\hfil\cr
\tabletoprule
\bf Building&   \bf Height\hidewidth&
\bf Stories\hidewidth\cr
\tablerule
Empire State&           1,250\rlap{~ft.}&   102\cr
Chicago Civic Center&   662&                31&
\invis{\bf ories}\cr
\tablebottomrule}
```

Building	Height	Stories
Empire State	1,250 ft.	102
Chicago Civic Center	662	31

Putting Horizontal Rules across Only a Few Columns

Sometimes you do not want the rule to go all the way across the table. For this, use \hrulefill, a plain TeX macro that typesets a horizontal rule inside an hbox, and therefore can be used in the entries of a table.

If a rule is the only thing on a line, you need to use \offinterlineskip. This plain TeX macro stops TeX from adding interlineskip glue between lines of text. TeX normally adds interlineskip glue between any lines of text, both inside a paragraph and inside an \halign table.[1] If you do not say \offinterlineskip when you use \hrulefill in a table this way, TeX places that rule a \baselineskip down from the baseline of the previous line of text.

To limit the effect of \offinterlineskip, put this instruction and the entire \halign table inside a group. If you forget to put \offinterlineskip inside a group, the baselines in your paragraphs after the table are no longer a \baselineskip apart. One way to keep \offinterlineskip inside a group is to use the \begintable and \endtable macros in Chapter 23. Since those two macros use the sandwich structure, you do not have to nest another group inside \begintable...\endtable.

---

[1] Generally speaking, TeX always adds interlineskip glue between boxes in order to place their baselines a \baselineskip apart. TeX behaves this way in both of its vertical modes and inside \halign tables.

Whenever you declare **\offinterlineskip**, you also need a **\strut** in the first-column template to make sure that each line is a **\baselineskip** apart. A **\strut** is a plain TeX macro that makes an invisible vertical rule. This invisible rule puts the same amount of space between lines as the **\baselineskip** does. (Section 31.6 explains the **\strut** and how to adjust its size to match your **\baselineskip**.)

Last but not least, when an **\hrulefill** spans two or more columns, use **\tabskip** glue instead of explicit **\hskip** space between columns. If the templates have an hskip between those particular columns, TeX puts white space there—and you have two **\hrulefill** lines instead of one.

```
{\offinterlineskip
\halign{#\strut\hfil\tabskip=2em&
#\hfil&  #\hfil&  #\hfil&
#\hfil&  #\hfil\tabskip=0pt\cr
\tabletoprule
\bf State&
\multispan{2}\hfil\bf January\hfil&
\multispan{2}\hfil\bf July\hfil&
\bf Average\cr
\omit& \multispan{2}\hrulefill
& \multispan{2}\hrulefill\cr
& Max.& Min.&   Max.& Min.&
\bf Precip.\cr
\tablerule
Alaska&   30&  20&  63&  48&  54.62 in.\cr
Florida&  74&  65&  87&  79&  39.99\cr
Nevada&   40&  15&  92&  50& \08.63\cr
\tablebottomrule}}
```

State	January		July		Average Precip.
	Max.	Min.	Max.	Min.	
Alaska	30	20	63	48	54.62 in.
Florida	74	65	87	79	39.99
Nevada	40	15	92	50	8.63

The **\omit** in this table prevents TeX from typesetting a **\strut** on that line of the table. If you do not say **\omit**, TeX adds a **\baselineskip** of space to that line.

\hrulefill can also be used in a template or column entry.

```
\halign{#\hfil&  \qquad#\hfil&  \qquad#\hfil&
\qquad\hrulefill#\hrulefill\hfil\cr
\bf Name&  \bf Size&  \bf Hue&  \bf Speed/Gait\cr
Tufted Framish& \hrulefill&  Vermillion& Clumsy\cr
Speckled Egron& Small&       Dusty Red&  Swift\cr}
```

Name	Size	Hue	Speed/Gait
Tufted Framish	⎯⎯	Vermillion	⎯Clumsy⎯
Speckled Egron	Small	Dusty Red	⎯Swift⎯

22.2   Putting Vertical Rules in a Table

To put vertical rules in a table, use **\vrule**, a TEX primitive. The easiest
approach is to make a separate column template for each **\vrule**. This
template is very simple:

If you use **\tabskip** glue: `\vrule#`

If you do not: `\quad\vrule#\quad`

Since the entries in these **\vrule** columns will not contain any text, you do
not need an **\hfil** to make them flushleft, flushright, or centered.

To make sure that each **\vrule** abuts the one above and below it, use
\offinterlineskip and put both **\offinterlineskip** and the table inside a
group. You also need a **\strut** in the first column template to keep the
baselines a **\baselineskip** apart.

```
{\offinterlineskip
\tabskip=1pc
\halign{\strut#\hfil&  \vrule#&  \hfil#\cr
Bald Eagles&&      435\cr
Buffalos&&       7,437\cr}}
```

Bald Eagles	435
Buffalos	7,437

If you are absolutely sure that you want vertical rules throughout your
table, you can put your **\vrule** into the regular templates instead of making
a separate template for each. The following **\halign** preamble has two
templates, containing three **\vrule**s.

```
\halign{\vrule  \quad#\hfil\quad&
        \vrule  \quad#\hfil\quad  \vrule\cr
```

If the **\vrule** is part of a larger template, you must add space between the
\vrule and the **#**. When each **\vrule** has its own template, the **\tabskip**
glue separates the rules from the text entries.

Using a separate template for each **\vrule** lets you **\omit** that template when you do not want a **\vrule** in a particular place. The following fast-food example omits three of the vertical rules between headings. It also uses **\noalign{\hrule}** to put horizontal rules between lines.

```
{\offinterlineskip
\halign{\strut\tabskip=0.6pc
\vrule#&  #\hfil&  \vrule#&  \hfil#&
\vrule#&  \hfil#&  \vrule#&  \hfil#&  \vrule#&  \hfil#&
\vrule#\tabskip=0pt\cr
\noalign{\hrule}
& \bf Food& \omit& \bf Gms.&&
\bf Prot.&  \omit& \bf Carb.& \omit& \bf Fat&\cr
\noalign{\hrule}
&Hamburger, 1/4 lb&&    174&&   24.9&&   37.6&&   21.1&\cr
\noalign{\hrule}
&French fries, 3 oz&&    85&&    3.4&&   33.1&&   14.2&\cr
\noalign{\hrule}
&Choc. shake, 10 oz&&  283&&    9.6&&   57.9&&   10.5&\cr
\noalign{\hrule}}}
```

Food	Gms.	Prot.	Carb.	Fat
Hamburger, 1/4 lb	174	24.9	37.6	21.1
French fries, 3 oz	85	3.4	33.1	14.2
Choc. shake, 10 oz	283	9.6	57.9	10.5

When you have **\vrule**s in a table, you cannot use the **\tablerule** macro to make horizontal rules. The **\smallskip**s add vertical space above and below the **\hrule**, thereby interrupting the **\vrule**s.

Oops! A Missing \vrule

It is easy to get out of sync and forget one of the ampersands (**&**) for these vertical rules.

The example below shows what happens when you have missing ampersands. The **Hamburger** line has a missing ampersand at the end of the line, just before the **\cr**. The only effect there is to omit the **\vrule** at the end of that line. When an ampersand is missing in the middle of a line, however (after **283** in the **Choc. shake** line), the text entries are typeset in the **\vrule** column instead of the text column.

```
\noalign{\hrule}
& \bf Food& \omit& \bf Gms.&&
\bf Prot.&  \omit& \bf Carb.& \omit& \bf Fat&\cr
\noalign{\hrule}
&Hamburger&&    174&&   24.9&&   37.6&&   21.1\cr
\noalign{\hrule}
&French fries&&  85&&    3.4&&   33.1&&   14.2&\cr
\noalign{\hrule}
&Choc. shake&&  283&     9.6&&   57.9&&   10.5&\cr}}
\noalign{\hrule}
```

Food	Gms.	Prot.	Carb.	Fat
Hamburger	174	24.9	37.6	21.1
French fries	85	3.4	33.1	14.2
Choc. shake	283 9.6		57.9	10.5

The only other differences between these two fast-food examples are the
size of the **\tabskip** (**0.5pc** instead of **0.6pc**) and shorter text in the first
column.

Adding Only a Few Vertical Rules

If you need only a few vertical rules here and there, put the **\vrule** into the
table itself, instead of the template. The following genealogy example shows
how.

```
\halign{\strut\tabskip=3.5pt
\hfil#\hfil&   \hfil#\hfil&   \hfil#\hfil&
\hfil#\hfil&   \hfil#\hfil&   \hfil#\hfil&
\hfil#\hfil&   \hfil#\hfil&   \hfil#\hfil\tabskip=0pt\cr
Ole&&&&      Grand\cr
Fudd&  \multispan{2}\hrulefill&  Doremi&&
Paw&    \multispan{2}\hrulefill&  Fasola\cr
&  \vrule&  \vrule&&&  \vrule&  \vrule\cr
&  Minnie&   Maxi&   \multispan{3}\hrulefill
&  Teedoh&  Hen3ry\cr
&&&  \vrule&  \vrule&  \vrule\cr
&&&  Uno&    DOS&     Trey\cr}
```

Do not forget the \strut. Without it, the \vrule has no height and disappears. (**Hen3ry** is not a typo; I am an ardent fan of Tom Lehrer's songs.)

Review and Related Matters

This chapter shows how to put both horizontal and vertical rules anywhere in your tables. When you use \hrule and \vrule, you often need to use \offinterlineskip as well. When you use \offinterlineskip, put both \offinterlineskip and the table inside a group and put a \strut at the beginning of the first template in the preamble.

To span only a few columns with a horizontal rule, use \hrulefill instead of \hrule. When you use \hrulefill, you must use \tabskip glue between those columns instead of explicit \hskips.

Chapter 21 shows how to put headings in your tables. It also shows how to make headings that are aligned differently from the column below.

Chapter 23 shows how to make material that can float to the top of the same page, the top of the next page, or to an entire page by itself. This is very useful for both tables and figures, so a set of general macros for tables and figures are defined together. These include begin-and-end sandwich-style macros, caption macros and macros for figure and table notes.

CHAPTER 23

Tables and Figures, Both Floating and Stationary

Tables and figures need to be set off from the rest of the text with space above and/or below them. Many tables and figures also need a caption, and are often numbered consecutively throughout a section, chapter, or entire document. Sometimes a particular table or figure needs to appear at a particular place in the text. Other times, it is better to allow a table or figure to *float*—to the top of the same page, to the top of the next page, or to a page by itself. This chapter shows how to accomplish all these tasks.

To understand this chapter, you must be familiar with the following:

- changing the font size (Chapter 7);
- sandwich-style macros and **displaybreak** (Chapter 12); and
- making, using, and advancing counters (Section 14.5 or 17.4).

 In LATEX, use the **table** and **figure** environments, described in Section 3.5.1 on pages 59–60 of Lamport's LATEX book. LATEX's **caption** macro is used the same way in both environments.

23.1   Simple Macros for Tables and Figures

The simplest table and figure macros begin or end a group and put a \displayskip between the text and the table or figure. Since a table or figure might follow another macro that ends with a \displayskip, use \displaybreak instead of \displayskip.

```
\def\beginTable{\begingroup\displaybreak}
\def\endTable{\displaybreak\endgroup}

\def\beginFigure{\begingroup\displaybreak}
\def\endFigure{\displaybreak\endgroup}
```

\displaybreak makes sure that you do not get more than a \displayskip of space, even if a \beginTable or \beginFigure follows directly after another \displayskip in your document. Section 12.5 explains how \displaybreak works.

Captions and Notes

Many people prefer to put table captions above the table, and figure captions below. For simple caption macros, begin a new paragraph for the caption with \noindent and add the appropriate amount of space above or below. Our \aboveCaption and \belowCaption macros both take one input: the text of the caption.

```
\def\aboveCaption#1{\noindent #1\medskip}
\def\belowCaption#1{\medskip \noindent #1}
```

The same general idea works well for both table notes and figure notes. If you have long notes, a sandwich structure is preferable—such as the following \beginTablenotes and \endTablenotes pair. If you might have more than one table note, you probably need to change the \parskip and \parindent.

```
\def\beginTablenotes{\begingroup
    \medskip
    \parindent=0pt
    \parskip=\medskipamount
    \noindent}
\def\endTablenotes{\par\endgroup}
```

In this approach, the text of all the notes goes between \beginTablenotes and \endTablenotes. Each note goes into a separate paragraph.

If you prefer, the text of each note can be the input for a separate \figurenote macro. Then you can have as many \figurenotes below a figure as you want.

```
\def\figurenote#1{\smallskip\noindent#1\par}
```

If you want to draw lines in your tables or figures, Chapter 22 describes how to put lines in your tables, and Chapter 31 describes how to draw lines generally.

23.2 Let TeX Do the Numbering for Tables and Figures

Tables and figures often evolve along with a document. One figure may become two. New figures may appear—or old ones disappear—seemingly overnight. The same is true of tables. Numbering this changing landscape by hand is a major nuisance. Luckily, TeX can do all the work for you.

Sections 14.5 and 17.4 describe the details of how to make a counter and \advance it. We use the same TeXnique here.

```
\newcount\tablenumber
\newcount\figurenumber
```

Since our numbered captions are likely to appear inside a group, we use the primitive \global to make sure the counter is advanced outside the group as well. \global tells TeX to post the new information on the innermost level of the bulletin board.

The following two caption macros have minor differences in the way they are numbered and whether the caption goes above or below the table or figure. \TableNumberedCaption is simple and straightforward. It takes one input: the text of the caption.

```
\def\TableNumberedCaption#1{%
   \global\advance\tablenumber by 1
   \noindent{\bf Table \the\tablenumber}\quad #1
   \medskip\nobreak}

\TableNumberedCaption{Effects of Captioning on
a Captive Audience}
\halign{#\hfil&   \qquad\hfil#&  #\hfil\cr
Rapt&          18.5&   %\cr
Interested&    32.7\cr
Bored&         43.8\cr
No response&    5.0\cr}
```

Table 1   Effects of Captioning on a Captive Audience

Rapt	18.5%
Interested	32.7
Bored	43.8
No response	5.0

The caption in **\FigureNumberedCaption** starts on a new line, and the figure number includes the chapter number. **\FigureNumberedCaption** also takes one input: the text of the caption.

```
\def\theFigureNumber{%
    \the\chapternumber.\the\figurenumber}
\def\FigureNumberedCaption#1{%
    \global\advance\figurenumber by 1
    \medskip\nobreak
    \noindent{\bf Figure \theFigureNumber}\eol
    #1\par}

\FigureNumberedCaption{Figure Eights in Skating}
```

> **Figure 23.1**
> Figure Eights in Skating

Oops!

If your **\tablenumber** or **\figurenumber** stays the same for each table or figure, you are advancing it inside a group. Put **\global** in front of **\advance**.

23.3   Using Insertions for Floating Material

Whenever you have long tables or figures, deciding where to put them can be a major hassle. Keeping the table or figure close to its corresponding text—without generating large amounts of blank space in the process—can be quite a challenge. The following three plain TeX macros can *float* material to other nearby locations. This makes the task of positioning your tables and figures much easier.

\midinsert	puts material here if it can; if not, floats to top of next available page.
\topinsert	puts material at top of current page if it can; if not, floats to top of next available page.
\pageinsert	puts material by itself on next available page.

The term *next available page* means that TeX may be working with more than one insertion at the same time. If so, TeX handles them in a queue (as if they were waiting in line for a bus) and floats the inserts in the same order they appear in your document.

All three insertion macros have **\par\begingroup**, so they act as begin-sandwich macros. The corresponding end-sandwich macro for all three is **\endinsert**.

\midinsert	\topinsert	\pageinsert	floating
⋮	⋮	⋮	⟵ material
\endinsert	\endinsert	\endinsert	goes here

Each of these insertion macros puts the floating material into a **\vbox**. Chapter 28 explains about TEX's boxes. The main consequences here are that TEX cannot start a new page inside a vbox, and you cannot put any footnotes inside a vbox. (If you need a footnote inside a floating table or figure, use **\vfootnote**, described in Section 19.5.)

When a float appears in the midst of a page, TEX automatically puts a **\bigskip** above and below it. When a float appears at the top of a page, TEX puts a **\bigskip** below it. When a float appears on a page by itself, it is vertically centered inside a vbox that is the same length as the **\vsize**; TEX places glue above and below the float.

The **\bigskip** in these insertions means that we cannot use our begin-and-end table and figure macros with the insertion macros. If we try this anyway, we wind up with extra space—either in the float or in the text. Instead, we must make new begin-and-end floating table and figure macros.

23.4   Macros for Floating Tables

Our first step toward making a floating table macro is to use **\topinsert**. If all your tables float to the top of a page, the following **\beginTopTable** macro is exactly what you need.

\beginTopTable does not need to add any vertical space since the **\topinsert** does that for us. However, we do need to **\advance** the **\tablenumber** and give **\beginTopTable** one input: the caption for the table. This makes sure that all the tables have the same appearance.

Both **\TableCaption** and **\beginTopTable** take one input: the text of the caption.

```
\def\TableCaption#1{\noindent
   {\bf Table \the\tablenumber}\quad #1}
\def\beginTopTable#1{%
   \topinsert
   \global\advance\tablenumber by 1
   \TableCaption{#1}\medskip}
\def\endTopTable{\endinsert}
```

When we use these sandwich macros with an **\halign** table, the result looks like this (placed at the top of a page):

```
\beginTopTable{Spinning one's wheels}
\halign{#\hfil&   \qquad#\hfil&   \qquad#\hfil\cr
\bf Wheel&        \bf Radius&   \bf Weight\cr
Gotchall 60R13&      13 inches&    19 lbs.\cr
Tigertooth 75R15&    15 inches&    26 lbs.\cr}
\endTopTable
```

Table 2   Spinning one's wheels

Wheel	Radius	Weight
Gotchall 60R13	13 inches	19 lbs.
Tigertooth 75R15	15 inches	26 lbs.

However, this strategy requires three macros: **\beginMidTable**, **\beginTopTable**, and **\beginPageTable**. Life would be much simpler with only one **\beginFloatTable** macro that takes a different kind of input: the word **mid** or **top** or **page**. TeX can do this too.

The primitives **\csname** and **\endcsname** take a string of characters and convert it into a control sequence.[1] The following two instructions have the same effect:

```
\TeX
\csname TeX\endcsname
```

\endcsname shows TeX where the string of characters ends. **\csname** is short for <u>c</u>ontrol-<u>s</u>equence <u>name</u> and **\endcsname** for <u>end</u> <u>c</u>ontrol-<u>s</u>equence <u>name</u>.

We can use **\csname** and **\endcsname** in our floating-table macro to make whichever type of insertion we want. Here is the definition of **\beginFloatTable**. Its main difference from **\beginTopTable** is the way that it uses input **#1** to make the insert. The second input is the text for the caption.

```
\def\beginFloatTable#1#2{%
%   #1 is type of insert
%   #2 is caption text
    \csname #1insert\endcsname
    \global\advances\tablenumber by 1
    \TableCaption{#2}\medskip}
\def\endFloatTable{\endinsert}
```

Using **\beginFloatTable** makes it easy to specify which kind of float you want for a particular table, and to change from one kind to another in midstream.

---

[1]More precisely, **\csname** converts a *token list* into a control sequence.

```
\beginFloatTable{mid}{Drifting along; sinking fast}
\halign{#\hfil&  \qquad\hfil#&  #\hfil\cr
\tabletoprule
\bf Material&  \bf Specific gravity\hidewidth\cr
\tablerule
Styrofoam&      0.02&  \hskip 55pt\cr
Cork&           0.15\cr
Maple&          0.49\cr
Oak&            0.77\cr
Quartz&         2.65\cr
Lead&          11.34\cr
Gold&          19.30\cr
\tablebottomrule}
\endFloatTable
```

Table 3 Drifting along; sinking fast

Material	Specific gravity
Styrofoam	0.02
Cork	0.15
Maple	0.49
Oak	0.77
Quartz	2.65
Lead	11.34
Gold	19.30

23.5   Macros for Floating Figures

Writing macros for a floating figure is slightly different, because the caption
usually needs to go at the bottom of the figure instead of the top. However,
it is awkward to make the caption an input to \endFloatFigure. It is
easier to see and read when the caption is an input to \beginFloatFigure.

We solve this dilemma with \theCaption, a macro that is defined by
\beginFloatFigure and used by \endFloatFigure. \FigureCaption takes
one input: the text for the caption. \beginFloatFigure takes two inputs:
the type of insert and caption text.

```
\def\FigureCaption#1{\noindent
   {\bf Figure \theFigureNumber}\eol #1}
\def\beginFloatFigure#1#2{%
   \global\advance\figurenumber by 1
   \def\theCaption{#2}
   \csname #1insert\endcsname}
\def\endFloatFigure{\displayskip
   \FigureCaption{\theCaption}\par
   \endinsert}
```

Here is what happens to input **#2** in **\beginFloatFigure**. Let's suppose your text file has

```
\beginFloatFigure{top}{Typical flotsam shapes}
```

When TEX expands **\beginFloatFigure**, it defines **\theCaption** as **Typical flotsam shapes**. When TEX reaches **\endFloatFigure**, it also expands **\theCaption**. Thus, **\FigureCaption{\theCaption}** is expanded to

```
\noindent{\bf Figure 23.2}\hfil\break
Typical flotsam shapes
```

Here is an example of our floating-figure macros at work. (Again, this figure would normally appear at the top of a page.)

```
\beginFloatFigure{top}{A variety of 'big-o's}
\noindent$\displaystyle
\bigoplus \qquad \bigodot \qquad \bigotimes$
\endFloatFigure
```

Figure 23.3
A variety of 'big-o's

If the figures in your document are pasted into your printout by hand, measure the drawings and add the appropriate **\vskip** to each figure. If all your figures are pasted in, you can design your figure macro accordingly. The following **\makefigure** macro takes two inputs: glue for the **\vskip** and text for **\FigureCaption**.

```
\def\makefigure#1#2{\topinsert
   \vskip #1
   \displayskip
   \FigureCaption{#2}\endinsert}

\makefigure{3.25in}{Busts of Julius Caesar}
```

If the figures in your document are created by things other than TEX (such as PostScript, MacDraw, or Lisp), it may be possible to incorporate them using **\special**—a primitive that puts instructions for the driver into your **.dvi** file. Explanations of **\special** are beyond the scope of this book. Ask your TEX wizards for assistance.

Oops!

When a **\topinsert** or **\midinsert** is longer than a page, TEX continues floating it all the way to the end of your document. If you have many floats, this fills up TEX's memory very rapidly. TEX says **capacity exceeded, sorry**, just before it quits. If you cannot break the **\topinsert** or **\midinsert** into smaller pieces, change it into a **\pageinsert**.

If TEX complains about an underfull vbox in your **\pageinsert**, put a **\vfil** between the floating material and **\endinsert**.

Review and Related Matters

This chapter begins with some simple sandwich-style table and figure macros, and gives a variety of caption macros. TEX can number your tables and figures automatically with counters.

You can also use **\midinsert**, **\topinsert**, and **\pageinsert** to let TEX float your tables and figures to a different place in the document. Putting a footnote into a floating table or figure requires **\vfootnote**, so you need to check your printout to make sure that the footnote appears on the correct page.

Chapter 20 shows how to make tables with **\halign**. Chapter 21 shows how to put headings in your tables. Chapter 22 shows how to put lines in your tables.

Chapter 28 describes how to work with TEX's boxes: **\hbox**, **\vbox**, and **\vtop**. Each of these boxes changes TEX's mode, so you may also want to read Chapter 33.

CHAPTER 24

Using Math Mode

Math mode is very similar to horizontal (paragraph-making) mode. Instead of assembling characters into words and spaces, math mode assembles characters into formulas and spaces. Math mode also uses a different set of rules for where the spaces go, and how big those spaces should be. For the most part, the result of these rules is mathematically correct—but when it is wrong, you can correct the spacing even if you do not know what TeX's rules are.

This chapter shows how to use math mode. Section 24.8 explains the spacing rules for those of you who want to know them.

To understand this chapter, you must be familiar with the following:

- writing macros (Chapter 5), and

- using groups and changing fonts (Chapter 6).

24.1   How to Use Math Mode

To start math mode, type a dollar sign. Then type the math mode material. To stop math mode, type a second dollar sign.

```
The distance $D$ that a car travels in time
$t$ is determined by its velocity $v$ as
follows: $D=vt$.
```

> The distance D that a car travels in time t is determined by its velocity v as follows: $D = vt$.

LATEX Notes

In LaTeX, use \(...\) or **\begin{math}**...**\end{math}** to use math mode. These two sandwich-style methods make sure you do not get a Math Oops Mode Bug (page 16). However, both are what LaTeX calls *fragile*. If you prefer, the math mode **$** toggles work exactly the same in LaTeX as in TeX, and have the advantage of being *robust*. *Robust* versus *fragile* LaTeX commands are described in Section 2.2.3 on page 24, in Section 2.5 on page 33, and in Section C.1.3 on pages 151–52 of Lamport's LaTeX book.

Oops!

Do not use math mode as a "quickie italics." If you compare the math italic and text italic font tables on pages 365 and 367, the $differences$ (**$differences$**) between them are important and glaring.

- Math italic letters are wider.
- The math italic font does not have ligatures (see Section 2.3).
- The numbers are different. The numbers in the math italic font are **\oldstyle** roman (0123456789); numbers in the text italic font are italic. (Unless you specify **\oldstyle**, however, TeX typesets numbers from the roman font when it is in math mode.)
- Some symbols in the fonts are quite different. Math italic includes lowercase Greek letters; text italic has a variety of accents and other symbols.

24.2 Display Math Mode

Some math formulas need to be displayed, either because they need more height than a single text line normally provides, or because they are important and need to stand out visually from the rest of the text. TeX's display math mode centers the formula horizontally and puts vertical space above and below the formula. Display math mode also uses a larger version of some of the symbols and puts a little more vertical space into the formulas.

Use double dollar signs (**$$**) to start display math mode, and a second set of double dollar signs to end it.

```
DeMorgan's Theorem states that
$$\neg(P \wedge Q) \equiv (\neg P \vee \neg Q)$$
and is a cornerstone of symbolic logic,
as any mathematician can tell you.
```

DeMorgan's Theorem states that

$$\neg(P \wedge Q) \equiv (\neg P \vee \neg Q)$$

and is a cornerstone of symbolic logic, as any mathematician can tell you.

If your text file has blank lines above and below the display math material (thus making the math easier to read), put a \noindent in front of a continuing paragraph after the display. However, TEX is always willing to break a page between paragraphs, so the display can wind up at the top of a page—an arrangement that math publishers frown upon. (Section 32.1 explains how TEX decides to break a page in the vicinity of a math display.)

A better option is to put the double dollar signs on separate lines, with the display math material between them.

```
As most of us learned and then promptly forgot
after the math test:
$$
(x+y)^{2} = x^{2} + 2xy + y^{2}.
$$
How wonderful to have a practical use for it!
```

> As most of us learned and then promptly forgot after the math test:
> $$(x + y)^2 = x^2 + 2xy + y^2.$$
> How wonderful to have a practical use for it!

Since TEX is willing to break a page after a math display, it usually does not matter whether you continue the paragraph immediately after the second set of **$$** toggles or type a blank line and **\noindent**.

Do not use blank lines and **\noindent** after a math display if you are using **\item**, **\hangindent**, or **\parshape**. If you do, the unusual paragraph shape is lost.

 To use display math mode in LATEX, use \[...\] or the **displaymath** environment. These are both fragile.

Also, LATEX's flushleft equation system (the optional **[fleqn]** input to **\documentstyle**) does not work if you use TEX's **$$** toggles instead of LATEX's \[...\] or **displaymath** environment.

24.3　Adjusting Space above and below Math Displays

TeX has four primitive reporters that govern the size of the skips above and below a math display. Plain TeX establishes the sizes of these skips as follows:

```
\abovedisplayskip = 12pt plus 3pt minus 9pt
\belowdisplayskip = 12pt plus 3pt minus 9pt
\abovedisplayshortskip = 0pt plus 3pt
\belowdisplayshortskip = 7pt plus 3pt minus 4pt
```

TeX uses **\abovedisplayskip** and **\belowdisplayskip** unless the line of text above the display is short. Here, *short* means that the text is shorter than the space between the margin and the math material being displayed. If this is the case, TeX uses **\abovedisplayshortskip** and **\belowdisplayshortskip** instead.

The example on page 239 with $(x + y)^2 = x^2 + 2xy + y^2$ has a short line above the math display. If TeX had used **\abovedisplayskip** and **\belowdisplayskip** instead of **\abovedisplayshortskip** and **\belowdisplayshortskip**, there would have been roughly twice as much white space above the display as below it.

If you have changed the **\baselineskip**, these above and below displayskips can lead to odd-looking spacing that you need to adjust with an additional **\vskip**, or by changing these displayskips.

24.4　Adjusting Horizontal Space in Math Mode

In both of its math modes, TeX ignores the spaces you type and uses its own rules for where the spaces go and how big they should be. (Of course, you must still type a space after a control sequence if the character that follows is a letter.)

```
Math teachers thrive on exercises like the
following: If $ 2 x+   3y =97$ cents and
$ 2 7 sheep+ 2d o g s =may hem$, prove that
Lassie comes home on Sunday.
```

> Math teachers thrive on exercises like the following: If $2x + 3y = 97$ cents and $27sheep + 2dogs = mayhem$, prove that Lassie comes home on Sunday.

TeX uses three sizes of horizontal spaces in math mode: a *thin space*, *medium space*, and *thick space*. In the example above, there are thick spaces around the equals signs, medium spaces around the plus signs, and no spaces anywhere else.

There are two practical implications of TEX's spacing rules. First, you can type spaces in math mode material in any fashion you like—so go ahead and use spaces to make it easier to read. Second, when the spacing TEX puts into a formula is incorrect, you can fix it by using the following control symbols for these thin, medium, and thick spaces.

\,	thin space	$1/6$ of a quad
\>	medium space	$2/9$ of a quad
\;	thick space	$5/18$ of a quad
\!	negative thin space	$-1/6$ of a quad

For example, TEX never puts space between two ordinary characters in math mode, so it fails to put the correct amount of space in front of the "dx" in calculus. Add a thin space.

`$\int a\,dx = ax$` $\int a\,dx = ax$

You can also use any of the horizontal skips from Chapters 9 and 10 in math mode. **\quad**, **\qquad**, **\hskip**, **\hfil**, and **\hfill** are the most useful.

In math mode, TEX puts a thin space after commas. If you want a number with a comma to be typeset normally, put braces around the comma. Also, TEX puts space in front of the colon—just as it does for an equals sign. If you need an ordinary colon, use **\colon**. (See page 245 for a description of how TEX treats punctuation marks in math mode.)

`$165,702x + 3y$` $165,702x + 3y$
`$165{,}702x + 3y$` $165{,}702x + 3y$

`$f: M \rightarrow N$` $f : M \rightarrow N$
`$f\colon M \rightarrow N$` $f\colon M \rightarrow N$

24.5   Math Mode Begins and Ends a Group

Any changes you make inside math mode are local. When you change the font, give a reporter new information, or define new macros inside math mode, these changes stop when you end math mode.

```
With Cartesian coordinates,
$\bf x^2 + y^2 = 5$ defines a circle.
```

With Cartesian coordinates, $\mathbf{x^2 + y^2 = 5}$ defines a circle.

The numbers became boldface as well as the letters, but the plus and equals signs did not. In TEX's math modes, the font-changing macros such as **\rm** and **\bf** affect only the letters **A**–**Z** and **a**–**z**, the digits **0**–**9**, uppercase Greek letters **\Gamma** to **\Omega**, and math accents such as **\hat** and **\tilde**. (**\hat** and **\tilde** are shown in Section 25.3.) To see exactly which math symbols are available in which typefaces, look at the font tables in Appendix A (pages 364 through 368).

To make a limited change, use braces to begin and end another group inside the math mode group.

```
Does $ c {\bf A} b = b{\bf A}c$?
```

$$\text{Does } c\mathbf{A}b = b\mathbf{A}c?$$

If you change a reporter or define a macro inside math mode but want that reporter or macro to stay the same when you stop math mode, use the primitive **\global** (see page 169). **\global** tells TeX to post the new information on the innermost layer of the bulletin board.

24.6 Delimiters

Mathematics uses *delimiters* to show where part of a formula begins and ends, or to show which pieces should be done first. The main delimiters are ( ), [ ], and { }, but people are always inventing new things, so TeX has other symbols that are also used as delimiters. Twelve of TeX's delimiters form pairs.

$$() \qquad [] \qquad \{\} \qquad \lfloor\rfloor \qquad \lceil\rceil \qquad \langle\rangle$$

Another ten symbols can also be used as delimiters.

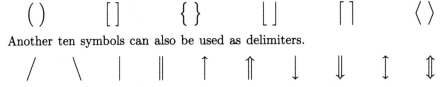

Here are the control sequences (or characters to type) for each of these delimiters. The parentheses (( )), brackets ([ ]), and slash (/) can be used outside of math mode as part of ordinary text. All the others can be used only in math mode.

(	(	{	\{ or \lbrace	⌊	\lfloor
)	)	}	\} or \rbrace	⌋	\rfloor
[	[or \lbrack	⟨	\langle	⌈	\lceil
]	] or \rbrack	⟩	\rangle	⌉	\rceil
/	/	↑	\uparrow	⇑	\Uparrow
\	\backslash	↕	\updownarrow	⇕	\Updownarrow
|	| or \vert	↓	\downarrow	⇓	\Downarrow
‖	\\| or \Vert				

Lamport redefined \{ and \} so they can also be used outside of math mode.

These delimiters come in five different sizes (and most can grow even larger to be whatever size you need). You can specify the size directly or allow TEX to choose.

The simplest way is to let TEX decide. **\left** and **\right** are primitives that take one input—the delimiter—and figure out what size to make it.

```
$$ f(n) = 1 + \left( {2n+xy \over z^2} \right] $$
```

$$ f(n) = 1 + \left(\frac{2n + xy}{z^2} \right] $$

The delimiters you choose do not have to match. However, if you have a \left, you must also have a \right. To get an opening delimiter with no closing, or a closing delimiter with no opening, type a period instead of a delimiter for the one that needs to be blank (\left. or \right.).

Sometimes, though, TEX chooses a delimiter size that is too large or too small. Then you need one of the following sixteen plain TEX macros:

- **\bigl**, **\Bigl**, **\biggl**, and **\Biggl** create *opening* delimiters in progressively larger sizes.

- **\bigr**, **\Bigr**, **\biggr**, and **\Biggr** create *closing* delimiters in progressively larger sizes.

- **\bigm**, **\Bigm**, **\biggm**, and **\Biggm** create progressively larger "middle delimiters" that can be used in the middle of formulas. TEX treats these delimiters as *relations*—the same way it does an equals sign.

- **\big**, **\Big**, **\bigg**, and **\Bigg** create progressively larger delimiters that act like an *ordinary* character (just like 2 and x and A).

The distinction among these *openings, closings, relations,* and *ordinary* characters is that TEX puts different amounts of space around them. Section 24.8 explains TEX's math mode spacing rules.

Each of these sixteen macros takes one input: the delimiter, either as a character or a control sequence. Here are their sizes:

```
$$\Biggl( a \biggl[ b \Bigl\lceil c \bigl\lfloor
        d \langle e \rangle f
    \bigr\rfloor g \Bigr\rceil h \biggr] i \Biggr)$$
```

$$ \left(a \left[b \left\lceil c \left\lfloor d \langle e \rangle f \right\rfloor g \right\rceil h \right] i \right) $$

Several more unusual delimiters are available: see \arrowvert, \Arrowvert, \bracevert, \lgroup, \rgroup, \lmoustache, and \rmoustache on page 150 of *The T_EXbook*.

24.7   Writing Macros for Math Mode

Generally speaking, macros for math mode are no different from any other kind of macro. Put into the definition whatever you would type in the text. If you type something often, it deserves its own macro. One good candidate is a subscripted letter or expression, such as the following:

```
\def\Ek{{\cal E}_k}

When $x + \Ek = 0$, the remaining \dots
```

When $x + \mathcal{E}_k = 0$, the remaining . . .

Another is a pattern like the following: $a_1, a_2, \ldots, a_n$. Our **\series** macro takes two inputs. The first input is the letter or expression being subscripted (such as a or x in these examples). The second input is the final subscript of the series (such as n or k).

```
\def\series#1#2{#1_{1},
                #1_{2}, \ldots,
                #1_{#2}}

For the series $\series{x}{k}$, we know \dots
```

For the series $x_1, x_2, \ldots, x_k$, we know . . .

24.8   Math Mode Spacing Rules

When T_EX is assembling a math list, instead of converting characters and control sequences into words, T_EX converts characters and control sequences into *atoms*. Atoms have a variety of characteristics. Only one is relevant to the math mode spacing rules: its type. There are eight basic types of atoms.

- *Ordinary* characters. This category includes all the letters, numbers, Greek letters, and some miscellaneous symbols.
- *Large operators.* These include the $\sum$ and $\int$ signs, plus all the others having two different sizes for regular and display math. Also, the large operators can take *limits*, such as the zero and infinity symbol in $\int_0^\infty f(x)\,dx$.

- *Binary operations.* This category includes the $+$ and $-$ signs and a variety of other symbols that act in a similar way. These symbols are called *binary* because they connect two smaller pieces into larger formulas, and *operations* because they perform a specified kind of operation between the two pieces.

- *Relations.* Here we have $=$, $<$, $>$, and other symbols that state a relationship between two sides of the entire formula. Relations can be negated ($\neq$). All of TeX's arrows are in this category.

- *Openings.* These are left delimiters, such as (, [, and {.

- *Closings.* These are right delimiters, such as),], and }.

- *Punctuation.* This category includes commas and semicolons, but does not include the period, colon, exclamation point, or question mark.

- *Inner.* These are delimited subformulas.

The amount of space that TeX puts between any two math atoms depends on which type is on the left and which on the right. TeX uses the following table to decide how much space to put between them. In this table, 0 means no space, 1 means a thin space, 2 means a medium space, and 3 means a thick space. The parentheses mean that space is inserted only in display and text styles, not script or scriptscript styles. An asterisk means that this combination of atoms is not possible.

Atom on the left:	Atom on the right:							
	Ord	Op	Bin	Rel	Open	Close	Punct	Inner
Ord	0	1	(2)	(3)	0	0	0	(1)
Op	1	1	*	(3)	0	0	0	(1)
Bin	(2)	(2)	*	*	(2)	*	*	(2)
Rel	(3)	(3)	*	0	(3)	0	0	(3)
Open	0	0	*	0	0	0	0	0
Close	0	1	(2)	(3)	0	0	0	(1)
Punct	(1)	(1)	*	(1)	(1)	(1)	(1)	(1)
Inner	(1)	1	(2)	(3)	(1)	0	(1)	(1)

Punctuation

The comma (,) and semicolon (;) are punctuation in math mode. TeX puts a thin space after them. If you want no space after the comma or semicolon, put braces around them.

TeX treats the colon (:) as a relation in math mode. To get an ordinary colon, use **\colon**.

Since mathematicians do not put space after a period in math formulas, TeX treats the period (.) as an ordinary character. TeX also treats the exclamation point, question mark, and all the other punctuation marks as ordinary characters.

24.9   Making Math-Mode-Only Macros

If you need to make sure that TeX puts the correct amount of space around a macro, specify the type of atom you want the macro to be. Use

- **\mathord** for an ordinary character,
- **\mathop** for a large operator,
- **\mathbin** for a binary operation,
- **\mathrel** for a relation,
- **\mathopen** for an opening delimiter,
- **\mathclose** for a closing delimiter,
- **\mathpunct** for punctuation, or
- **\mathinner** for an inner, delimited subformula.

For example, if you want a **\clubsuit** symbol that behaves like a binary operation instead of an ordinary character, use **\mathbin** in your macro definition.[1]

```
\def\clubin{\mathbin{\clubsuit}}

$ 5x \clubsuit 2y = 6$, but
$ 3x \clubin 39 y = 15$.
```

$$5x\clubsuit 2y = 6, \text{ but } 3x \clubsuit 39y = 15.$$

When you use one of these math-atom categorizers in a macro, that macro can be used only in math mode.

Review and Related Matters

This chapter shows the basic aspects of using math mode and display math mode. It describes how to adjust the vertical spacing above and below math displays and the horizontal spacing inside both math modes. Math mode has

---

[1]The **\clubin** binary operation in this example has no arithmetic, algebraic, or other meaning.

implicit grouping: Changes you make inside math mode are local. Delimiters come in many shapes and sizes. You can specify the size or let TEX decide which size to use.

Writing macros with math mode symbols is the same basic process as writing macros for text. If you want TEX to complain if it finds a particular macro when it is not in math mode, use one of TEX's eight math-atom categorizers.

Instead of assembling characters into words and spaces, math mode assembles characters into atoms and spaces. The size of a space between two atoms depends on the types of those atoms. There are eight basic types of atoms: ordinary, large operator, binary operation, relation, opening, closing, punctuation, and inner.

Chapter 25 gives all the symbols TEX uses in math mode and shows how to use them. Chapter 26 shows how to make fractions, typeset multiline equations, include equation numbers, and use similar display math TEXniques. Chapter 27 describes how to use TEX's font-family system so you can use math mode in your headings or footnotes as well as in your text.

CHAPTER 25

Math Mode Symbols

This chapter presents all the symbols of math mode (except delimiters), and shows how to use them.

To understand this chapter, you must be familiar with the following:

- how macros take inputs (page 55), and
- most of Chapter 24.

An understanding of the eight types of math mode atoms (Section 24.8) is helpful but not necessary.

LaTeX uses the same symbols and spacing rules as TeX.

25.1   Subscripts and Superscripts

Mathematicians, scientists, and engineers use subscripts and superscripts all the time. The underline character (_) makes a subscript, and the circumflex (^) creates a superscript. The _ and ^ characters can be used only in math mode.

```
Einstein's energy equation is $E = mc^2$.
```

Einstein's energy equation is $E = mc^2$.

Both _ and ^ take one input: the next object that follows. If there is more than one character in the subscript or superscript, put them inside braces. In fact, putting braces around a single-character subscript or superscript never hurts and is a useful habit.

```
The Fibonacci numbers satisfy
$F_{n} = F_{n-1} + F_{n-2}$, for $n\geq 2$.
```

> The Fibonacci numbers satisfy $F_n = F_{n-1} + F_{n-2}$, for $n \geq 2$.

Math mode uses an extensive and comprehensive set of special mathematical symbols like $\geq$. This chapter shows how to use them.

The **\prime** superscript appears so often that Knuth made an abbreviation for it:

`$a'$ and $x^\prime$`	a' and x'
`$c_{n}''$ and $y_{n}^{\prime\prime}$`	c_n'' and y_n''
`$e'''_{n}$ and $z^{\prime\prime\prime}_{n}$`	e_n''' and z_n'''

As this example shows, when you need both a subscript and a superscript, it does not matter which you put first. However, since mathematicians say "x-sub-n squared" instead of "x-squared sub n," you may want to develop the habit of typing the subscript first.

Occasionally, you may need to change the way TEX places a subscript or superscript after a tall letter. You may also need a superscript "of nothing" in your text. To do this, type an empty group in front of the subscript and/or superscript.

`$P_{2}^{2}$ versus $P{}_{2}^{2}$`	P_2^2 versus P_2^2
`the ${}^{\dagger}$ symbol`	the † symbol
`staggered $Q_{m}{}^{ij}{}_{n}$`	staggered $Q_m{}^{ij}{}_n$

A subsubscript is simply a subscript of a sub- or superscript, and similarly for a supersuperscript.

`$x^{n^3}$`	x^{n^3}
`$y_{k^2}$`	y_{k^2}
`$z_{n_i}^{ax^{b+1}}$`	$z_{n_i}^{ax^{b+1}}$

25.2   Roots

Square roots are done with **\sqrt**, cube and other roots with **\root**. Both are plain TEX macros and can be used only in math mode.

`$\sqrt a$`	$\sqrt{a}$
`$\sqrt{-1}$`	$\sqrt{-1}$
`$\sqrt{a_{n} + 2x^{2}}$`	$\sqrt{a_n + 2x^2}$
`$\root n-1 \of a$`	$\sqrt[n-1]{a}$
`$\root 5 \of {100}$`	$\sqrt[5]{100}$
`$\root j+1 \of {x^{2} + y^{2}}$`	$\sqrt[j+1]{x^2 + y^2}$

\sqrt takes one input—the next object that follows. To put more than one character under the square root sign, put braces around the entire formula.

\root takes two inputs and uses **\of** to separate them. The first input, between **\root** and **\of**, is placed in the upper left corner of the root sign. The second input is the object after **\of** and is placed under the root sign. If the second input contains more than one character, put braces around them.

The size of the root sign expands to fit whatever is underneath it.

Do not use **\root** in LATEX. Instead, give **\sqrt** an optional argument. **\sqrt[n−1]{a}** produces $\sqrt[n-1]{a}$.

25.3   Vectors, Accents, Overbars, and Underbars

Mathematics often uses arrows, accent marks, or lines over characters, and sometimes uses lines below them as well.

A vector is a special number that has both size and direction, so mathematicians put arrows over vectors. If the vector's name is just one letter, you can use the **\vec** accent. For a longer arrow, use **\overrightarrow**. Both **\vec** and **\overrightarrow** are plain TEX macros and take one input. **\imath** and **\jmath** are plain TEX macros that typeset a dotless $\imath$ and $\jmath$ (see Section 25.5).

```
\dots\ for the addition of vectors,
$$
\overrightarrow{P_{1} P_{2}}
= (x_{2} - x_{1}) \vec\imath
+ (y_{2} - y_{1}) \vec\jmath
+ (z_{2} - z_{1}) \vec k
$$
```

. . . for the addition of vectors,

$$\overrightarrow{P_1P_2} = (x_2 - x_1)\vec{\imath} + (y_2 - y_1)\vec{\jmath} + (z_2 - z_1)\vec{k}$$

Since the **\vec** accent and **\overrightarrow** have slightly different appearances, you may prefer to use **\overrightarrow** on all your vectors. TEX also has an **\overleftarrow** that points leftward instead of rightward.

Altogether, TEX has ten math accents. They are different from the accents used for regular text (shown on page 24), because the spacing is different in math mode. All of them are plain TEX macros and can be used only in math mode.

$\acute{n}$	\acute n	$\hat{n}$	\hat n	$\breve{n}$	\breve n
$\grave{n}$	\grave n	$\check{n}$	\check n	$\bar{n}$	\bar n
$\dot{n}$	\dot n	$\tilde{n}$	\tilde n	$\vec{n}$	\vec n
$\ddot{n}$	\ddot n				

The **\hat** and **\tilde** accents have versions that can grow wider, depending on the width of their input: **\widehat** and **\widetilde**.

`$\widehat x, \widetilde x$`	$\widehat{x}, \widetilde{x}$
`$\widehat{xy}, \widetilde{xy}$`	$\widehat{xy}, \widetilde{xy}$
`$\widehat{xyz}, \widetilde{xyz}$`	$\widehat{xyz}, \widetilde{xyz}$

If you need a line wider than the **\bar**, use **\overline**, a primitive that puts a line over its input. **\overline** can be used only in math mode.

`$ \overline M $`	$\overline{M}$
`$ \overline{x_{1} y_{1}} $`	$\overline{x_1y_1}$
`$ \overline{a'b} $`	$\overline{a'b}$

If you want all the overlines at the same height, you can use **\mathstrut**, a plain TEX macro that puts an invisible, zero-width parenthesis into the formula. The **\mathstrut** comes in handy whenever you need to have uniform vertical spacing in a math formula.

TeX also has **\underline**, another primitive that can be used only in math mode.

```
$ \underline Q $
$ \underline{m_{2} n_{2}} $
$ \underline{c'd} $
```

$$Q$$
$$m_2 n_2$$
$$c'd$$

Oops!

\underline does not work well as a "quickie underline" for text. If you insist on having underlined words instead of italics in your text, use the plain TeX macro **\underbar** or write your own macro instead. The following example shows the difference between **\underline** and **\underbar**.

```
$\underline{\rm Underline}$
$\underline{\rm Questions}$.
\underbar{Query}   \underbar{All}
\underbar{Authors}.
```

<u>Underline</u> <u>Questions</u>. <u>Query</u> <u>All</u> <u>Authors</u>.

25.4   Greek and Calligraphic Letters

Mathematicians, scientists, and engineers also love Greek letters, so TeX has a full set of them.

```
The Pythagorean identity is
$1 - \sin^{2}\theta = \cos^{2}\theta$.
```

The Pythagorean identity is $1 - \sin^2 \theta = \cos^2 \theta$.

TeX has all the lowercase Greek letters—except *omicron*, which is the same as the **o** in the math italic font—plus six variant lowercase letters. All of these plain TeX macros can be used only in math mode.

α	\alpha	ι	\iota	ρ	\rho
β	\beta	κ	\kappa	σ	\sigma
γ	\gamma	λ	\lambda	τ	\tau
δ	\delta	μ	\mu	υ	\upsilon
ϵ	\epsilon	ν	\nu	ϕ	\phi
ζ	\zeta	ξ	\xi	χ	\chi
η	\eta	o	o	ψ	\psi
θ	\theta	π	\pi	ω	\omega

The six variants are as follows:

ε	\varepsilon	ϖ	\varpi	ς	\varsigma
ϑ	\vartheta	ϱ	\varrho	φ	\varphi

TEX also has the eleven uppercase Greek letters that are different from the \rm font's uppercase letters, in both upright and slanted form.

Γ	\Gamma	Ξ	\Xi	Φ	\Phi
Δ	\Delta	Π	\Pi	Ψ	\Psi
Θ	\Theta	Σ	\Sigma	Ω	\Omega
Λ	\Lambda	Υ	\Upsilon		

Mathematics generally uses the upright version of the uppercase Greek letters. If you need to use the italic ones instead, say **\mit** in front of the letter, just like **\rm** or **\bf** and the other font-changing macros. **\mit** stands for math italic. The italic uppercase Greek letters are in the math italic font. The upright uppercase Greek letters are in the roman font.

For those of you who are unfamiliar with the appearance of uppercase Greek letters, here they are, in alphabetical order:

$$A\ B\ \Gamma\ \Delta\ E\ Z\ H\ \Theta\ I\ K\ \Lambda\ M\ N\ \Xi\ O\ \Pi\ P\ \Sigma\ T\ \Upsilon\ \Phi\ X\ \Psi\ \Omega$$

If you need to define your own **\Alpha**, do it like this:

```
\def\Alpha{\mathord{\rm A}}
```

Because this **\Alpha** macro is defined with **\mathord**, it can be used only in math mode. TEX treats **\Alpha** like an ordinary character. If you try to use **\Alpha** outside of math mode, TEX complains, goes into math mode, and proceeds from there. (**\mathord** is explained in Section 24.9.)

All of the Greek letters are defined with **\mathord**, so they behave as ordinary characters in TEX's math mode spacing rules.

Calligraphic Letters

You can also get the following calligraphic letters by saying **\cal** in math mode.

$$\mathcal{A\ B\ C\ D\ E\ F\ G\ H\ I\ J\ K\ L\ M\ N\ O\ P\ Q\ R\ S\ T\ U\ V\ W\ X\ Y\ Z}$$

25.5   Miscellaneous Ordinary Symbols

TEX has another thirty symbols that are ordinary characters for the math mode spacing rules. All are plain TEX macros that can be used only in math mode.

$\aleph$	\aleph	$'$	\prime	$\forall$	\forall
$\hbar$	\hbar	$\emptyset$	\emptyset	$\exists$	\exists
$\imath$	\imath	∇	\nabla	$\neg$	\neg
$\jmath$	\jmath	$\surd$	\surd	$\flat$	\flat
ℓ	\ell	$\top$	\top	$\natural$	\natural
$\wp$	\wp	$\bot$	\bot	$\sharp$	\sharp
$\Re$	\Re	$\|$	|	$\clubsuit$	\clubsuit
$\Im$	\Im	$\angle$	\angle	$\diamondsuit$	\diamondsuit
∂	\partial	$\triangle$	\triangle	$\heartsuit$	\heartsuit
∞	\infty	$\backslash$	\backslash	$\spadesuit$	\spadesuit

When you need an accent over an i or a j, use **\imath** and **\jmath**, which have no dots to interfere with the accent. These two dotless letters are also available in Computer Modern's roman, boldface, slanted, and typewriter fonts. (See positions 16 and 17 in the corresponding font tables of Appendix A.)

25.6 Sums and Integrals

TeX has two sizes of sum and integral signs, one for regular math mode and another for display math. Use _ and ^ to typeset their *limits*. These *limits* are the information placed above and below the symbols. This information is positioned differently in the two math modes. In regular math mode,

`$ \sum x_{n} $`	$\sum x_n$
`$ \sum_{n=1}^{m} x_{n} $`	$\sum_{n=1}^{m} x_n$
`$ \int a\,dx $`	$\int a\,dx$
`$ \int_{0}^{\infty} a\,dx $`	$\int_0^\infty a\,dx$

In display math mode,

`$$ \sum^{m}_{n=1} x_{n} $$`	$$\sum_{n=1}^{m} x_n$$
`$$ \int^{\infty}_{0} a\,dx $$`	$$\int_0^\infty a\,dx$$

Again, it does not matter which you put first, the lower limit or the upper one (the subscript or superscript).

For TeX's math mode spacing rules (see Section 24.8), both the **\sum** and **\integral** symbols are *large operators*.

25.7 Other Symbols with Limits

TeX has another twelve symbols that come in two sizes and can take limits. These are also large operators for TeX's math mode spacing rules.

$\prod$ $\prod$	\prod	$\bigcap$ $\bigcap$	\bigcap	$\bigodot$ $\bigodot$	\bigodot
$\coprod$ $\coprod$	\coprod	$\bigcup$ $\bigcup$	\bigcup	$\bigotimes$ $\bigotimes$	\bigotimes
$\oint$ $\oint$	\oint	$\bigvee$ $\bigvee$	\bigvee	$\bigoplus$ $\bigoplus$	\bigoplus
$\bigsqcup$ $\bigsqcup$	\bigsqcup	$\bigwedge$ $\bigwedge$	\bigwedge	$\biguplus$ $\biguplus$	\biguplus

Overbrace and Underbrace

Another pair of symbols that can take limits are the **\overbrace** and **\underbrace**. Both are plain TeX macros that can be used only in math mode.

$$\overbrace{x_1 + \cdots + x_n}^{n=\psi}$$

```
$ \overbrace{x_{1}+\cdots+x_{n}}^{n=\psi} $
$ \underbrace{a+b+c+d}_{\forall\Re} $
```

$$\underbrace{a+b+c+d}_{\forall\Re}$$

Both are also large operators for TeX's math mode spacing rules.

25.8 Text Words in Math Mode

Some words—such as **sin**, **log**, and **lim**—should be in roman type, not italic, and should also have space around them. Many of these words occur so often in mathematics that it makes sense to write macros for them, and Knuth did exactly that.

```
Does $\sin30^\circ = \cos 60^\circ$?      Does $\sin 30° = \cos 60°$?
```

Since **30** is a nonletter, TeX can see where the control sequence **\sin** ends. For **\sin x**, either put a space between **\sin** and **x**, or put braces around the **x**.

Plain TeX has thirty-two such macros. All of them can be used only in math mode.

arccos	\arccos	dim	\dim	log	\log
arcsin	\arcsin	exp	\exp	max	\max
arctan	\arctan	gcd	\gcd	min	\min
arg	\arg	hom	\hom	Pr	\Pr
cos	\cos	inf	\inf	sec	\sec

cosh	\cosh	ker	\ker	sin	\sin
cot	\cot	lg	\lg	sinh	\sinh
coth	\coth	lim	\lim	sup	\sup
csc	\csc	lim inf	\liminf	tan	\tan
deg	\deg	lim sup	\limsup	tanh	\tanh
det	\det	ln	\ln		

All of these macros are defined with **\mathop**, so they behave as large operators for TEX's math mode spacing rules. However, they only come in one size, and only ten of them can take limits:

\det	\inf	\liminf	\max	\Pr
\gcd	\lim	\limsup	\min	\sup

Use a subscript for their limits, just as you did for the other large operators.

Using an Hbox for Text Words

Another method of getting text words in math mode is to put them in an hbox. This TEXnique is especially useful in display math mode.

```
$$ 3n + 2x = 2x + 3n
\qquad\hbox{for all $n$ and all $x$.}
$$
```

$$3n + 2x = 2x + 3n \qquad \text{for all } n \text{ and all } x.$$

Inside an hbox, TEX uses text spacing rules instead of math mode spacing rules. Thus, if you need only a few **\rm** letters in a math expression, put them inside a group and change the font: {**\rm ax**}. If you need actual words instead, put them inside an hbox.

The potential pitfall here is that the hbox uses the current font, which might be italic or slanted or bold instead of roman. This is often the correct thing to do, but if you need to be sure of using the **\rm** font, use the following **\tbox** macro (for text hbox). Our **\tbox** macro takes one input: the text.

```
\def\tbox#1{\hbox{\rm#1}}
```

Now we can use this **\tbox** instead of an **\hbox**, and be sure that text will be typeset in the **\rm** font.

For roman or bold subscripts or superscripts, use a group to change the font inside the subscript or superscript. Do not use an hbox to change the font of a subscript or superscript. (If you do, you get the **\textfont** size instead of the **\scriptfont** size. Chapter 27 explains the **\textfont** and **\scriptfont** sizes.)

25.9   Binary Operation Symbols

Binary means that something has two parts. *Operation* means using a rule to transform those two parts into a third thing. In $1 + 2 = 3$, the two parts are the numbers 1 and 2. The binary operation is addition, which takes the numbers 1 and 2 and uses a rule to arrive at the number 3.

Subtraction, multiplication, and division are also binary operations. Putting space around the symbols $+$, $-$, $\times$, and $\div$ makes them easier to see, so the math mode spacing rules treat binary operations differently from the ordinary characters. As Section 24.8 shows, TeX puts a medium space on both sides of all binary operations.

Besides $+$ and $-$, TeX has thirty-two symbols that act as binary operations in the math mode spacing rules. Type them as you would any other control sequence.

```
$ 2x \cup 3y \vee 4z = 8a \odot 3b \star 7c $
```

$$2x \cup 3y \vee 4z = 8a \odot 3b \star 7c$$

These thirty-two binary operations are all plain TeX macros that can be used only in math mode.

$\pm$	\pm	$\ominus$	\ominus	$\amalg$	\amalg
$\mp$	\mp	$\oslash$	\oslash	$\cap$	\cap
$\setminus$	\setminus	$\triangleleft$	\triangleleft	$\cup$	\cup
$\cdot$	\cdot	$\triangleright$	\triangleright	$\sqcap$	\sqcap
$\times$	\times	$\wr$	\wr	$\sqcup$	\sqcup
$\ast$	\ast	$\bigcirc$	\bigcirc	$\vee$	\vee
$\div$	\div	$\bigtriangleup$	\bigtriangleup	$\wedge$	\wedge
$\star$	\star	$\bigtriangledown$	\bigtriangledown	$\odot$	\odot
$\diamond$	\diamond	$\dagger$	\dagger	$\oplus$	\oplus
$\circ$	\circ	$\ddagger$	\ddagger	$\otimes$	\otimes
$\bullet$	\bullet			$\uplus$	\uplus

Oops!

Except for the **\sqcap**, all the symbols in the right-hand column have large-operator cousins. Be sure to use the correct version. If you use the wrong symbol, the spacing around it will be wrong too. Knuth says that "Large operators usually occur at the beginning of a formula or subformula, and they usually are subscripted; binary operations usually occur between two symbols or subformulas, and they rarely are subscripted."

Two of these binary operation symbols also have ordinary cousins. The difference between **\bigtriangleup** (binary: $x \bigtriangleup x$) and **\triangle** (ordinary: $x\triangle x$) is the way that TeX typesets space around them. Similarly, do not confuse **\setminus** (binary: $x \setminus x$) and **\backslash** (ordinary: $x\backslash x$).

The **\nabla** and **\bigtriangledown** are different symbols: The top and left sides of the **\nabla** (∇) are heavier than those of the **\bigtriangledown** ($\bigtriangledown$).

25.10   Relation Symbols

A *relation* describes the relationship between two mathematical formulas. They might be equal, equivalent, or similar. One might be larger or smaller than the other. All these are relations.

Because a relation separates a math expression into two distinct parts, TeX puts more space around relations than any other symbol. Besides $=$, $<$, and $>$, TeX has thirty-three relations, another twenty-one negated relations, and thirty-one arrow-type relations. All are plain TeX macros that can be used only in math mode.

Relations

$\leq$	\leq	$\geq$	\geq	$\equiv$	\equiv
$\prec$	\prec	$\succ$	\succ	$\sim$	\sim
$\preceq$	\preceq	$\succeq$	\succeq	$\simeq$	\simeq
$\ll$	\ll	$\gg$	\gg	$\approx$	\approx
$\subset$	\subset	$\supset$	\supset	$\cong$	\cong
$\subseteq$	\subseteq	$\supseteq$	\supseteq	$\asymp$	\asymp
$\sqsubseteq$	\sqsubseteq	$\sqsupseteq$	\sqsupseteq	$\bowtie$	\bowtie
$\in$	\in	$\ni$	\ni	$\propto$	\propto
$\vdash$	\vdash	$\dashv$	\dashv	$\models$	\models
$\smile$	\smile	$\mid$	\mid	$\doteq$	\doteq
$\frown$	\frown	$\parallel$	\parallel	$\perp$	\perp

\mid and **\parallel** are relations. | ($|$) and \| ($\|$) behave as ordinary characters.

Negated Relations

\not is a plain TeX macro that puts a slash through whatever follows it. **\not** is defined as a relation of width **0pt**.

$\not<$ \not<	$\not>$ \not>	$\neq$ \not=
$\not\leq$ \not\leq	$\not\geq$ \not\geq	$\not\equiv$ \not\equiv
$\not\prec$ \not\prec	$\not\succ$ \not\succ	$\not\sim$ \not\sim
$\not\preceq$ \not\preceq	$\not\succeq$ \not\succeq	$\not\simeq$ \not\simeq
$\not\subset$ \not\subset	$\not\supset$ \not\supset	$\not\approx$ \not\approx
$\not\subseteq$ \not\subseteq	$\not\supseteq$ \not\supseteq	$\not\cong$ \not\cong
$\not\sqsubseteq$ \not\sqsubseteq	$\not\sqsupseteq$ \not\sqsupseteq	$\not\asymp$ \not\asymp

Arrow Relations

The up and down arrows can grow larger as needed, as the delimiters do.

←	\leftarrow	⟵	\longleftarrow
⇐	\Leftarrow	⟸	\Longleftarrow
→	\rightarrow	⟶	\longrightarrow
⇒	\Rightarrow	⟹	\Longrightarrow
↔	\leftrightarrow	⟷	\longleftrightarrow
⇔	\Leftrightarrow	⟺	\Longleftrightarrow
↦	\mapsto	⟼	\longmapsto
↑	\uparrow	⇑	\Uparrow
↓	\downarrow	⇓	\Downarrow
↕	\updownarrow	⇕	\Updownarrow
↖	\nwarrow	↗	\nearrow
↙	\swarrow	↘	\searrow
↩	\hookleftarrow	↪	\hookrightarrow
↼	\leftharpoonup	⇀	\rightharpoonup
↽	\leftharpoondown	⇁	\rightharpoondown
⇌	\rightleftharpoons		

If you need to typeset something over an arrow or other relation, use
\buildrel.

$$\buildrel \alpha\beta \over \longrightarrow$$ `$\buildrel \alpha\beta \over \longrightarrow$`

In LATEX, use **\stackrel** instead of **\buildrel**. The **\stackrel** macro takes two inputs, and is shown in Section 3.3.6 on page 52 of Lamport's LATEX book.

Numbers

To get italic, boldface, or old-style numbers in math mode, change the font.

`${\it 0 1 2 3 4 5 6 7 8 9}$`	*0123456789*
`${\bf 0 1 2 3 4 5 6 7 8 9}$`	**0123456789**
`${\oldstyle 0 1 2 3 4 5 6 7 8 9}$`	0123456789

Alternate Names

$\neq$	`\neq`	same as `\not=`
$\rightarrow$	`\to`	same as `\rightarrow`
$\leftarrow$	`\gets`	same as `\leftarrow`
$\ni$	`\owns`	same as `\ni`
$\wedge$	`\land`	same as `\wedge`
$\vee$	`\lor`	same as `\vee`
$\neg$	`\lnot`	same as `\neg`
$\iff$	`\iff`	same as `\;\Longleftrightarrow\;`

Nonmath Symbols

The following four symbols are from the **cmsy** math mode font but can be used outside of math mode.

§	`\S`	¶	`\P`	†	`\dag`	‡	`\ddag`

Review and Related Matters

This chapter presents all of TeX's math mode symbols (except the delimiters) and shows how to use them.

Chapter 24 describes how to use math mode, adjust spacing, use delimiters, and write macros for math mode. It also explains the math mode spacing rules for the *ordinary* characters, *large operators*, *binary operations*, and *relations* shown in this chapter.

Chapter 26 shows how to make fractions, typeset multiline equations, include equation numbers, and use similar display math TeXniques.

Chapter 27 describes how to use TeX's font-family system so you can use math mode in your headings or footnotes as well as in your text.

CHAPTER 26

Fractions and Multiline Math Displays

Mathematics often contains fractions, both simple and complex. Some equations are short; others are long and need to be split onto two or more lines. Equation numbers are often used to identify particular equations and refer to them in the text. This chapter covers each of these tasks.

To understand this chapter, you must be familiar with the following:

- most of Chapter 24 (Section 24.8 is helpful but not necessary), and
- all of Chapter 25.

Also, familiarity with **\halign** (Chapter 20) is helpful but not necessary.

26.1   Fractions

Simple fractions can go into the text. The primitive **\over** separates the numerator (formula on top) from the denominator (formula on bottom). Put the entire fraction inside braces so TeX can see where it begins and ends.

```
There are 101${2\over3}$ ways to cook tofu.
```

There are $101\frac{2}{3}$ ways to cook tofu.

More complex fractions need to be displayed.

```
$$
{ dy \over dx } = Nx^{N-1}
$$
```

$$\frac{dy}{dx} = Nx^{N-1}$$

TEX also has \atop, a primitive that behaves like \over except that there is no fraction line, and \choose, a plain TEX macro that behaves like \atop except that it puts parentheses around the formula.

```
$$
{M_1 + M_2 \atop M_m} =
{y^u mm_y \choose t^u_ms}
$$
```

$$\frac{M_1 + M_2}{M_m} = \binom{y^u mm_y}{t^u_m s}$$

Finally, there is \above, a primitive that takes one input: a dimension specifying the thickness of the fraction line.

```
Newton's Law of Gravitation is
$$
F = { G m_{1} m_{2} \above 1pt r^{2} }
$$
```

Newton's Law of Gravitation is

$$F = \frac{Gm_1 m_2}{r^2}$$

Since TEX ignores spaces in math mode, type your fractions in any way that makes them easier to read in your text file.

LATEX has a macro called \frac that takes two inputs: the numerator and denominator. It makes a fraction: \frac{a+b}{2x} produces $\frac{a+b}{2x}$. \frac can be used only in math mode.

26.2   Matrixes

A more complicated array with columns and rows is called a *matrix*. Not surprisingly, the plain TeX macro that typesets these columns and rows is called \matrix.

\matrix takes one input: the entire array. Type an ampersand (&) to separate each column entry. Type \cr at the end of each row. In the following example, C_1 is column 1, C_2 is column 2, and C_c is column c; R_1 is row 1, R_2 is row 2, and R_r is row r. We also use our \tbox macro (defined on page 257) to get ordinary text spacing in math mode.

```
$$ \tbox{my matrix} =
\matrix{
C_{1} R_{1}&   C_{2} R_{1}&   \ldots&  C_{c} R_{1}\cr
C_{1} R_{2}&   C_{2} R_{2}&   \ldots&  C_{c} R_{2}\cr
C_{1} R_{3}&   C_{2} R_{3}&   \ldots&  C_{c} R_{3}\cr
\vdots&        \vdots&        \ddots&  \vdots\cr
C_{1} R_{r}&   C_{2} R_{r}&   \ldots&  C_{c} R_{r}\cr}
$$
```

$$\text{my matrix} = \begin{matrix} C_1R_1 & C_2R_1 & \ldots & C_cR_1 \\ C_1R_2 & C_2R_2 & \ldots & C_cR_2 \\ C_1R_3 & C_2R_3 & \ldots & C_cR_3 \\ \vdots & \vdots & \ddots & \vdots \\ C_1R_r & C_2R_r & \ldots & C_cR_r \end{matrix}$$

The \matrix macro uses \halign to create the array. Each entry in a matrix is centered within its column. To make an entry flushright or flushleft instead, use \hfill to overwhelm the fil glue. (This is the same TeXnique that we used with table headings in Section 21.2.)

You can put more than one matrix in the same display. \matrix makes a box the same size as the material inside it. This box is centered vertically within the display. In math mode, TeX aligns boxes along an *axis*—an invisible line that runs through the middle of the plus sign—instead of along their baselines as shown in the examples in Chapters 11 and 33. All other characters have a corresponding axis position. \matrix uses \vcenter, a primitive that makes a vbox (vertical box) whose top and bottom edges are the same distance away from the axis.

Since TeX typesets each \matrix entry in math mode, it does not matter if you type extra spaces in those entries. However, putting no space between the end of an entry and the following & is a good habit to cultivate because you need this same habit for \halign tables with text (as shown in Chapter 20). TeX ignores spaces after the & in any \halign.

Altogether, TeX has four ellipses that can be used only in math mode:

\ldots	on the baseline: between characters
\cdots	centered (on the axis): between plus signs and similar symbols
\vdots	vertically: between rows
\ddots	diagonally: between both rows and columns

All four of these macros can be used only in math mode. Here is an example of **\cdots**:

```
$$
{1\over2} + {1\over4} + {1\over8} + \cdots =
\sum_{k=1}^{\infty}
\left( {1\over2} \right)^{k}
$$
```

$$\frac{1}{2} + \frac{1}{4} + \frac{1}{8} + \cdots = \sum_{k=1}^{\infty} \left(\frac{1}{2}\right)^k$$

LATEX Notes

LATEX has an **array** environment. It is similar to the **tabular** environment but creates a **\matrix** instead of an **\halign**. The **array** environment can be used only in math mode, but does not automatically start math mode if TEX is not already in math mode.

Matrixes with Delimiters

Matrixes often have delimiters around them. You can let TEX choose the delimiter size: **\left[...\right]**; or you can choose the size yourself: **\Bigl\lgroup...\Bigr\rgroup**. If you want parentheses around the matrix, use **\pmatrix**, a plain TEX macro that inserts the parentheses automatically.

```
$$
\bigoplus_{\alpha}^{\omega} =
\pmatrix{\alpha\beta&    \ldots&   \alpha\omega\cr
         \beta\beta&     \ldots&   \beta\omega\cr
         \vdots&         \ddots&   \vdots\cr
         \psi\beta&      \ldots&   \psi\omega\cr}
$$
```

$$\bigoplus_{\alpha}^{\omega} = \begin{pmatrix} \alpha\beta & \ldots & \alpha\omega \\ \beta\beta & \ldots & \beta\omega \\ \vdots & \ddots & \vdots \\ \psi\beta & \ldots & \psi\omega \end{pmatrix}$$

If you need to put information above and to the left of a matrix, use **\bordermatrix** (see page 177 of *The TEXbook*).

Cases

Some mathematical expressions have more than one solution or have different values under different circumstances. The plain TEX macro **\cases** shows the possible alternatives.

A good example is $|x|$ (the absolute value of x). $|x|$ is always a positive number (zero or higher) and the same amount as x. When x is a positive number, $|x|$ and x are the same ($|4| = 4$). When x is negative, however, $|x|$ is $-x$. Mathematically speaking, $|-5| = (-1) * (-5) = 5$.

```
$$ |x| = \cases{x,&  if $x \geq 0$;\cr
            -x,&  otherwise.\cr}
$$
```

$$|x| = \begin{cases} x, & \text{if } x \geq 0; \\ -x, & \text{otherwise.} \end{cases}$$

\cases typesets the open brace and two columns. Each entry in the left column is typeset in math mode. Each entry in the right column is typeset in an hbox, as text. Thus, to put math mode material in a right column entry, you must use the math mode toggles **$...$**. You can have as many rows as you want.

26.3   Equation Numbers

To put an equation number at the right margin of a display, use the primitive **\eqno**. Type **\eqno** after the equation or formula, then type the equation number itself, followed by the end display math **$$** toggle.

```
$$
\int \log x\,dx = x \log x - x
\eqno(26.1)
$$
```

$$\int \log x\, dx = x \log x - x \eqno(26.1)$$

Since spaces are ignored in math mode, this example puts the **\eqno** where it is easy to see: on a line by itself in your text file.

A corresponding **\leqno** puts an equation number at the left margin. Use the same pattern for **\leqno**: **$$***equation* **\leqno** *(equation number)***$$**.

You can also use LaTeX's **equation** environment to make an automatically numbered displayed formula. LaTeX's **equation** environment automatically starts display math mode.

Let TeX Make the Equation Number

Just as we made counters for items, headings, tables, and figures, we can make a counter for the equation number and let TeX do all the work. Sections 14.5 and 17.4 explain the details of making and using counters.

```
\newcount\equationnumber

\def\theEquationNumber{%
    \the\chapternumber.\the\equationnumber}

\def\makeEquationNumber{%
    \global\advance\equationnumber by 1
    (\theEquationNumber)}
```

Since math mode begins and ends a group, we must use **\global** to make sure the counter stays advanced when we end the group.

Now we can use our **\makeEquationNumber** macro.

```
$$
\int e^{x}\,dx = e^{x} + C
\eqno\makeEquationNumber
$$
```

$$\int e^x\,dx = e^x + C \qquad (26.2)$$

If you use this **\theEquationNumber** macro, set the **\equationnumber** back to zero at the beginning of each chapter. The simple way to do this is inside your **\chapter** macro.

```
\def\EquationNumberedChapter#1{...
    \equationnumber=0
    ...}
```

Sometimes a display has more than one equation. The plain TEX macro **\displaylines** allows you to put more than one line into a display. Type **\cr** at the end of each equation.

```
$$\openup 1\jot
\displaylines{
\left( {\delta z \over \delta x} \right) P_{1}
      = {c \over \sqrt{2} \, a}\cr
x = {-b \pm \sqrt{b^{2} - 4ac} \over 2a}\cr}
$$
```

$$\left(\frac{\delta z}{\delta x} \right) P_1 = \frac{c}{\sqrt{2}\, a}$$

$$x = \frac{-b \pm \sqrt{b^2 - 4ac}}{2a}$$

When the lines are too close together, use **\openup**, a plain TEX macro that increases the **\baselineskip**.[1] **\openup** takes one input: the size of the increase. A convenient dimension for this purpose is the **\jot**, a plain TEX reporter for **3pt**.

Oops!

You cannot use **\eqno** or **\leqno** with **\displaylines** because **\eqno** and **\leqno** can be used only in *display math mode*—not regular math mode. The **\displaylines** macro uses **\halign**, regular math mode, and **\displaystyle** to achieve its effects. To get an equation number in a multiline display, you must use either **\eqalignno** or **\leqalignno**, which are explained in Section 26.5.

Aligning the Equals Signs or Other Symbols

\displaylines has one possible disadvantage: All the lines are centered. If you want the equals signs (or other symbols) to be aligned, use the plain TEX macro **\eqalign** instead.

\eqalign makes two columns. Use an ampersand (**&**) to separate the columns, and end each line with **\cr**. Also, put the equals sign in the second column, after the ampersand, to get the correct spacing around it.

---

[1]The **\openup** macro also increases the **\lineskip** and **\lineskiplimit**.

```
$$
\eqalign{
f'(x)& = {dy \over dx}\cr
&       = \lim_{\Delta x \rightarrow 0}
          {\Delta y \over \Delta x}\cr
&       = c\cr}
$$
```

$$
\eqalign{
f'(x) &= \frac{dy}{dx} \\
&= \lim_{\Delta x \to 0} \frac{\Delta y}{\Delta x} \\
&= c
}
$$

\eqalign does not exist in LaTeX. Use the **eqnarray** or **eqnarray*** environments instead. The **eqnarray** environment automatically generates equation numbers; the **eqnarray*** environment does not. You can prevent **eqnarray** from making an equation number on any line where you do not want one. Both **eqnarray** and **eqnarray*** automatically start display math mode.

One Equation on Two or More Lines

You can also use \eqalign to break one long equation onto two or more lines. When you do, the second line often begins with a plus sign that is too close to the character that follows.

In mathematics, the plus sign has two possible meanings: addition or a positive number. When TeX finds **$a+b$** $(a + b)$, it decides the plus sign means addition and is therefore a binary operation. When TeX finds **$+N$** $(+N)$ instead, it decides the plus sign means a positive number, so it typesets the plus sign as an ordinary symbol, with no space after it. This problem occurs with the minus sign as well.

To fix the spacing, put \null in front of the plus (or minus) sign. \null is a plain TeX macro that makes an empty hbox and therefore has zero width. Since it follows the **$a+b$** pattern, however, TeX puts the proper amount of space after the plus (or minus) sign.

Better still, add a \quad or \qquad as well:

```
$$\eqalign{\tbox{snag coefficient}&
   = 47\nu_{x} + acx + \cdots \cr
& \quad\null + {\tbox{random}\over 4Q}
   + \tbox{nada}_{me}^{2} \cr}$$
```

$$\text{snag coefficient} = 47\nu_x + acx + \cdots$$
$$+ \frac{\text{random}}{4Q} + \text{nada}_{me}^2$$

More Than One \eqalign

You can have more than one **\eqalign** on the same line or equation. **\eqalign** is similar to **\matrix**. It makes a box the same size as the material inside it. Knuth gives the example

```
$$
\left\{
    \eqalign{\alpha& = f(z)\cr
            \beta& = f(z^2)\cr
            \gamma& = f(z^3)\cr}
\right\} \qquad \left\{
    \eqalign{x& = \alpha^2 - \beta\cr
            y& = 2\gamma\cr}
\right\}.
$$
```

$$
\left\{
\begin{matrix}
\alpha = f(z) \\
\beta = f(z^2) \\
\gamma = f(z^3)
\end{matrix}
\right\}
\quad
\left\{
\begin{matrix}
x = \alpha^2 - \beta \\
y = 2\gamma
\end{matrix}
\right\}.
$$

Oops!

You cannot use **\eqno** or **\leqno** to label individual lines in an **\eqalign**. To get an equation number in a multiline display, use either **\eqalignno** or **\leqalignno**, which are explained in the next section.

26.5   Equation Numbers in Multiline Displays

When you need equation numbers in a multiline display, use **\eqalignno** to put the number at the right margin, or **\leqalignno** for the left margin. **\eqalignno** and **\leqalignno** have a third column for the equation number.

Type the equation number after a second **&** and before the **\cr**. You can type the actual number directly, or use **\makeEquationNumber** (defined on page 268).

```
$$\openup 1\jot
\eqalignno{
\tbox{circumference}&  = 2 \pi r&        (26.3)\cr
\tbox{area}&             = \pi r^{2}\cr
\tbox{volume}&           = {4\over3}\, \pi r^{3}&
   \makeEquationNumber\cr}
$$
```

$$\text{circumference} = 2\pi r \qquad\qquad (26.3)$$

$$\text{area} = \pi r^2$$

$$\text{volume} = \frac{4}{3}\,\pi r^3 \qquad\qquad (26.4)$$

For lines that do not need an equation number, you can type \cr after the second column, as shown for the area-of-a-circle equation in the example above.

\eqalignno and \leqalignno do not exist in LATEX. Use the **eqnarray** environment instead.

26.6 Adding Space or Words between Lines in a Display

Just as we used **\noalign** to add vertical material to an **\halign**, we can use this same TEXnique with **\displaylines**, **\eqalign**, **\eqalignno**, and **\leqalignno**.

Use **\noalign{\vskip** *dimension*} to add the amount of vertical space you specify in any of these four multiline displays. Let's suppose that you have two equations in the same display, but the first equation takes up two lines. To separate the two equations visually, you want to put a **\medskip** between them. The best approach for putting the first equation on two lines is to use **\eqalign**. Thus, put the **\noalign{\medskip}** between the second and third lines, as shown in the following example:

```
$$\eqalign{
A&  = bx + cx^2 + dx^3 + ex^4 - Fx^{n}\cr
&\quad\null + \cdots
+ G \, {\alpha + \beta \over \gamma - \delta}\cr
\noalign{\medskip}
H_{i+1}&  = {J m_{1} n_{2} \over 3k}\,\pi\omega\cr}
$$
```

$$A = bx + cx^2 + dx^3 + ex^4 - Fx^n$$

$$+ \cdots + G\,\frac{\alpha + \beta}{\gamma - \delta}$$

$$H_{i+1} = \frac{Jm_1 n_2}{3k}\,\pi\omega$$

Next, let's suppose that you want to typeset a few words at the left margin between two or more equations—but you also want to align the equals sign below these words with the equals sign above these words.

You cannot use **\eqalign** for this purpose, because the **\eqalign** box is not as wide as the **\hsize**. The **\eqalign** box does not reach from margin to margin; it is only as wide as the material that goes inside it. However, you can use **\eqalignno** or **\leqalignno**. TEX makes these boxes the same width as the **\hsize** so it can place the equation number flush against the right or left margin.[2]

Use **\noalign{\tbox{**words**}}** to add a few words at the margin between equations. Here, using **\tbox** in the equations means that TEX uses text spacing rules for these words and phrases.

```
The Pythagorean Theorem states that
$$
\eqalignno{
c& = \sqrt{a^{2} + b^{2}}\cr
\noalign{\tbox{where}}
\tbox{$a$ and $b$}&
   = \tbox{sides of the right triangle}\cr
c& = \tbox{hypotenuse}.\cr}
$$
```

The Pythagorean Theorem states that

$$c = \sqrt{a^2 + b^2}$$

where

$$a \text{ and } b = \text{sides of the right triangle}$$
$$c = \text{hypotenuse}.$$

---

[2]More precisely, TEX makes the **\eqaligno** and **\leqalignno** boxes the same width as the **\displaywidth**. **\displaywidth** is a primitive reporter that remembers the width of the display area. TEX gives **\displaywidth** a new value just before each display is processed. The **\displaywidth** is usually the same as the **\hsize**, but can be different depending on the circumstances. In the paragraph after an **\item**, for example, the **\displaywidth** is **\hsize** minus the **\parindent**.

Since the equation in this example did not have an equation number, we did not need to use **\eqalignno**'s third column.

26.7   Controlling the Size of Characters and Symbols

Math mode uses four different styles in typesetting math. Generally speaking, TeX uses display style in a display, text style in a paragraph, script style for subscripts and superscripts, and scriptscript style for subsubscripts and supersuperscripts. These styles control the size of the font that TeX uses in a display, text, sub/superscript, and subsub/supersuperscript. TeX generally uses smaller and smaller styles as you build fractions, subscripts, and superscripts.

To force TeX to use a different style than it normally would, say **\displaystyle**, **\textstyle**, **\scriptstyle**, or **\scriptscriptstyle** in front of the material you want to change. These four primitives override TeX's usual style choice. For example, you can use the display style symbols inside a paragraph.

```
By the time they reached their marriage bed,
'twas indeed a consummation $\displaystyle
\sum_{\rm midnight}^{\rm noon}$ devoutly wished.
```

By the time they reached their marriage bed, 'twas indeed a consummation $\displaystyle \sum_{\rm midnight}^{\rm noon}$ devoutly wished.

You can also maintain the display style inside compound fractions. Knuth gives the following example on page 142 of *The TeXbook*.

```
$$
a_0 + {1 \over\displaystyle
        a_1 + {\strut 1 \over\displaystyle
                a_2 + {\strut 1 \over\displaystyle
                        a_3 + {\strut 1 \over
                                a_4}}}
$$
```

$$
a_0 + \cfrac{1}{a_1 + \cfrac{1}{a_2 + \cfrac{1}{a_3 + \cfrac{1}{a_4}}}}
$$

The **\strut** makes each denominator taller than usual, so the **1**'s do not bump into the fraction lines above and below them. Each new **\displaystyle** is necessary because TEX would otherwise choose a smaller style.

Here is the same fraction without the **\strut**s and **\displaystyle**.

```
$$ a_0 + {1 \over a_1
       + {1 \over a_2
       + {1 \over a_3
       + {1 \over a_4}}}}
$$
```

$$a_0 + \cfrac{1}{a_1 + \cfrac{1}{a_2 + \cfrac{1}{a_3 + \frac{1}{a_4}}}}$$

The style you select is active until TEX reaches the end of the group, formula, or subformula—or until you select another style. The numerator and denominator are separate subformulas. Thus, in a complex expression, you may need to experiment until you get the effect you want.

(*Formula* is just a term for any mathematical expression. If a formula contains an equals sign, it can also be called an equation. A *subformula* is simply a smaller piece of the overall formula.)

Review and Related Matters

This chapter deals with fractions and a variety of multiline display tasks. The control sequences **\over**, **\atop**, **\choose**, and **\above** make fractions and fraction-like formulas. More complex arrays are done with **\matrix**, **\pmatrix**, **\bordermatrix**, and **\cases**. **\displaylines** makes multiline displays. **\eqalign** lines up the equals signs (or other symbols) in multiline displays.

\eqno and **\leqno** put equation numbers into a one-line display. In a multiline display, you must use either **\eqalignno** or **\leqalignno**. Since the equation-number counter is advanced inside a group, you need to use **\global**.

Math mode uses four different styles: **\displaystyle**, **\textstyle**, **\scriptstyle**, and **\scriptscriptstyle**.

Chapter 24 describes how to use math mode, adjust spacing, use delimiters, and write macros for math mode. It also explains the math mode spacing rules. Chapter 25 gives all the symbols TeX uses in math mode and shows how to use them. Chapter 27 describes how to use TeX's font-family system so you can use math mode in your headings or footnotes as well as in your text.

CHAPTER 27

Fonts for Math Mode

Some documents need math mode in more than one font size, such as in footnotes or headings as well as text. To use math mode in any size other than TEX's set of Computer Modern 10-point fonts, you must use TEX's font-family system. Otherwise, you get TEX's standard 10-point math mode fonts instead.

If you want to use fonts in math mode that are not usually available, such as sans serif, you must make these fonts accessible to TEX's font-family system. Otherwise, TEX simply does not know how to find the font you want to use. As a result, you get either nothing at all or a math italic font instead of the one you want.

This chapter explains how to use TEX's font-family system. To understand this chapter, you must be familiar with the following:

- reporters (Chapter 3.10),

- loading fonts with \font and scaled (Chapters 6 and 7), and

- computer filenames for the Computer Modern fonts (page 73).

27.1   TEX's Font Families

TEX has a family number for each different typeface style. Roman fonts are family 0. Math italic fonts are family 1. Math symbol fonts are family 2. Math extension fonts are family 3. TEX uses reporters to remember the other family numbers. Text italic fonts are family \itfam, slanted fonts are family \slfam, boldface fonts are family \bffam, and typewriter fonts are family \ttfam.

For those of you who are curious, here are the actual numbers:

```
Family number itfam is \the\itfam.
Family number slfam is \the\slfam.
Family number bffam is \the\bffam.
Family number ttfam is \the\ttfam.
```

Family number itfam is 4.   Family number slfam is 5.
Family number bffam is 6. Family number ttfam is 7.

To use a font in math mode, that font must have a family number. If the font does not already have such a number, use **\newfam**, a plain TeX macro that creates a new family-number reporter. Here, we make one for the sans serif family:

```
\newfam\ssffam
Family number ssffam is \the\ssffam.
```

Family number ssffam is 8.

\newfam automatically gives the new family-number reporter the next available family number. In other words, since family numbers 0–7 are already being used, our new **\ssffam** number is 8.

27.2   How TeX Uses Font Families

TeXnically speaking, **\rm** is not the name of a font. Instead, it is a plain TeX macro defined as follows:

```
\def\rm{\fam=0\tenrm}
```

This definition of **\rm** accomplishes two things:

- It gives new information to **\fam**—the primitive reporter that remembers the current font-family number.
- It changes the current font to **\tenrm**—the fontname TeX uses for **cmr10**.

When TeX is typesetting a paragraph or hbox (in a horizontal mode), the **\fam** number is irrelevant, and TeX uses the current font. But in math mode, the opposite is true: The current font is irrelevant and TeX uses the current **\fam** number.

Thus, when you change to **\rm** in math mode, the **\fam=0** part of the definition tells TeX which font-family number to use. If we want to use a sans serif font in math mode, we must define a new **\ssf** macro (change to the sans serif font) as

```
\def\ssf{\fam=\ssffam\tenssf}
```

27.3   Math Mode Uses Three Different Font Sizes

TEX uses three different font sizes in math mode. The ordinary characters (such as the letters in $F = ma$) use one size, the subscripts and superscripts use another size, and the subsubscripts and supersuperscripts use a third size. These three sizes have names. The ordinary-character size is the *textfont*. The sub/superscript size is the *scriptfont*. The subsub/supersuperscript size is the *scriptscriptfont*.

To make a font accessible to TEX's math mode, we must say which size and family it belongs to. Plain TEX specifies this for family 0, the roman family, as follows:

```
\textfont0=\tenrm
\scriptfont0=\sevenrm
\scriptscriptfont0=\fiverm
```

These three instructions say that when **\fam** reports **0**, the textfont is **\tenrm**, the scriptfont is **\sevenrm**, and the scriptscriptfont is **\fiverm**.

Similarly, plain TEX establishes the math italic family 1 as follows:

```
\textfont1=\teni
\scriptfont1=\seveni
\scriptscriptfont1=\fivei
```

When TEX is in math mode and finds a font-changing macro such as **\rm**, the active font-family number changes (in this case to **0**). Each time TEX typesets a character in math mode when the font-family number is **0**, TEX uses **\textfont0** for text, **\scriptfont0** for subscripts and superscripts, and **\scriptscriptfont0** for subsubscripts and supersuperscripts.

This is true of each font-family number. When TEX typesets a character in math mode and the active font-family number is N, it uses **\textfont**N for text, **\scriptfont**N for subscripts and superscripts, and **\scriptscriptfont**N for subsubscripts and supersuperscripts.

We use this same pattern to make our sans serif font family available for math mode in all three sizes:

```
\textfont\ssffam=\tenssf
\scriptfont\ssffam=\sevenssf
\scriptscriptfont\ssffam=\fivessf
```

One corner of TEX's bulletin board holds a math-mode-fonts table. This table has a separate column for each size, and as many rows as we want to provide (up to 15). When we say **\textfont\ssffam=\tenssf**, the **\textfont** primitive stores this new information in the pigeonhole that corresponds to the **\ssffam** family. Here are plain TEX's specifications for each family and size, plus our own specification for the sans serif family (\ssffam) on the last row.

\fam	\textfont	\scriptfont	\scriptscriptfont
0	\tenrm	\sevenrm	\fiverm
1	\teni	\seveni	\fivei
2	\tensy	\sevensy	\fivesy
3	\tenex	\tenex	\tenex
\itfam	\tenit		
\slfam	\tensl		
\ttfam	\tentt		
\bffam	\tenbf	\sevenbf	\fivebf
\ssffam	\tenssf	\sevenssf	\fivessf

When TeX is in math mode, it uses this table to decide which font to use. TeX uses the column for the size it needs and the row for the family number. If that pigeonhole is blank, TeX uses the **\nullfont** instead. **\nullfont** is a primitive that stands for a font that contains no characters. Since most users are unlikely to need sub/superscripts or subsub/supersuperscripts in the text italic, slanted, or typewriter fonts, plain TeX does not provide them.

27.4   An Entire Set of Twelve-Point Fonts

If we want to use math mode in both 12-point text and 10-point footnotes, we need to load an entire set of fonts for our 12-point text. We also need two macros—**\twelvepoint** and **\tenpoint**—that change the definitions of **\rm**, **\it**, and the rest. For any font you want to use in math mode, you must assign that font to a specific font size and family number, using **\textfont**, **\scriptfont**, and **\scriptscriptfont**.

Loading the Fonts We Need

We begin by loading a set of roman, boldface, text italic, slanted, typewriter, and three math fonts, **scaled\magstep1**. The following example uses **xii** instead of **twelve** for the font names since **xii** is easier and quicker to type.

```
\font\xiirm=cmr10    scaled\magstep1    % roman
\font\xiibf=cmbx10   scaled\magstep1    % bold
\font\xiiit=cmti10   scaled\magstep1    % text italic
\font\xiisl=cmsl10   scaled\magstep1    % slanted
\font\xiitt=cmtt10   scaled\magstep1    % typewriter

\font\xiimi=cmmi10   scaled\magstep1    % math italic
\font\xiisy=cmsy10   scaled\magstep1    % math symbol
\font\xiiex=cmex10   scaled\magstep1    % math extended

\skewchar\xiimi='177
\skewchar\xiisy='060
```

The \skewchar instructions for the \xiimi and \xiisy fonts make sure that math accents are positioned properly over the characters in these two fonts. Do this whenever you load a **cmmi** or **cmsy** font.

Now we need some fonts for the \scriptfont and \scriptscriptfont sizes. We can use TeX's standard, already loaded 10-point fonts for the \scriptfont size, but we need to load some 8-point fonts for the \scriptscriptfont size. Follow the pattern for \eightrm if you need additional fonts in the \scriptscriptfont size.

```
\font\eightrm=cmr8
\font\eightmi=cmmi8   \skewchar\eightmi='177
\font\eightsy=cmsy8   \skewchar\eightsy='060
```

Now we load a set of sans serif fonts in the two larger sizes.

```
\font\xiissf=cmss10    scaled\magstep1  % sans serif
\font\xiissi=cmssi10   scaled\magstep1  % sans serif italic
\font\xiissb=cmssdc10  scaled\magstep1  % sans serif bold

\font\tenssf=cmss10
\font\tenssi=cmssi10
\font\tenssb=cmssdc10

\def\tenmi{\teni}      % to prevent confusion
```

Writing a \twelvepoint Macro

Now we write our \twelvepoint macro, as shown on the following page. For each font family, \twelvepoint defines the font-changing macro and establishes at least the \textfont size for that family. \twelvepoint also establishes a \normalbaselineskip and a new size for the \strutbox.

The percent sign after each close brace makes sure you do not get a Peek-A-Boo Space Bug (see page 333). The percent signs are necessary because TeX could be in horizontal mode when you use the \twelvepoint macro. (If \obeyspaces might be in effect as well, remove all the spaces between control sequences and at the beginnings of the lines.)

To switch to the 12-point set of fonts, type \twelvepoint before the text in your document. You also need to make a similar \tenpoint macro to typeset your footnotes in the 10-point set of fonts. Otherwise, TeX continues to use the 12-point fonts in the footnotes as well.

The \tenpoint macro needs to provide the same information as the \twelvepoint macro, but with different sizes. When TeX finds \tenpoint in your file, it does not erase the entire \twelvepoint math-fonts table and build a new \tenpoint math-fonts table. Instead, each slot keeps its current information until you give the relevant font-size reporter new information for a particular family number.

```
\def\twelvepoint{\def\rm{\fam=0\xiirm}%
\textfont0=\xiirm\scriptfont0=\tenrm\scriptscriptfont0=\eightrm
\textfont1=\xiimi\scriptfont1=\tenmi\scriptscriptfont1=\eightmi
\textfont2=\xiisy\scriptfont2=\tensy\scriptscriptfont2=\eightsy
\textfont3=\xiiex\scriptfont3=\tenex\scriptscriptfont3=\tenex
\textfont\itfam=\xiiit    \def\it{\fam=\itfam\xiiit}%
\textfont\slfam=\xiisl    \def\sl{\fam=\slfam\xiisl}%
\textfont\ttfam=\xiitt    \scriptfont\ttfam=\tentt
\def\tt{\fam=\ttfam\xiitt}%
\textfont\bffam=\xiibf    \scriptfont\bffam=\tenbf
\def\bf{\fam=\bffam\xiibf}%
\textfont\ssffam=\xiissf  \scriptfont\ssffam=\tenssf
\def\ssf{\fam=\ssffam\xiissf}%
\textfont\ssifam=\xiissi  \scriptfont\ssifam=\tenssi
\def\ssi{\fam=\ssifam\xiissi}%
\textfont\ssbfam=\xiissb  \scriptfont\ssbfam=\tenssb
\def\ssb{\fam=\ssbfam\xiissb}%
\normalbaselineskip=15pt
\setbox\strutbox=\hbox
   {\vrule height 10.65pt depth 4.35pt width 0pt}%
\normalbaselines\rm}
```

Review and Related Matters

This chapter describes TEX's method of deciding which font to use when it
is in math mode. Each type style has a family number. TEX uses reporters
such as **\ttfam** to remember all the font-family numbers except for the **\rm**
family and the three math-font families. **\newfam** creates a new font-family-
number reporter.

In math mode, TEX uses three different font sizes for ordinary characters,
for subscripts or superscripts, and for subsubscripts or supersuperscripts.
These sizes are called the textfont, scriptfont, and scriptscriptfont,
respectively.

To use a font in math mode, it must have a font-family number and be
either the textfont for that number, the scriptfont for that number, or the
scriptscriptfont for that number.

Chapter 6 describes how to change fonts and how to load additional
fonts beyond TEX's standard set of 10-point **\rm**, **\it**, **\sl**, **\bf**, and **\tt**.
Chapter 7 shows how to load and use different font sizes.

Chapter 24 shows how to use math mode. Chapter 25 gives all the
symbols TEX uses in math mode and shows how to use them. Chapter 26
shows how to put together fractions, typeset multiline equations, include
equation numbers, and use similar display math TEXniques.

PART IV

STEEPER SLOPES

CHAPTER 28

Boxes

TEX uses boxes implicitly all the time. You can also use them explicitly to accomplish a variety of special tasks. A few such tasks are preventing line breaks or page breaks in awkward places, and putting text in unusual places on the page.

This and the next two chapters explain how to use boxes, control their size, and move them to a different place on the page. Boxes and modes are intertwined in TEX. There is no simple way of explaining them separately. The chapters about boxes contain brief references to TEX's modes. Chapter 33 explains modes more thoroughly and shows what they do with TEX's boxes.

To understand this chapter, you must be familiar with the following:

- sandwich-structure macros (Chapter 12),
- using **global** (page 169), and
- how TEX makes a page (Chapter 11).

 LATEX has several macros that create special kinds of boxes. See **mbox**, **makebox**, **fbox**, **framebox**, **parbox**, and the **minipage** environment in Section 5.4.3 on pages 96–100 of Lamport's LATEX book. You can also use any of TEX's boxes as described in this and the following chapters.

28.1   What Are TEX's Boxes?

As described in Chapter 11, boxes are rectangles with a baseline across their middle. They have height, depth, and width. The height of a box is how far it extends above the baseline. The depth is how far it extends below the baseline. The width is how far it extends horizontally. Boxes also have a reference point: the point where the baseline meets the left edge of the box.

The following box contains a "y" from a 25-point font. The height of this box is **11.51219pt**, its depth is **4.83777pt**, and its width is **13.93115pt**.[1]

reference point ⟶ y ⎯⎯⎯ baseline

When TEX is typesetting letters into words and words into lines and lines into pages, it does all this work with boxes. TEX views each letter as a box whose size is determined by the information in the font files. TEX sticks these character-boxes together horizontally to make words (thus the name *horizontal mode*) and puts glue between the words.

At the end of the paragraph, TEX breaks this long list of words plus glue into lines, and puts each line into an enclosing hbox (horizontal box). TEX then puts interlineskip glue between these hboxes and stacks them vertically on the page (thus the name *vertical mode*).

Any changes you make inside a box are local: They stay inside that box. For example, I typeset the large "y" above by saying

```
\hbox{\largefont\seethebox{y}}
```

This switch to **\largefont** stays inside the box. **\seethebox** is a special macro that I wrote for this book. It draws the lines of the enclosing box around the letter(s) inside it.

When you are inside a box, use **\global** if you need to make a change global (outside the box). For example, if you **\advance** a counter inside a box or want to change a reporter, type something like the following:

```
\vbox{...
    \global\advance\itemcounter by 1
    \global\hsize=6.125in
    ...}
```

28.2 Preventing Awkward Line Breaks with an Hbox

TEX's **\hbox** is a primitive. It takes one input: whatever you want to put inside the hbox.

The text inside an hbox is typeset according to the same rules for typesetting words within a paragraph, except that all the text stays on the same line. If the text inside the hbox is wider than the **\hsize**, it sticks out into the margin and TEX sends you an overfull hbox warning.

---

[1]No, I did not measure it; TEX gave me these dimensions. To find out the height, depth, and width of a box, use the primitives **\setbox**, **\ht**, **\dp**, and **\wd**. For example, make a test file that says **\setbox0=\hbox{text}** and **The height is \the\ht0, the depth is \the\dp0, the width is \the\wd0.** Then run TEX on this test file and look at the printout.

You can use \hbox to prevent TEX from choosing an awkward line-break point. This characteristic of an hbox is useful in several situations. One is in math mode. You can force TEX to choose a different line-break point by putting the math mode material inside the hbox. In the following example, TEX normally breaks the line after the equals sign.

```
\dots\ I traveled rather quickly to the post
office.  Since \hbox{$E=mc^2$}, I was relieved
to find all my matter intact.
```

> . . . I traveled rather quickly to the post office. Since $E = mc^2$, I was relieved to find all my matter intact.

A similar use for \hbox comes up when the last word on a page is hyphenated. This forces the reader to do extra work: remembering part of the word while turning the page. Placing this particular word in an hbox forces TEX to break the line in a different place. (See page 47 for an example of this).

Macros with \hbox to Prevent Line Breaks

You can also use \hbox to make sure that TEX never hyphenates a particular type of word in your document. TEX automatically does not hyphenate words starting with a capital letter, such as the names of people, streets, ships, programming languages, and the like. However, you might not want TEX to hyphenate other kinds of words, such as the names of control sequences. You might also want short pieces of computer code to stay on the same line. For these purposes, use \hbox in a macro instead of directly in your text.

The following improved version of our \code macro (page 70) takes one input: the text to be typeset in the \tt font inside the hbox.

```
\def\code#1{\leavevmode\hbox{\tt#1}}

To have \TeX\ make a \code{.dvi} file, type
\code{tex filename}.
```

> To have TEX make a .dvi file, type tex filename.

Thus, the entire instruction **tex filename** cannot be broken onto two separate lines.

\leavevmode is a plain TEX macro that starts a new paragraph if TEX happens to be in vertical (page-making) mode, but does nothing if TEX is in horizontal (paragraph-making) mode. If you do not include \textbf{\textbackslash leavevmode} in macros like \textbf{\textbackslash code} that start with an hbox, a Text by Itself Bug appears if one of these macros is the first thing in a paragraph. The following \textbf{\textbackslash oopsbox} macro takes one input: the text to be typeset in the emphasis font and placed inside an hbox.

```
\def\oopsbox#1{\hbox{\em#1}}

\oopsbox{Murphy} delights in crossing the i's
and dotting the t's.
```

> *Murphy*
> delights in crossing the i's and dotting the t's.

Text by Itself Bug

An **\hbox** can be used in any mode, so it does not start a new paragraph. When TEX is in horizontal (paragraph-making) mode, it adds the hbox to the list of words it is assembling for the paragraph. When TEX is in vertical (page-making) mode, it adds the hbox to the bottom of its current page, with the box's left edge against the left margin (as it did in the example above). TEX does not start a new paragraph until it encounters the text that follows the hbox (**"delights"** in the example above).

To fix this bug, we need to be sure that TEX is in horizontal (paragraph-making) mode before it typesets the **\hbox**. However, we cannot use \textbf{\textbackslash indent} at the beginning of the macro, because it always adds a \textbf{\textbackslash parindent} of white space, even if the \textbf{\textbackslash indent} appears in the middle of a paragraph. We cannot use \textbf{\textbackslash noindent}, because we might be at the beginning of a new paragraph and therefore need the \textbf{\textbackslash parindent}.

The \textbf{\textbackslash leavevmode} macro solves this problem. \textbf{\textbackslash leavevmode} does not start a new paragraph if TEX is already in horizontal mode, but does start one if TEX is in vertical mode. (See Chapter 33 for a full explanation of TEX's modes.)

LATEX's **\mbox** macro is equivalent to **\leavevmode\hbox**.

28.3   Preventing Awkward Page Breaks with a Vbox

TeX has two primitives that create a vbox (vertical box): **\vbox** and **\vtop**. Material inside either of these vboxes cannot be broken across pages.

For example, you might want to stop TeX from starting a new page in the middle of a small quotation. If there are only one or two such places in your document, go ahead and put the quotation (or other paragraph) inside a vbox directly, just as we put a word inside an hbox to prevent an awkward line break. (Putting only part of a paragraph into the vbox does not work. If you try it, you get truly strange effects.)

However, it is often easier and simpler to include the vbox in your macro whenever you want to keep material on the same page. The following **\samePageQuote** macro takes one input: the quotation text that goes inside the vbox and therefore stays on the same page.

```
\def\samePageQuote#1{\vtop{\narrower
    \noindent #1\strut}}

\samePageQuote{Experience is the child of
Thought, and Thought is the child of Action.  We
cannot learn men from books [Benjamin Disraeli,
{\em Vivian Grey}, 1826].}
```

> Experience is the child of Thought, and Thought is the child of Action. We cannot learn men from books [Benjamin Disraeli, *Vivian Grey*, 1826].

\samePageQuote uses a **\vtop** instead of a **\vbox** to prevent a Disappearing Topskip Bug (pages 185 and 291). The **\strut** prevents a Scrunched Baseline Bug (page 291).

28.4   Choosing between \vbox and \vtop

The only difference between **\vbox** and **\vtop** is the relative size of their height and depth. Both of the vboxes can expand vertically to hold more than one line of text. In a **\vbox**, the height expands; in a **\vtop**, the depth expands. The following example shows a **\vbox** on the left and a **\vtop** on the right. The line through the boxes shows their baselines, which are aligned.

This is a vbox. Its *baseline* is the same as the baseline of the bottom line of text in the box. Its *depth* is the same as the depth of the largest descender in the bottom line of the box. Its *height* expands to hold the rest of the text. (If the bottom line has no descender, the depth is zero points.)

This is a vtop box. Its *baseline* is the same as the baseline of the first line of text in the box. Its *height* is the same as the height of the tallest letter on the top line of the box. Its *depth* expands to hold the rest of the text.

Thus, use **\vbox** to align the bottom line of a vbox with other text, and **\vtop** to align the top line of a vbox with other text. (This is why we used **\vtop** to put a paragraph of text into a table in Section 20.3.)

TeX's vboxes can be used in any mode. When TeX is in vertical mode, it adds the vbox to the bottom of its current page. When TeX is in horizontal mode (as it is in the examples above and below), it adds the vbox to the list of words it is assembling for the paragraph.

```
\TeX\ assembles boxes
%
\vtop{\hsize=70pt\noindent\it
of different sizes and shapes}
%
\vbox{\hsize=78pt\noindent\sl
having as many words as you wish}
%
into paragraphs and pages---as this example
clearly shows.
```

TeX assembles boxes *of different sizes and shapes* having as many words as you wish into paragraphs and pages—as this example clearly shows.

In the example above, TeX aligned the boxes along their baselines. First, the characters **\TeX\ assembles boxes** are treated as ordinary characters in an ordinary paragraph. Next, the baseline of the **\vtop** box is the same as the baseline for **of different sizes**. Finally, the baseline of the **\vbox** is the same as the baseline for **words as you wish**.

Specifying the \hsize inside the vbox controls the width of that vbox, as explained in Chapter 29. Also, you do not need a \par at the end of a vbox to end the paragraph in that vbox.

Oops! The Topskip Glue Disappeared

Another reason for using \vtop instead of \vbox is to prevent the Disappearing Topskip Bug.

If you have a \vbox instead of a \vtop at the top of a page, and if the \vbox has more than one line of text, you can get a Disappearing Topskip Bug if you increased the \topskip glue.

Disappearing Topskip Bug

TeX puts glue between the top edge of the page's body vbox (containing the text on that page) and the first box of text on the page. TeX then adjusts this glue so that the baseline of the box of text is a \topskip away from the top edge of the enclosing vbox.

TeX does this in order to place the first baseline of text at the same place on each page. However, this allows the height of a \vbox to reduce the size of this glue. Thus, if the \vbox has more than one line of text, TeX places the top of the vbox too close to the \headline.

Since the height of a \vtop box is the same height as its first line of text, it does not stick up into the \topskip area (unless something in that line is very tall). Thus, if a macro containing a vbox might be the first thing on a page, use \vtop instead of \vbox.

Putting \struts in Your Vboxes

The example above also shows what happens when you do not put a \strut into your vbox: a Scrunched Baseline Bug. There is too little white space between **and shapes** and **pages---as**.

Scrunched Baseline Bug

When a vbox has more than one line of text, the height + depth of the box is larger than the \baselineskip. This means that TeX places the vbox too close to the box either above or below it.

In a \vtop box, the additional lines of text are below the baseline, so the bottom of the \vtop box touches the box below it. In a \vbox, the additional lines are above the baseline, so the top of the box touches the box above it. In either case, the lines of text in adjacent boxes are too close.

To fix this bug, we need to increase the depth of a \vtop (or the height of a \vbox) to move this scrunched baseline the correct distance away from the baseline on the adjacent line. We do that by adding a \strut at the beginning or end of the box. In the example above, the \strut goes after **and shapes**.

```
\vtop{...
of different sizes and shapes\strut}
```

In a \vbox, the problem is at the other end of the box, so we put the \strut at the beginning instead of the end.

```
\vbox{...\strut
having as many words as you wish}
```

If you might change your mind later about which type of box to use, put \struts at both the beginning and the end. They do no harm and can often do some good.

The \strut is an invisible line (rule) whose height + depth is the same as the \baselineskip. Section 31.6 explains the \strut and how to adjust its size.

Make sure you change the size of the \strut whenever you change the \baselineskip. Section 31.6 shows how to do this. A good place to change both the \baselineskip and the size of the strut is in macros that change the font size (see the bottom of **\twelvepoint** on page 282).

28.5   Making Sandwich Macros with Vboxes

Whenever you have more than a few lines of text, it makes sense to use the sandwich structure instead of a jelly-doughnut macro. (The sandwich and jelly-doughnut macro structures are described in Chapter 12.) However, if you have an open brace ({) to begin the vbox's input, you must also have a matching close brace (}) in that same definition.

To solve this problem, Knuth created **\bgroup** and **\egroup**. These are clones of the open brace and close brace. Like **\begingroup** and **\endgroup**, they can also be put into separate macro definitions.

```
\def\beginSamePageQuote{\displaybreak
    \vtop\bgroup \narrower\noindent}
\def\endSamePageQuote{\strut\egroup\displaybreak}
```

Because they are clones, you can always use **\bgroup** instead of {, and **\egroup** instead of }. However, you cannot use **\begingroup** or **\endgroup** in any situation where TeX expects to find an open brace or close brace.

28.6   Boxes and Modes

\hbox starts *restricted horizontal mode*, which is similar to TeX's ordinary horizontal (paragraph-making) mode but has a few differences. Both \vbox and \vtop start *internal vertical mode*, which is similar to TeX's ordinary vertical (page-making) mode but again has a few differences. Chapter 33 explains these similarities and differences in detail.

Review and Related Matters

This chapter describes TeX's boxes and shows the basic methods of using them. Changes inside a box are local to the box. To make such changes global, use \global. Text inside an hbox stays on the same line; text inside a vbox stays on the same page. Both can be used in macros.

The control sequences \bgroup and \egroup make it possible to write macros that use boxes in sandwich-structure macros. Use \bgroup instead of { when you begin a box in the begin-sandwich macro. Use \egroup instead of { to end that box in the corresponding end-sandwich macro.

The \vbox has an expandable height, and its baseline is the same as the bottom line of text in the box. The \vtop has an expandable depth, and its baseline is the same as the top line of text in the box.

A box at the beginning of a paragraph creates a Text by Itself Bug. Use \leavevmode to make sure that TeX is in horizontal mode. A \vbox at the beginning of a page can create a Disappearing Topskip Bug. Use a \vtop instead. Use a \strut at the beginning of a \vbox and at the end of a \vtop box to prevent getting a Scrunched Baseline Bug. Make sure you change the size of the \strut when you change your \baselineskip (Section 31.6 shows how to do this).

Chapter 29 says how to control the size of your boxes. Chapter 30 describes methods of moving boxes to different places on the page. Chapter 33 explains TeX's horizontal, vertical, and math modes in detail.

CHAPTER 29

Controlling the Size of Your Boxes

The previous chapter showed how to make boxes. This one shows how to control their size. To understand this chapter, you must be familiar with the following:

- keywords (Chapter 7),
- glue (Chapter 10),
- meat-and-potatoes and jelly-doughnut macros (Chapter 12), and
- boxes (Chapter 28).

 LaTeX's \makebox and \framebox can take optional inputs that control their width. \parbox and the minipage environment both require an input that specifies their width. Only one of LaTeX's box-making macros takes an input that controls its vertical size: \raisebox can take two optional inputs for its height and depth.

29.1   The Natural Size of a Box

An \hbox expands in width to cover the characters inside it plus the natural space of its interword glue. Therefore, the unstretched glue inside an hbox is likely to be *narrower than the stretched glue* on the same line outside that hbox. The height and depth of an hbox are the same as the largest height and depth of the characters (or boxes) inside it.

A \vbox expands in height to hold whatever is inside it, usually the hboxes created for the paragraph(s) it contains. Its depth is the same as the deepest box on its bottom line, usually the depth of the deepest character on that bottom line. A \vtop expands in depth to hold whatever is inside it, usually the hboxes of one or more paragraphs. Its height is the same as the highest box on its top line, usually the height of the tallest letter on that top line.

The width of a vbox is the same as the widest box inside it. Since text inside a vbox is typeset as one or more paragraphs, the natural width of a vbox is generally the same as the \hsize. It becomes wider than the \hsize if the paragraph(s) inside the vbox contain an overfull hbox.

A vbox can be narrower than the \hsize under two circumstances. You can specify a smaller width using the TeXniques described in the next section. Also, if you nest other boxes inside the vbox (see Section 30.4), its natural width is the same as the widest of these boxes.

29.2   Specifying a Particular Size for a Box

Instead of allowing your boxes to expand to their natural width, height, or depth, you can specify the size you want. The keyword **to** says how big to make the box. The keyword **spread** says how much to add to the box's natural size.

In the examples in the rest of this chapter, the \hbox, \vbox, and \vtop control sequences did not draw the lines around the boxes. I made them myself (using TeX's \hrule and \vrule) so you can see the edges of these boxes.

For an hbox, you can specify the width. The following example shows three hboxes. The first is **2.5in** wide. The second is **1in** wider than its natural width. The third is its natural width; it shows the natural width of the text inside the second hbox so you can compare the widths of the second and third hboxes.

```
\hbox to 2.5in{This hbox is 2.5in wide.}

\medskip\noindent
\hbox spread 1in{This hbox is 1in wider than normal.}

\medskip\noindent
\hbox{This hbox is 1in wider than normal.}
```

This   hbox   is   2.5in   wide.

This   hbox   is   1in   wider   than   normal.

This hbox is 1in wider than normal.

For a vbox, you can specify the total height + depth. The following example shows two vboxes. The first is **.75in** from the top edge to the bottom edge. The second is **0.25in** deeper than its natural depth.

```
\vbox to .75in{The height + depth of this box
totals .75in, no matter how much or how little I
put in it.
\vfil
Its width is the hsize.}

\medskip
\vtop spread 0.25in{The height + depth of this
box is 0.25in larger than normal, and its width
is the hsize.}
```

> The height + depth of this box totals .75in, no matter how much or how little I put in it.
>
>
> Its width is the hsize.

> The height + depth of this box is 0.25in larger than normal, and its width is the hsize.

(The printout part of all the examples has a special **\hsize** of **255pt**.)

29.3 Specifying Both Horizontal and Vertical Size

Sometimes you need to control both the width and the height + depth of a box. To do this, use a vbox, and specify its width.

To control the width of a vbox, specify a different **\hsize** inside the box. To stop TeX from adding paragraph indentation at the beginning of the text in the vbox, use **\noindent**.

```
\vbox{\hsize=3in\noindent
Some use a shoebox as their cash box, which is
probably a better strategy than burying one's
cash in the sandbox.}
```

> Some use a shoebox as their cash box, which is probably a better strategy than burying one's cash in the sandbox.

To write a macro that specifies a box's width and height + depth, we use a **\vtop** in case it appears at the top of a page, the **to** keyword to specify the height + depth, and **\hsize** to specify the width. The following **\rectangle** macro takes three inputs—for the width, height + depth, and text.[1]

```
\def\rectangle#1#2#3{%
%    #1 is width
%    #2 is height + depth
%    #3 is text
    \vtop to #2{\hsize=#1
                \noindent #3}}
```

Putting information about a macro's inputs into its definition is always a good idea, especially when there are many inputs. Then you do not need to puzzle through the definition to remember what the inputs are for.

The lines in the following example show the edges of our **\rectangle** box.

```
\rectangle{3in}{0.5in}{When I get on my soapbox,
I can fill this bandbox to overflowing with the
words that tumble from my mouth.  I'm fortunate
that no one boxes my ears for this.}
```

When I get on my soapbox, I can fill this band-box to overflowing with the words that tumble from my mouth. I'm fortunate that no one boxes my ears for this.

In this example, the text does not fit inside the box. It overflows into the space below, making an overfull vbox. When TEX makes an overfull vbox, it sends you an error message. The message for this particular box looked like this:

```
Overfull \vbox (6.80945pt too high) detected at line 186.
```

Use a **\rectangle** when you want to center some text inside a specific area. The following example shows how to place centered text inside a **\rectangle**. (Again, these control sequences do not draw the lines. The only purpose of these lines is to show the size of the box.)

The **\vfils** center the text vertically. **\centerline** is a preview of coming attractions: a plain TEX macro that places a single line of text in the middle of the **\hsize**. **\centerline** is described in the next section.

---

[1] I used the first input for the width and the second input for the height + depth because that matches the order of Cartesian coordinates: x, y.

```
\rectangle{3in}{0.5in}{\vfil
    \centerline{My hatbox}
    \vfil}
```

My hatbox

29.4   Some Special Hboxes with Special Sizes

Making specially sized boxes is a very useful TEXnique, so useful that TEX already has six of them: **\line**, **\leftline**, **\rightline**, **\centerline**, **\rlap**, and **\llap**.

The \line Hbox

\line is a plain TEX macro that makes an hbox the same width as the **\hsize**. Here is its definition and an example of how to use it.

```
\def\line{\hbox to \hsize}

\line{Put this line---\hfil---in your toolbox.}
```

Put this line—   —in your toolbox.

If the text plus glue inside a **\line** is narrower than the hbox, the last piece of text is typeset flush against the right side of the box and the interword glue is stretched to fit. Thus, if we remove the **\hfil** from the **\line** above, we get an underfull hbox because TEX stretches the glue farther than its **plus** amount.

If the text plus glue inside a **\line** is wider than the hbox, we get an overfull hbox. The extra text sticks out into the right margin.

\line is not a jelly-doughnut macro, even though the example seems to show it taking an input. Instead, **\line** is a meat-and-potatoes macro, and the text that follows **\line** is actually an input to **\hbox to \hsize**. When TEX finds **\line**, it first expands the macro to its definition: **\hbox to \hsize**. TEX then continues and finds the input for **\hbox** that it expects.

LATEX's **\line** is a macro that draws a line in the **picture** environment. It has no relationship at all to plain TEX's **\line** macro.

\leftline, \rightline, and \centerline

\leftline, \rightline, and \centerline do what their names imply. Each puts text inside a \line, and places that text at the left, right, or center of that \line. Here are some examples of \leftline, \rightline, and \centerline.

```
\leftline{Put your left foot forward.}
\rightline{So right you are.}
\centerline{Fence-straddling is an art form.}
```

Put your left foot forward.

So right you are.

Fence-straddling is an art form.

These three plain TeX macros use \line in their definitions. All of them need to take inputs, because they put glue inside their \lines. The jelly-doughnut structure is the simplest way of making sure that the glue and the text are positioned properly.

Here are the definitions of \leftline, \rightline, and \centerline. These three macros use \hss, a special kind of glue that is explained below.

```
\def\leftline#1{\line{#1\hss}}
\def\rightline#1{\line{\hss#1}}
\def\centerline#1{\line{\hss#1\hss}}
```

\hss is a primitive. It makes infinitely stretchable and shrinkable horizontal glue that is equivalent to **0pt plus 1fil minus 1fil** glue. Its vertical counterpart is called \vss.

```
\hbox to 2.5in{This special glue\hss is stretchy.}

\medskip
\hbox to 2.5in{It also shrinks as far\hss
    as you need it to shrink.}

\medskip
\vbox to 0.5in{\noindent The vertical variety of
    \vss\noindent
    this special glue is also stretchy.}

\medskip
\vbox to 0.5in{\noindent The vertical variety also
    shrinks as far as you need it to shrink.  Thus,
    \vss\noindent
    the contents of the box are never larger than
    the size of the box, even if something winds
    up overlapping.}
```

| This special glue is stretchy. |

| It also shrinks asafaryou need it to shrink. |

| The vertical variety of

this special glue is also stretchy. |

| The vertical variety also shrinks as far as you need it to shrink. Thus,
the contents of the box are never larger than the size of
the box, even if something winds up overlapping. |

These two special glues can be used only inside a box. If you use them in horizontal or vertical mode (inside an ordinary paragraph or between paragraphs), TeX sends you an error message.

Using \hss in \leftline, \rightline, and \centerline makes it impossible for them to be overfull or underfull, no matter how much or little text you put inside them. If the text is narrower than the \hsize, the \hss glue stretches; if the text is wider than the \hsize, the \hss glue shrinks down past 0pt to compensate.

\leftline, \rightline, and \centerline do work correctly in LaTeX. Lamport defined another macro that he uses instead of \line for his definitions of these three box-making macros.

In the examples on page 300, the text was narrower than the \hsize. In the examples below, the text is wider. The lines show the actual sizes and positions of these hboxes.

```
\leftline{At supermarkets and theatre queues,
    the line forms on the left.}

\medskip\noindent
\rightline{In school, the correct response is
    rewarded as an indication of mastery.}

\medskip\noindent
\centerline{When following the yellow stripe in
    the center of the road, be cautious!}
```

> At supermarkets and theatre queues, the line forms on the left.

> In school, the correct response is rewarded as an indication of mastery.

> When following the yellow stripe in the center of the road, be cautious!

In these three examples, the **\hss** glue at the ends of the hboxes shrinks, and thereby reduces the width of these hboxes to match the **\hsize**.

\rlap and \llap

\rlap and **\llap** make hboxes that are **0pt** wide. These plain TEX macros can put one piece of text over another, put notes in the margins, and perform similar kinds of tasks. The **\rlap** macro puts its input on the right of its position on the page, and the **\llap** macro on the left.

The following example uses **\rlap** to put a slash through the next character.

```
All music boxes are on \rlap{/}sale this week!
```

> All music boxes are on /sale this week!

Here are the definitions of **\rlap** and **\llap**. Each takes one input: the text that overlaps to the right or the left.

```
\def\rlap#1{\hbox to 0pt{#1\hss}}
\def\llap#1{\hbox to 0pt{\hss#1}}
```

In these two macros, the **\hss** glue shrinks to a negative amount. Since the hboxes are specified as having **0pt** width, TEX shrinks this glue so that

$$\text{width of text} + \text{shrinking glue} = 0 \text{ points}$$

Therefore,

$$\text{shrinking glue} = -\text{width of text}$$

In **\rlap**, the shrinkable glue is on the right of the input, so the text in the box flows rightward—into/over/on top of this shrinking glue. (Yes, the metaphor is a bit sticky here. Just keep in mind that the text always goes on the same side as the glue: rightward, leftward, upward, or downward. If the **\hss** or **\vss** glue is on both sides, the text is centered.)

Knuth's definition of **\item** uses **\llap** to place the item's label an **\enspace** to the left of the text.[2] You can use this same TEXnique to put an asterisk or other identifier in the margin at the beginning of a paragraph.

---

[2]More precisely, Knuth's **\item** macro uses **\textindent**, and **\textindent** uses **\llap**.

For example, an asterisk can indicate which exercises have answers in an appendix.

```
\def\answered{\leavevmode\llap{$*$\enspace}}
\def\exercise{\leavevmode{\bf Exercise
   \theExerciseNumber}\eol}

\answered\exercise
If a jukebox contains $R$ records, and the
coffee shop contains $N$ teenagers, how long
will it take for the teenagers to play all the
records?
```

> * **Exercise 29.1**
> If a jukebox contains R records, and the coffee shop contains N teenagers, how long will it take for the teenagers to play all the records?

Both **\answered** and **\exercise** must start with **\leavevmode**, because either of them might be the first thing in the paragraph (see the Text by Itself Bug, page 288). When **\answered** is first, the **\leavevmode** in **\exercise** has no effect. **\leavevmode** only nudges TEX into horizontal (paragraph-making) mode if TEX is in a vertical mode. **\eol** is our end-of-line macro on page 108.

Review and Related Matters

This chapter shows various ways of controlling the size of your boxes. The keywords **to** and **spread** affect the width of an hbox or the height + depth of a vbox. To change the width of a vbox, specify a different **\hsize** inside the vbox.

Since an **\hbox to \hsize** is such a useful tool, TEX has four of them: **\line**, **\leftline**, **\rightline**, and **\centerline**. A **0pt** wide hbox allows you to overlap things. TEX has two such hboxes: **\rlap** and **\llap**.

Chapter 28 describes TEX's boxes and shows the basic methods of using them. Chapter 30 describes methods of moving boxes to different places on the page. Chapter 33 explains TEX's horizontal, vertical, and math modes in detail.

CHAPTER 30

Moving Your Boxes

There are two basic methods of putting a box in a nonstandard place on the page. You can skip to the place you want and then do the box, or you can use one of TeX's four box-moving primitives: \raise, \lower, \moveright, and \moveleft.

TeX's boxes can be used in any mode, but the control sequences that move them cannot. To place your boxes where you want them, you must know which mode TeX is in and how to change from one mode to another. Chapter 33 explains TeX's modes in detail. I recommend that you read it in addition to the material in this chapter.

The next three sections show how to move boxes in each of TeX's modes. Section 30.4 shows how to nest one box inside another.

To understand this chapter, you must be familiar with the following:

- making and using new dimension reporters (Chapters 9 and 10),
- using fillers, especially \hfil, \hfill, \vfil, and \vfill (Chapter 10),
- boxes (Chapter 28), and
- modes (Chapter 33).

 LaTeX has a \raisebox macro (see page 100 of Lamport's LaTeX book). Otherwise, use the TeXniques described in this chapter.

30.1 Moving Boxes in Math Mode

To move a box in either of TeX's two math modes, use the methods described below for horizontal mode.

In either of the horizontal modes (making a paragraph or inside an hbox), TeX sticks letters and boxes together horizontally, along their baselines. If there is a space between the letters or boxes, TeX also adds interword glue. To move a box horizontally, use **\hskip**. (You can also use **\hfil** or **\hfill**.) To move a box vertically, use **\raise** or **\lower**.

\hskip, **\hfil**, **\hfill**, **\raise**, and **\lower** are all *inherently horizontal*. If you use them in a vertical mode, TeX changes to horizontal mode. However, you can use **\hskip**, **\hfil**, **\hfill**, **\raise**, and **\lower** in TeX's math modes.

Many business letters are done entirely flushleft, but personal letters often place the date and closing on the right side of the page. Moving the date is simple. Since the date and closing need to be the same distance from the left margin, we make a new reporter called **\letterskip** to remember this dimension and make sure our letters are consistent. We also use **\noindent** in our **\date** macro to make sure that TeX does not add a **\parindent** as well.

```
\newdimen\letterskip \letterskip=3.5in
\def\date{\noindent \hskip\letterskip}

\date 1 April 1984
\beginaddress
Dr.\ Ken Essex \dots
```

> 1 April 1984
>
> Dr. Ken Essex . . .

The **\letterskip** in this example is **2.5in** instead of **3.5in** because of the size of this book's page.

Now we do the same thing for the closing, except that we move an entire vbox instead of just the date.

```
\def\sincerely{\bigskip
   \noindent \hskip\letterskip
   \vtop{\hsize=2in \noindent
        Sincerely,
        \vskip 3pc \noindent
        Ell O. Quent}}
```

\bigskip both ends the previous paragraph (in case we forget to type a blank line above **\sincerely**) and adds vertical space to the page. **\noindent** nudges TeX into horizontal mode and makes sure that TeX does not add paragraph indentation.

Saying **\hsize=2in** inside the **\vtop** makes sure that this vbox does not stick out into the margin and create an overfull hbox. When we said **\noindent\hskip\letterskip**, we began a new paragraph, so this example puts the vbox inside a paragraph. If the **\letterskip** plus the width of the **\vtop** box is wider than the **\hsize**, this line turns into an overfull hbox.

Now we can use **\sincerely** in a letter. (The **\letterskip** in the following example is also **2.5in**.)

```
An SASE is enclosed, and I look forward to seeing
it in my mailbox.

\sincerely
```

>   An SASE is enclosed, and I look forward to seeing it in
>   my mailbox.

>   Sincerely,

>   Ell O. Quent

\raise and **\lower** are primitives that move a box up or down. They need two inputs: a dimension and a box. For a few scattered special effects, go ahead and use them directly.

```
\dots\ going up into the \raise5pt\hbox{witness
box}, and then down to look under the \lower 5pt
\hbox{icebox}.
```

>   . . . going up into the ^{witness box}, and then down to look
>   under the _{icebox}.

When you write a macro that you plan to use in a horizontal or math mode, use **\hskip**, **\hfil**, **\hfill**, **\raise**, and **\lower** to move boxes in that macro. Here is a macro that makes some **\stairs**.

```
\def\stairs{s\raise2pt\hbox{t}\raise4pt
    \hbox{a}\raise6pt\hbox{i}\raise8pt
    \hbox{r}\raise10pt\hbox{s}}

Take these \stairs\ to the press box.
```

Take these s$t^{a^{i^{r^s}}}$ to the press box.

Without the control space after \stairs, TEX does not typeset a space between the box and to.

30.3   Moving Boxes in Vertical Mode

In either of the vertical modes (making a page or inside a vbox), TEX stacks the boxes vertically, putting their left edges against the left margin.

To move a box vertically, put a \vskip before the box. (To move upward, give \vskip a negative dimension: \vskip−20pt.) You can also use \vfil or \vfill to put infinitely stretchable glue above or below a box. To move a box horizontally, use \moveright or \moveleft. \moveright and \moveleft are primitives and take two inputs: a dimension and a box. These control sequences are all *inherently vertical*. You cannot use them in TEX's horizontal or math modes.

Our \sincerely macro moved the box in horizontal mode. The following \truly macro accomplishes this same task in vertical mode. Here, \letterskip is the input for \moveright instead of \hskip.

```
\def\truly{\bigskip
   \moveright\letterskip
   \vtop{\hsize=2in \noindent
        Very truly yours,
        \vskip 3pc \noindent
        Eppie Sode}}
```

The only significant difference between \truly and \sincerely is on the second line—the mode used to move the box.

When you write a macro that you plan to use in a vertical mode, use \vskip, \vfil, \vfill, \moveright, and \moveleft to move a box.

The following \FigureBox macro takes two inputs. The first input specifies the height + depth of the vbox. The second input is the figure title.

```
\def\FigureBox#1#2{\par
   \vtop to #1{%
   \vfil
   \moveright 1.5in\hbox{Figure goes here: #2}}
   \vfil}}
```

Everything except the text inside the \hbox is done in a vertical mode.

The \par at the beginning of the macro definition makes \FigureBox goof-proof. It does not matter if someone forgets to put a blank line above \FigureBox.

```
\dots\ completely ruined my voice box.
```

```
\FigureBox{3pc}{Filigree snuffbox}
```

     . . . completely ruined my voice box.

                   Figure goes here: Filigree snuffbox

30.4   Nesting One Box inside Another

As the **\FigureBox** macro shows, you can put any of TEX's boxes inside
another box. This TEXnique of nesting boxes inside other boxes often makes
a simpler macro.

For example, instead of specifying an **\hsize** of **2in** in the **\sincerely**
(page 306) and **\truly** (page 308) macros, we can write a general **\closing**
macro that nests two hboxes inside the vbox. **\closing** takes two inputs: the
closing words and the sender's name.

```
\def\closing#1#2{\bigskip
   \moveright\letterskip
   \vtop{\hbox{#1,}
         \vskip 3pc
         \hbox{#2}}}
```

Since the natural size of an hbox is the same as the text inside it, we do
not need to specify the **\hsize**. Also, since an hbox does not cause TEX to
start a new paragraph, we do not need the **\noindent**s.

In the following example, the **\letterskip** is again **2.5in**.


```
\dots\ and thanks so much for the lovely saucebox.
```

```
\closing{Yours truly}{M. Penny Trubble}
```

     . . . and thanks so much for the lovely saucebox.

                       Yours truly,

                       M. Penny Trubble

You can also nest vboxes inside an hbox, or vboxes inside a vbox.

Review and Related Matters

This chapter shows how to \raise and \lower your boxes in horizontal mode and how to use \moveleft and \moveright in vertical mode. You can also use \hskip, \hfil, and \hfill in horizontal mode to put horizontal white space before a box. Similarly, \vskip, \vfil, and \vfill can put vertical white space above and below a box. Using a negative dimension with \vskip moves upward instead of down. This chapter also shows how to nest one or more boxes inside another box.

Chapter 28 describes TEX's boxes and shows the basic methods of using them. Chapter 29 shows how to control the size of your boxes. Chapter 33 explains TEX's horizontal, vertical, and math modes in detail.

CHAPTER 31

Drawing Lines (Rules) in Your Text

Lines on the page have an immediate visual impact: They separate one part of the page or text from another. This makes them a powerful tool. This chapter shows how to put them into your text.

Since the word *line* can also mean a line of type, printers and typesetters use the word *rule* instead of *line*—and TeX does, too. The words *rule* and *ruler* both come from a Latin word meaning "straightedge." TeX has two kinds of rules: horizontal (**hrule**) and vertical (**vrule**).

To understand this chapter, you must be familiar with the following:

- using keywords (Chapter 7),

- adding space to the line or page with **hskip** and **vskip**, (Chapters 9 and 10), and

- making and using dimension reporters (Chapters 9 and 10).

Some familiarity with TeX's boxes (Chapters 28 and 29) is occasionally helpful but not necessary. A modest understanding of TeX's modes (Chapter 33) is also helpful.

31.1 Using Horizontal Rules

Putting a rule across the page is easy. Type an **hrule** between paragraphs, and put some **vskip** space above and below the rule.

```
\dots\ following the golden rule.

\medskip\hrule\medskip

Among the Aldebarans, however, \dots
```

. . . following the golden rule.

Among the Aldebarans, however, . . .

You Can Specify a Rule's Height, Depth, and Width

\hrule is a primitive. You can change its size with three keywords: **height**, **depth**, and **width**.

These keywords need a dimension as input. As usual, it does not matter whether you put a space between the keyword and the dimension. Also, you can specify these keywords in any order you want.

```
\medskip \hrule height 3pt   width 2in
\medskip \hrule depth1pt      height0pt   width1in
\medskip \hrule height1.5pt depth1.5pt width 2in
\medskip \hrule width 5pt    height 5pt
```

Naturally, you can also use a dimension reporter as the input for these keywords.

```
How shall we subdue the ruling passions?

\hrule width\parindent

This question has no easy answer.
```

How shall we subdue the ruling passions?
This question has no easy answer.

Oops!

TeX does not put any space between an **\hrule** and the text above or below it, or between two adjacent **\hrule**s. You must add space to separate an **\hrule** from the text, or to separate two **\hrule**s from each other.

TeX places each line of a paragraph in an hbox. The natural height of an hbox is the same as the tallest letter (or box) inside it, and the natural depth of an hbox is the same as the deepest letter (or box) inside it. Thus, a rule above an hbox touches the tallest letters in that box, and a rule below an hbox touches the deepest letters in that box.

31.2   Using Vertical Rules

TeX also has a **\vrule**. This primitive is designed to be used inside paragraphs instead of between them. If you use **\vrule** in a vertical mode, TeX starts a new paragraph. (Chapter 33 describes how TeX changes modes.) Again, you must add space to separate the **\vrule** from the text, or to separate two **\vrule**s from one another.

```
The rule of the road in the U.S.A.\quad
\vrule\thinspace\vrule\quad
is to drive on the right of the yellow line.
```

> The rule of the road in the U.S.A. ‖ is to drive on the right of the yellow line.

Making a Short, Multiple-Choice Rule

You can specify the size of a **\vrule** in the same way as an **\hrule**. Since you cannot use an **\hrule** inside a paragraph, use a **\vrule** to make check-off-your-choice rules.

```
\def\checkRule{\vrule
    height 0.4pt depth 0pt width 1pc}

Was Charlemagne a ruler \checkRule\ a traveling
singer \checkRule\ or a horse trainer
\checkRule~?
```

> Was Charlemagne a ruler ___ a traveling singer ___ or a horse trainer ___ ?

31.3   Making Fill-in-the-Blank Rules

The difficulty with specifying the width of a **\vrule** is that you do not always know how wide the rule should be. For example, the rules on a form after **Name** and **Address** should extend to the margin, but measuring those widths is a nuisance and cannot be entirely accurate.

To solve this problem, TeX has **\hrulefill**, a plain TeX macro that you can use in a paragraph or hbox (either of TeX's horizontal modes).

```
{\baselineskip=24pt
\noindent
Name \hrulefill\break
\line{Address \hrulefill}\par}
\noindent
(Please print clearly.)
```

Name ⸻⸻⸻⸻⸻⸻⸻⸻⸻

Address ⸻⸻⸻⸻⸻⸻⸻⸻
(Please print clearly.)

\hrulefill acts like glue. Something must pull on it to stretch it across the space you want to fill. This example shows two different ways of stretching the rule (or glue).

- In horizontal (paragraph-making) mode:

    \break forces TeX to break the line at that point, so it also pulls the **\hrulefill** to the end of that line. Without that **\break**, TeX typesets only the **Name**, an interword space, and the **\line** with the **Address** and **\hrulefill**. (The **Name** plus the interword space plus the **\line** are wider than the **\hsize**, so TeX also typesets an overfull hbox and sends you a warning.)

- In restricted horizontal mode (inside an **\hbox**):

    Since the **\line** hbox is the same width as the **\hsize**, TeX stretches the **\hrulefill** to fill the hbox in the same way that it ordinarily fills the right side of a **\line** with glue.

\hrulefill is one particular kind of *leader*—something that leads the eye across a space. Tables of contents sometimes use a row of dots to accomplish this same purpose. **\dotfill** is a plain TeX macro that fills a space with periods.

```
\line{Julius Caesar \dotfill\ 37}
\line{MacBeth \dotfill\ 296}
```

Julius Caesar 37
MacBeth 296

Both **\hrulefill** and **\dotfill** are made with **\leaders**—a primitive that fills a space with multiple copies of a box or rule.[1]

31.4   The Usual Size of TEX's Rules

Unless you specify otherwise, the height, depth, and width of TEX's **\hrule** and **\vrule** are as follows:

	\hrule	\vrule
height	0.4pt	⇑
depth	0.0pt	⇓
width	⟺	0.4pt

In the table above, the arrows show that the rule goes all the way to the edge of the box that encloses it. In the "golden rule" example on page 312, the enclosing box is a vbox in the **\showPrintout** macro that I wrote for this book, so the **\hrule** was the same width as the **\printoutwidth**, my reporter for the **\hsize** inside that vbox. In the "rule of the road" example on page 313, the enclosing box was the hbox containing that line of text in the paragraph, so the **\vrule**s were the same height and depth as the text.

31.5   Making Invisible Rules

To be visible, a rule must have both a positive width and a positive height + depth (*positive* means larger than **0pt**). Thus, there are two ways of making a rule invisible: with a **0pt** dimension or with a negative dimension. Invisible rules are helpful in a variety of tasks, such as the following:

- A **\vrule** with a negative width acts like a backspace.
- An invisible **\hrule** above or below a **\vskip** changes the amount of space that TEX puts between the rule and the text on the other side of the **\vskip**.
- A **\strut** is an invisible **\vrule** that we can use to make a box's height + depth at least as large as the **\baselineskip**.

Removing Unwanted Space from a Vskip

Book designers often specify an exact amount of vertical space above and below section headings. If your **\section** macro begins with a **\vskip** or **\vglue** and continues with a box or a **\noindent**ed paragraph, you can tear

---

[1]See *The TEXbook*, pp. 223–25, to learn how to use **\leaders**.

your hair out trying to get rid of the seemingly extra space in the printout between the previous section's text and the new section's title.

For example, the following **\extraVspaceSection** macro places more than $1/4$ inch between the bottom of the **p** in **spaced** and the top of **Moon Walkers**. It also places more than $1/8$ inch of space between the bottom of **Moon Walkers** and the top of **Upon lunar**. **\extraVspaceSection** takes one input: the text for the section title.

```
\def\extraVspaceSection#1{%
   \vskip 0.25in
   \hbox{\bf#1}
   \vskip 0.125in}
\dots\ spaced-out cadets.

\extraVspaceSection{Moon Walkers}

Upon lunar arrival, walkers must move carefully
and cautiously.  Jumping is never wise.
```

. . . spaced-out cadets.

Moon Walkers

Upon lunar arrival, walkers must move carefully and cautiously. Jumping is never wise.

Too Much Space Bug

A **\vskip** between boxes adds a specific amount of space between their baselines. Thus, if you put a **\vskip 12pt** between two paragraphs when the **\baselineskip** is **12pt**, the distance between the baselines on each side of the **\vskip** is **24pt**.

Normally, this is exactly what you want. When you need a specific amount of space between the bottom and top edges of two lines of text, however, the **\vskip** adds a smidgeon too much space.

To fix this bug, put an invisible **\hrule** between the text and the **\vskip**. TEX always typesets an **\hrule** snugly against the box(es) above or below it. To make an invisible **\hrule**, we give it either a negative or a **0pt** width.

```
\def\invisRule{\hrule width-1pt}
```

Now we use this **\invisRule** in our **\exactSpaceSection** macro. **\exactSpaceSection** takes one input: the text for the section title.

```
\def\exactSpaceSection#1{
    \vskip 0.25in
    \invisRule
    \hbox{\bf#1}
    \invisRule
    \vskip 0.125in}

\dots\ precision in all things.

\exactSpaceSection{The Joys of Exactitude}

One pound of flesh---no more, no less---was
Shylock allowed, nay, {\em commanded\/} to
remove, but not a single drop of blood.
```

... precision in all things.

The Joys of Exactitude

One pound of flesh—no more, no less—was Shylock allowed, nay, *commanded* to remove, but not a single drop of blood.

It is not necessary to put an **\invisRule** at the end of the previous section's text or at the beginning of the new section's first paragraph.

31.6   The \strut

The **\strut** is a plain TEX macro that makes an invisible **\vrule**. The **\strut**'s width is **0pt**, and its height + depth is the same as the **\baselineskip**. Thus, you can use it to extend the height or depth of a vbox to match the **\baselineskip** above or below it. **\strut**s are also necessary in tables when you use **\offinterlineskip**. When **\offinterlineskip** is in effect, TEX does not add any glue between lines, which means there is no space between the bottom of one line and the top of the next.

Because the **\strut** is designed to match the **\baselineskip**, make sure that you change the size of the **\strut** when you change your **\baselineskip**. To do this, change the size of the rule in the **\strutbox**. Here is plain TEX's **\strutbox**:

```
\setbox\strutbox=\hbox{%
    \vrule height 8.5pt depth 3.5pt width 0pt}
```

This **\strutbox** is designed for TEX's startup **\baselineskip** of **12pt**. To change the size of the **\strut**, keep the same proportion of height and depth.

Height	8.5pt	.708	× new \baselineskip = new height
Depth	3.5pt	.292	× new \baselineskip = new depth
Total	12.0pt	1.000	new \baselineskip

If your new **\baselineskip** is **15pt**, the new height for your **\strut** is .708 × 15 = **10.62pt**, and the new depth is .292 × 15 = **4.38**.

Checking this arithmetic is a nuisance at best. At worst, it is another opportunity for Murphy to hire you to make mistakes, so let TeX do the math. After you establish the **\baselineskip** for your document, use it to change the **\strutbox**, like this:

```
\setbox\strutbox=\hbox{\vrule
    height .708\baselineskip
    depth  .292\baselineskip
    width  0pt}
```

31.7   Moving Rules

To move a rule, put it in a box and move the box. Inside an hbox, use a **\vrule**. Inside a vbox, use an **\hrule**.

If you use **\hrule** in horizontal mode, TeX ends the paragraph and goes back to vertical mode. If you use **\hrule** inside an hbox, TeX says **! You cannot use '\hrule' here except with leaders.** (You can use **\hrulefill** inside an hbox.) If you use **\vrule** in a vertical mode, TeX starts a new paragraph.

Review and Related Matters

This chapter shows how to put **\hrule**s and **\vrule**s into your document. Use **\hrule** between paragraphs (in a vertical mode), and **\vrule** inside paragraphs or hboxes (in a horizontal or math mode).

The size of a rule can be controlled with the keywords **height**, **depth**, and **width**. You can make invisible rules with a **0pt** or negative width, or with a **0pt** or negative height + depth. The **\strut** is an invisible **\vrule** the same height + depth as the **\baselineskip**. **\hrulefill** can be used inside an hbox to fill a space with a horizontal rule.

The next chapter shows how to fix awkward page breaks. Chapter 33 explains TeX's modes.

CHAPTER 32

Adjusting Awkward Page Breaks

Most of the time, TeX chooses a page-break point that humans find aesthetically pleasing—but not always. TeX sometimes puts huge gaps of white space between various paragraphs on a page. When there are no good break points, TeX takes the least awful break point it can find and stretches all the vertical glue. The result is an underfull vbox.

TeX sometimes puts only the last line of a paragraph at the top of a page or the first line of a paragraph at the bottom of a page. These are called *widow* and *orphan* lines.

This chapter presents several methods of changing the page break when you do not like the one TeX chose. To understand this chapter, you must be familiar with the following:

- reporters (Section 3.10), and
- using glue, especially **\vskip**, **\vfil**, and **\vfill** (Chapters 9 and 10).

Some knowledge of vboxes (Chapters 28 and 29) is helpful.

32.1   Widow and Orphan Lines

TeX's willingness or reluctance to typeset a widow or orphan line is governed by the reporters called **\widowpenalty** and **\clubpenalty**. The **\widowpenalty** affects the top of the page; the **\clubpenalty** the bottom.

When TeX starts up, both **\widowpenalty** and **\clubpenalty** are **150**. To make TeX more reluctant to typeset widow or orphan lines, increase these reporters. The largest number you can give these reporters is **10000**. Saying

```
\widowpenalty=10000
\clubpenalty=10000
```

stops TeX from typesetting any widow or orphan lines at all.

Page Breaks above and below Math Displays

TeX is always willing to break a page between paragraphs, so if there are blank lines above and below your display math material, the display can be the first thing TeX puts on a page. When the display math material is part of the paragraph, TeX prefers to put at least one line of text above the display math material.

Three primitive reporters influence TeX's page-breaking decisions in the vicinity of math displays. TeX's willingness to break a page is affected by **\predisplaypenalty** just above a math display and by **\postdisplaypenalty** below. The **\displaywidowpenalty** affects TeX's willingness to put a widow line of text as the first thing on a page before a math display.

When TeX starts up, these reporters are

```
\predisplaypenalty=10000
\postdisplaypenalty=0
\displaywidowpenalty=50
```

Thus, if there is no blank line between your display math material and the text above it, TeX never puts the math display at the top of a page unless you change the **\predisplaypenalty**. TeX is also only mildly reluctant to put a widow line above a math display.

The best way to force a page break after display math material is

```
$$
\postdisplaypenalty = -10000
math material
$$
```

TeX automatically puts **\belowdisplayskip** glue below a math display. If you say **\eject** after the display, the page is too short because this glue stays on the page. Saying **\postdisplaypenalty=−10000** forces TeX to break the page right after the display *and* pulls the math display box down to the bottom of the page.

The **\postdisplaypenalty** reporter governs TeX's page-breaking behavior, so you need to put this change inside a group. If you do not, TeX continues breaking pages immediately after all the math displays. Since display math begins and ends a group, putting the change inside the display math toggles (**$$**) is the most convenient way of doing this.

32.2   Making Ragged-Bottom Pages

Sometimes a document uses ragged-bottom pages. The plain TEX macro **\raggedbottom** tells TEX to put fill glue at the bottom of the page when it chooses a page-break point. A corresponding **\normalbottom** macro restores TEX's usual behavior of pulling the bottom line of text down to the bottom of the page.

When you use **\raggedbottom**, sometimes you find an underfull page that has a big piece of white space at the top.

Ragged Top Bug

\raggedbottom increases the **\topskip** glue by **plus 60pt**. Thus, when TEX is forced to stretch the finite glue on the page, this includes the **\topskip** glue.

To fix this Ragged Top Bug, change the **\topskip** back to its usual **10pt** after you say **\raggedbottom**. (If you also want to increase the space between the header and the text, change the **\topskip** to the new value after you say **\raggedbottom**.)

LATEX's **\raggedbottom** does not create a Ragged Top Bug.

32.3   Making a Paragraph Longer or Shorter

If you need to adjust a page by only a line or two, look for a long paragraph before the awkward page break. Then use the TEX primitive **\looseness** to make that paragraph longer or shorter.

To increase the number of lines in a paragraph, choose a paragraph whose last line is almost as wide as the page.

> The garrulous old man sat on the park bench and talked about the days when belts were loose during the Depression. "Pants were baggy, like tents flapping in the breeze," he said. "Back then, you knew what you'd lost."

Then give **\looseness** a positive number, as we do here:

```
\looseness=1
The garrulous old man sat on the park bench and
talked about the days when belts were loose
during the Depression.  ''Pants were baggy, like
tents flapping in the breeze,'' he said.  ''Back
then, you knew what you'd lost.''
```

> The garrulous old man sat on the park bench and talked about the days when belts were loose during the Depression. "Pants were baggy, like tents flapping in the breeze," he said. "Back then, you knew what you'd lost."

To reduce the number of lines in a paragraph, choose a paragraph whose last line is relatively short—preferably only a word or two. Then give **\looseness** a negative number.

\looseness=2 tells TEX to make that paragraph two lines longer than normal. **\looseness=−2** says to make the paragraph two lines shorter. However, if you want to change the length of a paragraph by two (or more) lines, the paragraph must be long and the **\tolerance** high. Otherwise, TEX cannot do what you want.

\looseness affects only one paragraph. After that paragraph, the **\looseness** becomes **0** again.

32.4   Adding or Subtracting White Space

Sometimes the solution is to add or subtract some white space between specific paragraphs that normally have little or no glue between them. Use **\vskip** with a positive dimension to increase the space, or a negative dimension to decrease it. **\vfil** and **\vss** can also be helpful if you want TEX to adjust several spots of glue evenly. (**\vss** can be used only inside a vbox.)

32.5   Breaking the Page Earlier

If you are working on a book where the bottoms of the pages need to be the same length, sometimes the way to achieve this is to go back a few pages and break the pages a line or two earlier. This moves one or more lines to a later page and helps fill up those white gaps.

There are several ways of breaking a page earlier than usual. You can put an explicit **\eject** or **\newpage** into your text file. **\eject** is a plain TEX macro that forces a page break. **\eject** also pulls the last line of text down to the bottom of the page, thereby stretching the glue. **\newpage** is a macro defined on page 108, and it also forces a page break. However, **\newpage** first fills the bottom of the page with fill glue, so the rest of the glue on the page is not stretched.

Sometimes it is awkward to use \eject or \newpage directly, especially if you want to break the page in the middle of a paragraph. The solution is to use \vadjust{\eject} or \vadjust{\newpage}, as follows:

```
The egg-shell adjuster paused in his assessment
of the DDT levels in the eagle's egg.  ''This
is\vadjust{\eject}
a definite improvement, but still not sufficient
to save the eagles.  Perhaps we can bathe the
shells in whiffle-dust, the new razzle-dazzletry
from Nook's End.''
```

\vadjust is a primitive that takes one input. After TeX chooses the line-break points in the paragraph, TeX acts on \vadjust's input after the line break that follows the \vadjust. In other words, if you say \vadjust{\newpage}, TeX does a \newpage after the line break that follows the \vadjust.

The input for \vadjust can be any sort of vertical-mode material. (See Chapter 33 for an explanation of TeX's modes.) Here, we use it to break the page with \eject or \newpage.

32.6   Breaking the Page Later

To put more on a page than TeX normally allows, use a vbox. Everything inside a vbox stays on the same page. The following example shows how to start and end such a vbox in the middle of paragraphs. Since this vbox goes at the top of a page, use \vtop instead of \vbox to avoid a Disappearing Topskip Bug (pages 185 and 291).

```
Springing forth from his box, the box elder
mounted a box camera on his box kite and flew it
past the\break\par\vtop{\noindent
box seats at the social box \dots

When the box score of box pleats became
stalled,\break}\noindent
the wellbeing of the box turtle was jeopardized.
```

page 1:   Springing forth from his box, the box elder mounted a box camera on his box kite and flew it past the

page 2:   box seats at the social box . . .

When the box score of box pleats became stalled,

page 3:   the wellbeing of the box turtle was jeopardized.

In the first part of this example,

- \break pulls the text to the right margin,
- \par ends the paragraph (and resumes vertical mode),
- \vtop{ starts the vbox, and
- \noindent starts the long page with a nonindented paragraph.

At the end of the long page,

- \break again pulls the text to the right margin, [1]
- the close brace } ends the the vbox (and therefore the paragraph), and
- \noindent starts the next page with a nonindented paragraph.

If you prefer, use the following macros:

```
\def\beginLongPage{\break\par
   \vtop\bgroup
   \noindent}
\def\endLongPage{\break\egroup
   \noindent}
```

When you make a long page, do not put a space between the last word on a page and the \break, \beginLongPage, or \endLongPage. If you do, TeX typesets that space as the last character on the page.

 In LaTeX, you can use the **minipage** environment to keep text on the same page. You can also use the \samepage, \nopagebreak, and \pagebreak macros described in Section 5.2.2 on page 90 of Lamport's LaTeX book to control the ways that LaTeX chooses page breaks.

32.7 Inserts on a Page with a Vbox

All inserted material disappears when you put it inside a vbox. Thus, you must move any \topinsert or \pageinsert material either above or below the vbox. \midinsert material should be converted into text if you want to keep it inside the box. Otherwise, change it to a \topinsert. For the same reason, you cannot have footnotes inside a vbox. Use \vfootnote instead.

When you want to add a line to a page that has a float on it, you must give the vbox a size that is smaller than its natural size. Otherwise, TeX does not put the vbox and the float on the same page. A good rule of

---

[1]Actually, using \hfilneg\null\par is better than \break, because it prevents TeX from placing an extra blank line at the bottom of the vbox. In most circumstances, however, this extra blank line is invisible and therefore irrelevant.

thumb here is to count the number of text lines that TeX put on the page and use that as the size of the vbox. Then add the lines you wanted to include from the subsequent page.

```
... critters.\break\par
\vtop to 13\baselineskip{\noindent
'Twas brillig, and the slithy toves did gyre and
gimble in the wabe; all mimsy were the borogoves,
and the mome raths outgrabe....
\vss}
```

End the vbox with **\vss**, the infinitely shrinking glue, to avoid getting an overfull vbox warning.

You can also use a **\vtop to 0pt**, and say **\newpage** after the vbox.

LaTeX's **\parbox** macro and **minipage** environment both create a vbox. LaTeX's **figure** and **table** environments are inserted material (floats) and disappear from a **\parbox**, **minipage**, or vbox. Move them either above or below the vbox.

You can use **\footnote** inside a **minipage**, but the footnote appears just below the **minipage** box. (Of course, this might be exactly what you want.)

\vfootnote does not exist in LaTeX. Use **\footnotemark** and **\footnotetext** instead.

32.8   Stopping the Overfull and Underfull Vbox Warnings

When a vbox is longer than the **\vsize**, TeX sends you an overfull vbox warning, just as it told you about overfull hboxes in your paragraphs. TeX sends these warnings only when the extra size of the overfull vbox exceeds the **\vfuzz**. Thus, if you do not like seeing overfull vbox messages and are not concerned about fixing pages that are longer than the **\vsize**, give **\vfuzz** a larger dimension to remember—perhaps

```
\vfuzz=2\baselineskip
```

When TeX stretches finite glue on a page farther than the **plus** amounts allow, it sends you an underfull vbox warning. If you do not like seeing these messages, give **\vbadness** a larger number. TeX's largest **\vbadness** number is **10000**, so if you say **\vbadness=10000**, you never see another underfull vbox warning again. Since pages with a **\vbadness** of **10000** are likely to be very ugly indeed, a better strategy is to say

```
\vbadness=9999
```

When TeX starts up, the **\vbadness** is **1000**.

This chapter shows several ways of adjusting awkward page breaks. TeX has several reporters that influence TeX's willingness to break a page at a particular place.

\widowpenalty	single line at the top of a page
\clubpenalty	single line at the bottom of a page
\predisplaypenalty	page break above a math display
\postdisplaypenalty	page break after a math display
\displaywidowpenalty	single line at the top of a page above a math display

A high number discourages TeX from choosing these page-break points (**10000** makes that choice impossible). A negative number encourages TeX to choose such points (**−10000** forces TeX to use that page break point).

You can also change the page-break point by adding or removing glue with a **\vskip** at specific places on the page. Similarly, **\eject** and our own **\newpage** macro force TeX to break the page at a particular place. To tell TeX to "break this page after you break this line," say **\vadjust**{**\eject**} or **\vadjust**{**\newpage**}.

To put more text on a page than TeX normally would, put the entire page inside a vbox. Our **\beginLongPage** and **\endLongPage** macros (page 324) are especially helpful for this. To make a longer-than-normal page that includes a float, put the text inside a **\vbox to 0pt** and put **\newpage** after the vbox. The floating material must go immediately above the vbox. To include a footnote on a long page, use **\vfootnote**.

To get fewer overfull and underfull vbox warnings on your screen and in the transcript file, increase the **\vfuzz** (for overfull warnings) and the **\vbadness** (for underfull warnings).

TeX's **\raggedbottom** macro puts fill glue at the bottom of each page. To avoid getting a Ragged Top Bug, change the **\topskip** glue back to **10pt** after you say **\raggedbottom**.

To make a specific paragraph one line longer, make **\looseness=1** for that paragraph. Similarly, **\looseness=−1** makes a paragraph one line shorter.

Chapter 4 shows how to fix overfull hboxes (awkward line breaks) and prevent TeX from breaking the page in the middle of a hyphenated word.

CHAPTER 33

How TEX Works: Modes, Tokens, Mouth, and Stomach

Altogether, TEX has six modes. Most of the time, TEX does the right thing automatically, so you do not need to think about which mode TEX is using. Sometimes, however, strange effects can appear in your printout if you do not understand how these modes work. This chapter explains all six of TEX's modes and the fine points of using them effectively.

To understand this chapter, you must be familiar with the following:

- how TEX assembles pages (Chapter 11), and
- boxes (Chapter 28).

 LATEX has the same modes but uses different names for two of them. LATEX's paragraph mode is TEX's horizontal mode, and LATEX's LR mode is TEX's restricted horizontal mode.

33.1 TEX's Main Modes: Horizontal, Vertical, and Math

In horizontal mode, TEX makes paragraphs. It assembles letters into words, puts glue between the words, decides where to break the lines, and puts each line into an hbox (horizontal box) that has the same width as the text on the page (the \hsize).

When TeX is in horizontal mode, it aligns letters and boxes horizontally along their baselines. Repeating the example from Chapter 11,

These are words

In vertical mode, TeX makes pages. It adds each of the paragraph's hboxes to the bottom of the current page. When TeX is accumulating boxes to make a page, it aligns them vertically along their reference points. TeX also adds interlineskip glue between the hboxes of a paragraph so the baselines are \baselineskip apart. Here is the example from Chapter 11:

Some words on this page
are wider than other words
on page seven.

When TeX has more than enough text to fill a page—including any insertion (floating) material it has been saving—it decides where to break the page and activates the *output routine*. The output routine assembles the entire page by putting the insertion material in the appropriate spot(s) and adding the headline and footline. The output routine then sends the finished page to the **.dvi** file.

In math mode, TeX typesets math. It uses a special set of rules for deciding where to put spaces and how large those spaces should be. These math mode spacing rules are described in Section 24.8.

Placement of Boxes in Vertical Mode

In vertical mode, TeX adds interlineskip glue between boxes to place their baselines one \baselineskip apart. It does not matter whether these are hboxes or one-line vboxes. TeX still places them according to the \baselineskip.

If the height of a \vbox or depth of a \vtop makes the baseline-to-baseline dimension larger than the \baselineskip, TeX then uses \lineskiplimit and \lineskip to decide how much glue to put between the boxes. The primitive reporter \lineskiplimit says how close the adjacent edges of two boxes can be before there is a problem. The primitive reporter \lineskip says how much white space to add between boxes that are closer than the \lineskiplimit.

In other words, if placing boxes one \baselineskip apart puts the edges of the boxes closer than the \lineskiplimit, TeX does not use the \baselineskip to position the second box. Instead, TeX separates those boxes by putting a \lineskip between them. TeX's startup \lineskiplimit is 0pt, and the startup \lineskip is 1pt.

33.2 How TeX Changes from One Mode to Another

TeX starts out in vertical mode. If you \input a macro file at the beginning of your text file, TeX is in vertical mode while it processes all the definitions and instructions.

When TeX is in vertical mode, it changes to horizontal mode (starts a new paragraph) if it sees one of the following:

- text: a character token (any letter, number, or punctuation);
- the control sequences \indent, \noindent, or \leavevmode;
- a control space (\ );
- a math mode toggle ($)—whereupon it also changes to math mode;
- horizontal glue: \hskip, \hfil, \hfill, \hss, or \hfilneg;
- a \vrule;
- any other inherently horizontal control sequence: \char, \unhbox, \unhcopy, \valign, \noboundary, \accent, \discretionary, and \-.

TeX ends horizontal mode and returns to vertical mode if it finds one of the following:

- a blank line (two consecutive carriage returns);
- the control sequences \par or \endgraf;
- vertical glue: \vskip, \bigskip, \medskip, \smallskip, \vfil, \vfill, \vss, or \vfilneg;
- an \hrule;
- any other inherently vertical control sequence: \unvbox, \unvcopy, \halign, \end, and \dump.

TeX starts math mode when it finds a math mode toggle ($) and stops math mode when it finds another math mode toggle. If TeX finds a math-mode-only macro when it is not in math mode, it pauses, inserts a $ so it can start math mode, and then continues with the math-mode-only macro and whatever comes next. TeX also stops math mode if it reaches the end of a paragraph when it is still in math mode.

33.3   List Building: A Closer Look at TeX's Modes

Since computers do their work with numbers, there are no actual boxes or glue inside the machine. These are metaphors that help our human brains understand how TeX works. What TeX actually does is build lists. It builds a different kind of list in each mode.

In vertical mode, TeX adds things to the main vertical list. Usually, these things are either glue or the hboxes of a paragraph, but they can also be an \hrule, display math mode material, an hbox made explicitly with \hbox, or a vbox (vertical box made with \vbox or \vtop).[1]

Every time TeX finishes a paragraph and returns to vertical mode, it checks to see if the main vertical list (including any pending insertions) is long enough to make a complete page. If not, TeX simply continues with the next task—usually another paragraph. If the list is long enough, TeX decides where to break the page and sends the result to the output routine. Then it puts the "leftovers" at the top of the newly emptied main vertical list.

In horizontal mode, TeX adds boxes and glue to a horizontal list. When TeX reaches the end of a paragraph, it selects line-break points in that list and converts the list into a series of hboxes.[2]

In math mode, TeX builds a list of mathematical symbols. This list includes *penalties*—information that rates the desirability of the possible break points. When the math list is complete, it is added to the horizontal list. When TeX reaches the end of a paragraph, the penalties in the math list allow TeX to choose line-break points for the entire paragraph.

Penalties govern the way TeX breaks lines and pages. A penalty can be as low as **−10000**, which forces a break, or as high as **10000**, which prevents a break.

---

[1]TeX can also add a penalty, kern, insertion, mark, or whatsit to the main vertical list. A *penalty* describes the desirability or undesirability of a particular break point. A *kern* is like glue, except it cannot be stretched, shrunk, or broken across pages. An *insertion* is a footnote or a float. A *mark* contains material that TeX adds to the main vertical list in a special way. A *whatsit* allows TeX to do things that are external to TeX, such as read and write information from auxiliary files or incorporate PostScript material in a figure.

[2]TeX can also add a penalty, kern, math-on or math-off, discretionary break, or whatsit to the horizontal list. TeX can also add material to the vertical list from \insert, \vadjust, or \mark. A *penalty* in horizontal mode describes the desirability of a line-break point instead of a page-break point. A *kern* in horizontal mode cannot be broken across lines. *Math-on* and *math-off* are created by the math mode toggles (**$**). The *discretionary break* is an allowable break point inside a word. TeX's hyphenation program inserts discretionary breaks into words automatically, or you can add them yourself with \-. \insert is the primitive that creates floats. TeX typesets floats in vboxes and stores them in its memory until they are needed. The output routine then adds them to the page. \vadjust provides vertical-mode material or instructions for TeX to perform at the next line-break point.

33.4   TEX's Three Specialist Modes

TEX's other three modes are specialized versions of the horizontal, vertical, and math modes. Each of them also builds a list, but in a slightly different way for a specialized purpose.

Restricted Horizontal Mode

TEX uses restricted horizontal mode inside an hbox, and builds a horizontal list for an hbox instead of a paragraph. TEX typesets words inside an hbox as it does inside a paragraph, but with a few important differences.

- TEX does not break the line in restricted horizontal mode. Everything inside an \hbox stays on the same line. (This makes \hbox a handy tool for preventing hyphenation of particular words.)

- When you start restricted horizontal mode, you are not starting a new paragraph. Thus, TEX does not add paragraph indentation to the beginning of this horizontal list.

- If a space is the first thing inside \hbox's input, TEX typesets that space. Normally, this is not a problem unless an extraneous space appears during the expansion of a macro. For example, if the definition of \xiipt has an extraneous space, this space is typeset if you say \hbox{\xiipt...}. (See the Peek-a-Boo Space Bug, page 333.)

- You cannot nest display math mode material inside an \hbox. If you type \hbox{This is text $$ x+y=2 $$ in an hbox}, TEX typesets an empty math formula on each side of x+y=2, and the x+y=2 is typeset as ordinary text.

If you add an hbox to the main vertical list, you can put a footnote inside it. However, if you place this hbox inside a paragraph, the footnote disappears.

Internal Vertical Mode

TEX uses internal vertical mode inside a vbox, and builds a vertical list for a vbox instead of for the page. There are two main differences between the two vertical modes.

- TEX does not break the page in internal vertical mode. Everything inside a \vbox or \vtop stays on the same page. It does not matter how long that page is—although if it includes the rest of your file, TEX is likely to run out of memory before it reaches the end of the file.

- If you put insertions into a vbox, they disappear. Insertions are footnotes and floats (see Chapters 19 and 23).

The other differences between vertical mode and internal vertical mode are esoteric and beyond the scope of this book.

Display Math Mode

Display math mode puts an **\abovedisplayskip** and **\belowdisplayskip** above and below the displayed math material—or a **\abovedisplayshortskip** and **\belowdisplayshortskip**. It also uses the larger size of symbols like the integral and sum. Display math mode behaves slightly differently depending on which mode TeX is in when it finds the display math toggles (**$$**).

- In vertical or internal vertical modes, changing to display math mode adds three things to the vertical list: the **\abovedisplayskip** glue, the math material typeset in display style, and the **\belowdisplayskip** glue.

- In horizontal mode, changing to display math mode first breaks the current paragraph into lines and returns to the enclosing vertical or internal vertical mode. TeX then adds the **\abovedisplayskip** glue, typesets the math material in display style, and adds the **\belowdisplayskip** glue. Finally, TeX resumes horizontal mode again with an empty list, which means with no paragraph indentation.

- In restricted horizontal mode, changing to display math mode puts an empty math formula into the text at each of the **$$** toggles.

These characteristics of display math mode make it possible to put display math material either inside or between paragraphs.

```
Einstein's energy equation $$E=mc^2$$ was an
extraordinary find.
```

Einstein's energy equation

$$E = mc^2$$

was an extraordinary find.

33.5   Oops! Mode Bugs

When TeX is in a vertical mode, it is not typesetting anything. Therefore, all spaces at the beginnings and ends of lines are ignored.

When TeX is in a horizontal mode, it does not typeset spaces at the beginning of lines and after control sequences, but it does typeset any spaces after a close brace (or an open brace). This difference in TeX's behavior can lead to a Peek-a-Boo Space Bug: Sometimes you get an extra space, sometimes you do not.

Peek-a-Boo Space Bug

In a horizontal mode, TEX typesets a space that follows a brace. In a vertical mode, it ignores that space.

Thus, when a macro contains spaces after an open brace or close brace and you use that macro in a vertical mode, no extra spaces appear in your printout—but in a horizontal mode, they do. Section 34.5 also describes this bug and shows how it looks.

To fix this bug, make sure that any macro you might use in a horizontal mode has no spaces that can be typeset. If a close brace is the last character on a line, put a percent sign after it. Similarly, if an open brace is the last character on a line, put a percent sign after it too. Since the macros that change the font size are especially vulnerable to this bug, the following copy of our \eightpoint macro from Chapter 7 shows how to remove all the spaces and make such macros goof-proof.

```
\def\eightpoint{%
\def\rm{\eightrm}%
\def\it{\eightit}%
\def\sl{\eightsl}%
\def\bf{\eightbf}%
\def\tt{\eighttt}%
\rm}
```

If you might use a macro while \obeyspaces is in effect, make sure you remove *all the spaces* in its definition. Put a % at the ends of all the lines, and do not type any spaces at the beginnings of lines or after control sequence names.

33.6   TEX's Digestive Tract: Eyes, Mouth, and Stomach

TEX goes through the following three stages as it processes your text file and creates the **.dvi** file:

- Eyes: Characters in your text file are converted into *tokens*.
- Mouth: Macros are expanded until all the control sequences are primitives.
- Stomach: Everything is organized into lists: horizontal lists, math lists, and vertical lists.

Eyes: Convert to Tokens

As TEX processes your text file, its first step is to convert the characters you typed into tokens. A token is either a control sequence or a single character with a *category code*. The category code tells TEX what sort of character it is dealing with, such as a letter, space, subscript, math shift, or escape character.

Thus, if your text file says **\hbox to 20pt{pooh}**, TEX converts this to

$$\boxed{\textbf{hbox}}\quad t_{11}\quad o_{11}\quad\; {}_{10}\quad 2_{12}\quad 0_{12}\quad p_{11}\quad t_{11}\quad \{_1\quad p_{11}\quad o_{11}\quad o_{11}\quad h_{11}\quad \}_2$$

The control sequence $\boxed{\textbf{hbox}}$ does not have a category code because it is a control sequence. Only characters need to have category codes.

TEX has sixteen different category codes:

Category	Meaning	
0	Escape character	\
1	Beginning of group	{
2	End of group	}
3	Math shift	$
4	Alignment tab	&
5	End of line	$\boxed{\text{CARRIAGE-RETURN}}$
6	Parameter	#
7	Superscript	^
8	Subscript	_
9	Ignored character	⟨null⟩
10	Space	(a space)
11	Letter	A–Z, a–z
12	Other character	none of the above or below
13	Active character	such as ~
14	Comment character	%
15	Invalid character	⟨delete⟩

Most of these are self-explanatory, and you almost never need to know which category code is which.

Mouth: Expand the Macros

TEX's second step is to expand the macros until all the control sequences are primitives. In the example above, the $\boxed{\textbf{hbox}}$ token is already a primitive, but a token such as $\boxed{\textbf{bigskip}}$ would be expanded into $\boxed{\textbf{vskip}}$ and $\boxed{\textbf{bigskipamount}}$.

Stomach: Make the Lists

TEX now does the actual work. It processes paragraphs into horizontal lists, chooses line-break points, and puts the resulting lines into hboxes. It processes math mode material into math lists, then converts the math lists into a horizontal list for a paragraph, or into the appropriate form for a math display. In vertical modes, TEX builds vertical lists of boxes, rules and glue, and adds them to the page or vbox. When the main vertical list is long enough, TeX breaks the page and sends it to the output routine.

Coordination among Eyes, Mouth, and Stomach

Even though these three stages are distinct, what happens in one part of TeX's digestive tract can affect what TeX does in another.

For example, \obeylines changes the behavior of TeX's eyes. Instead of converting the $\boxed{\text{END-OF-LINE}}$ character into a space (category code 10), TeX now converts it into a $\boxed{\text{par}}$ token—or, if you use the \beginCode macro developed in Chapter 16, into a $\boxed{\text{startline}}$ token. However, if you try to use \obeylines in a jelly-doughnut macro, TeX has already converted all the $\boxed{\text{END-OF-LINE}}$ characters of the input into spaces. Thus, the Disobedient Bug (page 165) is really a digestive-system bug.

Review and Related Matters

TeX has three main modes: vertical, horizontal, and math—and three specialist modes: internal vertical, restricted horizontal, and display math. In vertical mode, TeX adds to the list of things on the page. In horizontal mode, TeX builds a horizontal list that it converts into a series of hboxes for a paragraph. In math mode, TeX builds a math list.

Material inside an hbox is typeset according to the rules of *restricted horizontal mode*. Restricted horizontal mode is similar to ordinary horizontal mode but cannot be broken across lines, does not start a new paragraph, and does not allow a change to display math mode.

Material inside a vbox is stacked vertically in *internal vertical mode*. Internal vertical mode is similar to ordinary vertical mode but cannot be broken across pages.

TeX does its work in three stages. The eyes convert everything into tokens. The mouth expands macros until all the control sequences are primitives. The stomach does the actual work of building lists.

Chapters 28 through 30 describe TeX's boxes, how to control their size, and how to move them to different places on the page.

PART V

BACK AT THE LODGE

CHAPTER 34

Bug Diagnosis: Tips and Strategies

Trying to figure out what sort of bug you are dealing with can be a very frustrating experience. Sometimes the problem is obvious and easy to solve. You misspelled the name of a control sequence or forgot the **$** to end math mode. Sometimes you recognize the symptoms ("Oh yes, that's a Disappearing Topskip Bug"), but you cannot remember what to do about it or where it appears in this book. Sometimes the symptoms look vaguely familiar, but you do not remember which bug causes it. Sometimes the problem seems completely baffling.

This chapter provides help for finding and recognizing bugs. It describes several new bugs, including the Chameleon Bug that can mimic many different types of bugs. It also describes two useful strategies for finding elusive bugs. In particular, the divide-and-conquer strategy can help you find any kind of bug, and is often essential for finding the Chameleon Bug.

The next chapter lists the symptoms of each of the bugs in this book, and explains how to interpret and use TeX's error messages.

To understand this chapter, you must be familiar with the following:

- how macros take inputs (Section 5.3), and
- groups (Section 6.2).

Some familiarity with boxes and modes (Chapters 28 and 33) is helpful but not necessary.

Whenever you are baffled about what kind of bug you are grappling with—especially if you are convinced that this problem cannot happen!—it may well be a Mismatched Brace Bug. This bug can produce so many different kinds of effects that it deserves to be called a Chameleon Bug. It also appears more frequently than any other type of bug.

There are two different kinds of Mismatched Brace Bugs. One is caused by an open brace with no matching close brace. The other is caused by a close brace with no matching open brace. These bugs usually creep into your document via a typo: typing [or] instead of { or }, and typing { or } instead of \{ or \}.

The close-brace variety of this bug often has puzzling symptoms but is much easier to find and fix.

Mismatched Close-Brace Bug

When a close brace appears without a matching open brace, TEX says "! **Too many }'s.**" If this happens inside a group that began with an open brace, TEX ends this group prematurely—so the error message does not appear until TEX encounters the next close brace: the one that is not really mismatched.

The Mismatched Close-Brace Bug is relatively easy to recognize and find. The strange effects are usually limited to a small section of your document. TEX sends the **too many** }'s message either at the place where it finds the extraneous brace or at the next unmatched close brace it finds, which is usually not far away. The following is a typical example:

```
To quote Henry James:

\medskip
{\narrower\noindent\sl
However incumbent it may be on most of us to do our
duty, there is \dots\ nothing in the world that
anyone is under the least obligation to like---not
even (one braces one's self to risk the declaration}
a particular kind of writing [Flaubert, 1893].\par}
```

> To quote Henry James:
>
> *However incumbent it may be on most of us to do our duty, there is . . . nothing in the world that anyone is under the least obligation to like—not even (one braces one's self to risk the declaration a particular kind of writing [Flaubert, 1893].*

The mismatched close brace is the one after **declaration**. It should be a close parenthesis instead. TEX sends the error message when it finds the close brace after **\par**. Also, since the mismatched } ended the group prematurely, the **\narrower** margin change is no longer in effect at the end of the paragraph. Thus, the bug in this particular example mimics the Ignores My Command Bug (page 129).

The Mismatched Open-Brace Bug is much trickier than its sibling to recognize and find. It can result in an entire slew of error messages that have nothing to do with the real problem.

Mismatched Open-Brace Bug

When you begin a group but do not end it, whatever changes you make inside that group continue throughout the rest of your document. Also, when the close brace is missing at the end of an input, TEX does not see that something is wrong until it reaches the end of the current paragraph. (If you use **\long** with the macro definition, TEX does not notice that anything is wrong until it reaches the end of your document or runs out of memory space.)

The Mismatched Open-Brace Bug is difficult to recognize because the symptoms depend on what is happening inside the group. For example, if you change to the **\tt** typewriter font inside an unending group, you start getting many overfull hboxes. If you do not notice that all of the overfull text lines start with **\tentt**, you might spend a lot of time fixing the overfull hboxes before you actually make a printout and realize that half your document was typeset in the **\tt** font.

The Mismatched Open-Brace Bug does have one clearcut symptom that never changes. If you begin a group and do not end it, TEX always says **\end occurred inside a group** when it reaches the end of your text file. This message also says how many groups are still open: **at level 1** means one open group, **at level 2** means two open groups, and so on. Thus, whenever you see this error message, you know you have a Mismatched Open-Brace Bug.

Since the Mismatched Open-Brace Bug can mimic so many other kinds of bugs, it is usually a good idea to let TEX finish processing your entire document before you start debugging it. However, this is not always possible. TEX might get stuck in an Endless Loop Bug, or might have such a narrow **\hsize** that the printout would be thousands of pages long. Even when TEX does reach the end of your document and tells you that **\end occured inside a group**, this gives you no clues about where the problem is. The best way of finding a Mismatched Brace Bug is to use the following divide-and-conquer strategy.

34.2   The Divide-and-Conquer Diagnostic Strategy

The divide-and-conquer strategy is useful for finding any kind of elusive bug, and sometimes is the only way of finding a Mismatched Brace Bug. When you either know or suspect that the problem is caused by an unending group (or possibly a prematurely ended group), type \bye halfway through your document. (Choose a place that is between paragraphs, not inside any other groups, and not inside a box.)

If TEX again says that \end occured inside a group, you know the problem is located in the first half of your document. If you do not see this error message, the problem is somewhere in the second half.

Now move \bye half way through the part where the problem is—to either the one-quarter or three-quarter point of the document—and run it through TEX again. Repeat this divide-and-conquer process until you have narrowed the problem to an area that is small enough to examine carefully and find the bug.

A variation on the divide-and-conquer strategy could be called a toss-it strategy. Copy your text file as **junk.tex** (or whatever you prefer), and then eliminate the parts of **junk.tex** that work until you have a small section that still generates the error message.

34.3   Other Mismatched Begin-and-End-Group Bugs

The Mismatched Brace Bug is only one variety of a more general type of Chameleon Bug. Each begin-a-group character or control sequence has a matching end-a-group character or control sequence. In other words, when you begin a group with one of these, you must end that same group with its matching counterpart. These matching group-making pairs are

```
        {...}
\begingroup...\endgroup
    \bgroup...\egroup
        $...$
        $$...$$
```

Thus, you cannot say {...\begingroup...}...\endgroup. Instead, you must say {...\begingroup...\endgroup...} or \begingroup...{...}...\endgroup. The same is true of all these group-making characters and control sequences.[1]

Whenever one of these begin-and-end group-makers appears in your text file without its matching counterpart, TEX gets out of sync with what you

---

[1] Actually, since **\bgroup** and **\egroup** are clones, you can also say **\bgroup**...} or {...**\egroup**. Since that is a good way to confuse yourself, I do not recommend it.

intended and sends you error messages. Your printout probably looks rather odd too.

The Mismatched Group-Maker Bugs are essentially the same as the Mismatched Brace Bugs. The symptoms in your printout depend on the changes you made in the unending group or the prematurely ended group. The error messages you get depend on what type of group-maker is mismatched, what mode TeX is in when it finds the mismatched group-maker, and what sorts of things TeX is doing in the places where it experiences a glitch.

Here is one example of a Mismatched Group-Maker Bug. First, we write a pair of mismatched sandwich macros, together with a **\who** macro that takes one input—the name of the character—and typesets that input in italics.

```
{\obeylines%
\global\def\beginOopsVerse{\medskip\begingroup\obeylines}%
\global\def\endOopsVerse{\egroup\medskip}}

\def\who#1{{\it#1}}
```

Next, we use our mismatched sandwich macros. Since the group that began in **\beginOopsVerse** does not end, **\obeylines** continues and each line is typeset as a separate paragraph.

```
From {\it Henry IV, Part I:}

\beginOopsVerse
\who{Glendower:} I can call spirits from the vasty deep.
\who{Hotspur:} Why, so can I, or so can any man;
But will they come when you do call for them?
\endOopsVerse

In this exchange, Shakespeare delves
into the philosophy of \dots
```

> From *Henry IV, Part I:*
>
> > *Glendower:* I can call spirits from the vasty deep.
> > *Hotspur:* Why, so can I, or so can any man;
> > But will they come when you do call for them?
> >
> > In this exchange, Shakespeare delves
> > into the philosophy of . . .

In this example, when TeX sees the **\egroup** from **\endOopsVerse**, it says **! Extra }, or forgotten \endgroup**. If you ask for the help message, TeX also says that it **deleted a group-closing symbol because it seems** to be **spurious**. So the group that began in **\beginOopsVerse** never ends. At the end of the document, TEX tells you that **\end occurred inside a group**.

In some of these Mismatched Group-Maker Bugs, TEX knows that something is wrong and has some built-in tactics for getting back into sync. For example, when TEX is in math mode and reaches the end of a paragraph, TEX inserts a **missing $** to end math mode before it ends the paragraph (see the Math Oops Mode Bug, page 16). The following list shows the error messages you might see when there is a Mismatched Group-Maker Bug in your text:

```
! Missing } inserted.
! Missing $ inserted.
! Missing \endgroup inserted.
! Too many }'s.
! Extra \endgroup.
! Extra }, or forgotten \endgroup.
! Extra }, or forgotten $.
```

Depending on what else TEX is doing at the time it finds a problem, you may see other error messages as well.

Chameleon Bugs with TEX's Boxes

All three of TEX's box-making primitives also begin and end a group (**\hbox**, **\vbox**, and **\vtop**). Thus, you cannot begin a group inside a box and end it outside that box. If you try, TEX complains and gets out of sync, resulting in yet another variety of Mismatched Group-Maker Bug.

For an **\hbox** with no close brace after its input, TEX realizes that something is wrong when it finds a control sequence that can be used only in a vertical mode—usually a **\vskip**, but possibly an **\hrule** or other inherently vertical control sequence. TEX then inserts a **missing }** to end the hbox before it continues with the vertical material. (Chapter 33 explains TEX's modes and what *inherently vertical* means. Chapter 28 explains TEX's boxes.)

A vbox with no close brace after its input continues forever, or at least until TEX finds **\bye**. TEX then says you cannot **use \end in internal vertical mode**, which means inside a vbox. (**\end** is part of the definition of **\bye**.)

If **\bye** was at the end of your text file, TEX now sends the single-asterisk prompt to your screen and waits for instructions. Type

```
}\bye
```

The } ends the vbox. **\bye** finishes the job and sends you back to top level.

34.4   When Does an Input Need Braces?

When people are learning TeX, the question of when to use braces around an input can be confusing (especially if they are learning both TeX and LaTeX at the same time). Luckily, the rules are simple:

- TeX's primitives are "smart" and can find their own inputs.
- All macros are "dumb" and need help.

Braces show a macro where its input begins and ends. Just in case these terms are still fuzzy,

- a *primitive* is a control sequence written in a programming language, such as C or Pascal;
- a *macro* is a control sequence written in TeX and created by **\def**.

There is one exception to these "primitives are smart" and "macros are dumb" rules. A few TeX primitives also need help because it is not obvious where their input ends. **\def** is a good example. The end of the new macro's name is clear, but the end of its definition is not. **\hyphenation** also needs help finding its input. There could be only one hyphenation example, or two, or twenty. Thus, all these where-does-my-input-end primitives also need braces around that input.

Oops!

Sooner or later, you will use the braces incorrectly (even if it is just a typo). Here is what happens when you do:

- If you use braces when the control sequence does not need them, TeX's error message usually tells you what kind of input it expected but did not find. For example, if you type **\hskip{20pt}** instead of **\hskip20pt**, TeX complains about a **missing number** and an **illegal unit of measure**. When this happens, TeX uses **0** for the number and **pt** as the unit.
- If you do not use braces when the control sequence does need them, TeX may or may not complain, but it does not do what you want and may do something odd instead.

If TeX does not behave properly with an input, try it the other way. If you put braces around the input, take them out. If you did not use braces, put them in. See if that fixes the problem.

When a control sequence expects a dimension and gets a group instead, it cannot unwrap the group or see inside. It just knows it did not get its muffin! So it complains.

34.5   An Intermittent Space Bug

The Peek-a-Boo Space Bug (page 333) is also very baffling. It puts an extra space into your printout, but when you look at your text file, you are sure it contains no extra space. This bug seems to appear in a variety of different situations. It has an erratic, now you see it, now you don't quality.

The problem is a space in your macro definition that is typeset when TeX is in a horizontal mode (inside a paragraph or hbox), but is not typeset when TeX is in a vertical mode (inside a vbox or while making the page). A typical example of this Peek-a-Boo Space Bug occurs when you use the following **\oopsFontsize** macro inside a paragraph or an hbox.

```
\def\oopsFontsize{%
   \def\rm{\fam=0\twelverm}
   \textfont0=\twelverm \scriptfont0=\tenrm
   \textfont1=\twelvemi \scriptfont1=\teni
   \textfont2=\twelvesy \scriptfont2=\tensy
   \textfont3=\twelveex \scriptfont3=\tenex
   \def\bf{\fam=\bffam\twelvebf}
   \textfont\bffam=\twelvebf
   \scriptfont\bffam=\tenbf
   \baselineskip=14pt
   \rm}
```

Now we use **\oopsFontsize** in an **\oopsSection** macro. **\oopsSection** takes one input: the text of the section heading.

```
\def\oopsSection#1{\bigbreak
   \noindent
   {\oopsFontsize\bf #1}
   \medskip}

\oopsSection{Peek-a-Boo Games}

\noindent
The peek-a-boo game gives the parent as much
pleasure as it does the child.  This timeless
activity \dots
```

Peek-a-Boo Games

The peek-a-boo game gives the parent as much pleasure as it does the child. This timeless activity . . .

Searching for the source of the extra space in front of **Peek-a-Boo Games** can be very frustrating. This situation calls for the following mark-it-up strategy.

When you are not sure where an extra space is coming from, adding markers to the macro can help identify the source. There might be several possible sources in our \oopsSection macro, so we remove the space after \noindent and put markers around each possible source in the heading itself. The following \diagnoseSection macro takes one input: the text of the section heading.

```
\def\diagnoseSection#1{\bigskip
    \noindent{[\oopsFontsize](\bf #1)}
    \medskip}

\diagnoseSection{Clarity Emerges}

\noindent
When Clarity came out of her dressing room,
everyone immediately understood \dots
```

[ ](Clarity Emerges)

When Clarity came out of her dressing room, everyone immediately understood . . .

The extra space is between the first, normal-size bracket and the second, larger bracket, and therefore comes from the \oopsFontsize macro.

When TEX is typesetting a paragraph or an hbox, it typesets a space after a close brace. In \oopsFontsize, the culprits are the END-OF-LINE characters after the close braces for the definitions of \rm and \bf. When TEX expands and processes the definition of \oopsFontsize, it converts these END-OF-LINE characters into spaces. Since TEX is typesetting a paragraph at the time, these spaces are typeset and appear in the printout.

To remove these spaces, put a percent sign at the ends of the two lines, like this:

```
\def\correctFontsize{%
    \def\rm{\fam=0\twelverm}%
    ...
    \def\bf{\fam=\bffam\twelvebf}%
    ...}
```

Any open or close brace at the end of a line can create a Peek-a-Boo Space Bug when TEX is making a paragraph or an hbox.

Brackets are good markers for this purpose. An better marker is the \vrule since TEX puts no space on either side of it.

34.7   Another Space Bug

Another kind of space bug can appear in your printout when TeX typesets the space after a close brace. If a macro typesets nothing at that point in your document, make sure you do not have spaces on both sides of the macro.

```
As Mark Twain said, few things are harder to
\ignorethis{so true, so true}
put up with than a good example.
```

> As Mark Twain said, few things are harder to put up with than a good example.

Doubled-Up Space Bug

When TeX is in a horizontal mode (making a paragraph or an hbox), it typesets the space after a close brace. When TeX is in a vertical mode (making a page or a vbox), it does not.

In the example above, TeX converts two $\boxed{\text{END-OF-LINE}}$ characters into spaces: the ones after **harder to** and **true}**. Since TeX is making a paragraph and there is something between those spaces, it typesets both of them. If **\ignorethis{...true}** appears between paragraphs instead of inside one, TeX is in a vertical mode and therefore does not typeset any spaces.

To fix this bug, remove one of the spaces. Put a percent sign after the close brace, or put **\ignorethis** immediately after **harder to**.

Review and Related Matters

Finding and fixing the bugs in your text or macro definitions can be tricky, especially if you are dealing with the elusive Chameleon Bug. This chapter describes several new bugs that can appear in a wide range of layout tasks. It also presents three strategies for locating bugs: divide and conquer, toss it, and mark it up. This chapter also gives more information about using braces to show a control sequence where its input begins and ends.

The next chapter lists all the bugs in this book by their symptoms. It also shows how to read and use TeX's error messages.

CHAPTER 35

Bug Diagnosis: Symptoms and Error Messages

When you cannot remember the name of a bug or where it was described, the first section of this chapter lists bug symptoms and can help you find a particular bug again. Since some bugs have more than one symptom, those bugs are repeated in each of the relevant areas. The other sections of this chapter describe how to understand and use TeX's error messages.

35.1   Diagnostics: Identifying a Bug by Its Symptoms

In this section, symptoms and their corresponding bugs are organized into seven areas describing the problem you are trying to solve: spaces between words, other white-space problems, something disappears or is missing, something extra or unexpected appears, something is in the wrong place, font problems, and other problems.

Any baffling or hard-to-find bug might turn out to be a Chameleon Bug (see Sections 34.1 through 34.3).

Spaces between Words

- Two or more consecutive spaces are typeset as a single space. See the Disappearing Space Bug, page 11.

- Spaces between words disappear, letters are typeset in italics, and the error messages say, **Missing $ inserted**. See the Math Oops Mode Bug, page 16. See also the Chameleon Bug, Sections 34.1 through 34.3.

- Fil level glue disappears between words. See the Disappearing Glue Bug, page 109.

- Spaces at the beginning of a line disappear, even though you said **\obeyspaces**. See the Ignores My Spaces Bug, page 168.

- A space appears in front of text that spans several columns in an **\halign** table. See the Multispanned Space Bug, page 216.

- A space appears between a hyphen and the rest of the word. See the Hyphen- ated Bug, page 9.

- Extra space appears in your printout that does not seem to be present in the text file or the macros. See the Peek-A-Boo Space Bug, page 333, and Sections 34.5 and 34.6.

- There are two spaces in the printout where you want only one, and there is a macro between those two spaces in the text file. See the Doubled-Up Space Bug, page 348.

Other White Space Problems

- Even though you put a **\vskip** at the top of a page to move the text down, TeX still puts the text at the top of the page. See the Does Not Skip at the Top Bug, page 175.

- A **\vskip** adds more space than you want between paragraphs or boxes. See the Too Much Space Bug, page 316.

- Glue disappears. See the Disappearing Glue Bug, page 109.

- Baselines are too close together. (Glue disappears between baselines.) See the Scrunched Baseline Bug, page 291.

- The text starts too high on the page, too close to the header. See the Disappearing Topskip Bug, pages 185 and 291.

- There is extra white space above the text on some of the pages. (The text starts below its normal position on these pages.) See the Ragged Top Bug, page 321.

Something Disappears or Is Missing

- Spaces between words disappear, letters are typeset in italics, and the error messages say, **Missing $ inserted**. See the Math Oops Mode Bug, page 16. See also the Chameleon Bug, Sections 34.1 through 34.3.

- Text in your text file does not appear in your printout. If you used % instead of \\%, you have a Disappearing Text Bug (page 19). If the missing text was an input for a macro, the macro definition does not have a slot that says what to do with that particular input (see Section 5.3).

- TEX puts the text at the top of the page even though you put a **\\vskip** at the top to move the text down. See the Does Not Skip at the Top Bug, page 175.

- A footnote is missing. See the Disappearing Footnote Bug, page 192.

- Glue disappears. See the Disappearing Glue Bug, page 109.

- The brace you typed does not appear in the printout, and weird things happen. See the Missing Brace Bug, page 20, and the Chameleon Bug, Sections 34.1 through 34.3.

- The words **plus** or **minus** are missing from your text. TEX sends you an error message about a missing number and illegal unit of measurement. See the Plus or Minus Bug, page 110.

Something Extra or Unexpected Appears

- Glue is typeset as text (the words **plus** something or **minus** something appear in your printout). See the Glue in Your Text Bug, page 111.

- A **\\vskip** adds more space than you want between paragraphs or boxes. See the Too Much Space Bug, page 316.

- There is extra white space above the text on some of the pages. (The text starts below its normal position on these pages.) See the Ragged Top Bug, page 321.

- An interword space appears between a hyphen and the rest of the word. See the Hyphen- ated Bug, page 9.

- An interword space appears in your printout that does not seem to be present in the text file or the macros. See the Peek-A-Boo Space Bug, page 333, and Sections 34.5 and 34.6.

- There are two interword spaces in the printout where you want only one, and there is a macro between those two spaces in the text file. See the Doubled-Up Space Bug, page 348.

Something Is in the Wrong Place

- The text starts too high on the page, too close to the header. See the Disappearing Topskip Bug, pages 185 and 291.

- Text in an hbox at the beginning of a paragraph is not typeset with the paragraph. Instead, it appears by itself flush against the margin, and the word after the hbox is indented for a new paragraph. See the Text by Itself Bug, page 288.

- Text that spans several columns in an \halign table is off center. See the Off-Center Multispanned Bug, page 215.

- Text in an \halign table extends farther than the rules in the table. See the Dangled Heading Bug, page 220.

- The first or last line in a ragged-left or centered paragraph is in the wrong place. See Sections 13.2 or 13.3 respectively.

- A \midinsert or \topinsert floats to the end of the document. See the **Oops!** section, page 235.

- The \underline below words in your text is placed at different levels. See the **Oops!** section, page 253.

- A line (rule) touches your text. TeX puts no space between a rule and box. See the **Oops!** section, page 312.

Font Problems

- Letters are typeset in italics, spaces between words disappear, and the error messages say, **Missing $ inserted**. See the Math Oops Mode Bug, page 16. See also the Chameleon Bug, Sections 34.1 through 34.3.

- You say \eightpoint or \twelvepoint, but the font does not change. See the Font Does Not Change Bug, page 79.

- The footnote is typeset in the wrong font. See the Wrong Font in Footnote Bug, page 191.

Other Problems

- The shape of a paragraph does not change, even though you changed the corresponding reporter. See the Ignores My Command Bug, page 129.

- The shape of a paragraph changes, but not in the way you expect. See the Cart Before the Horse Bug, page 135.

- The brace you typed does not appear in the printout, and weird things happen. See the Missing Brace Bug, page 20, and the Chameleon Bug, Sections 34.1 through 34.3.

- TeX treats the first subdirectory of a file's full pathname as a control sequence. TeX either does what that control sequence says to do, or complains about an undefined control sequence. See the DOS Backslash Filename Bug, page 32.

- TEX insists it cannot find a file named **whatever**, because there is no **whatever.tex** file. See the Broken Record Filename Bug, page 32.

- TEX prints a single-asterisk prompt and waits for instructions. You probably forgot to say **\bye** at the end of your file. See the Waiting Patiently Bug, page 36.

- A reporter does not change when you give new information to another reporter. (For example, you change **\normalbaselineskip**, and **\baselineskip** stays the same.) See the Reporter Did Not Change Bug, page 92.

- The figure or table numbers stay the same, even though you **\advance** the counter in the **\begintable** or **\beginfigure** macro. See the **Oops!** section, page 230.

- Even though you say **\obeylines** in a macro, TEX does not typeset each line separately. See the Disobedient Bug, page 165.

- Even though you say **\obeyspaces**, TEX does not typeset spaces at the beginning of a line. See the Ignores My Spaces Bug, page 168.

- TEX complains about a **bad character code**. You probably have a Bad Character Code Bug, page 362.

35.2   TEX's Error Messages

TEX can generate more than one hundred different error messages, so I cannot possibly explain all of them here. Instead, this section describes the structure and main ingredients of TEX's error messages so you can use the information in those messages to figure out what is wrong.

Some types of mistakes are very difficult to make, so you are not likely to see them. Some of the error messages are variations on the same theme, such as the ones you are likely to see with the Chameleon Bug:

```
! Missing } inserted.
! Missing $ inserted.
! Missing \endgroup inserted.
! Too many }'s.
! Extra \endgroup.
! Extra }, or forgotten \endgroup.
! Extra }, or forgotten $.
```

Sections 34.1 through 34.3 give information and strategies for the Chameleon Bug.

The Structure of TEX's Error Messages

TEX's error messages all have a similar structure. The first line begins with an exclamation point and describes the nature of the problem. The message also shows exactly where TEX stopped when it found the problem. The following example shows the error message that you see whenever you misspell the name of a control sequence.

```
That's such \malarkie{tripe and bunkum}
```

Message on your screen and in the transcript file:

```
! Undefined control sequence.
1.328 That's such \malarkie
                            {tripe and bunkum}
?
```

In the example above, TEX was on line 328 of your text file when it found the undefined control sequence. TEX has already read **... such \malarkie** and has not yet read {**tripe and bunkum**}.

The question-mark prompt shows that TEX is waiting for you to say what it should do next. (Your options about what TEX can do next are described in Section 3.7. If you have already switched to **\scrollmode**, **\nonstopmode**, or **\batchmode**, you do not see the question-mark prompt. TEX just sends the error message and continues.)

If the problem that TEX found was a misspelling or other typographic error, you can insert the correction (such as **i\malarky**) and continue. If you do need to define **\malarkie**, type the definition after the question-mark prompt just as you ordinarily would, perhaps as

```
i\def\malarkie#1{{\bf#1}}\malarkie
```

The reason for typing the second **\malarkie** after the definition is that TEX has already read the first one. If you do not type this second **\malarkie**, TEX typesets {**tripe and bunkum**} as ordinary text instead of the input to **\malarkie**.

If you prefer, you can just hit RETURN each time TEX finds **\malarkie**, and correct your text file later.

¡To Be Read Again¿

Some of TEX's other error messages contain additional information about material **<to be read again>**.

TEX has some built-in expectations about various things. For example, it knows that glue should follow a **\vskip**. So when TEX sees a **\vskip**, it looks first for a number, and then for a two-character keyword for the unit of length. However, TEX cannot just say "AHA!" when it sees the first digit or the **p**. There might be another digit, and the **p** might become **pt** or **pc** or something else entirely. Thus, TEX needs a place to accumulate things until it can tell if it has what it expects to find.

When TeX finds a problem instead of what it needs, the error message includes information about the *tokens* it has accumulated but has not yet processed. (A token is either a character or a control sequence.) Each accumulated token is shown on a separate line after **<to be read again>**.

```
! Illegal unit of measure (pt inserted).
<to be read again>
                     w
l.383 The \vskip 2 w
                     as interesting.
?
```

The example above has only one accumulated token, the **w** character, because none of TeX's dimension keywords start with a **w**.

Whenever TeX expects a dimension or glue and does not find a legitimate keyword, it automatically uses points (**pt**). So TeX has already done **\vskip 2pt**. If you press RETURN after the above error message, TeX processes the **w** from its **<to be read again>** accumulator and continues with **as interesting**.

Instead of pressing RETURN, you can insert a new instruction that corrects the size of the **\vskip** in your printout. For example, if you wanted a **\vskip** of **2pc**, you can add the additional **22pt** of space by typing **i\vskip 22pt** after the question-mark prompt. (**2pc** = **24pt**. Since TeX has already done a **\vskip** of **2pt**, you need another **22pt** to get a total of **24pt**.)

¡Inserted Text¿

In the example above, TeX has already inserted the **pt** and gone on, so you cannot back up and change the **pt** to **in** or **pc** or whatever else you wanted it to be. In the next example, you can change what TeX inserts because it has not yet processed the inserted text.

The following error message has two lines that we have not seen before: **<inserted text>** and the **$**.

```
! Missing $ inserted.
<inserted text>
                     $
<to be read again>
                     \pi
l.375 Everyone had \pi
                      \ and smacked their lips.
?
```

This error message has four pieces of information: the nature of the problem, the inserted text, the token to be read again, and the line where

TEX found the problem. The message also shows TEX's current state and what it intends to do next.

TEX was processing line 375 and had read **Everyone had** \pi when it found a problem. The problem is that \pi can be used only in math mode. To fix this problem, TEX put the \pi into its **<to be read again>** accumulator and inserted the math mode toggle so it can start math mode before it processes the \pi. However, TEX also sent you this error message both to notify you about the problem and to let you solve the problem differently if you prefer.

The line after **<inserted text>** shows the material that TEX inserted: the math mode toggle **$**. The line after **<to be read again>** tells you that TEX has not yet processed the \pi. If you press RETURN, TEX processes the **$\pi** and then continues with \ **and smacked**.

Since a Math Oops Mode Bug is happening here, you might prefer to take the **$\pi** out of the queue and insert the correct text. To do this, first type **2** (and RETURN).

TEX removes the next two tokens that it intends to process (**$** and \pi) and sends you a status report on its current state. \pi is a single token because it is a control sequence. (Chapter 33 explains TEX's tokens.)

```
<recently read> \pi

l.375 Everyone had \pi
                       \ and smacked their lips.
    ?
```

Now type the correction: **iπ**. TEX typesets the rest of the line correctly.

Removing Tokens from the Queue

When you type a number after TEX's question-mark prompt, TEX discards that number of tokens from whatever it normally would do next. (TEX does not toss these tokens into the garbage. Instead, it reads but does not act on them, just as if a percent sign had been typed in front of them.)

How can you tell how many tokens to discard? TEX puts each **<to be read again>** token on a separate line. Thus, if there are three **<to be read again>** lines, type a **3** to discard all three tokens. If there are two **<to be read again>** lines and one line of **<inserted text>**, again type a **3** to discard all three tokens.

35.3   Endless Loops

There are several ways that TEX can get stuck in an endless loop.

- When TeX cannot find a file that you want to \input, it insists on getting the name of a file. (See the Broken-Record Filename Bug, page 32.)

- When you define a control sequence and put the name of that control sequence inside the definition, TeX goes into an endless loop.

- When the tokens in the **<to be read again>** accumulator cause TeX to continue to insert new tokens, TeX never processes the accumulated tokens, and gets stuck in a **<to be read again>** loop.

To break out of an endless loop and make TeX stop, you can always use your operating system's abort command. Some common abort commands are

CONTROL-**C**   CONTROL-**G**   CONTROL-**Z**   CONTROL-BREAK

In TeXtures, click the mouse on the PAUSE box in the **.log** window, then click on QUIT.

If none of these abort sequences work for you, ask colleagues or your systems wizards what to do. If you are working at home, look for *abort sequence* or *stop* in your operating system's instruction manual. If all else fails, turn the computer off.

The Broken-Record Filename Bug

When TeX insists on getting the name of a file to \input and you cannot supply a filename that TeX can recognize, you can usually type **null**. (See the Broken-Record Filename Bug, page 32.)

Most versions of TeX come with a **null.tex** file that contains either nothing or the control sequence \relax (which means to do nothing). If your version of TeX does not have a **null.tex** file, make one and place it in a directory where TeX always looks. If you are not sure what directory that might be, see the installation instructions for your version of TeX.

Recursion

If you use the name of a control sequence inside the definition of that same control sequence, TeX goes into an endless loop. For example, the following \endlessloop macro

```
\def\endlessloop{%
   Why is \TeX\ in an \endlessloop?}
```

expands into

```
Why is \TeX\ in an Why is \TeX\ in an Why is \TeX\ in an ...
```

and never reaches the question mark at the end of the definition.

You might think that TeX would go on forever if you put this \endlessloop in your text file. Instead, TeX runs out of memory. According to *The TeXbook*, you then see the following error message:

```
! TeX capacity exceeded, sorry [input stack size=80]
\endlessloop -> Why is \TeX\ in an \endlessloop
                                                 ?
\endlessloop -> Why is \TeX\ in an \endlessloop
                                                 ?
...
```

My own experiment produced **! TeX capacity exceeded, sorry [main memory size=0]** instead, so the exact details of this message varies among the different installations of TeX. Also, the transcript file contained 173,490 bytes, and 1714 lines of **\endlessloop -> Why is \TeX\ in an \endlessloop?** It took longer to print the transcript file on the screen than it took for TeX to run out of memory!

To-Be-Read-Again Loops

If the error messages seem to be caught in a cycle and TeX does not move to the next line, it is probably stuck in a to-be-read-again loop. If TeX waits for instructions from you when it finds errors, you can simply type **x** to make TeX stop there. However, if you have changed to **\scrollmode**, **\nonstopmode**, or **\batchmode**, then you may need to use your operating system's abort command to make TeX stop.

If TeX finds 100 errors before it reaches the end of a paragraph, TeX stops and tells you

```
! That makes 100 errors; please try again.
```

Sometimes TeX does move on, but very slowly. It may send four or six error messages about one piece of text, then another four or six error messages about the next piece of text, and so on. In this situation, it usually makes sense to stop TeX here and look at the text file to see if you can spot the problem and solve it. Since a Chameleon Bug is one likely cause of this problem, you may need to use the divide-and-conquer or toss-it strategies to find the bug and fix it.

Thankfully, these loops are rare.

35.4   Some Other Error Messages and Their Causes

- **Only one # is allowed per tab.** See the Too Many Number Signs Bug, page 204.
- **Extra alignment tab has been changed to \cr.** See the Extra Alignment Tab Bug, page 204.

- **Undefined control sequence**. This is usually the result of a typo in your text file. However, you may have forgotten to define a **\thetitle** or **\theauthor** macro (see the **Oops!** section, page 176), or a **\theSectionTitle** macro (see the **Oops!** section, page 184).

- **You can't use \eqno or \leqno in math mode**. The difficulty is that you must be in *display math mode* to use **\eqno** or **\leqno**, not regular math mode. See the **Oops!** section, page 269, and use **\eqaligno** or **\leqaligno** instead of **\displaylines** or **\eqalign**.

Review and Related Matters

Even though the bugs in this book have descriptive names, not all of those names are easy to remember. Thus, this chapter lists the bugs by similar types of symptoms. This chapter also explains the structure of TeX's error messages and shows how to use them. It also shows what to do when TeX gets stuck in an endless loop.

The previous chapter describes how to find and fix the bugs in your text or macro definitions, including three strategies for finding elusive bugs. It also presents several general types of bugs that can appear in a wide range of layout tasks.

APPENDIX A

Font Tables

This appendix contains eight font tables—for the roman, math italic, math symbol, math extension, text italic, slanted, bold, and typewriter fonts—in Section A.2. Each font also has its own size of interword space, intersentence space, the **em** and **ex**, and a dimension that TeX uses to place accent marks in the correct position. These dimensions are called \fontdimen parameters. Section A.3 describes ways of using these \fontdimen parameters to fine tune the size of spaces in your documents, and contains a table showing these parameters for all the text fonts plus the math italic font.

Section A.1 describes how to use \char, the TeX primitive that goes and gets a character from the current font table.

A.1   Using \char

When you want to typeset a character that does not appear on the keyboard, you can use \char to go get that character from the font table. \char is a primitive and takes one input: the number that shows the character's position on the font table.

For example, in the roman font shown on page 364, the open bracket [is in position 91, and the close bracket] is in position 93. Thus, if your keyboard does not have brackets, you can use \char instead, as follows:

```
The party was no fun.  I was bracketed by bores:
dodos \char91~me~\char93\ deadbeats.
```

> The party was no fun. I was bracketed by bores: dodos [me] deadbeats.

In effect, \char typesets a character from the current font table.[1]

To determine a character's position, add the numbers at the left of the row and the top of the column. Both [and] are in the 90 row. The [is in the 1 column and the] is in the 3 column. So [is in position 91, and] in position 93.

Whenever you need a character from the font table on a regular basis, it makes sense to write a macro. That way, you do not have to remember or look up the position number every time you want to use that character.

```
\def\circumflex{{\char94}}
\def\Tilde{\char126\relax}
```

(TeX already has a \tilde control sequence; it typesets a tilde accent in math mode.)

Oops!

When you write a macro with \char, make sure you put \relax after the number or put a second set of braces around \char and its input. Otherwise, you get a Bad Character Code Bug whenever a number follows this macro in your text file.

Bad Character Code Bug

The spaces after a control sequence are gobbled up in showing where that control sequence ends. Let's suppose you defined \oopstilde as

```
\def\oopstilde{\char126}
```

and said \oopstilde 5 in your text file. TeX expands the \oopstilde macro into \char126—but the next character is a 5, so \char looks for a character in position 1265 on the font tables. Since this position does not exist, TeX sends you an error message.

```
! Bad character code (1265).
```

The error message also shows the line number and the line of text where TeX found this problem.

The solution is simple. When you write a macro with \char, put \relax after the number, or put the entire instruction inside braces as shown in the definition of \circumflex above.

---

[1]More precisely, \char *accesses* that character, which enables you to do whatever you want with it. Normally, what you want to do is typeset that character—but there are other possibilities, such as putting it into a \phantom hbox.

Oops!

If you change fonts, **\char** sometimes gets a character that is different from the one you wanted. This happens only when the current font table is different from the one you had in mind. For example, if you define an **\emdash** macro as

```
\def\emdash{{\char124}}
```

and then use this **\emdash** in the typewriter font or in math mode, you get the following:

```
He was such a dashing fellow\emdash always on the
run.  He must have known $4\times101\emdash
404\heartsuit$ ways of spicing up ordinary
activities, which is {\tt quite an
accomplishment\emdash under any circumstances}.
```

> He was such a dashing fellow—always on the run. He must have known $4 \times 101|404\heartsuit$ ways of spicing up ordinary activities, which is `quite an accomplishment|under any circumstances.`

To fix this problem, change the font to the one you need, such as **\rm** or **\bf**.

Using Octal and Hexadecimal Numbers for \char

\char also recognizes octal and hexadecimal numbers, and the font tables in *The TEXbook* have eight columns instead of ten. That makes it simple to use octal (base 8) and hexadecimal (base 16) numbers instead of decimal (base 10).

I decided to use decimal format for the font tables in this book because everyone understands base 10 numbers. The rest of this section explains how to use octal or hexadecimal numbers as the input number for **\char**, for those of you who want to learn.

Put an apostrophe (') in front of an octal number and a typewriter quote (") in front of a hexadecimal one. To find the octal number of a character's position in *The TEXbook*'s font tables, use the same strategy described above for decimal numbers. Take the number at the left of that row, and substitute the number from the top of that column for the x. To find the hexadecimal number, take the number at the right of that row, and substitute the number from either the top or bottom of that column for the x.

For example, page 427 of *The TeXbook* also contains the roman font table, laid out in eight columns instead of ten. The octal number for [is **'133** and for] is **'135**. The hexadecimal number for [is **"5B** and for] is **"5D**. (These font tables contain two rows for each hexadecimal layer. In the row above the brackets, the hexadecimal numbers for **S** and **U** are **"53** and **"55**, respectively.)

Thus, a pair of bracket macros could be defined as follows:

```
\def\openbracket{{\char'133}}
\def\closebracket{\char"5D\relax}
```

The numbers for **\char** correspond to the ASCII numbers for the characters. *The TeXbook*'s Appendix C explains ASCII numbers and codes in detail, as well as how TeX uses them.

A.2 The Font Tables

The roman font: \rm, \textfont=0, \fam=0.

	0	1	2	3	4	5	6	7	8	9
0	Γ	Δ	Θ	Λ	Ξ	Π	Σ	Υ	Φ	Ψ
10	Ω	ff	fi	fl	ffi	ffl	ı	j	`	´
20	˘	ˇ	¯	˚	¸	ß	æ	œ	ø	Æ
30	Œ	Ø	´	!	"	#	$	%	&	'
40	(	)	*	+	,	-	.	/	0	1
50	2	3	4	5	6	7	8	9	:	;
60	¡	=	¿	?	@	A	B	C	D	E
70	F	G	H	I	J	K	L	M	N	O
80	P	Q	R	S	T	U	V	W	X	Y
90	Z	[	"	]	^	·	`	a	b	c
100	d	e	f	g	h	i	j	k	l	m
110	n	o	p	q	r	s	t	u	v	w
120	x	y	z	–	—	"	~	¨		

The math italic font: `\mit, \textfont=1, \fam=1.`

	0	1	2	3	4	5	6	7	8	9
0	Γ	Δ	Θ	Λ	Ξ	Π	Σ	Υ	Φ	Ψ
10	Ω	α	β	γ	δ	ϵ	ζ	η	θ	ι
20	κ	λ	μ	ν	ξ	π	ρ	σ	τ	υ
30	ϕ	χ	ψ	ω	ε	ϑ	ϖ	ϱ	ς	φ
40	$\leftharpoonup$	$\leftharpoondown$	$\rightharpoonup$	$\rightharpoondown$	$\check{\ }$	$\acute{\ }$	$\triangleright$	$\triangleleft$	0	1
50	2	3	4	5	6	7	8	9	.	,
60	$<$	$/$	$>$	$\star$	∂	A	B	C	D	E
70	F	G	H	I	J	K	L	M	N	O
80	P	Q	R	S	T	U	V	W	X	Y
90	Z	$\flat$	$\natural$	$\sharp$	$\smile$	$\frown$	ℓ	a	b	c
100	d	e	f	g	h	i	j	k	l	m
110	n	o	p	q	r	s	t	u	v	w
120	x	y	z	$\imath$	$\jmath$	$\wp$	$\vec{\ }$	$\frown$		

The math symbol font: `\cal, \textfont=2, \fam=2.`

	0	1	2	3	4	5	6	7	8	9
0	$-$	$\cdot$	$\times$	$*$	$\div$	$\diamond$	$\pm$	$\mp$	$\oplus$	$\ominus$
10	$\otimes$	$\oslash$	$\odot$	$\bigcirc$	$\circ$	$\bullet$	$\asymp$	$\equiv$	$\subseteq$	$\supseteq$
20	$\leq$	$\geq$	$\preceq$	$\succeq$	$\sim$	$\approx$	$\subset$	$\supset$	$\ll$	$\gg$
30	$\prec$	$\succ$	$\leftarrow$	$\rightarrow$	$\uparrow$	$\downarrow$	$\leftrightarrow$	$\nearrow$	$\searrow$	$\simeq$
40	$\Leftarrow$	$\Rightarrow$	$\Uparrow$	$\Downarrow$	$\Leftrightarrow$	$\nwarrow$	$\swarrow$	$\propto$	$\prime$	∞
50	$\in$	$\ni$	$\triangle$	$\bigtriangledown$	$/$	$\prime$	$\forall$	$\exists$	$\neg$	$\emptyset$
60	$\Re$	$\Im$	$\top$	$\bot$	$\aleph$	$\mathcal{A}$	$\mathcal{B}$	$\mathcal{C}$	$\mathcal{D}$	$\mathcal{E}$
70	$\mathcal{F}$	$\mathcal{G}$	$\mathcal{H}$	$\mathcal{I}$	$\mathcal{J}$	$\mathcal{K}$	$\mathcal{L}$	$\mathcal{M}$	$\mathcal{N}$	$\mathcal{O}$
80	$\mathcal{P}$	$\mathcal{Q}$	$\mathcal{R}$	$\mathcal{S}$	$\mathcal{T}$	$\mathcal{U}$	$\mathcal{V}$	$\mathcal{W}$	$\mathcal{X}$	$\mathcal{Y}$
90	$\mathcal{Z}$	$\cup$	$\cap$	$\uplus$	$\wedge$	$\vee$	$\vdash$	$\dashv$	$\lfloor$	$\rfloor$
100	$\lceil$	$\rceil$	$\{$	$\}$	$\langle$	$\rangle$	$\mid$	$\parallel$	$\updownarrow$	$\Updownarrow$
110	$\backslash$	$\wr$	$\surd$	$\amalg$	∇	$\int$	$\sqcup$	$\sqcap$	$\sqsubseteq$	$\sqsupseteq$
120	$\S$	$\dagger$	$\ddagger$	$\P$	$\clubsuit$	$\diamondsuit$	$\heartsuit$	$\spadesuit$		

The math extension font: `\textfont=3, \fam=3.`

	0	1	2	3	4	5	6	7	8	9
0	(	)	[	]	⌊	⌋	⌈	⌉	{	}
10	⟨	⟩	|	‖	/	\	(	)	(	)
20	[	]	⌊	⌋	⌈	⌉	{	}	⟨	⟩
30	/	\	(	)	[	]	⌊	⌋	⌈	⌉
40	{	}	⟨	⟩	/	\	/	\	(	)
50	⌈	⌉	⌊	⌋	|	|	(	)	(	)
60	{	}	.	|	(	)	|	|	⟨	⟩
70	⊔	⊔	∮	∮	⊙	⊙	⊕	⊕	⊗	⊗
80	Σ	Π	∫	∪	∩	⊎	∧	∨	Σ	Π
90	∫	∪	∩	⊎	∧	∨	⊔	⊔	⌢	⌢
100	⌢	~	~	~	[	]	⌊	⌋	⌈	⌉
110	{	}	√	√	√	√	√	|	⌈	‖
120	↑	↓	⌐	`	`	´	⇑	⇓		

The text italic font: `\it, \textfont=\itfam, \fam=\itfam.`

	0	1	2	3	4	5	6	7	8	9
0	Γ	Δ	Θ	Λ	Ξ	Π	Σ	Υ	Φ	Ψ
10	Ω	ff	fi	fl	ffi	ffl	ı	j	`	´
20	ˇ	˘	¯	°	˛	ß	æ	œ	ø	Æ
30	Œ	Ø	˙	!	”	#	£	%	&	'
40	(	)	*	+	,	-	.	/	0	1
50	2	3	4	5	6	7	8	9	:	;
60	¡	=	¿	?	@	A	B	C	D	E
70	F	G	H	I	J	K	L	M	N	O
80	P	Q	R	S	T	U	V	W	X	Y
90	Z	[	"	]	^	·	'	a	b	c
100	d	e	f	g	h	i	j	k	l	m
110	n	o	p	q	r	s	t	u	v	w
120	x	y	z	–	—	"	~	¨		

The slanted font: `\sl, \textfont=\slfam, \fam=\slfam.`

	0	1	2	3	4	5	6	7	8	9
0	Γ	Δ	Θ	Λ	Ξ	Π	Σ	Υ	Φ	Ψ
10	Ω	ff	fi	fl	ffi	ffl	ı	j	`	´
20	ˇ	˘	¯	°	˛	ß	æ	œ	ø	Æ
30	Œ	Ø	˙	!	”	#	$	%	&	'
40	(	)	*	+	,	-	.	/	0	1
50	2	3	4	5	6	7	8	9	:	;
60	¡	=	¿	?	@	A	B	C	D	E
70	F	G	H	I	J	K	L	M	N	O
80	P	Q	R	S	T	U	V	W	X	Y
90	Z	[	"	]	^	·	'	a	b	c
100	d	e	f	g	h	i	j	k	l	m
110	n	o	p	q	r	s	t	u	v	w
120	x	y	z	–	—	"	~	¨		

The bold font: `\bf, \textfont=\bffam, \fam=\bffam.`

	0	1	2	3	4	5	6	7	8	9
0	Γ	Δ	Θ	Λ	Ξ	Π	Σ	Υ	Φ	Ψ
10	Ω	ff	fi	fl	ffi	ffl	ı	J	`	´
20	˘	ˇ	¯	˚	¸	ß	æ	œ	ø	Æ
30	Œ	Ø	-	!	"	#	$	%	&	'
40	(	)	*	+	,	-	.	/	0	1
50	2	3	4	5	6	7	8	9	:	;
60	¡	=	¿	?	@	A	B	C	D	E
70	F	G	H	I	J	K	L	M	N	O
80	P	Q	R	S	T	U	V	W	X	Y
90	Z	[	"	]	^	˙	`	a	b	c
100	d	e	f	g	h	i	j	k	l	m
110	n	o	p	q	r	s	t	u	v	w
120	x	y	z	–	—	"	~	¨		

The typewriter font: `\tt, \textfont=\ttfam, \fam=\ttfam.`

	0	1	2	3	4	5	6	7	8	9
0	Γ	Δ	θ	Λ	Ξ	Π	Σ	Υ	Φ	Ψ
10	Ω	↑	↓	'	i	¿	ı	J	`	´
20	˘	ˇ	¯	˙	¸	ß	æ	œ	ø	Æ
30	Œ	Ø	␣	!	"	#	$	%	&	'
40	(	)	*	+	,	-	.	/	0	1
50	2	3	4	5	6	7	8	9	:	;
60	<	=	>	?	@	A	B	C	D	E
70	F	G	H	I	J	K	L	M	N	O
80	P	Q	R	S	T	U	V	W	X	Y
90	Z	[	\	]	^	_	`	a	b	c
100	d	e	f	g	h	i	j	k	l	m
110	n	o	p	q	r	s	t	u	v	w
120	x	y	z	{	|	}	~	¨		

A.3   The \fontdimen parameters

Each font has its own size of interword space, intersentence space, the **em** and **ex**, and a dimension that TEX uses to place accent marks in the correct position. These dimensions are called **\fontdimen** parameters. The following table shows these **\fontdimen** parameters for **cmr10** (roman), **cmbx10** (bold), **cmsl10** (slanted), **cmti10** (text italic), **cmtt10** (typewriter), and **cmmi10** (math italic).

#	Meaning	cmr10	cmbx10	cmsl10	cmti10	cmtt10	cmmi10
1	slant per point	0.00pt	0.00pt	0.17pt	0.25pt	0.00pt	0.25pt
2	interword space	3.33pt	3.83pt	3.33pt	3.58pt	5.25pt	0.00pt
3	interword stretch	1.67pt	1.92pt	1.67pt	1.53pt	0.00pt	0.00pt
4	interword shrink	1.11pt	1.28pt	1.11pt	1.02pt	0.00pt	0.00pt
5	x-height (**1ex**)	4.31pt	4.44pt	4.31pt	4.31pt	4.31pt	4.31pt
6	quad width (**1em**)	10.00pt	11.50pt	10.00pt	10.22pt	10.50pt	10.00pt
7	extra space	1.11pt	1.28pt	1.11pt	1.02pt	5.25pt	0.00pt

Here is an explanation of each **\fontdimen**.

- **\fontdimen1** is the slant parameter. TEX uses this dimension to place accent marks in the correct position. This dimension is **0pt** in the upright fonts, **0.25pt** in both italic fonts, and **0.17pt** in the slanted font.

- **\fontdimen2** is the normal size of a space between words. In **cmmi10**, this dimension is **0pt**. That is one reason why TEX puts no space between "words" in math mode. In **cmtt10**, this dimension is the same as the width of all the other characters in the font.

- **\fontdimen3** is the amount of stretchable glue that TEX can normally use in a space between words. In both **cmtt10** and **cmmi10**, this is **0pt**.

- **\fontdimen4** is the amount of shrinkable glue that TEX normally uses in a space between words. In both **cmtt10** and **cmmi10**, this is **0pt**.

- **\fontdimen5** is the height of **1ex**. The roman, slanted, italic, and typewriter fonts have the same x-height. Only the bold font is different.

- **\fontdimen6** is the width of **1em**, or one quad width. These are the same in **cmr10**, **cmsl10**, and **cmmi10**—and slightly larger in the others.

- **\fontdimen7** is the extra space that TEX puts between sentences. (It also puts a proportion of this space after colons, semicolons, and commas.) In **cmtt10**, this dimension is the same as the interword space. In **cmmi10**, this dimension is **0pt**.

None of these dimensions is carved in stone, although it is not wise to change them unless you have a good reason. One dimension that I always change is **fontdimen4**. I prefer to use a high **tolerance** and **pretolerance** in most of my documents, but I also want to prevent TeX from shrinking the spaces. Thus, I always give my fonts a **fontdimen4** of **0pt**.

The time to change a **fontdimen** is when you load the font. For example, here are the 8-point text fonts that I loaded for this book:

```
\font\eightrm=cmr8     \fontdimen4\eightrm=0pt
\font\eightbf=cmbx8    \fontdimen4\eightbf=0pt
\font\eightit=cmti8    \fontdimen4\eightit=0pt
\font\eightsl=cmsl8    \fontdimen4\eightsl=0pt
```

Knuth's *TeXbook* says that the math symbol fonts have at least twenty-two **fontdimen** parameters instead of seven, and the math extension fonts have at least thirteen. (These are explained in *The TeXbook*'s Appendix G, for those of you who want to know.)

APPENDIX B

TEX's Reporters

This appendix lists most of TEX's reporters and all the doers that handle dimensions or glue. It also shows the default (startup) values of each of these reporters. A complete list of TEX's reporters (parameters) is on pages 272–75 of *The TEXbook*.

B.1   Count Reporters (Integer Parameters)

The following reporters were described in earlier chapters of this book:

- **\pretolerance=100**: affects the width of spaces that TEX accepts during its first pass through a paragraph looking for line-break points, before it hyphenates the words in the paragraph. (Chapter 4)

- **\tolerance=200**: affects the width of spaces that TEX accepts during its second pass through a paragraph looking for line-break points, after it hyphenates the words in the paragraph. (Chapter 4)

- **\hbadness=1000**: the level where TEX sends error messages about underfull hboxes. (Chapter 4)

- **\vbadness=1000**: the level where TEX sends error messages about underfull vboxes. (Chapter 32)

- **\looseness=0**: the number of lines to add to or subtract from the length of a paragraph. A positive number increases the number of lines in the paragraph, making it "looser." A negative number reduces the number of lines, making it "tighter." (Chapter 32)

- **\hangafter=1**: the number of lines that use hanging indentation. This reporter affects only one paragraph and is reset to its default value of **1** after TEX completes that paragraph. A positive number means that hanging indentation starts after that line and continues for the rest of the paragraph. A negative number uses hanging indentation for that number of lines at the top of the paragraph. (Chapter 15)

- **\fam=0**: the current font family number. The **\fam** number specifies which font TeX uses in math mode. (Chapter 27)

TeX also keeps track of the time, with reporters for the **\time** (current time of day in minutes since midnight), **\day**, **\month**, and **\year**.

TeX uses penalties to decide where to break lines and pages. A high penalty discourages TeX from using a particular break point. A penalty of zero means that TeX has no preference one way or the other. A negative penalty encourages TeX to use that break point. TeX's highest penalty number is **10000**, the lowest is **−10000**.

The following penalties were described in Chapter 32:

- **\clubpenalty=150**: putting a single line at the bottom of a page.
- **\widowpenalty=150**: putting a single line at the top of a page.
- **\predisplaypenalty=10000**: breaking the page just before a math display.
- **\postdisplaypenalty=0**: breaking the page just after a math display.
- **\displaywidowpenalty=50**: putting a single line at the top of a page before a math display.

TeX has several penalties that deal with hyphens. A high positive number inhibits this behavior; a negative number encourages it.

- **\hyphenpenalty=50**: breaking a line after a discretionary hyphen (\-).
- **\exhyphenpenalty=50**: breaking a line after an explicit hyphen (-).
- **\brokenpenalty=100**: breaking the page after a line that ends with a hyphen.
- **\doublehyphendemerits=10000**: having two consecutive lines that end with hyphens.
- **\finalhyphendemerits=5000**: having the second to last line on a page end with a hyphen.
- **\lefthyphenmin=2**: smallest size of the word fragment in front of the hyphen, in number of characters.
- **\righthyphenmin=3**: smallest size of the word fragment after the hyphen, in number of characters.

You may also want to explore the following penalties. Again, a high penalty number discourages this behavior; a negative number encourages it.

- **\interlinepenalty=0**: additional penalty for breaking the page inside a paragraph. Giving **\interlinepenalty** a high number discourages page breaks inside a paragraph and encourages page breaks between paragraphs.

- **\binoppenalty=700**: penalty for breaking a line after a binary operation in math mode.

- **\relpenalty=500**: penalty for breaking a line after a math relation in math mode.

- **\floatingpenalty=0**: penalty for splitting an insertion (footnote) onto two or more pages.

B.2   Dimension Reporters (Dimension Parameters)

The following dimension reporters were described in earlier chapters of this book:

- **\hfuzz=0.1pt**: extra width that TEX accepts for an overfull hbox without sending error messages. (Chapter 4)

- **\vfuzz=0.1pt**: extra length that TEX accepts for an overfull vbox without sending error messages. (Chapter 32)

- **\hsize=6.5in**: the width of the hboxes that TEX makes while typesetting a paragraph (in horizontal mode). (Chapter 8)

- **\vsize=8.9in**: the height + depth of the vbox that contains the body, or text portion of the page. (Chapter 8)

- **\overfullrule=5pt**: the width of the black box that TEX typesets at the right edge of an overfull hbox. (Chapter 4)

- **\lineskiplimit=0pt**: the threshold where TEX puts **\lineskip** glue between the hboxes in a paragraph, instead of placing their baselines **\baselineskip** apart. (Chapter 24)

- **\parindent=20pt**: the width of the indentation TEX puts at the beginning of a new paragraph. **\indent** uses this dimension. (Chapter 8)

- **\hangindent=0pt**: the size of the hanging indentation for a paragraph. This reporter affects only one paragraph and is automatically reset to **0pt** after TEX finishes that paragraph. (Chapter 15)

- **\hoffset=0pt**: the distance that TEX moves the text to the right. Most printers place 1 inch of white space between the left edge of the paper and the text, so the **\hoffset** is in addition to this inch. (Chapter 8)

- **\voffset=0pt**: the distance that TEX moves the text down on the page. Most printers place 1 inch of white space between the top edge of the paper and the text, so the **\voffset** is in addition to this inch. (Chapter 8)

Here are some additional dimension reporters you may want to explore:

- **\emergencystretch=0pt**: a dimension that TEX adds to the stretchiness of spaces between words during a third pass through a paragraph, to distinguish between poor line-break points and atrocious ones. This is done only if **\emergencystretch** is higher than **0pt**, and only if TEX cannot find acceptable line-break points during the second pass through the paragraph using **\tolerance**.
- **\scriptspace=0.5pt**: extra space after a subscript or superscript.
- **\mathsurround=0pt**: space that TEX puts before and after math mode material in a paragraph. Using a larger **\mathsurround** makes mathematical formulas stand out from the rest of the text.
- **\predisplaysize**: the width of the hbox immediately above a math display. TEX sets this for each math display, so there is no default size.
- **\displaywidth**: the width of the line for a displayed equation. TEX sets this for each math display, so there is no default size.
- **\displayindent**: the indentation at the front of the line for a displayed equation. TEX sets this for each math display, so there is no default size.

B.3   Glue Reporters (Glue Parameters)

All of TEX's glue reporters have the word *skip* in their names. The following reporters were described in earlier chapters of this book:

- **\baselineskip=12pt**: the vertical distance between baselines of the hboxes in a paragraph. Also, the vertical distance that TEX normally puts between the baselines of all boxes when TEX is in a vertical mode. (Chapter 8)
- **\parskip=0pt plus 1pt**: vertical glue that TEX adds to the page just before starting a new paragraph. (Chapter 8)
- **\abovedisplayskip=12pt plus 3pt minus 9pt**: vertical glue that TEX puts above a math display, unless the text in the line just above the display is short. (Chapter 24)
- **\belowdisplayskip=12pt plus 3pt minus 9pt**: vertical glue that TEX puts below a math display, unless the text in the line just above the display is short. (Chapter 24)
- **\abovedisplayshortskip=0pt plus 3pt**: vertical glue that TEX puts above a math display when the text in the line above the display is short. (Chapter 24)
- **\belowdisplayshortskip=7pt plus 3pt minus 4pt**: vertical glue that TEX puts below a math display when the text in the line above the display is short. (Chapter 24)

- **\leftskip=0pt**: horizontal glue that TEX puts at the left edge of an hbox, before the text. The effect is to change the apparent left margin of one or more paragraphs of text. (Chapter 13)

- **\rightskip=0pt**: horizontal glue that TEX puts between the text and the right edge of an hbox. The effect is to change the apparent right margin of one or more paragraphs of text. (Chapter 13)

- **\topskip=10pt**: vertical glue that TEX puts between the header and the text. More specifically, TEX puts glue between the top edge of the body (vbox containing the text on a page) and the first box inside that body (usually the first hbox of a paragraph). TEX adjusts this glue so the **\topskip** specifies the distance from the top edge of the body's vbox to the baseline of the first line of text. (Chapter 18)

- **\lineskip=1pt**: vertical glue that TEX puts between boxes when **\baselineskip** is not feasible. In other words, if placing two boxes 1\baselineskip apart makes their adjacent edges closer than the **\lineskiplimit**, TEX places a **\lineskip** between the boxes instead. (Chapter 33)

- **\tabskip=0pt**: horizontal glue that TEX puts between the columns of an **\halign**. TEX also puts **\tabskip** glue before the first column and after the last column of the **\halign**. (Chapter 20)

Here are all of TEX's remaining glue reporters:

- **\parfillskip=0pt plus 1fil**: horizontal glue that TEX puts on the last line at the end of a paragraph.

- **\splittopskip=10pt**: vertical glue that TEX puts at the top of split pages (pages having more than one body vbox).

- **\spaceskip=0pt**: horizontal glue that TEX puts between words, if **\spaceskip** is not zero.

- **\xspaceskip=0pt**: horizontal glue that TEX puts between sentences, if **\xspaceskip** is not zero.

Specifying a different **\spaceskip** and **\xspaceskip** is another way of controlling the size of interword spaces and intersentence spaces.

B.4 Other Reporters

The following glue reporters are not included in TEX's list of parameters (on pages 272–75 of *The TEXbook*).

- **\bigskipamount**: the glue for **\bigskip**. (Chapter 8)
- **\medskipamount**: the glue for **\medskip**. (Chapter 8)
- **\smallskipamount**: the glue for **\smallskip**. (Chapter 8)

- \normalbaselineskip: the normal size of \baselineskip. (Chapter 8)
- \normallineskip: the normal \lineskip. (Chapter 24)

TEX also has three math-glue reporters. Math glue is called *muglue*, so the following three reporters are called *muglue parameters*. The unit of length for muglue is called a **mu** (for *math unit*) instead of **pt** or **cm** or **in** and the like.

- \thinmuskip=3mu: thin math space.
- \medmuskip=4mu plus 2mu minus 4mu: medium math space.
- \thickmuskip=5mu plus 5mu: thick math space.

TEX uses these thin, medium, and thick spaces in formulas. Thin muglue spaces do not stretch or shrink. Medium muglue spaces can stretch a little or shrink to zero. Thick spaces can stretch to twice their normal size, but cannot shrink.

B.5 Dimension and Glue Doers

Last but not least, here is a list of doers that deal with dimensions and glue.

- \hskip: add horizontal glue (to this line or inside an hbox).
- \vskip: add vertical glue (to this page or inside a vbox).
- \kern: add either a horizontal or vertical dimension of space to this line or page. A kern cannot be stretched or shrunk.
- \hfil: add horizontal fil glue.
- \hfill: add horizontal fill glue.
- \vfil: add vertical fil glue.
- \vfill: add vertical fill glue.
- \bigskip: add the \bigskipamount of vertical glue.
- \medskip: add the \medskipamount of vertical glue.
- \smallskip: add the \smallskipamount of vertical glue.
- \enskip: macro defined as \hskip 0.5em\relax.
- \enspace: macro defined as \kern 0.5em.

The \enskip can only be used in a horizontal mode. If TEX is in a vertical mode, an \enskip causes TEX to change to horizontal mode. However, the \enspace can be used in any mode, because the \kern creates horizontal space in horizontal modes, and vertical space in vertical modes.

The following three doers create new reporters:

- **\newcount**: make a new count reporter.
- **\newdimen**: make a new dimension reporter.
- **\newskip**: make a new glue reporter.

And for those who enjoy nonstraight margins:

- **\raggedbottom**: a macro that creates ragged-bottom pages.
- **\normalbottom**: a macro that restores TeX's usual behavior of pulling text down to the bottom of the body-vbox pages.
- **\raggedright**: a macro that creates ragged right margins instead of straight (justified) ones.

Index

Note: Entries with no page numbers are TEX commands described in *The TEXbook* but not here. Having a complete list of their names in this index helps you avoid using these names when you make a new control sequence.

\ (prim: control space), 11, 329
(parameter character), 53, 196
\# (plain: number sign), 13–14, 21
(plain), 207
$ (math mode toggle), 14–17, 237, 329
$, in a macro definition, 58–59
\$ (plain: dollar sign), 13–14, 16
$$ (display math mode toggles), 238–39, 332
% (comment character), 19–20, 78, 170, 334
\% (plain: percent sign), 13–14, 19
& (alignment tab character), 196, 265, 269–70
\& (plain: ampersand), 13–14, 20
' (with octal number), 363–64
' (′), 250
\' (plain: acute accent ó), 24
\` (plain: grave accent ò), 24
" (with hexadecimal number), 363–64
   see also quotation marks
\" (plain: dieresis or umlaut accent ö), 24
}, *see* braces, groups
\} (plain: delimiter), 242–43
   in LATEX, 243
{, *see* braces, groups
\{ (plain: delimiter), 242–43
   in LATEX, 243

+, *see* plus sign
\+ (plain)
−, *see* minus sign
\- (prim: discretionary hyphen), 43, 160, 329
--, *see* en dash
---, *see* em dash
* (single asterisk prompt), 36, 38, 353
** (double asterisk prompt), 31, 38
* (plain: discretionary ×)
/ (as delimiter), 242–43
\/ (plain: italic correction), 68–69
| (absolute value sign), 23
| (delimiter), 242–43
\| (plain: ‖), 255
\ (escape character), 4–5, 13–14
\\ (Snow: as macro for backslash), 52
   in LATEX, 52, 108
=, *see* equals sign
\= (plain: macron accent ō), 24
\, (plain: math thin space), 241
\. (plain: dot accent ȯ), 24
\; (plain: math thick space), 241
\! (plain: math negative thin space), 241
_ (subscripts), 249–50
_ (underscore), 13–14, 17–18
^ (circumflex), 13–14, 16–18
^ (superscripts), 249–50
\^ (plain: circumflex accent ô), 24

\alpha (plain: α), 253
\Alpha (Snow), 254
alternatives, *see* \cases
am fonts, 73
\amalg (plain: II), 258
ampersand, *see* &, \&
\angle (plain: ∠), 255
\answered (Snow), 303
\approx (plain: ≈), 259
arabic-numeral page numbers, 182–83
\arccos (plain: arccos), 256
\arcsin (plain: arcsin), 256
\arctan (plain: arctan), 256
argument, 15
  see also inputs, runaway
  arguments
\arg (plain: arg), 256
array environment (LaTeX), 266
arrays, 265–67
\arraystretch (LaTeX), 206
arrows, 260
\arrowvert (plain), 244
\Arrowvert (plain), 244
ASCII file, *see* plain-text file
ASCII numbers, 364
ASCII system, 7
\asciinum (Snow), 151
\ASCIInumber (Snow), 179
assignments, 147, 161
\ast (plain: ∗), 258
asterisk prompts, *see* * and **
\asymp (plain: ≍), 259
at (plain: keyword), 79–80
atoms, in math mode, 244–45
\atop (prim: $\frac{a}{b}$), 264
\atopwithdelims (prim)
\author (Snow), 175–76
auxiliary files, 330
axis, of characters in math mode, 265

\b (plain: bar-under accent o̠), 24
backslash (escape character), 4–5,
  13–14
\backslash (plain: \ ), 242–43, 255,
  259
\badness (prim)
badness number, 44–46
\bar (plain: math accent n̄), 252
bars over letters, 251–52

base 8 or 16, 363–64
baseline of a vbox, 290
baseline-sized skips, 99–100
baselines, 285–86
\baselineskip (prim), 90–93, 328, 374
\baselinestretch (LaTeX), 93
\batchmode (prim), 36
\begin{document} (LaTeX), 6
\begin{*environment*} (LaTeX), 128
\beginABC (Snow), 151–52
\beginBibliography (Snow), 157
\beginBullets (Snow), 148–49
\beginCenter (Snow), 141
\beginCode (Snow), 167–71
\beginFigure (Snow), 228
\beginFloatFigure (Snow), 233–34
\beginFloatTable (Snow), 232
\beginFlushList (Snow), 152–53
\beginFlushRight (Snow), 138
\beginGlossary (Snow), 159
\begingroup (prim), 127
\beginIndentedFlushList (Snow),
  154
\beginIndentedQuote (Snow), 137
\beginLongPage (Snow), 324
\beginNoSpaceCode (Snow), 167–68
\beginNumbers (Snow), 151
\beginOopsVerse (Snow), 343
\beginQuotation (Snow), 132
\beginQuote (Snow), 127
\beginRaggedOops (Snow), 135
\beginRaggedQuote (Snow), 134
\beginReferencedQuote (Snow),
  128
\beginRightQuote (Snow), 138–39
\beginRigidVerse (Snow), 172
\beginSamePageQuote (Snow), 292
\beginSkipBullets (Snow), 149
\beginStubbornCode (Snow), 169
\beginTable (Snow), 228
\beginTablenotes (Snow), 228
\beginTopTable (Snow), 231
\beginVerse (Snow), 164
\belowCaption (Snow), 228
\belowdisplayshortskip (prim), 374
\belowdisplayskip (prim), 374
Berry, Karl, x
\beta (plain: β), 253

\gg (plain: ≫), 259
\global (prim), 169–70, 286
global vs. local, 169
\globaldefs (prim)
\gloss (Snow), 159
glossaries, 159–60
\glossary (LaTeX), 155
\glossaryindent (Snow), 159
\glue (plain)
glue, 105–112
   at the top of a page, 175, 291
   how it stretches on a page, 106
   how to use it, 105–08
   in math mode, 375
   infinite, 106–07, 300–01
   inside an hbox, 295
   interlineskip, *see* interlineskip glue
   interword, *see* space between words
   levels of, 108–09, 137, 140
   natural space of, 105
   shrinkable, 109–10
   stretch-only or shrink-only, 107
     see also levels of glue
glue register, 151
glue reporters/parameters, 374–75
\goodbreak (plain)
\grave (plain: math accent $\grave{n}$), 252
Greek letters, 253–54
groups, 66–68
   bugs, 340–44
   how to nest them, 67–68
   in math mode, 241–42
   margin changes inside, 124–25, 127–28
   redefined \item inside, 148–51

\H (plain: long Hungarian umlaut á), 24
\halign (prim), 195–208, 329
   width of, 203–04
\hang (plain)
\hangafter (prim), 160–62, 371
\hangindent (prim), 156, 159, 162, 373
hanging indentation, 155–62, 371, 373
Hargreaves, Kathryn, x
\hat (plain: math accent $\hat{n}$), 252
\hbadness (prim), 46, 371
\hbar (plain: ℏ), 255

\hbox (prim), 286–88, 295, 331, 344
headers, 117–18, 181–87
   blank on title pages, 186–87
   changing the font, 182–83
   multiline, 187
\headheight (LaTeX), 185
\heading (Snow), 174
\headingfont (Snow), 183
headings, 173–79
   of table columns, 209–17
   shape of, 179
   with larger typeface, 174
   with numbers or letters, 176–79
\headline (plain), 181–82
\headsep (LaTeX), 185
\heartsuit (plain: ♡), 255
height (plain: keyword), 312–13
height,
   of a box, 285–86, 295–99
   of a rule, 315
   of a vbox, 289–90
help, 34
hexadecimal numbers, 363–64
\hfil (prim), 107–09, 329, 376
\hfill (prim), 107–09, 329, 376
\hfilll (Snow), 109
\hfilneg (prim), 324, 329
\hfuzz (prim), 43–44, 373
\hglue (plain), 175
\hideskip (plain)
\hidewidth (plain), 211–14
\hoffset (prim), 87–88, 373
\holdinginserts (prim)
\hom (plain: hom), 256
\hookleftarrow (plain: ↩), 260
\hookrightarrow (plain: ↪), 260
horizontal list, 330, 332, 334
horizontal mode, 116, 286, 327–30
   moving boxes in, 306–08
horizontal rules, 311–13
   in a table, 219–23
horizontal skips, 101
\hphantom (plain)
\hrule (prim), 219–20, 311–13, 329
\hrulefill (plain), 221–23, 314–15
\hsize (prim), 87–88, 327, 373
   of examples in this book, 297
\hskip (prim), 97–98, 329, 376
   in an \halign, 201–02

\mark (prim)

mark, 330

mark-it-up bug diagnosis strategy, 347

\markboth (LaTeX), 186

\markright (LaTeX), 186

\MartianEyeColor (Snow), 55

math accents, 251–52

math-atom categorizer, 246

math displays, page breaks, 320–21

math environment (LaTeX), 238

math extension font table, 366

math italic font table, 365

math list, 330, 334

math mode, 14–15, 237–242, 244–46, 327–30

   changing fonts in, 68, 241–42

   having text words in, 256–57

   space around, 374

   spacing rules, 244–46

   symbols, 249–61

   when TeX stops and starts, 329

math mode and macros, 58–59

math mode fonts, 277–82

math mode space, 240–41

math mode toggles, *see* **$**

math-off, 330

math-on, 330

math symbol font table, 365

\mathaccent (prim)

\mathbin (prim), 246

\mathchar (prim)

\mathchardef (prim)

\mathchoice (prim)

\mathclose (prim), 246

\mathcode (prim)

\mathhexbox (plain)

\mathinner (prim), 246

\mathop (prim), 246

\mathopen (prim), 246

\mathord (prim), 246, 254

\mathpalette (plain)

\mathpunct (prim), 246

\mathrel (prim), 246

\mathstrut (plain), 252

\mathsurround (prim), 374

\matrix (plain), 265–66

matrixes with delimiters, 266–67

\max (plain: max), 256

\maxdeadcycles (prim)

\maxdepth (prim)

\maxdimen (plain), 44

\mbox (LaTeX), 285, 288

\meaning (prim)

meat-and-potatoes structure for macros, 124–25

\medbreak (plain), 131

\medHskip (Snow), 102

\medmuskip (prim), 376

\medskip (plain), 99, 329, 376

\medskipamount (plain), 99–100, 106, 375

memory exceeded, when TeX quits, 9, 235, 331, 341, 358

\message (prim)

metrics files for fonts, 74

\mid (plain: |), 259

\midinsert (plain), 230–31, 235

millimeter, 84

\min (plain: min), 256

minipage environment (LaTeX), 285, 295, 324, 325

   with footnote, 325

minus (plain: keyword), 105–06, 110–11

minus sign (−), 23

   at wrong place in multiline equation, 270–71

   in dimensions, 85

missing number error message, 345

missing something, bugs, 349–51

\mit (plain), 254, 365

\MIT (Snow), 51–52, 59

\mkern (prim)

mm (plain: keyword), 84

\models (plain: ⊨), 259

modes, 327–33

   scroll, nonstop, quiet, and stop-for-errors, 35

\month (prim), 372

\moveleft (prim), 308

\moveright (prim), 308–09

moving a box, 305–309

moving a rule, 318

\mp (plain: ∓), 258

\mskip (prim)

\mu (plain: μ), 253

mu (plain: math unit glue keyword), 376

quiet mode, 35
\quotation (Snow), 124–25
quotation environment (LaTeX), 124
quotation marks, 21–22
quotations, macros for, 124–27, 289, 292
quote environment (LaTeX), 124
\quotethis (Snow), 125

\radical (prim)
\raggedbottom (plain), 321, 377
\raggedcenter (plain)
\raggedHeading (Snow), 179
\raggedleft (Snow), 137–38
\raggedright (plain), 134, 377
\raise (prim), 306–08
\raisebox (LaTeX), 295, 305
\rangle (plain: $\rangle$), 242–43
\rbrace (plain: }), 242–43
\rbrack (plain:]), 242–43
\rceil (plain: $\rceil$), 242–43
\Re (plain: $\Re$), 255
\read (prim)
\rectangle, 298–99
recto, 185–86
recursion, 357–58
redefining a macro, 56–57, 59–60
redefining \footnote, 192
redefining \item, 147, 150–54
reference mark for footnotes, 189–90, 193–94
reference point of a box, 286
register, 37
relations, in math mode, 245, 259–60
\relax (prim), 102, 110–11, 362
\relbar (plain)
\Relbar (plain)
\relpenalty (prim), 373
\removelastskip (plain)
\renewcommand (LaTeX), 60
\repeat (plain)
reporter, 37–38, 161–62
    change inside a paragraph, 129–30
    doesn't change, 353
    giving new information to, 92–94
reporters, list of, 371–77
restricted horizontal mode, 331
\rfloor (plain: $\rfloor$), 242–43
\rgroup (plain: Γ), 244

\rho (plain: ρ), 253
\rhook (plain)
\right (prim), 243
right margin, see margins, \raggedright
\rightarrow (plain: $\rightarrow$), 260
\Rightarrow (plain: $\Rightarrow$), 260
\rightarrowfill (plain)
\rightcol (Snow), 206–07
\rightharpoondown (plain: $\rightharpoondown$), 260
\rightharpoonup (plain: $\rightharpoonup$), 260
\RightHead (Snow), 186
\righthyphenmin (prim), 372
\rightleftharpoons (plain: $\rightleftharpoons$), 260
\rightline (plain), 300–02
\rightskip (prim), 135–36, 375
\rigidspaces (Snow), 172
\rlap (plain), 302–03
    in a table, 212
\rm (plain: font-changing macro), 65, 278, 364
\rmoustache (plain), 244
robust vs. fragile LaTeX commands, 238
roman font table, 364
roman-numeral page numbers, 182–83
\romannumeral (prim)
\root (plain: $\sqrt[n]{a}$), 251
row of dots, see \dotfill
rules, 311–18
    fill-in-the-blank, 313–14
    how to move them, 318
    in a table, 219–26
    in text, 311–18
    touch adjacent box(es), 313
    usual size of, 315
runaway arguments, 126
running heads and feet, 181–87

\S (plain: §), 261
\samepage (LaTeX), 324
\samePageQuote (Snow), 289
sandwich macros with vboxes, 292
sandwich structure for macros, 127–28
sans serif fonts, 71–73, 278–81
\sb (plain)
\sc (Snow, LaTeX: font-changing macro), 72
scaled (plain: keyword), 79–80

space (continued),
    between header and text, 184–85,
        291, 375
    between \item and its input,
        144–45
    between macros, extra and
        unwanted, 131
    between paragraphs, 89–90, 374
    between rules, 312
    between rules and text, 312
    between sentences, 18–19, 369, 375
    extra skip above items, 149
    too much at a \vskip, 315–17
space between lines, 90–93, 286,
        291–92, 328, 374
    adding exact amount of, 98
    in display math, 272–73
    with \obeylines, 165–66, 170–71
        see also interlineskip glue,
        \vskip, \bigskip, \medskip,
        \smallskip, \baselineskip
space between words, 45–46, 171–72,
        369–71, 374–375
    bugs, 349–50
    disappearing, 10
    extra and unwanted, 158–59,
        346–48
    in \halign entry, 197
    inside an hbox, 295
    more than one, 11
    size of, 44–46, 160, 171–72, 371
    unbreakable, 18
        see also \tolerance, \spaceskip,
        \xspaceskip, \pretolerance,
        \emergencystretch,
        \obeyspaces
space bugs, general, 350
space in a table,
    between columns, 200–03, 375
    between rows, 205–06
space on a page, adding or removing,
        322
space-and-a-half, see space between
        lines
\spacefactor (prim)
spaces,
    at beginning of line, 9, 167–68, 177,
        353
    before and after & in \halign, 197

spaces (continued),
    in math mode, 240–41, 244–46
    intermittent, 333
    when TEX ignores or typesets
        them, 332–33
\spaceskip (prim), 171–72, 375
\spadesuit (plain: ♠), 255
\span (prim), 207
spanning columns in a table, 214–16
\special (prim), 235
special effects, using boxes to make,
        300–03
\splitbotmark (prim)
\splitfirstmark (prim)
\splitmaxdepth (prim)
\splittopskip (prim), 375
spread (plain: keyword), 296–97
\sqcap (plain: ⊓), 258
\sqcup (plain: ⊔), 258
\sqrt (plain: $\sqrt{-1}$), 251
\sqsubseteq (plain: ⊑), 259
\sqsupseteq (plain: ⊒), 259
square roots, 251
\ss (plain: ß), 24
\ssb (Snow), 72
\ssf (Snow), 72, 278
\ssffam (Snow), 278, 280
\ssi (Snow), 72
\stackrel (LATEX), 260
\stairs (Snow), 307–08
\star (plain: ⋆), 258
\startline (Snow), 168–70
startup settings, 56, 371–376
stopping TEX, 32, 34, 357
\string (prim)
\strut (plain), 200, 222, 225, 274–75,
        291–92, 315, 317–18
\strutbox (plain), 281–82, 317–18
style files in LATEX, 95
subdirectory, file is in different, 31
subformula, 275
\subparagraph (LATEX), 173
subscripts, 249–50, 374
    font used for, 279–80
    size of characters in, 274–75
\subsection (LATEX), 173
\subsectionnumber (Snow), 177
\subset (plain: ⊂), 259
\subseteq (plain: ⊆), 259

\valign (prim), 329
\varepsilon (plain: ε), 254
\varphi (plain: φ), 254
\varpi (plain: ϖ), 254
\varrho (plain: ϱ), 254
\varsigma (plain: ς), 254
\vartheta (plain: ϑ), 254
\vbadness (prim), 325, 371
\vbox (prim), 289–92, 296, 344
vboxes, 289–92, 331
\vcenter (prim), 265
\vdash (plain: $\vdash$), 259
\vdots (plain: $\vdots$), 265–66
\vec (plain: math accent $\vec{n}$), 251–52
vectors, 251–52
\vee (plain: $\vee$), 258
verbatim environment (LaTeX), 163
verse, 163–66, 171–72
verse environment (LaTeX), 163
\verseskip (Snow), 166
verso, 185–86
\vert (plain: |), 242–43
\Vert (plain: ‖), 242–43
vertical list, 330, 332, 334
vertical mode, 117–18, 286, 327–30
    moving boxes in, 308–09
vertical rules,
    in a table, 223–26
    in text, 313–15
\vfil (prim), 107–09, 329, 376
\vfill (prim), 107–09, 329, 376
\vfilll (Snow), 109
\vfilneg (prim), 329
\vfootnote (plain), 193
\vfuzz (prim), 325, 373
\vglue (plain), 175
\voffset (prim), 89, 373
\voidb@x (plain)
\vphantom (plain)
\vrule (prim), 223, 225, 313–15, 329
\vsize (prim), 89, 373
\vskip (prim), 97–98, 322, 329, 376
\vspace (LaTeX), 98
\vsplit (prim)
\vss (prim), 300–01, 322, 325, 329
\vtop (prim), 289–92, 296, 323–24, 344

\wd (prim), 286
\wedge (plain: $\wedge$), 258
What-You-See-Is-What-You-Get, see
    WYSIWYG
whatsit, 330
\who (Snow), 343
\widehat (plain: math accent $\widehat{mm}$),
    252
\widetilde (plain: math accent $\widetilde{mm}$),
    252
widow line, 319–20
\widowpenalty (prim), 319–20, 372
width (plain: keyword), 312–13
width,
    of a box, 285–86, 295–99
    of a rule, 315
    of an \halign, 203–04
    of text on a page, 327–28
wizard, system, 28
wizard, TeX, ix
\wlog (plain)
word processing, 3
\wp (plain: $\wp$), 255
\wr (plain: $\wr$), 258
\write (prim)
\wrongboat (Snow), 71
WYSIWYG, 3–4
WYSIWYG effects, 163, 171

\xdef (prim)
\xi (plain: ξ), 253
\Xi (plain: Ξ), 254
\xiibold, loading 12-point fonts, 79
\xleaders (prim)
\xspaceskip (prim), 171–72, 375

\year (prim), 372

\z@ (plain)
\z@skip (plain)
zero in dimensions, 85
\zeta (plain: ζ), 253
\zip (Snow), 199